Oracle Core

Essential Internals for DBAs and Developers

Jonathan Lewis

Apress®

Oracle Core: Essential Internals for DBAs and Developers

ISBN-13 (pbk): 978-1-4302-3954-3

ISBN-13 (electronic): 978-1-4302-3955-0

President and Publisher: Paul Manning
Lead Editor: Jonathan Gennick
Development Editor: James Markham
Technical Reviewer: Tanel Põder
Editorial Board: Steve Anglin, Mark Beckner, Ewan Buckingham, Gary Cornell, Morgan Ertel, Jonathan Gennick, Jonathan Hassell, Robert Hutchinson, Michelle Lowman, James Markham, Matthew Moodie, Jeff Olson, Jeffrey Pepper, Douglas Pundick, Ben Renow-Clarke, Dominic Shakeshaft, Gwenan Spearing, Matt Wade, Tom Welsh
Coordinating Editor: Jessica Belanger
Copy Editor: Kimberly Burton
Production Support: Patrick Cunningham
Indexer: SPi Global
Artist: SPi Global
Cover Designer: Anna Ishchenko

Distributed to the book trade worldwide by Springer Science+Business Media, LLC, 233 Spring Street, 6th Floor, New York, NY 10013. Phone 1-800-SPRINGER, fax (201) 348-4505, e-mail orders-ny@springer-sbm.com, or visit www.springeronline.com.

For information on translations, please e-mail rights@apress.com, or visit www.apress.com.

Apress and friends of ED books may be purchased in bulk for academic, corporate, or promotional use. eBook versions and licenses are also available for most titles. For more information, reference our Special Bulk Sales–eBook Licensing web page at www.apress.com/bulk-sales.

Any source code or other supplementary materials referenced by the author in this text is available to readers at http://www.apress.com. For detailed information about how to locate your book's source code, go to http://www.apress.com/source-code/.

Contents at a Glance

Contents

About the Author

Jonathan Lewis is a qualified teacher with a mathematics degree from Oxford University. Although his interest in computers came to light at the tender age of about 12—in the days when high-technology meant you used a keyboard, rather than a knitting needle to punch holes in cards—it wasn't until he was four years out of university that he moved into computing professionally. Apart from an initial year as an incompetent salesman (apparently the correct answer to any question is "Yes," not "Yes, but it's going to take several weeks of configuration and programming"), he has been self-employed his entire career in the computer industry.

Jonathan's initiation into Oracle was on version 5.1 running on a PC, which he used to design and build a risk-management system for the crude-trading floor of one of the major oil companies. (He had written the first version of the system using a PC program called dBase III—which did use tables and indexes and made some claims to being a relational database management system.) With Oracle, he found out what a proper relational database management system ought to be able to do, and was immediately hooked.

Since that day of revelation, Jonathan has focused exclusively on the use and abuse of the Oracle RDBMS. After three or four years of contract work helping to build large systems, he decided to move from the "contractor" market to the "consultant" market, and now shares his time evenly between short-term consultancy work, holding seminars, and "research."

Jonathan is well-known in the international Oracle scene, having worked in 50 different countries and a dozen US states in the course of the last 10 years. He is a strong supporter of user groups—particularly the UK user group (`www.ukoug.org`), of course—and whenever the opportunity arises, he tries to find time for speaking to user groups outside the United Kingdom, sometimes as short, evening events at the end of a day's consultancy work. He also has a blog about Oracle (`http://jonathanlewis.wordpress.com`) and contributes regularly (when he's not fully occupied writing books) to various magazines, forums and discussion groups.

Jonathan just celebrated his silver wedding anniversary to Diana (currently a primary school teacher and head of mathematics after many years of being an accountant). They have two children: Anna (now in her final year at Oxford University) and Simon (in his first year at York University). Despite the numerical backgrounds and mathematical skills of their parents, neither of the younger generation is the slightest bit interested in a career in computing.

About the Technical Reviewer

Tanel Põder is an internationally-acclaimed Oracle performance specialist, having helped solve complex problems for customers in more than twenty countries on five continents. He specializes in advanced performance tuning, end-to-end troubleshooting, and other complex (and, therefore, interesting) tasks, such as migrating very large databases with minimal downtime. Tanel has optimized the performance of Exadata installations starting from Exadata V1, and he plans to go even deeper with his current Exadata performance and troubleshooting research. He is a co-author of *Expert Oracle Exadata* (Apress, 2011).

Tanel is one of the world's first Oracle Certified Masters, an Oracle ACE Director, and a proud member of the OakTable Network. He regularly speaks at conferences worldwide and publishes his articles, scripts, and tools in his blog at `http://blog.tanelpoder.com`.

Acknowledgments

Above and beyond all others I have to thank my wife Diana for the support she has given me while I was writing. Without her love and patience, there would have been no book. I can't count the number of cups of tea prepared (and often left to go cold), the late nights (or early mornings) suffered, or the suppression of complaints over the things I should have done instead of write; this book required a lot of focus, and without someone at my side to deal with all the distractions of life, I wouldn't have got it written.

A technical book requires good reviewers, of course, and I'd like to thank Tanel Põder (`http://tech.e2sn.com/` and `http://blog.tanelpoder.com/`) who was my official technical reviewer. His comments, questions and corrections were most helpful and instructive.

I also had a couple of "unofficial" reviewers in Martin Widlake (`http://mwidlake.wordpress.com`) and Timur Akhmadeev (`http://timurakhmadeev.wordpress.com/`), who have also been most helpful in making the book what it is. The role I gave them was to tell me what was missing, what needed to be removed, and what bits were ambiguous; inevitably, though, they were also most useful at pointing out technical errors. If you like the diagrams in this book, you can thank Martin, in particular, because he kept telling me he wanted a visual image of some of the things I had described.

Andrey Nikolaev (`http://andreynikolaev.wordpress.com/`) was a special reviewer for Chapter 4. There is a huge volume of information about the private workings of Oracle on the Internet—and a large part of that volume is simply repetition of material that has slowly been going out of date for years. The information available about latching is the best demonstration of this phenomenon; partly, no doubt, because it is a very difficult thing to investigate. Andrey has done far more than any other author I have seen on the internet to bring our understanding of latches (and mutexes) up to date—so I asked him if he would review what I had said on the topic in Chapter 4. I am most grateful for the comments and corrections he made.

Despite the excellence of my reviewers, you will still find errors and omissions in this book—the blame for any such errors and omissions is mine. Some examples will be deliberate simplifications, some will simply be things that I got wrong. A huge fraction of this book is about internal mechanisms, and neither I nor my reviewers have any access to special internal documentation that tells us about those mechanisms; we're just ordinary people who apply the scientific method to the things we can observe and measure. Over time, and with peer group review, we get to a consensus about how things work—until new evidence appears.

There are many other people whose names I could mention, and some whose names I never knew; people who have contributed some fragment to the content of this book either by supplying answers, by asking questions, or by hiring me to look at interesting problems. There are always plenty of questions on forums, such as OTN (`http://forums.oracle.com`) and Oracle-L (`www.freelists.org/archive/oracle-l`), describing real-world issues with Oracle, and lots of people with the knowledge and experience to offer insights and solutions. Without a continuous flow of new questions, it's easy to get stuck in a rut and think you know it all—so I can safely say that much of my knowledge about Oracle has been learned because of research than has been prompted by the questions I see on the internet

Introduction

When I wrote *Practical Oracle 8i,* there was a three-week lag between publication and the first e-mail asking me when I was going to produce a 9i version of the book—thanks to Larry Ellison's timing of the launch of 9i. That question has been repeated many times (with changes in version number) over the last 12 years. This book is about as close as I'm going to come to writing a second edition of the book—but it only covers the first chapter (and a tiny bit of the second and third) of the original.

There were two things that encouraged me to start writing again. First, was the number of times I saw questions of the form: *How does Oracle do XXX?* Second, was the realization that it's hard to find answers to such questions that are both adequate and readable. Generally, you need only hunt through the manuals and you will find answers to many of the commonly-asked questions; and if you search the internet, you will find many articles about little features of how Oracle works. What you won't find is a cohesive narrative that put all the right bits together in the right order to give you a picture of how the whole thing works and why it has to work the way it does. This book is an attempt to do just that. I want to tell you the story of how Oracle works. I want to give you a narrative, not just a collection of bits and pieces.

Targets

Since this book is only a couple of hundred pages and the 11g manuals extend to tens of thousands of pages, it seems unlikely that I could possibly be describing "the whole thing," so let me qualify the claim. The book is about the core mechanics of the central database engine—the bit that drives everything else; essentially it boils down to undo, redo, data caching, and shared SQL. Even then I've had to be ruthless in eliminating lots of detail and interesting special cases that would make the book too long, turgid, and unreadable. Consider, for example, the simple question: *How does Oracle do a logical I/O?*, then take a look at structure `x$kcbsw`, which is a list of all the functions that Oracle might call to visit a block. You will find (for 11.2.0.2) that there are 1,164 different functions for doing a logical I/O—do you really want a detailed breakdown of all the options, or would a generic description of the common requirements be sufficient?

The problem of detail repeats itself at a different level—how much rocket science do you want to know; and how much benefit would anyone get from the book be if I did spend all my time writing about some of the incredibly intricate detail. Again, there's a necessary compromise to reach between completeness, accuracy, and basic readability. I think the image I've followed is one that I first saw expressed by Andrew Holdsworth of Oracle's Real-World Performance Group at Oracle OpenWorld in 2006. In a presentation about the optimizer and how to collect statistics, he talked about the 90/9/1 methodology, as follows:

- 90 percent of the time the default sample works
- 9 percent of the time a larger sample works
- 1 percent of the time the sample size is irrelevant

It's an enhancement of the famous 80/20 Pareto rule, and one that I think applies reasonably well to the typical requirement for understanding Oracle's internal mechanisms, but for the purposes of explaining this book, I want to rearrange the order as follows: 90 percent of the time you only need the barest information about how Oracle works to keep a system running adequately; 1 percent of the time you need to be a bit of a rocket scientist to figure out what's going wrong; and, I'm aiming this book at the 9 percent group who could get a little more out of their databases and lose a little less time if they had a slightly better idea of how much work is going on under the covers.

Where Next

Some time ago Tanel Põder (my technical reviewer) made the following comment in answer to the question of when he was going to write a book on Oracle internals:

"The answer is never, if talking about regular, old-fashioned, printed-on-paper books. I think the subject just changes too fast. Also, it takes at least a year of full-time work to come up with a book that would be any good, and by the time of publishing, many details would already be outdated."

This is a good answer, and adds weight to my comments about avoiding the 1 percent and sticking to the general requirements and approximations. Tanel's response to the problem is his "living book" at `http://tech.e2sn.com/oracle`.

But paper is nice (even if it's electronic paper)—and I believe the imposition of the book format introduces a difference between the content of a collection of internet articles (even very good ones) and the content a book. Again it comes back to narrative; there is a continuity of thought that you can get from a book form that doesn't work from collating short articles. As I write this introduction, I have 650 articles on my blog (a much greater volume of text than I have in this book); and although I might be able to draw a few articles together into a mini-series, if I tried to paste the whole lot together into a single book, it wouldn't be a terrible book—even if I spent days trying to write linking paragraphs between articles. Even technical books need a cohesive narrative.

To address the problems of a "non-living" book, I've posted a set of pages on my blog at `http://jonathanlewis.wordpress.com/oracle-core/`, one page for each chapter of the book. Over time, this will report any errors or brief additions to the published version; but as a blog it will also be open for questions and comments. When asked about a second edition for my other books, I said there wouldn't be any. But with feedback from the readers, I may find that with this book, some of the topics could benefit from further explanation, or that there are popular topics I've omitted, or even whole new areas that demand a chapter or appendix of their own.

I've offered my opening gambit to satisfy a popular requirement—now it's up to you, the reader, to respond.

CHAPTER 1

Getting Started . . .

Where to Begin

My goal in this book is to tell you just enough about the mechanics of Oracle to allow you to work out for yourself why your systems have problems. This means I have included only the details that really matter, at a level that makes them easy to understand. It also means I have omitted mention of all sorts of features, mechanisms, and interesting bits that don't really matter at all—without even explaining why they don't matter.

Trying to tell you "just enough" does make it hard to pick a starting point. Should I draw the process architecture somewhere on page 1 to give you the "big picture"? (I'd rather not, because most of the processes aren't really core.) Maybe I should start with transaction management. But I can't do that without talking about undo segment headers and interested transaction lists (ITLs), which means talking about undo and redo, which means talking about buffers and writers . . . so perhaps I should start with redo and undo, but that's a little difficult if I say nothing about transactional activity.

At the core, Oracle is very small, and there are only a few mechanisms you really need to understand to be able to recognize anything that has gone wrong—and you don't even have to understand all the minutiae and variations of those core mechanisms. Unfortunately, though, the bits hang together very tightly, leaving the hapless author with a difficult task. Describing Oracle is a bit like executing a transaction: from the outside you have to see none of it or all of it—there's no valid position in between.

I can't talk about read consistency without talking about system change numbers (SCNs) and undo records; I can't talk about undo records without talking about transactions; I can't talk about transactions without talking about ITL slots and SCNs; and so on, round and round in circles. This means the best way to explain Oracle (and the method I use in this book) is to visit each subject several times with increasing detail: start with a little bit of A so that I can tell you a little bit about B; once I've told you a bit about B I can tell you about C; and when you've got C I can tell you a little bit more about A, which lets me tell you a little more about B. Eventually you'll know all the details you really need to know about all the topics you really need to know.

Oracle in Processes

Figure 1-1 shows the simplest process diagram of Oracle you're likely to see and (probably) the most complicated process diagram of Oracle that you really need to understand. This, basically, is what the book is about; everything else is just the icing on the cake.

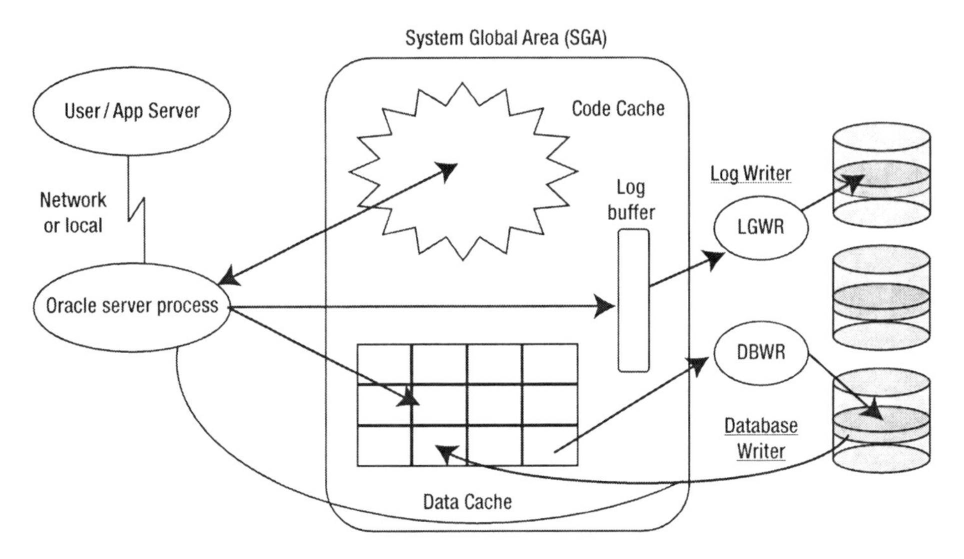

Figure 1-1. *The "just enough" diagram of Oracle Database processes*

Figure 1-1 shows two types of files. *Data files* are where our "real" data is kept, and *redo log files* (often just called *log files*) are where we record in a continuous stream a list of all the changes we make to the data files.

The data files are subject to random access. To allow random access to happen efficiently, each file has a unit I/O size, the *block size*, which may be 2KB, 4KB, 8KB (the commonest default), 16KB, or (on some platforms) 32KB. It is possible (and common) to group a number of data files into logical objects called *tablespaces*, and you can think of the tablespace as the natural "large-scale" unit of the database—a simple data object will be associated with a tablespace rather than a data file. There are essentially three types of tablespaces, which we will meet later on: undo tablespaces, temporary tablespaces, and "the rest."

Oracle introduced the concept of the temporary tablespace in Oracle 8, and the undo tablespace in Oracle 9. Prior to that (and back to version 6, where tablespaces were first introduced) all tablespaces were the same. Of "the rest" there are a couple of tablespaces that are considered special (even though they are treated no differently from all other tablespaces): the *system* tablespace and the *sysaux* tablespace, which should not be used for any end-user data. The sysaux tablespace appeared in Oracle 10*g* as a place for Oracle to keep the more dynamic, and potentially voluminous, data generated by its internal management and maintenance packages. The system tablespace is where Oracle stores the data dictionary—the metadata describing the database.

The log files are subject to sequential I/O, although they do have a minimum unit size, typically 512 bytes, for writes. Some log files, called *online* redo log files, are in fairly constant use. The rest, called *archived* redo log files, are simply copies of the online redo log files that are made as each file becomes full.

Note There are other types of files, of course, but we are going to ignore most of them. Chapter 6 does make some comments about the *control file*.

When the software is running under UNIX (or virtually any other operating system), a number of copies of the same oracle *process* are running in memory, and these copies share a large segment of memory. In a Windows environment, there is a single process called oracle with a number of independent *threads*. In this case it's a little easier to think of the threads sharing a large segment of memory. Technically, we refer to the data files as being the *database* and the combination of memory and running program(s) as an *instance*. In Real Application Clusters (RAC) we can configure several machines so that each manages a separate instance but all the instances share the same database.

The shared memory segment (technically the *System Global Area*, but sometimes called the *Shared Global Area*, and nearly always just the *SGA*) holds many pieces of information, but the most significant components are the *data cache*, a window onto the data files holding copies of some of the data blocks, the *log buffer*, a fairly small amount of memory used in a circular fashion to hold information that will soon be written to the log files, and the *library cache*, most significantly holding information about the SQL statements and PL/SQL blocks that have been executed in the recent past. Technically the library cache is part of the *shared pool*, but that term is a little flexible and sometimes is used to refer to any memory in the SGA that is currently unused.

■ **Note** There are a few other major memory components, namely the *streams pool*, the *java pool*, and the *large pool*, but really these are just areas of memory that have been isolated from the shared pool to handle particular types of specialized work. If you can cope with the shared pool, there's nothing particularly significant to learn about the other pools.

There is one memory location in the SGA that is particularly worth mentioning: the "clock" that the instance uses to coordinate its activity. This is a simple counter called the *System Change Number* (SCN) or, not quite correctly, the System Commit Number. Every process that can access the SGA can read and modify the SCN. Typically, processes read the current value of the location at the start of each query or transaction (through a routine named *kcmgss*—Get Snapshot SCN), and every time a process commits a transaction, it will increment the SCN (through a routine named *kcmgas*—Get and Advance SCN). The SCN will be incremented on other occasions, which is why System Change Number is a more appropriate name than System Commit Number.

There are then just three processes (or types of process) and one important fact that you really need to know about. The important fact is this: end-user programs don't touch the data files and don't even get to touch the shared memory.

There is a special process that copies information from the log buffer to the log files. This is the log writer (known as *lgwr*), and there is only ever one log writer in an instance. There is a special process that copies information from the data cache to the data files. This is the database writer (known as *dbwr*), and in many cases there will be only one such process, but for very large, busy systems, it is possible (and occasionally necessary) to configure multiple database writers, in which case they will be named *dbwN* (where the range of possible values for *N* varies with the version of Oracle).

Finally, there will be many copies of *server processes* associated with the instance. These are the processes that manipulate the SGA and read the data files on behalf of the end users. End-user programs talk through the pipeline of *SQL*Net* to pass instructions to and receive results from the server processes. The DBA (that's you!) can choose to configure the system for two different types of server processes, *dedicated* server processes and *shared* (formerly *multithreaded*) server processes; most systems use only dedicated servers, but some systems will do most of their lightweight work through shared servers, leaving the more labor-intensive tasks to dedicated servers.

Oracle in Action

So what do you really need to know about how Oracle works? Ultimately it comes down to this:

> *An end user sends requests in the form of SQL (or PL/SQL) statements to a server process; each statement has to be interpreted and executed; the process has to acquire the correct data in a timely fashion; the process may have to change data in a correct and timely fashion; and the instance has to protect the database from corruption.*

All this work has to take place in the context of a multiuser system on which lots of other end users are trying to do the same thing to the same data at the same time. This concurrent leads to these key questions: How can we access data efficiently? How can we modify data efficiently? How can we protect the database? How do we minimize interference from other users? And when it all breaks down, can we put our database back together again?

Summary

In the following chapters we will gradually build a picture of the work that Oracle does to address the issues of *efficiency* and *concurrency*. We'll start with simple data changes and the mechanisms that Oracle uses to record and apply changes, and then we'll examine how changes are combined to form transactions. As we review these mechanisms, we'll also study how they allow Oracle to deal with concurrency and read consistency, and we'll touch briefly on some of the problems that arise because of the open-ended nature of the work that Oracle can do.

After that we'll have a preliminary discussion of the typical memory structures that Oracle uses, and the mechanisms that protect shared memory from the dangers of concurrent modifications. Using some of this information, we'll move on to the work that Oracle does to locate data in memory and transfer data from disc to memory.

Once we've done that, we can discuss the mechanisms that transfer data the other way—from memory to disc—and at the same time fill in a few more details about how Oracle tracks data in memory. Having spent most of our time on data handling, we'll move on to see how Oracle handles its code (the SQL) and how the memory-handling mechanisms for code are remarkably similar to the mechanisms for handling data—even though some of the things we do with the code are completely different.

Finally we'll take a quick tour through RAC, identifying the problems that appear when different instances running on different machines have to know what every other instance is doing.

CHAPTER 2

Redo and Undo

The Answer to Recovery, Read Consistency, and Nearly Everything—Really!

In a conference session I call "The Beginners' Guide to Becoming an Oracle Expert," I usually start by asking the audience which bit of Oracle technology is the most important bit and when did it first appear. The answers I get tend to go through the newer, more exciting features such as ref partitioning, logical standby, or even Exadata, but in my opinion the single most important feature of Oracle is one that first appeared in version 6: the *change vector*, a mechanism for *describing* changes to data blocks, the heart of redo and undo.

This is the technology that keeps your data safe, minimizes conflict between readers and writers, and allows for instance recovery, media recovery, all the standby technologies, flashback mechanisms, change data capture, and streams. So this is the technology that we're going to review first.

It won't be long before we start looking at a few dumps from data blocks and log files. When we get to them, there's no need to feel intimidated—it's not rocket science, but rather just a convenient way of examining the information that Oracle has stored. I won't list all the `dump` commands I've used in line, but I've included notes about them in the Appendix.

Basic Data Change

One of the strangest features of an Oracle database is that it records your data twice. One copy of the data exists in a set of data files which hold something that is nearly the latest, up-to-date version of your data (although the newest version of some of the data will be in memory, waiting to be copied to disc); the other copy of the data exists as a set of instructions—the redo log files—telling you how to re-create the content of the data files from scratch.

Note When talking about data and data blocks in the context of describing the internal mechanism, it is worth remembering that the word "data" generally tends to include indexes and metadata, and may on some occasions even be intended to include undo.

The Approach

Under the Oracle approach to data change, when you issue an instruction to change an item of data, Oracle doesn't just go to a data file (or the in-memory copy if the item happens to be buffered), find the item, and change it. Instead, Oracle works through four critical steps to make the change happen. Stripped to the bare minimum of detail, these are

1. Create a description of how to change the data item.
2. Create a description of how to re-create the original data item if needed.
3. Create a description of how to create the description of how to re-create the original data item.
4. Change the data item.

The tongue-twisting nature of the third step gives you some idea of how convoluted the mechanism is, but all will become clear. With the substitution of a few technical labels in these steps, here's another way of describing the actions of changing a data block:

1. Create a *redo change vector* describing the change to the data block.
2. Create an *undo record* for insertion into an undo block in the undo tablespace.
3. Create a *redo change vector* describing the change to the undo block.
4. Change the data block.

The exact sequence of steps and the various technicalities around the edges vary depending on the version of Oracle, the nature of the transaction, how much work has been done so far in the transaction, what the states of the various database blocks were before you executed the instruction, whether or not you're looking at the first change of a transaction, and so on.

An Example

I'm going to start with the simplest example of a data change, which you might expect to see as you updated a single row in the middle of an OLTP transaction that had already updated a scattered set of rows. In fact, the order of the steps in the historic (and most general) case is not the order I've listed in the preceding section. The steps actually go in the order 3, 1, 2, 4, and the two redo change vectors are combined into a single redo change record and copied into the redo log (buffer) *before* the undo block and data block are modified (in that order). This means a slightly more accurate version of my list of actions would be

1. Create a *redo change vector* describing how to insert an *undo record* into an *undo* block.
2. Create a *redo change vector* for the *data* block change.
3. Combine the *redo change vectors* into a *redo record* and write it to the *log buffer.*
4. Insert the *undo record* into the *undo* block.
5. Change the *data* block.

Here's a little sample, taken from a system running Oracle 9.2.0.8 (the last version in which it's easy to create the most generic example of the mechanism). We're going to execute an update statement that updates five rows by jumping back and forth between two table blocks, dumping various bits of information into our process trace file before and after the update. I need to make my update a little bit complicated because I want the example to be as simple as possible while avoiding a few "special case" details.

■ **Note** The first change in a transaction includes some special steps, and the first change a transaction makes to each block is slightly different from the most "typical" change. We will look at those special cases in Chapter 3.

The code I've written will update the third, fourth, and fifth rows in the first block of a table but will update a row in the second block of the table between each of these three updates (see `core_demo_02.sql` in the code library on www.apress.com), and it'll change the third column of each row—a `varchar2()` column—from xxxxxx (lowercase, six characters) to YYYYYYYYYY (uppercase, ten characters).

Here's a symbolic dump of the fifth row in the block before and after the update:

```
tab 0, row 4, @0x1d3f
tl: 117 fb: --H-FL-- lb: 0x0  cc: 4
col  0: [ 2]  c1 0a
col  1: [ 2]  c1 06
col  2: [ 6]  78 78 78 78 78 78
col  3: [100]
30 30 30 30 30 30 30 30 … 30 30 30 30 30  (for 100 characters)

tab 0, row 4, @0x2a7
tl: 121 fb: --H-FL-- lb: 0x2  cc: 4
col  0: [ 2]  c1 0a
col  1: [ 2]  c1 06
col  2: [10]  59 59 59 59 59 59 59 59 59 59
col  3: [100]
 30 30 30 30 30 30 30 30 … 30 30 30 30 30  (for 100 characters)
```

As you can see, the third column (`col 2:`) of the table has changed from a string of 78s (x) to a longer string of 59s (Y). Since the update increased the length of the row, Oracle had to copy it into the block's free space to make the change, which is why its starting byte position has moved from `@0x1d3f` to `@0x2a7`. It is still row 4 (the fifth row) in the block, though; if we were to check the block's *row directory*, we would see that the fifth entry has been updated to point to this new row location.

I dumped the block before committing the change, which is why you can see that the *lock byte* (`lb:`) has changed from `0x0` to `0x2`—the row is locked by a transaction identified by the second slot in the block's interested transaction list (ITL). We will be discussing ITLs in more depth in Chapter 3.

■ **Note** For details on various debugging techniques such as block dumps, redo log file dumps, and so on, see the Appendix.

So let's look at the various change vectors. First, from a symbolic dump of the current redo log file, we can examine the change vector describing what we did to the table:

```
TYP:0 CLS: 1 AFN:11 DBA:0x02c0018a SCN:0x0000.03ee485a SEQ:  2 OP:11.5
KTB Redo
op: 0x02  ver: 0x01
op: C  uba: 0x0080009a.09d4.0f
KDO Op code: URP row dependencies Disabled
  xtype: XA  bdba: 0x02c0018a  hdba: 0x02c00189
itli: 2  ispac: 0  maxfr: 4863
tabn: 0 slot: 4(0x4) flag: 0x2c lock: 2 ckix: 16
ncol: 4 nnew: 1 size: 4
col  2: [10]  59 59 59 59 59 59 59 59 59 59
```

I'll pick out just the most significant bits of this change vector. You can see that the `Op code:` in line 5 is `URP` (update row piece). Line 6 tells us the block address of the block we are updating (`bdba:`) and the segment header block for that object (`hdba:`).

In line 7 we see that the transaction doing this update is using ITL entry 2 (`itli:`), which confirms what we saw in the block dump: it's an update to `tabn: 0 slot: 4` (fifth row in the first table; remember that blocks in a *cluster* can hold data from many tables, so each block has to include a list identifying the tables that have rows in the block). Finally, in the last two lines, we see that the row has four columns (`ncol:`), of which we are changing one (`nnew:`), increasing the row length (`size:`) by 4 bytes, and that we are changing column 2 to YYYYYYYYYY.

The next thing we need to see is a description of how to put back the old data. This appears in the form of an undo record, dumped from the relevant undo block. The methods for finding the correct undo block will be covered in Chapter 3. The following text shows the relevant record from the symbolic block dump:

```
*-----------------------------
* Rec #0xf  slt: 0x1a  objn: 45810(0x0000b2f2)  objd: 45810  tblspc: 12(0x0000000c)
*       Layer:  11 (Row)   opc: 1   rci 0x0e
Undo type:  Regular undo   Last buffer split:  No
Temp Object:  No
Tablespace Undo:  No
rdba: 0x00000000
*-----------------------------
KDO undo record:
KTB Redo
op: 0x02  ver: 0x01
op: C  uba: 0x0080009a.09d4.0d
KDO Op code: URP row dependencies Disabled
  xtype: XA  bdba: 0x02c0018a  hdba: 0x02c00189
itli: 2  ispac: 0  maxfr: 4863
tabn: 0 slot: 4(0x4) flag: 0x2c lock: 0 ckix: 16
ncol: 4 nnew: 1 size: -4
col  2: [ 6]  78 78 78 78 78 78
```

Again, I'm going to ignore a number of details and simply point out that the significant part of this undo record (for our purposes) appears in the last five lines and comes close to repeating the content of the redo change vector, except that we see the row size decreasing by 4 bytes as column 2 becomes xxxxxx.

But this is an undo record, written into an undo block and stored in the undo tablespace in one of the data files, and, as I pointed out earlier, Oracle keeps two copies of everything, one in the data files and one in the redo log files. Since we've put something into a data file (even though it's in the undo tablespace), we need to create a description of what we've done and write that description into the redo log file. We need another redo change vector, which looks like this:

```
TYP:0 CLS:36 AFN:2 DBA:0x0080009a SCN:0x0000.03ee485a SEQ:  4 OP:5.1
ktudb redo: siz: 92 spc: 6786 flg: 0x0022 seq: 0x09d4 rec: 0x0f
            xid:  0x000a.01a.0000255b
ktubu redo: slt: 26 rci: 14 opc: 11.1 objn: 45810 objd: 45810 tsn: 12
Undo type:  Regular undo       Undo type:  Last buffer split:  No
Tablespace Undo:  No
             0x00000000
KDO undo record:
KTB Redo
op: 0x02  ver: 0x01
op: C  uba: 0x0080009a.09d4.0d
KDO Op code: URP row dependencies Disabled
  xtype: XA  bdba: 0x02c0018a  hdba: 0x02c00189
itli: 2  ispac: 0  maxfr: 4863
tabn: 0 slot: 4(0x4) flag: 0x2c lock: 0 ckix: 16
ncol: 4 nnew: 1 size: -4
col  2: [ 6]  78 78 78 78 78 78
```

The bottom half of the redo change vector looks remarkably like the undo record, which shouldn't be a surprise as it is, after all, a description of what we want to put into the undo block. The top half of the redo change vector tells us where the bottom half goes, and includes some information about the *block header* information of the block it's going into. The most significant detail, for our purposes, is the `DBA:` (data block address) in line 1, which identifies block `0x0080009a`: if you know your Oracle block numbers in hex, you'll recognize that this is block 154 of data file 2 (the file number of the undo tablespace in a newly created database).

Debriefing

So where have we got to so far? When we change a data block, Oracle inserts an undo record into an undo block to tell us how to reverse that change. But for every change that happens to a block in the database, Oracle creates a redo change vector describing how to make that change, and it creates the vectors before it makes the changes. Historically, it created the undo change vector before it created the "forward" change vector, hence, the following sequence of events (see Figure 2-1) that I described earlier occurs:

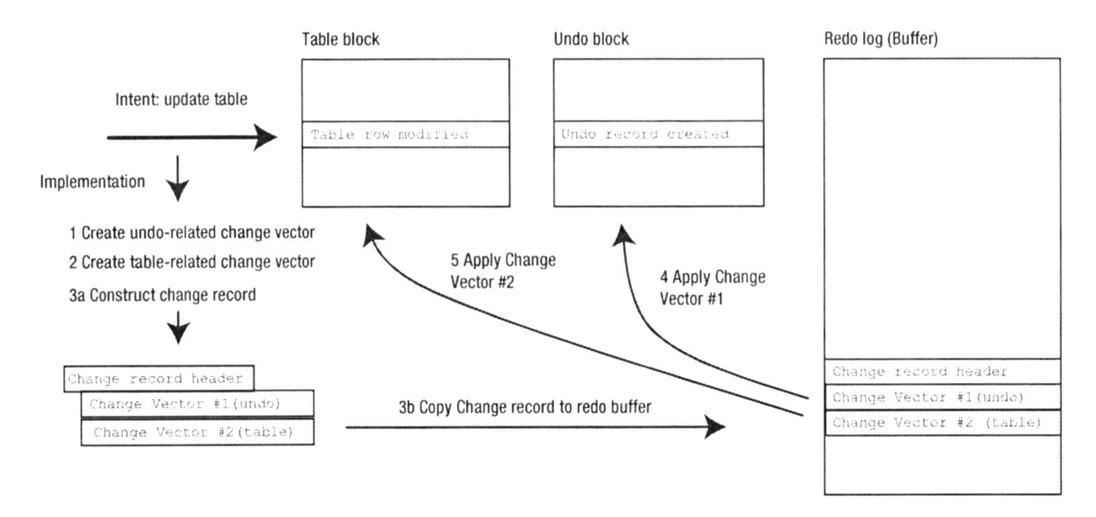

Figure 2-1. *Sequence of events for a small update in the middle of a transaction*

1. Create the change vector for the undo record.
2. Create the change vector for the data block.
3. Combine the change vectors and write the redo record into the redo log (buffer).
4. Insert the undo record into the undo block.
5. Make the change to the data block.

When you look at the first two steps here, of course, there's no reason to believe that I've got them in the right order. Nothing I've described or dumped shows that the actions must be happening in that order. But there is one little detail I can now show you that I omitted from the dumps of the change vectors, partly because things are different from 10g onwards and partly because the description of the activity is easier to comprehend if you first think about it in the wrong order.

■ **Note** Oracle Database 10*g* introduced an important change to the way that redo change vectors are created and combined, but the underlying mechanisms are still very similar; moreover, the new mechanisms don't apply to RAC, and even single instance Oracle falls back to the old mechanism if a transaction gets too large or you have enabled supplemental logging or flashback database. We will be looking at the new strategy later in this chapter. One thing that doesn't change, though, is that redo is generated before changes are applied to data and undo blocks—and we shall see why this strategy is a stroke of pure genius when we get to Chapter 6.

So far I've shown you our two change vectors only as individual entities; if I had shown you the complete picture of the way these change vectors went into the redo log, you would have seen how they were combined into a single *redo record*:

```
REDO RECORD - Thread:1 RBA: 0x00036f.00000005.008c LEN: 0x00f8 VLD: 0x01
SCN: 0x0000.03ee485a SUBSCN:  1 03/13/2011 17:43:01
CHANGE #1 TYP:0 CLS:36 AFN:2 DBA:0x0080009a SCN:0x0000.03ee485a SEQ:  4 OP:5.1
...
CHANGE #2 TYP:0 CLS: 1 AFN:11 DBA:0x02c0018a SCN:0x0000.03ee485a SEQ:  2 OP:11.5
...
```

It is a common (though far from universal) pattern in the redo log that change vectors come in matching pairs, with the change vector for an undo record appearing before the change vector for the corresponding forward change.

While we're looking at the bare bones of the preceding redo record, it's worth noting the `LEN:` figure in the first line—this is the length of the redo record: `0x00f8` = 248 bytes. All we did was change xxxxxx to YYYYYYYYYY in one row and it cost us 248 bytes of logging information. In fact, it seems to have been a very expensive operation given the net result: we had to generate two redo change vectors and update two database blocks to make a tiny little change, which looks like four times as many steps as we need to do. Let's hope we get a decent payback for all that extra work.

Summary of Observations

Before we continue, we can summarize our observations as follows: in the data files, every change we make to our own data is matched by Oracle with the creation of an undo record (which is also a change to a data file); at the same time Oracle puts into the redo log a description of how to make our change and how to make its own change.

You might note that since data can be changed "in place," we could make an "infinite" (i.e., arbitrarily large) number of changes to our single row of data, but we clearly can't record an infinite number of undo records without growing the data files of the undo tablespace, nor can we record an infinite number of changes in the redo log without constantly adding more redo log files. For the sake of simplicity, we'll postpone the issue of infinite changes and simply pretend for the moment that we can record as many undo and redo records as we need.

ACID

Although we're not going to look at transactions in this chapter, it is, at this point, worth mentioning the *ACID* requirements of a transactional system and how Oracle's implementation of undo and redo gives Oracle the capability of meeting those requirements. Table 2-1 lists the ACID requirements.

***Table 2-1.** The ACID Requirements*

Atomicity	**A transaction must be invisible or complete.**
Consistency	The database must be self-consistent at the start and end of each transaction.
Isolation	A transaction may not see results produced by another incomplete transaction.
Durability	A committed transaction must be recoverable after a system failure.

The following list goes into more detail about each of the requirements in Table 2-1:

- *Atomicity*: As we make a change, we create an undo record that describes how to reverse the change. This means that when we are in the middle of a transaction, another user trying to view any data we have modified can be instructed to use the undo records to see an older version of that data, thus making our work invisible until the moment we decide to publish (commit) it. We can ensure that the other user either sees nothing of what we've done or sees everything.
- *Consistency*: This requirement is really about constraints defining the legal states of the database; but we could also argue that the presence of undo records means that other users can be blocked from seeing the incremental application of our transaction and therefore cannot see the database moving from one legal state to another by way of a temporarily illegal state—what they see is either the old state or the new state and nothing in between. (The internal code, of course, can see all the intermediate states—and take advantage of being able to see them—but the end-user code never sees inconsistent data.)
- *Isolation*: Yet again we can see that the availability of undo records stops other users from seeing how we are changing the data until the moment we decide that our transaction is complete and commit it. In fact, we do better than that: the availability of undo means that other users need not see the effects of our transactions for the entire duration of their transactions, even if we start and end our transaction between the start and end of their transaction. (This is not the default *isolation level* in Oracle, but it is an available isolation level; see the "Isolation Levels" sidebar.) Of course, we do run into confusing situations when two users try to change the same data at the same time; perfect isolation is not possible in a world where transactions have to take a finite amount of time.

- *Durability*: This is the requirement that highlights the benefit of the redo log. How do you ensure that a completed transaction will survive a system failure? The obvious strategy is to keep writing any changes to disc, either as they happen or as the final step that "completes" the transaction. If you didn't have the redo log, this could mean writing a lot of random data blocks to disc as you change them. Imagine inserting ten rows into an `order_lines` table with three indexes; this could require 31 randomly distributed disk writes to make changes to 1 table block and 30 index blocks durable. But Oracle has the redo mechanism. Instead of writing an entire data block as you change it, you prepare a small description of the change, and 31 small descriptions could end up as just one (relatively) small write to the end of the log file when you need to make sure that you've got a permanent record of the entire transaction. (We'll discuss in Chapter 6 what happens to the 31 changed data blocks, and the associated undo blocks, and how recovery might take place.)

ISOLATION LEVELS

Oracle offers three isolation levels: read committed (the default), read only, and serializable. As a brief sketch of the differences, consider the following scenario: table `t1` holds one row, and table `t2` is identical to `t1` in structure. We have two sessions that go through the following steps in order:

1. Session 1: select from t1;
2. Session 2: insert into t1 select * from t1;
3. Session 2: commit;
4. Session 1: select from t1;
5. Session 1: insert into t2 select * from t1;

If session 1 is operating at isolation level read committed, it will select one row on the first select, select two rows on the second select, and insert two rows.

If session 1 is operating at isolation level read only, it will select one row on the first select, select one row on the second select, and fail with Oracle error "ORA-01456: may not perform insert/delete/update operation inside a READ ONLY transaction."

If session 1 is operating at isolation level serializable, it will select one row on the first select, select one row on the second select, and insert one row.

Not only are the mechanisms for undo and redo sufficient to implement the basic requirements of ACID, they also offer advantages in performance and recoverability.

The performance benefit of redo has already been covered in the comments on durability; if you want an example of the performance benefits of undo, think about isolation—how can you run a report that takes minutes to complete if you have users who need to update data at the same time? In the absence of something like the undo mechanism, you would have to choose between allowing wrong results and locking out everyone who wants to change the data. This is a choice that you have to make with some other database products. The undo mechanism allows for an extraordinary degree of concurrency because, per Oracle's marketing sound bite, "readers don't block writers, writers don't block readers."

As far as recoverability is concerned (and we will examine recoverability in more detail in Chapter 6), if we record a complete list of changes we have made to the database, then we could, in principle, start with a brand-new database and simply reapply every single change description to reproduce an up-to-date copy of the original database. Practically, of course, we don't (usually) start with a new database; instead we take regular backup copies of the data files so that we need only replay a small fraction of the total redo generated to bring the copy database up to date.

Redo Simplicity

The way we handle redo is quite simple: we just keep generating a continuous stream of redo records and pumping them as fast as we can into the redo log, initially into an area of shared memory known as the redo log buffer. Eventually, of course, Oracle has to deal with writing the buffer to disk and, for operational reasons, actually writes the "continuous" stream to a small set of predefined files—the *online redo log files*. The number of online redo log files is limited, so we have to reuse them constantly in a round-robin fashion.

To protect the information stored in the online redo log files over a longer time period, most systems are configured to make a copy, or possibly many copies, of each file as it becomes full before allowing Oracle to reuse it: the copies are referred to as the *archived redo log files*. As far as redo is concerned, though, it's essentially write it and forget it—once a redo record has gone into the redo log (buffer), we don't (normally) expect the instance to reread it. At the basic level, this "write and forget" approach makes redo a very simple mechanism.

Note Although we don't usually expect to do anything with the online redo log files except write them and forget them, there is a special case where a session can read the online redo log files when it discovers the in-memory version of a block to be corrupt and attempts to recover from the disk copy of the block. Of course, some features, such as Log Miner, Streams, and asynchronous Change Data Capture, have been created in recent years to take advantage of the redo log files, and some of the newer mechanisms for dealing with Standby databases have become real-time and are bound into the process that writes the online redo. We will look at such features in Chapter 6.

There is, however, one complication. There is a critical bottleneck in redo generation, the moment when a redo record has to be copied into the redo log buffer. Prior to 10*g*, Oracle would insert a redo record (typically consisting of just one pair of redo change vectors) into the redo log buffer for each change a session made to user data. But a single session might make many changes in a very short period of time, and there could be many sessions operating concurrently—and there's only one redo log buffer that everyone wants to access.

It's relatively easy to create a mechanism to control access to a piece of shared memory, and Oracle's use of the *redo allocation latch* to protect the redo log buffer is fairly well known. A process that needs some space in the log buffer tries to acquire (*get*) the redo allocation latch, and once it has exclusive ownership of that latch, it can reserve some space in the buffer for the information it wants to write into the buffer. This avoids the threat of having multiple processes overwrite the same piece of memory in the log buffer, but if there are lots of processes constantly competing for the redo allocation latch, then the level of competition could end up "invisibly" consuming lots of resources (typically CPU spent on latch *spinning*) or even lots of sleep time as sessions take themselves off the run queue after failing to get the latch on the first spin.

In older versions of Oracle, when the databases were less busy and the volume of redo generated was much lower, the "one change = one record = one allocation" strategy was good enough for most systems, but as systems became larger, the requirement for dealing with large numbers of concurrent allocations (particularly for OLTP systems) demanded a more scalable strategy. So a new mechanism combining *private redo* and *in-memory undo* appeared in 10g.

In effect, a process can work its way through an entire transaction, generating all its change vectors and storing them in a pair of private redo log buffers. When the transaction completes, the process copies all the privately stored redo into the public redo log buffer, at which point the traditional log buffer processing takes over. This means that a process acquires the public redo allocation latch only once per transaction, rather than once per change.

Note As a step toward improved scalability, Oracle 9.2 introduced the option for multiple log buffers with the `log_parallelism` parameter, but this option was kept fairly quiet and the general suggestion was that you didn't need to know about it unless you had at least 16 CPUs. In 10*g* you get at least two public log buffers (*redo threads*) if you have more than one CPU.

There are a number of details (and restrictions) that need to be mentioned, but before we go into any of the complexities, let's just take a note of how this changes some of the instance activity reported in the dynamic performance views. I've taken the script in `core_demo_02.sql`, removed the `dump` commands, and replaced them with calls to take snapshots of `v$latch` and `v$sesstat` (see `core_demo_02b.sql` in the code library). I've also modified the SQL to update 50 rows instead of 5 rows so that differences in workload stand out more clearly. The following results come from a 9*i* and a 10*g* system, respectively, running the same test. First the 9*i* results:

```
Latch                          Gets      Im_Gets
-----                          ----      -------
redo copy                         0           51
redo allocation                  53            0

Name                        Value
----                        -----
redo entries                   51
redo size                  12,668
```

Note particularly in the 9*i* output that we have hit the redo copy and redo allocation latches 51 times each (with a couple of extra gets on the allocation latch from another process), and have created 51 redo entries. Compare this with the 10*g* results:

```
Latch                              Gets      Im_Gets
-----                              ----      -------
redo copy                             0            1
redo allocation                       5            1
In memory undo latch                 53            1

Name                          Value
----                          -----
redo entries                      1
redo size                    12,048
```

In 10*g*, our session has hit the redo copy latch just once, and there has been just a little more activity on the redo allocation latch. We can also see that we have generated a single redo entry with a size that is slightly smaller than the total redo size from the 9*i* test. These results appear *after* the commit; if we took the same snapshot before the commit, we would see no redo entries (and a zero redo size), the gets on the In memory undo latch would drop to 51, and the gets on the redo allocation latch would be 1, rather than 5.

So there's clearly a notable reduction in the activity and the threat of contention at a critical location. On the downside, we can see that 10*g* has, however, hit that new latch called the *In memory undo latch* 53 times in the course of our test, which makes it look as if we may simply have moved a contention problem from one place to another. We'll take a note of that idea for later examination.

There are various places we can look in the database to understand what has happened. We can examine `v$latch_children` to understand why the change in latch activity isn't a new threat. We can examine the redo log file to see what the one large redo entry looks like. And we can find a couple of dynamic performance objects (`x$kcrfstrand` and `x$ktifp`) that will help us to gain an insight into the way in which various pieces of activity link together.

The enhanced infrastructure is based on two sets of memory structures. One set (called `x$kcrfstrand`, the *private redo*) handles "forward" change vectors, and the other set (called `x$ktifp`, the *in-memory undo pool*) handles the undo change vectors. The private redo structure also happens to hold information about the traditional "public" redo log buffer(s), so don't be worried if you see two different patterns of information when you query it.

The number of pools in `x$ktifp` (in-memory undo) is dependent on the size of the array that holds transaction details (`v$transaction`), which is set by parameter `transactions` (but may be derived from parameter `sessions` or parameter `processes`). Essentially, the number of pools defaults to `transactions / 10` and each pool is covered by its own "In memory undo latch" latch.

For each entry in `x$ktifp` there is a corresponding private redo entry in `x$kcrfstrand`, and, as I mentioned earlier, there are then a few extra entries which are for the traditional "public" redo threads. The number of public redo threads is dictated by the `cpu_count` parameter, and seems to be `ceiling(1 + cpu_count / 16)`. Each entry in `x$kcrfstrand` is covered by its own redo allocation latch, and each public redo thread is additionally covered by one redo copy latch per CPU (we'll be examining the role of these latches in Chapter 6).

If we go back to our original test, updating just five rows and two blocks in the table, Oracle would still go through the action of visiting the rows and cached blocks in the same order, but instead of packaging pairs of redo change vectors, writing them into the redo log buffer, and modifying the blocks, it would operate as follows:

1. Start the transaction by acquiring a matching pair of the private memory structures , one from `x$ktifp` and one from `x$kcrfstrand`.
2. Flag each affected block as "has private redo" (but don't change the block).
3. Write each undo change vector into the selected in-memory undo pool.

4. Write each redo change vector into the selected private redo thread.

5. End the transaction by concatenating the two structures into a single redo change record.

6. Copy the redo change record into the redo log and apply the changes to the blocks.

If we look at the memory structures (see `core_imu_01.sql` in the code depot) just before we commit the transaction from the original test, we see the following:

```
INDX  UNDO_SIZE UNDO_USAGE  REDO_SIZE REDO_USAGE
----- ---------- ---------- ---------- ----------
    0      64000       4352      62976       3920
```

This show us that the private memory areas for a session allow roughly 64KB for "forward" changes, and the same again for "undo" changes. For a 64-bit system this would be closer to 128KB each. The update to five rows has used about 4KB from each of the two areas.

If I then dump the redo log file after committing my change, this (stripped to a bare minimum) is the one redo record that I get:

```
REDO RECORD - Thread:1 RBA: 0x0000d2.00000002.0010 LEN: 0x0594 VLD: 0x0d
SCN: 0x0000.040026ae SUBSCN:  1 04/06/2011 04:46:06

CHANGE #1 TYP:0 CLS: 1 AFN:5 DBA:0x0142298a OBJ:76887
SCN:0x0000.04002690 SEQ:  2 OP:11.5
CHANGE #2 TYP:0 CLS:23 AFN:2 DBA:0x00800039 OBJ:4294967295
SCN:0x0000.0400267e SEQ:  1 OP:5.2
CHANGE #3 TYP:0 CLS: 1 AFN:5 DBA:0x0142298b OBJ:76887
SCN:0x0000.04002690 SEQ:  2 OP:11.5
CHANGE #4 TYP:0 CLS: 1 AFN:5 DBA:0x0142298a OBJ:76887
SCN:0x0000.040026ae SEQ:  1 OP:11.5
CHANGE #5 TYP:0 CLS: 1 AFN:5 DBA:0x0142298b OBJ:76887
SCN:0x0000.040026ae SEQ:  1 OP:11.5
CHANGE #6 TYP:0 CLS: 1 AFN:5 DBA:0x0142298a OBJ:76887
SCN:0x0000.040026ae SEQ:  2 OP:11.5
CHANGE #7 TYP:0 CLS:23 AFN:2 DBA:0x00800039 OBJ:4294967295
SCN:0x0000.040026ae SEQ:  1 OP:5.4
CHANGE #8 TYP:0 CLS:24 AFN:2 DBA:0x00804a9b OBJ:4294967295
SCN:0x0000.0400267d SEQ:  2 OP:5.1
CHANGE #9 TYP:0 CLS:24 AFN:2 DBA:0x00804a9b OBJ:4294967295
SCN:0x0000.040026ae SEQ:  1 OP:5.1
CHANGE #10 TYP:0 CLS:24 AFN:2 DBA:0x00804a9b OBJ:4294967295
SCN:0x0000.040026ae SEQ:  2 OP:5.1
CHANGE #11 TYP:0 CLS:24 AFN:2 DBA:0x00804a9b OBJ:4294967295
SCN:0x0000.040026ae SEQ:  3 OP:5.1
CHANGE #12 TYP:0 CLS:24 AFN:2 DBA:0x00804a9b OBJ:4294967295
SCN:0x0000.040026ae SEQ:  4 OP:5.1
```

You'll notice that the length of the undo record (`LEN:`) is `0x594` = 1428, which matched the value of the redo size statistic I saw when I ran this particular test. This is significantly smaller than the sum of the 4352 and 3920 bytes reported as used in the in-memory structures, so there are clearly lots of extra bytes involved in tracking the private undo and redo—perhaps as starting overhead in the buffers.

If you read through the headers of the 12 separate change vectors, taking note particularly of the `OP:` code, you'll see that we have five change vectors for code `11.5` followed by five for code `5.1`. These are the five forward change vectors followed by the five undo block change vectors. Change vector #2 (code `5.2`) is the start of transaction, and change vector #7 (code `5.4`) is the so-called *commit record*, the end of transaction. We'll be looking at those change vectors more closely in Chapter 3, but it's worth mentioning at this point that while most of the change vectors are applied to data blocks only when the transaction commits, the change vector for the start of transaction is an important special case and is applied to the *undo segment header block* as the transaction starts.

So Oracle has a mechanism for reducing the number of times a session demands space from, and copies information into, the (public) redo log buffer, and that improves the level of concurrency we can achieve . . . up to a point. But you're probably thinking that we have to pay for this benefit somewhere—and, of course, we do.

Earlier on we saw that every change we made resulted in an access to the In memory undo latch. Does that mean we have just *moved* the threat of latch activity rather than actually relieving it? Yes and no. We now hit only one latch (In memory undo latch) instead of two (redo allocation and redo copy), so we have at least halved the latch activity, but, more significantly, there are multiple child latches for the In memory undo latches, one for each in-memory undo pool. Before the new mechanism appeared, most systems ran with just one redo allocation latch, so although we now hit an In memory undo latch just as many times as we used to hit the redo allocation latch, we are spreading the access across far more latches.

It's also worth noting that the new mechanism also has two types of redo allocation latch—one type covers the private redo threads, one type covers the public redo threads, and each thread has its own latch. This helps to explain the extra gets on the redo allocation latch statistic that we saw earlier: our session uses a private redo allocation latch to acquire a private redo thread, then on the commit it has to acquire a public redo allocation latch, and then the log writer (as we shall see in Chapter 6) acquires the public redo allocation latches (and my test system had two public redo threads) to write the log buffer to file.

Overall, then, the amount of latch activity decreases and the focus of latch activity is spread a little more widely, which is a good thing. But in a multiuser system, there are always other points of view to consider—using the old mechanism, the amount of redo a session copied into the log buffer and applied to the database blocks at any one instant was very small; using the new mechanism, the amount of redo to copy and apply could be relatively large, which means it takes more time to apply to the database blocks, potentially blocking other sessions from accessing those blocks as the changes are made. This may be one reason why the private redo threads are strictly limited in size.

Moreover, using the old mechanism, a second session reading a changed block would see the changes immediately; with the new mechanism, a second session can see only that a block is subject to some private redo, so the second session is now responsible for tracking down the private redo and applying it to the block (if necessary), and then deciding what to do next with the block. (Think about the problems of referential integrity if you can't immediately see that another session has, for example, deleted a primary key that you need.) This leads to longer code paths, and more complex code, but *even if* the resulting code for read consistency does use more CPU than it used to, there is always an argument for making several sessions use a little more CPU as a way of avoiding a single point of contention.

■ **Note** There is an important principle of optimization that is often overlooked. Sometimes it is better for everyone to do a little *more* work if that means they are operating in separate locations rather than constantly colliding on the same contention point—competition wastes resources.

I don't know how many different events there are that could force a session to construct new versions of blocks from private redo and undo, but I do know that there are several events that result in a session abandoning the new strategy before the commit.

An obvious case where Oracle has to abandon the new mechanism is when either the private redo thread or the in-memory undo pool becomes full. As we saw earlier, each private area is limited to roughly 64KB (or 128KB if you're running a 64-bit copy of Oracle). When an area is full, Oracle creates a single redo record, copies it to the public redo thread, and then continues using the public redo thread in the old way.

But there are other events that cause this switch prematurely. For example, your SQL might trigger a recursive statement. For a quick check on possible causes, and how many times each has occurred, you could connect as SYS and run the following SQL (sample taken from 10.2.0.3):

```
select ktiffcat, ktiffflc from x$ktiff;

KTIFFCAT                                   KTIFFFLC
---------------------------------------- ----------
Undo pool overflow flushes                        0
Stack cv flushes                                 21
Multi-block undo flushes                          0
Max. chgs flushcs                                 9
NTP flushes                                       0
Contention flushes                               18
Redo pool overflow flushes                        0
Logfile space flushes                             0
Multiple persistent buffer flushes                0
Bind time flushes                                 0
Rollback flushes                                  6
Commit flushes                                13628
Recursive txn flushes                             2
Redo only CR flushes                              0
Ditributed txn flushes                            0
Set txn use rbs flushes                           0
Bitmap state change flushes                      26
Presumed commit violation                         0

18 rows selected.
```

Unfortunately, although there are various statistics relating to IMU in the `v$sysstat` dynamic performance view (e.g., `IMU flushes`), they don't seem to correlate terribly well with the figures from the `x$` structure—although, if you ignore a couple of the numbers, you can get quite close to thinking you've found the matching bits.

Undo Complexity

Undo is more complicated than redo. Most significantly, any process may, in principle, need to access any undo record at any time to "hide" an item of data that it is not yet supposed to see. To meet this requirement efficiently, Oracle keeps the undo records inside the database in a special tablespace known, unsurprisingly, as the undo tablespace; then the code has to maintain various pointers to the undo records so that a process knows where to find the undo records it needs. The advantage of keeping undo information inside the database in "ordinary" data files is that the blocks are subject to exactly the same buffering, writing, and recovery algorithms as every block in the database—the basic code to manage undo blocks is the same as the code to handle every other type of block.

There are three reasons why a process needs to read an undo record, and therefore three ways in which chains of pointers run through the undo tablespace. We will examine all three in detail in Chapter 3, but I will make some initial comments about the commonest two uses now.

Note *Linked lists* of undo records are used to deal with read consistency, rolling back changes, and deriving commit SCNs that have been "lost" due to *delayed block cleanout*. The third topic will be postponed until Chapter 3.

Read Consistency

The first, and most commonly invoked, use of undo is read consistency, and I have already commented briefly on read consistency. The existence of undo allows a session to see an older version of the data when it's not yet supposed to see a newer version.

The requirement for read consistency means that a block must contain a pointer to the undo records that describe how to hide changes to the block. But there could be an arbitrarily large number of changes that need to be concealed, and insufficient space for that many pointers in a single block. So Oracle allows a limited number of pointers in each block (one for each concurrent transaction affecting the block), which are stored in the ITL entries. When a process creates an undo record, it (usually) overwrites one of the existing pointers, saving the previous value as part of the undo record.

Take another look at the undo record I showed you earlier, after updating three rows in a single block:

```
*-----------------------------
* Rec #0xf  slt: 0x1a  objn: 45810(0x0000b2f2)  objd: 45810  tblspc: 12(0x0000000c)
*       Layer:  11 (Row)   opc: 1   rci 0x0e
Undo type:  Regular undo   Last buffer split:  No
Temp Object:  No
Tablespace Undo:  No
rdba: 0x00000000
*-----------------------------
KDO undo record:
KTB Redo
op: 0x02  ver: 0x01
op: C  uba: 0x0080009a.09d4.0d
KDO Op code: URP row dependencies Disabled
  xtype: XA  bdba: 0x02c0018a  hdba: 0x02c00189
itli: 2  ispac: 0  maxfr: 4863
tabn: 0 slot: 4(0x4) flag: 0x2c lock: 0 ckix: 16
ncol: 4 nnew: 1 size: -4
col  2: [ 6]  78 78 78 78 78 78
```

The table block holding the fifth row I had updated was pointing to this undo record, and we can see from the second line of the dump that it is record `0xf` in the undo block. Seven lines up from the bottom of the dump you see that this record has `op: C`, which tells us that it is the continuation of an earlier update by the same transaction. This lets Oracle know that the rest of the line `uba: 0x0080009a.09d4.0d` is part of the information that has to be used to re-create the older version of the block: as the xxxxxx (78s) are copied back to column 2 of row 4, the value `0x0080009a.09d4.0d` has to be copied back to ITL entry 2.

Of course, once Oracle has taken these steps to reconstruct an older version of the block, it will discover that it hasn't yet gone far enough, but the pointer in ITL 2 is now telling it where to find the next undo record to apply. In this way a process can gradually work its way backward through time; the pointer in each ITL entry tells Oracle where to find an undo record to apply, and each undo record includes the information to take the ITL entry backward in time as well as taking the data backward in time.

Rollback

The second, major use of undo is in rolling back changes, either with an explicit rollback (or *rollback to savepoint*) or because a step in a transaction has failed and Oracle has issued an implicit, statement-level rollback.

Read consistency is about a single block, and finding a linked list of all the undo records for that block. Rolling back is about the history of a transaction, so we need a linked list that runs through all the undo records for a transaction in the correct (which, in this case, means reverse) order.

Note Here is a simple example demonstrating why we need to link the undo records "backward." Imagine we update a row twice, changing a single column value from A to B and then from B to C, giving us two undo records. If we want to reverse the change, we have to change the C back to B before we can apply an undo record that says "change a B to an A"; in other words, we have to apply the second undo record before we apply the first undo record.

Looking again at the sample undo record, we can see signs of the linked list. Line 3 of the dump includes the entry `rci 0x0e`. This tells Oracle that the undo record created immediately before this undo record was number 14 (`0x0e`) in the same undo block. It's possible, of course, that the previous undo record will be in a different undo block, but that should be the case only if the current undo record is the first undo record of the undo block, in which case the `rci` entry would be zero and the `rdba:` entry four lines below it would give the block address of the previous undo record. If you have to go back a block, then the last record of the block will usually be the required record, although technically what you need is the record pointed at by the `irb:` entry. However, the only case in which the `irb:` entry might not point to the last record is if you have done a `rollback to savepoint`.

There's an important difference between read consistency and rolling back, of course. For read consistency we make a copy of the data block in memory and apply the undo records to that block, and it's a copy of the block that we can discard very rapidly once we've finished with it; when rolling back we acquire the current block and apply the undo record to that. This has three important effects:

- The data block is the current block, so it is the version of the block that must eventually be written to disc.
- Because it is the current block, we will be generating redo as we change it (even though we are "changing it back to the way it used to be").

- Because Oracle has crash-recovery mechanisms that clean up accidents as efficiently as possible, we need to ensure that the undo record is marked as "undo applied" as we use it, and doing that generates even more redo.

If the undo record was one that had already been used for rolling back, line 4 of the dump would have looked like this:

```
Undo type:  Regular undo    User Undo Applied  Last buffer split:  No
```

In the raw block dump, the `User Undo Applied` flag is just 1 byte rather than a 17-character string.

Rolling back involves a lot of work, and a rollback can take roughly the same amount of time as the original transaction, possibly generating a similar amount of redo. But you have to remember that rolling back is an activity that changes data blocks, so you have to reacquire, modify, and write those blocks, and write the redo that describes how you've changed those blocks. Moreover, if the transaction was a large, long-running transaction, you may find that some of the blocks you've changed have been written to disc and flushed from the cache—so they'll have to be read from disc before you can roll them back!

Note Some systems use Oracle tables to hold "temporary" or "scratchpad" information. One of the strategies used with such tables is to insert data without committing it so that read consistency makes it private to the session, and then roll back to make the data "go away." There are many flaws in this strategy, the potentially high cost of rolling back being just one of them. The ability to eliminate the cost of rollback is one of the things that makes global temporary tables useful.

There are other overheads introduced by rolling back, of course. When a session creates undo records, it acquires, pins, and fills one undo block at a time; when it is rolling back it gets one record from an undo block at a time, releasing and reacquiring the block for each record. This means that you generate more buffer visits on undo blocks to roll back than you generated when initially executing the transaction. Moreover, every time Oracle acquires an undo record, it checks that the tablespace it should be applied to is still online (if it isn't, Oracle will transfer the undo record into a *save undo* segment in the *system* tablespace); this shows up as get on the *dictionary cache* (specifically the dc_tablespaces cache).

We can finish the comments on rolling back with one last quirky little detail. If your session issues a rollback command, the step that completes the rollback is a commit. We'll spend a little more time on that in Chapter 3.

Summary

In some ways redo is a very simple concept: every change to a block in a data file is described by a *redo change vector*, and these change vectors are written to the redo log buffer (almost) immediately, and are ultimately written into the redo log file.

As we make changes to data (which includes index entries and structural metadata), we also create *undo records* in the undo tablespace that describe how to reverse those changes. Since the undo tablespace is just another set of data files, we create redo change vectors to describe the undo records we store there.

In earlier versions of Oracle, change vectors were usually combined in pairs—one describing the forward change, one describing the undo record—to create a single *redo record* that was written (initially) into the redo log buffer.

In later versions of Oracle, the step of moving change vectors into the redo log buffer was seen as an important bottleneck in OLTP systems, and a new mechanism was created to allow a session to accumulate all the changes for a transaction "in private" before creating one large redo record in the redo buffer.

The new mechanism is strictly limited in the amount of work a session will do before it flushes its change vectors to the redo log buffer and switches to the older mechanism, and there are various events that will make this switch happen prematurely.

While redo operates as a simple "write it and forget it" stream, undo may be frequently reread in the ongoing activity of the database, and undo records have to be linked together in different ways to allow for efficient access. Read consistency requires chains of undo records for a given block; rolling back requires a chain of undo records for a given transaction. (And there is a third chain, which will be addressed in Chapter 3.)

CHAPTER 3

Transactions and Consistency

Now You See Me, Now You Don't

In Chapter 2 you saw how Oracle uses redo change vectors to describe changes to data, undo records to describe how to reverse out those changes, and redo (again) to describe how to create the undo records—and then (apart from a concurrency optimization introduced in Oracle Database 10*g*) applies the changes in near real time rather than "saving them up" to the moment you commit.

Chapter 2 also commented on the way that undo records allow changes to the data to be kept "invisible" until everyone is supposed to see them, and how we can also use undo records to roll back our work if we change our minds about the work we've done.

Finally, Chapter 2 pointed out that redo is basically a "write and forget" continuous stream, while undo needs various linked lists running through it to allow different sets of records to be reused in different ways.

This chapter examines the mechanisms Oracle uses to create the linked lists through undo records and, most importantly, how the code locates the end points of those lists. It also examines the third type of linked list that was mentioned very briefly in Chapter 2, the linked list that gives us access to historic commit SCNs (and I'll describe how Oracle's "lazy processing" makes that linked list necessary).

We'll be looking at the transaction table that Oracle keeps in each undo segment header block to anchor one set of linked lists, and the interested transaction list (ITL) that Oracle keeps in every single data (and index) block as the anchor to another set of linked lists. Then we'll take a closer look into the undo segment header to examine the transaction table control section (hereinafter referred to as the *transaction control*) that Oracle uses as the anchor point for the final linked list.

We'll finish with a short note on LOBs (large objects), as Oracle deals with undo, redo, read consistency, and transactions differently when dealing with LOBs—or, at least, the LOB data that is stored "out of row."

Conflict Resolution

Let's imagine we have to deal with a system where there are just two users, you and I, who are constantly modifying and querying data in the small portion of a database.

If *you* are applying a transaction to a database and *I* am simply querying the database, I must not see *any* of your changes until the moment you tell me (by executing a `commit;` call) that I can see *all* of your changes. But even when you have committed your transaction, the moment at which I am allowed to see the changes you've made depends on my *isolation level* (see the sidebar "Isolation Levels" in Chapter 2) and the nature of the work I am doing. So, from an internal point of view, I have to have an efficient method for identifying (and ignoring) changes that are not yet committed as well as changes that have been committed so recently that I shouldn't yet be able to see them. To make things a little more challenging, I need to remember that "recently" might not be all that recent if I've been executing a long-running query, so I may have to do a lot of work to get an accurate idea of when your transaction committed.

Viewing the activity from the opposite perspective, when you commit your transaction (allowing your changes to become visible to other users), you need an efficient mechanism that allows you to let everyone see that you've committed that transaction, but you don't want to revisit and mark all the blocks that you have changed, because otherwise this step could take just as much time as the time it took to make the changes in the first place. Of course, if you decide to roll back your work rather than commit it, you will also need a mechanism that links together all the undo records for the changes you have made, in the order you made them, so that you can reverse out the changes in the opposite order. Since rolling back real changes is (or ought to be) a rare event compared to committing them, Oracle is engineered to make the commit as fast as possible and allows the rollback mechanism to be much slower.

One of the first things we need so that we can coordinate our activity is some sort of focal point for change. Since, in this scenario, you are the agent of change, you supply the focal point or, rather, two focal points—the first is a single entry in a special part of the database to act as the primary reference point for the transaction, and the second appears as an entry in every single table or index block that you change. We'll start by looking at the reference point for the transaction.

Transactions and Undo

When you create a database, you have to create an undo tablespace (and if you're using RAC, this is extended to one undo tablespace for each instance that will access the database). Unless you're using old-style manual rollback management, Oracle will automatically create several undo segments in that tablespace and will automatically add, grow, shrink, or drop undo segments as the workload on the database changes.

Transaction management starts with, and revolves around, the undo segments. The segment header block, which (for undo segments) is the first block of the segment, contains a lot of the standard structures that you will see in the segment header block of other types of segment—the extent map and the extent control header, for example—but it also contains a number of very special structures (see Figure 3-1), in particular the *transaction table* (*TRN TBL:*, a short list identifying recent transactions) and the *transaction table control section* (*TRN CTL::*, a collection of details describing the state and content of the transaction table).

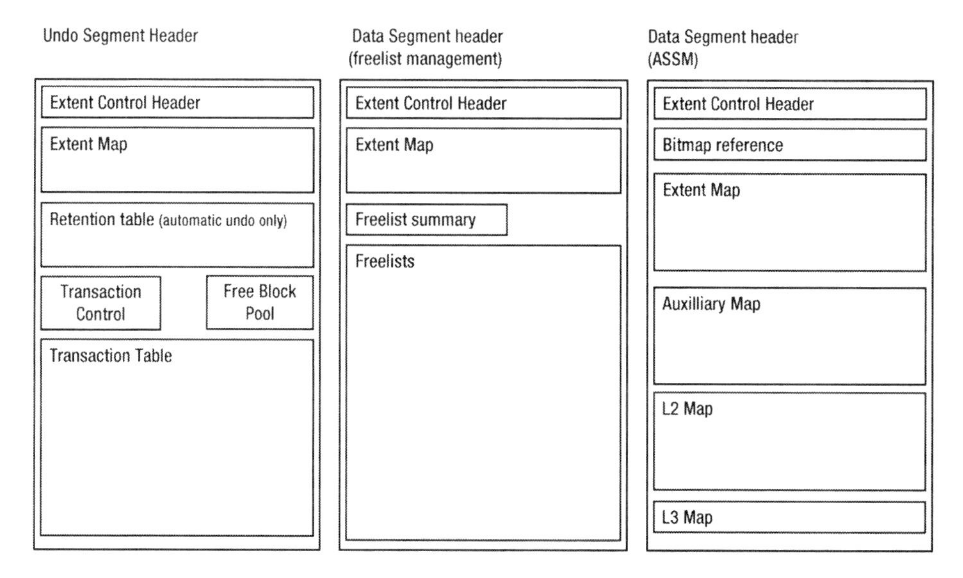

Figure 3-1. *Schematic comparing key content of different types of segment headers*

The following dump is an extract from a transaction table, restricted to just the first few and last few entries and hiding some of the columns we don't need to discuss. This extract includes one entry (`index = 0x02`) that represents an active transaction.

```
TRN TBL:

index state cflags  wrap#    uel         scn            dba            nub         cmt
------------------------------------------------------------------------------------
 0x00    9    0x00  0x2013 0x001b 0x0000.016f1fc1 0x0180083e 0x00000001 1302762364
 0x01    9    0x00  0x2014 0x001a 0x0000.016f1f54 0x0180083e 0x00000001 1302762364
 0x02   10    0x80  0x2013 0x0002 0x0000.016f20fc 0x0180083e 0x00000001          0
 0x03    9    0x00  0x200c 0x001c 0x0000.016f20d8 0x0180083e 0x00000001 1302762364
...
 0x20    9    0x00  0x200f 0x001f 0x0000.016f1c75 0x0180083f 0x00000001 1302762364
 0x21    9    0x00  0x2013 0x0010 0x0000.016f1e0c 0x0180083f 0x00000001 1302762364
```

This dump is from an 8KB block size using automatic undo management on a system running Oracle Database 11*g*, and the restrictions on space imposed by the 8KB block mean that the transaction table holds just 34 rows. (Earlier versions of Oracle held 48 entries in automatic undo segments and 96 entries in manually managed rollback segments—which didn't have an extent retention map—when using 8KB blocks).

Since there's only a limited number of entries in a transaction table and a limited number of undo segments in an undo tablespace, you can only record details about a relatively small number of recent transactions, and you will have to keep reusing the transaction table entries. Reusing the entries is where the column labeled `wrap#` becomes relevant; each time you reuse an entry in the table, you increment the `wrap#` for that entry.

Note Occasionally I hear the question, "Does the `wrap#` get reset every time the instance restarts?" The answer is no. As a general principle, any sort of counter that is stored on the database is unlikely to be reset when the instance restarts. Remember, every slot in every undo segment has its own `wrap#`, so it would be a lot of work at startup to reset them all.

Start and End of Transaction

When a session starts a transaction, it picks an undo segment, picks an entry from the transaction table, increments the `wrap#`, changes the `state` to "active" (value 10), and modifies a few other columns. Since this is a change to a database block, it will generate a redo change vector (with an `OP` code of 5.2) that will ultimately get into the redo log file; this declares to the world and writes into the database the fact that the session has an active transaction.

Similarly, when the transaction completes (typically through a `commit;` call), the session sets the state back to "free" (value 9) and updates a few other columns in the entry—in particular, by writing the current SCN into the `scn` column. Again, this constitutes a change to the database so it generates a redo change vector (with an `OP` code of 5.4) that will go into the redo log. This moment is also rather special because (historically) this is the "moment" when your session protects its committed changes by issuing a call to the log writer (lgwr) to write the current content of the redo log buffer to disc and then waiting for the log writer to confirm that it has finished writing. Once the log writer has written, you have a permanent record of the transaction—in the ACID jargon, the transaction is now *durable*.

Note You will often find comments on the Internet and in the Oracle documentation about the log writer "creating a commit record." There is no such action. When you commit, you modify a database block, specifically the undo segment header block holding the transaction table slot that you're using, and this block change first requires you to generate a redo change vector (historically as a stand-alone redo record) and copy it into the redo log buffer. It is this change vector that (very informally) could be called "the commit record"; but it's your session (not the log writer) that generates it and puts it into the redo log buffer, it's just a specific example of the standard logging mechanism. The only special thing about "the commit record" is that once it has been copied into the log buffer, the session calls the log writer to write the current contents of the log buffer to disk, and waits for that write to complete. There will be a more detailed description of the sequences of events in Chapter 6.

A transaction is defined by the entry it acquires in a transaction table and is given a transaction ID constructed from the undo segment number, the index number of the entry in the transaction table, and the latest `wrap#` of that entry—so when you see a transaction ID like `0x0009.002.00002013`, you can translate this into: undo segment 9, entry 2, `wrap#` `0x2013` (8,211 decimal). If you want to check which undo segment this is and the location of the header block, you can always query view `dba_rollback_segs` by `segment_id`.

This transaction ID will appear in several different places—a couple of the well-known places are in the dynamic performance views `v$transaction` and `v$lock`. The examples of dumps that I've printed so far came from an instance where nothing else was running, so when I ran the following queries, I knew they would return just one row which would be for the transaction I had started:

```
select xidusn, xidslot, xidsqn from v$transaction;

    XIDUSN    XIDSLOT     XIDSQN
---------- ---------- ----------
         9          2       8211

select trunc(id1/65536) usn, mod(id1,65536) slot, id2 wrap, lmode
from V$lock where type = 'TX';

       USN       SLOT       WRAP      LMODE
---------- ---------- ---------- ----------
         9          2       8211          6
```

You'll notice that the lock mode on this "transaction lock" is 6 (exclusive, or X, mode). While my transaction is active, no one else can change that entry in the transaction table, although, as you will see in Chapter 4, other sessions may try to acquire it in mode 4 (share, or S, mode) so that they can spot the moment the transaction commits (or rolls back). You'll also notice that where I've been talking about an "entry" in the transaction table, the view refers to it as a *slot*, and this is how I'll refer to it from now on.

The Transaction Table

Table 3-1 lists and describes the columns from the transaction table extract presented earlier in the chapter.

Table 3-1. *Columns in the Transaction Table*

Column	Description
`index`	Identifies the row in the transaction table and is used as part of the transaction id. This is known most commonly as the *transaction table slot* number. (It's not a value that's physically stored in the block, by the way—it's a value derived by position when we dump the block.)
`state`	The state of the entry: 9 is INACTIVE, and 10 is ACTIVE.
`cflags`	Bit flag showing the state of a transaction using the slot: `0x0` no transaction, `0x10` transaction is dead, `0x80` active transaction. (`0x90` – dead and being rolled back).
`wrap#`	A counter for the number of times the slot has been used. Part of the transaction id.
`uel`	A pointer to the next transaction table slot to use after this one goes active. In a new segment this will look very tidy, but as transactions come and go, the pointers will eventually turn into a fairly random linked list wandering through the slots.

Continued

Column	Description
scn	The commit SCN for a committed transaction. (Since a rollback call ends with a commit, this would also be used for the commit SCN at the end of a rollback). For most versions of Oracle, this column is also used as the start SCN when the transaction is active, but, strangely, my copy of 10.2.0.3 dumps this as zero for active transactions.
dba	Data Block Address of the last undo block that the transaction used to write an undo record. This allows Oracle (particularly on crash recovery) to find the last undo record generated by a transaction so that it knows where to start the process of rolling back.
nub	Number of undo blocks used by this transaction so far. (During a transaction rollback you can watch this number decrease.)
cmt	Commit time to the nearest second, measured as the number of seconds since midnight (UTC) of 1 January 1970. It is zero when the transaction is active. Since this seems to be a 32-bit number it has crossed my mind to wonder whether some systems may run into trouble in January 2038 if it's treated as a signed integer or in February 2106 if it's treated as unsigned.

In fact, you don't need to do block dumps to see the transaction table information because it's exposed in one of the x$ structures: `x$ktuxe`. This is one of the stranger structures in Oracle because a query against the structure will actually cause Oracle to visit each undo segment header block of each undo segment in the database. The formatting of the contents is different and the `cmt` column (transaction commit time) isn't available.

```
select
        indx,
        ktuxesta,
        ktuxecfl,
        ktuxesqn        wrap#,
        ktuxescnw       scnW,
        ktuxescnb       scnB,
        ktuxerdbf       dba_file,
        ktuxerdbb       dba_block,
        ktuxesiz        nub
from
        x$ktuxe
where
        ktuxeusn = 9
and     ktuxeslt <= 5
;
```

```
INDX KTUXESTA   KTUXECFL    WRAP#  SCNW      SCNB  DBA_FILE DBA_BLOCK   NUB
---- ---------- ---------- ------ ----- --------- --------- --------- -----
   0 INACTIVE   NONE         8211     0  24059841         6      2110     1
   1 INACTIVE   NONE         8212     0  24059732         6      2110     1
   2 ACTIVE     NONE         8211     0  24060156         6      2110     1
   3 INACTIVE   NONE         8204     0  24060120         6      2110     1
   4 INACTIVE   NONE         8212     0  24059364         6      2111     1
   5 INACTIVE   NONE         8212     0  24059497         6      2110     1
```

So what we have in a transaction table is a "focal point" that records a transaction ID as follows:

- A specific physical location stored in the database
- An indicator showing whether that transaction has committed or is still active
- The SCN for a committed transaction
- Information about where we can find the most recent undo record generated by the transaction
- The volume of undo generated by the transaction

This means we can typically access critical information about the most recent $N \times 34$ transactions (where N is the number of undo segments available to end-user processes, 34 is the number of transaction table slots in an undo segment in 11*g*, and assuming a fairly steady pattern of transactions) that have affected the database.

In particular, if a transaction has to roll back, or if a session is killed and `smon` (system monitor) has to roll its transaction back, or if the instance crashes and, during instance recovery, `smon` has to roll back all the transactions that were active at the moment of the crash, it is easy to spot any active transactions (`state = 10`) and find the last undo block (the `dba`) each transaction was using. Then we can start walking backward along the chain of undo blocks for each transaction, applying each undo record as we go, because (as you saw in Chapter 2) each undo record points to the previous undo record for the transaction. It isn't commonly realized, by the way, that when Oracle has applied all the relevant undo records, the last thing it does is update the transaction table slot to show that the transaction is complete—in other words, it commits.

■ **Note** It is possible to declare named *savepoints* in mid-transaction and then `rollback to savepoint X`. If you do this, your session keeps a list of the current savepoints in the session memory with the address of the last undo record created before the savepoint call was issued. This allows the session to apply undo records in reverse order and stop at the right place. An interesting (but perhaps undocumented) side effect of creating a savepoint in a transaction is that it seems to disable some of the array-processing optimization that sometimes takes place in the construction of undo records.

Reviewing the Undo Block

It's worth looking at a small extract from an undo block at this point, because there is a little detail about block "ownership" that you need to understand to complete the picture. Here's the start of an undo block dump showing the record directory and a little bit of the first and last records:

```
********************************************************************************
UNDO BLK:
xid: 0x0008.029.00002068  seq: 0x97a cnt: 0xc   irb: 0xc   icl: 0x0   flg: 0x0000

 Rec Offset      Rec Offset      Rec Offset      Rec Offset      Rec Offset
---------------------------------------------------------------------------
0x01 0x1f9c     0x02 0x1f4c     0x03 0x1ebc     0x04 0x1e88     0x05 0x1e2c
0x06 0x1db8     0x07 0x1d40     0x08 0x1cec     0x09 0x1c84     0x0a 0x1c28
0x0b 0x1bbc     0x0c 0x1b60

*-----------------------------
* Rec #0x1 slt: 0x17  objn: 2(0x00000002)  objd: 4294967295  tblspc: 12(0x0000000c)
*       Layer:  22 (Tablespace Bitmapped file)   opc: 3   rci 0x00
Undo type:  Regular undo    Begin trans    Last buffer split:  No

...

*-----------------------------
* Rec #0xc slt: 0x29  objn: 45756(0x0000b2bc)  objd: 45756  tblspc: 12(0x0000000c)
*       Layer:  11 (Row)   opc: 1   rci 0x0b
Undo type:  Regular undo   Last buffer split:  No
Temp Object:  No
```

Without looking too closely at the details, an undo block appears to be similar in many ways to an ordinary data block—there's a header section with some control information and metadata; there's a *row directory* that lists the locations of the items that have been stacked in the block, there's a heap of items (in this case, undo records) stacked up from the end of the block, and then there's the block free space in the middle. One important difference between table rows and undo records, though, is that undo records don't get changed (except in one special circumstance), so they always stay in the same place once they've been put into the block—unlike table rows, which, as you saw in Chapter 2, may get copied into the free space as they are updated, leaving tangled pointers and (temporary) holes in the block (see Figure 3-2).

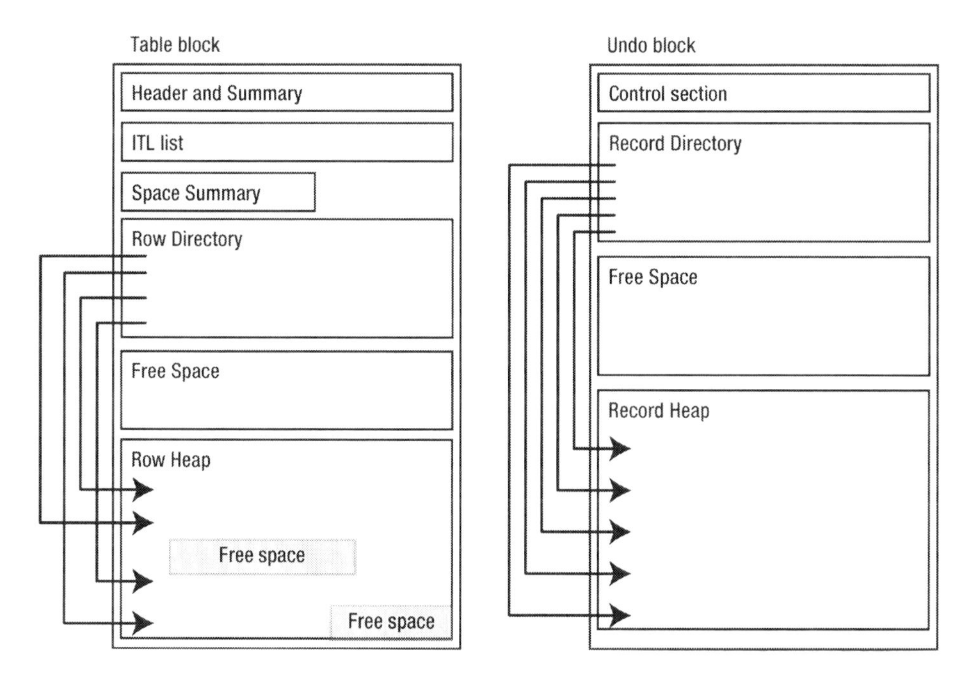

Figure 3-2. *Schematic comparison of an undo block and table block*

■ **Note** There is one case where undo records do get modified, but the modification is a change to a single byte flag, which means the record doesn't change size and therefore doesn't need to be copied for the modification. That single-byte change will still generate a few dozen bytes of redo. The change occurs when a session is rolling back a transaction (or rolling back to a savepoint) and, when it uses the undo record, it sets a flag byte in the record to a value for `User Undo Applied`. You can see this work reported in the statistic `rollback changes - undo records applied`.

Looking at the top line of the preceding block dump, the `xid:` (transaction ID) is `0x0008.029.00002068`, which means that this is undo segment 8 (`0x0008`), the "owner" of this undo block is currently a transaction that is using slot 41 (`0x029`) from the transaction table (since the slot number is over 34, we can infer that this is from an older version of Oracle, rather than 11*g*), and this is the 8,296th time (`0x00002068`) that the transaction slot has been used. We can also see from the incarnation number (`seq: 0x97a`) that the undo block itself has been wiped clean (*newed* in Oracle-speak) and reused 2,426 times.

Note When Oracle is about to reuse an undo block, it doesn't care about the previous content, so it doesn't bother to read it from disk before reusing it; it simply allocates a buffer and formats a new empty block in the buffer. This process is referred to as *newing* the block. If you have enabled Flashback Database, though, Oracle will usually decide that it needs to copy the old version of the block into the flashback log, so it will read it before newing it. This action can be seen in the statistic `physical reads for flashback new`. This mechanism isn't restricted to undo blocks – you will see the same effect when you insert new rows into a freshly truncated table, for example – but it is the most common reason for this statistic to start appearing when you enable database flashback.

There's an odd discrepancy, though, in the first line of record `#0x1`, where we can see the text `slt: 0x17`, which doesn't match the first line of the last record (`#0xC`) in the block, where we see the text `slt: 0x29`. This means the first record was put into this undo block by a transaction using slot 23 (`0x17`) of the transaction table while the last record was put there by the transaction using slot 41 (`0x29`)—which is what we expect since that's the one that "owns" the block.

It is a little-known fact that a single undo block may contain undo records from multiple transactions. This oversight is, I think, a misinterpretation of a comment in the Oracle documentation that transactions don't *share* undo blocks—a true, but slightly deceptive, statement. A transaction will acquire ownership of an undo block exclusively, pin it, and then use it until either the block is full (at which point the transaction acquires another undo block and updates its transaction table slot to point to the new block) or the transaction commits.

If there's still enough empty space left in the block when the transaction commits (approximately 400 bytes the last time I tested it), the block will be added to a short list in the undo segment header called the *free block pool*. If this happens, the next transaction to start in that undo segment is allowed to take the block from the pool and use up the remaining space. So active transactions will not write to the same undo block *at the same* time, but several transactions may have used the same undo block one after the other.

In general, then, the last record in an undo block will belong to the transaction that currently "owns" the block, but in extreme circumstances, any transaction that has put records into that block will be able to identify its own records because it has stamped its records with its slot number.

Note Occasionally people get worried about the number of `user rollbacks` their systems are recording, more often than not because they've looked at the statistic `Rollback per transaction %:` in an Automatic Workload Repository (AWR) or Statspack report. Don't worry about it until after you've looked at the instance activity statistics `transaction rollbacks` and `rollback changes - undo records applied`. It's quite possible that you've using one of those web application servers that issue a redundant `rollback;` call after every query to the database. This will result in lots of `user rollbacks` that don't turn into `transaction rollbacks`, but do no work.

So you know how to start and end a transaction and how to deal with rolling back a transaction, either voluntarily or after a session or system crash. There are lots more details we could investigate about the inner workings of transaction control, but we've covered the main activity that surrounds the transaction table. It's time now to look at undo from another perspective and turn our attention to the data blocks and the ITL structure that transactions use as the focal point for the changes they make to a block.

Data Block Visits and Undo

Any time your session looks at a data block, it needs to ensure that what you see is the appropriate version of the data. This means that, from an *external* point of view, your session should not see any uncommitted data, or data that was modified and committed since the start of your query (or DML statement or even transaction—depending on the isolation level). This is referred to as a *read-consistent version* of the data.

■ **Note** It's easy to forget that read consistency is also a necessary prerequisite to changing data. If your session is supposed to modify the data in a block, then, from an *internal* point of view, it has to see it in two different ways—it has to see the *current* version of the data, because that's the only thing that can legally change, and it has to see a *read-consistent* version of the data, because if there are critical differences between the two views, your session may have to wait, it may have to restart the current statement, or it may even have to fail and raise an error (typically `ORA-08177: can't serialize access for this transaction`).

We're going to walk through the details of how read consistency works in the next few sections, so we need to set up a little data, see exactly what it looks like, and then watch it very closely as one session makes changes and another session works to avoid seeing those changes.

Setting the Scene

We'll start with the example of querying the data. Imagine the following sequence of events in a multiuser environment where there are three other sessions apart from your own session connected to the database, and a table defined and loaded by the following SQL (see `core_03_ct.sql`, available in the Source Code/Download area of the Apress web site [`www.apress.com`]):

```
create table t1(id number, n1 number);

insert into t1 values(1,1);
insert into t1 values(2,2);
insert into t1 values(3,3);
commit;
```

Before allowing anything else to happen, let's take a look at a block dump of the single block in our table at this point. We need this dump so that we can watch the internal information changing as one session modifies the user data and another session tries to work backward toward a specific version of that data.

```
Block header dump:  0x00c0070a
 Object id on Block? Y
 seg/obj: 0x18317  csc: 0x00.1731c44  itc: 2  flg: O  typ: 1 - DATA
     fsl: 0  fnx: 0x0 ver: 0x01

 Itl           Xid                  Uba         Flag  Lck        Scn/Fsc
0x01   0x0001.001.00001de4  0x01802ec8.0543.05  --U-    3  fsc 0x0000.01731c46
0x02   0x0000.000.00000000  0x00000000.0000.00  ----    0  fsc 0x0000.00000000
bdba: 0x00c0070a
data_block_dump,data header at 0xc90225c
===============
tsiz: 0x1fa0
hsiz: 0x18
pbl: 0x0c90225c
     76543210
flag=--------
ntab=1
nrow=3
frre=-1
fsbo=0x18
fseo=0x1f85
avsp=0x1f6d
tosp=0x1f6d
0xe:pti[0]     nrow=3     offs=0
0x12:pri[0]    offs=0x1f97
0x14:pri[1]    offs=0x1f8e
0x16:pri[2]    offs=0x1f85
block_row_dump:
tab 0, row 0, @0x1f97
tl: 9 fb: --H-FL-- lb: 0x1  cc: 2
col  0: [ 2]  c1 02
col  1: [ 2]  c1 02
tab 0, row 1, @0x1f8e
tl: 9 fb: --H-FL-- lb: 0x1  cc: 2
col  0: [ 2]  c1 03
col  1: [ 2]  c1 03
tab 0, row 2, @0x1f85
tl: 9 fb: --H-FL-- lb: 0x1  cc: 2
col  0: [ 2]  c1 04
col  1: [ 2]  c1 04
end_of_block_dump
```

The detail we are really going to pursue in this section is the interested transaction list (ITL)—the tabular section near the top of this dump starting with a set of labels at line 5 and holding two rows of information

The Interested Transaction List

Table 3-2 lists and describes each item in the ITL.

Table 3-2. Columns in the Interested Transaction List

Column	Description
`Itl`	The array index for the list. The number isn't physically stored in the block; it's generated by the code that does the dump. This value is used in the *lock byte* (`lb:`) for a row to show which transaction has locked the row.
`Xid`	The transaction id of a recent transaction that has modified this block. The format is `undo segment . undo slot . undo sequence number`.
`Uba`	The undo record address—including the sequence (or incarnation) number—of the block of the most recent undo record generated by this transaction for this block. The format is `Absolute block address . block sequence number . record within block`. (The "b" in the label suggests byte or block, but neither of those interpretations is quite accurate.)
`Flag`	Bit flag identifying the apparent state of this transaction: `----`: active (or "never existed" if every field in the `Xid` is zero). `--U-`: Upper bound commit (also set during "fast commit"). `C---`: Committed and cleaned out (all associated lock bytes have been reset to zero). `-B--`: May be relevant to the recursive transactions for index block splits. I have seen comments that this flag means the UBA will point to a record holding the previous content of the ITL entry, but I have not managed to confirm this. `---T`: I have seen comments that this means the transaction was active during block cleanout, but I have not managed to confirm this.
`Lck`	Number of rows locked by this transaction in this block.
`Scn/Fsc`	Depending on the `Flag`, the commit SCN or the number of bytes of free space that would become available if this transaction committed (Free Space Credit).

We can see in the initial block dump that the ITL for our block contains two entries—this is the default number when creating a table or index in Oracle Database 9*i* or later. If you want to create (or rebuild) an object with a larger ITL in each block, which you might do to avoid contention at higher levels of concurrent modification, you can do so by setting the `initrans` parameter at object creation time—but the ITL in any block can grow dynamically if it needs to, provided there is enough free space available in the block.

The size of the ITL is limited by the `maxtrans` parameter (at least for earlier versions of Oracle), which has a syntactic limit of 255 but a hard limit dictated by the size of the object's data block. The syntactic limit is, unfortunately, ignored in versions 10*g* and later; and in the case of an 8KB block size, the hard limit is 169.

■ **Note** There are a few oddities with `initrans`. For an index, the value for `initrans` applies only to the leaf blocks—each branch block (which includes the root block) will get one ITL entry, which is used only for block splits. The first ITL of a leaf block is reserved for leaf block splits, and there is one special case: when you create a new index on an empty (or sufficiently small) table, the single block of the index has to behave both as a root (branch) and a leaf, so it gets two ITL entries—one because it's a branch and the second because it's also a leaf and therefore needs an ITL for actions other than block splits. Historically the default value of `initrans` for a table was 1, but in recent versions of Oracle this changed to 2 even though the data dictionary will still report the value as 1. (And if you load some blocks using direct path loads, you will find that they initially have three ITL entries.)

The ITL exists to identify transactions that recently changed a data block, but it takes space to identify a transaction, and Oracle likes to keep the ITL as short as possible. (Oracle doesn't shrink an ITL once it has grown; arguably, there's generally no good time to do so, but you may occasionally come across a few extreme cases where it seems to be an "obvious" thing to do.) Moreover, on an index leaf block split, the old ITL is copied forward into the new leaf block—and this strategy can end up wasting a lot of space.

■ **Note** There are two other SCNs recorded at fixed locations on each data block: the *cleanout SCN* (labeled in the dump as `csc:`), which records the SCN at which the block was last subject to full cleanout (see "Delayed Block Cleanout" later in this chapter), and the *last change SCN* (labeled in the dump as `scn:`), which records the SCN as at the most recent change to the block and is linked with an extra byte (labeled `seq:`) that records the number of times the block has changed at that SCN (if the `seq:` reaches 254, it rolls over to 1 and triggers an increment in the instance SCN).

So what we see in this block is a short list of recent transactions. In fact, this block is so new that one of those ITL entries hasn't even been used yet—every item in ITL entry `0x02` is zeroed out. But in ITL entry `0x01` we see that transaction `1.1.1de4` (undo segment 1, slot 1, sequence 7,652) changed the block recently. It committed at SCN `0x01731c46`, but the block has not yet been cleaned out properly because the flag is `--U-` for upper bound commit (we'll look at the different effects that can appear from a commit call in a little while), and the lock counter reports three rows locked. (If you glance further down the dump, you can see that all three rows in the block show `lb: 0x01`—the three rows in this block were all locked by the transaction currently reported at ITL entry `0x01`.) Finally, you can see from the `uba` that if you go to record 5 of block 11,976 of file 6 (which should have sequence number `0x0543`), you'll find a description of how to reverse out the most recent change applied by the transaction.

Without dumping all the relevant undo, I'll just let you know that record 5 from that undo block says "clear slot (row) `0x02` from the table block and change the `uba` for ITL entry 1 to read `0x01802ec8.0543.04` (i.e. point to record `0x04` in the current undo block)"; record 4 says: "clear slot (row) `0x01` from the table block and change the `uba` for ITL entry 1 to read `0x01802ec8.0543.03`"; and, finally, record 3 says "clear slot (row) `0x01` from the block and change ITL entry 1 to 'no previous use'."

Concurrent Action

Now that we have some data ready, and a block with one used and one empty ITL entry, let's start four separate sessions and take the following step—in exactly the following order:

```
Session 1:              update t1 set n1 = 101 where id = 1;
Session 2:              update t1 set n1 = 102 where id = 2;
                        commit;
My session:     set transaction read only;
Session 3:              update t1 set n1 = 99 where id = 3;
                        commit;
My session:     select id, n1 from t1;
```

The first call in the session that I've labeled "My session" sets the isolation level (see Chapter 2) to *read only*, in effect freezing the database (from my point of view) to a specific point in time or, to be a little more precise, to a specific SCN.

From that point onward, two restrictions apply to my session: first, I am not allowed to see any *uncommitted* changes made by any other user (which is the standard *read committed* behavior in Oracle anyway), and second, more stringently, I am not even allowed to see any *committed* changes made after that moment.

So when I run my select statement, the uncommitted change made by session 1 and the committed change made by session 3 must remain invisible, and I should see only the committed change made by session 2. My query has to return the result set: (1,1), (2,102), (3,3). On the other hand, because of the near-real-time nature of the way that Oracle changes blocks, all the changes will have been made to the copy of the block that is in memory before I actually start to run my query. So what's going on inside Oracle to make it possible for me to see the correct result?

This (stripped to a minimum) is what the block looks like after the three sessions have made their changes and just before my query starts to run:

```
Itl           Xid                  Uba         Flag  Lck        Scn/Fsc
0x01   0x000a.00e.00001b93  0x01800518.04f5.34  --U-    1  fsc 0x0000.01731c83
0x02   0x0004.00c.00001964  0x018036ad.05ff.3a  ----    1  fsc 0x0000.00000000

0x12:pri[0]    offs=0x1f7b
0x14:pri[1]    offs=0x1f71
0x16:pri[2]    offs=0x1f85

tab 0, row 0, @0x1f7b
tl: 10 fb: --H-FL-- lb: 0x2  cc: 2
col  0: [ 2]  c1 02
col  1: [ 3]  c2 02 02

tab 0, row 1, @0x1f71
tl: 10 fb: --H-FL-- lb: 0x0  cc: 2
col  0: [ 2]  c1 03
col  1: [ 3]  c2 02 03

tab 0, row 2, @0x1f85
tl: 9 fb: --H-FL-- lb: 0x1  cc: 2
col  0: [ 2]  c1 04
col  1: [ 2]  c1 64
```

I forced Oracle to write this block to disk with a call to `alter system checkpoint` before dumping it, to show that all the changes (including the uncommitted change from session 1) are not just in the buffered copy of the critical block but could also be on disk already. You might notice, by the way, that rows 0 and 1 are at a different location in the block (`0x1f7b` and `0x1f71` rather than the offsets `0x1f97` and `0x1f8d` that appeared in the previous dump) because their updates increased the row length, so Oracle had to copy the rows to the block's free space to make the change; on the other hand, row 2 is still in the same location (`0x1f85`) because the change to its value didn't change the length of the row, thus allowing Oracle to do the update in place.

Look carefully at the ITL: although we have executed three transactions affecting this block in the very recent past, there are *still* only two ITL entries. This is because Oracle tries to keep the ITL as short as possible, and will reuse ITL entries for committed transactions rather than extend the list. (The ITL entries will be reused in the order of oldest commit SCN first.)

ITL entry `0x01` is showing the effects of a *commit cleanout*, the rapid but incomplete cleanout that may get done to some of the changed blocks as a transaction commits. The flag is set to upper bound commit, but the lock count is still set to 1, and the `Scn/Fsc` label is still set to `fsc` even though the value itself is showing a commit SCN of `0x01731c83`. If we check the body of the block, we see that row 2 (the third row) is showing its lock byte (`lb:`) as `0x01`—row 2 is the one row that had been locked by the transaction in ITL 1. This ITL entry is the ITL entry for our third transaction, the one that changed `n1` to 99 for `id = 3` and then committed.

ITL entry `0x02` looks as if it is not yet committed. For reasons we will see later, this may be deceptive—it is possible that the transaction committed some time ago without Oracle doing anything to tidy up the mess and mark the transaction as committed. In fact, this ITL is recording our first, uncommitted transaction and we can see that it has one row locked (`Lck = 1` in the ITL) and that row 0 is the one row in the block that is locked by ITL `0x2` (`lb: = 0x2` in the body of the block).

It would be nice at this point to have an animated sequence of diagrams, showing the links between an ITL entry and the relevant parts of the associated undo segment, but the best I can do is Figure 3-3, which is a generic example showing how an ITL points to the related slot in the undo segment header's transaction table, while the `uba` points to a specific record in an undo block in that segment, and—if this happens to be the most recent block in the transaction—how the transaction table slot would also point to the same undo block.

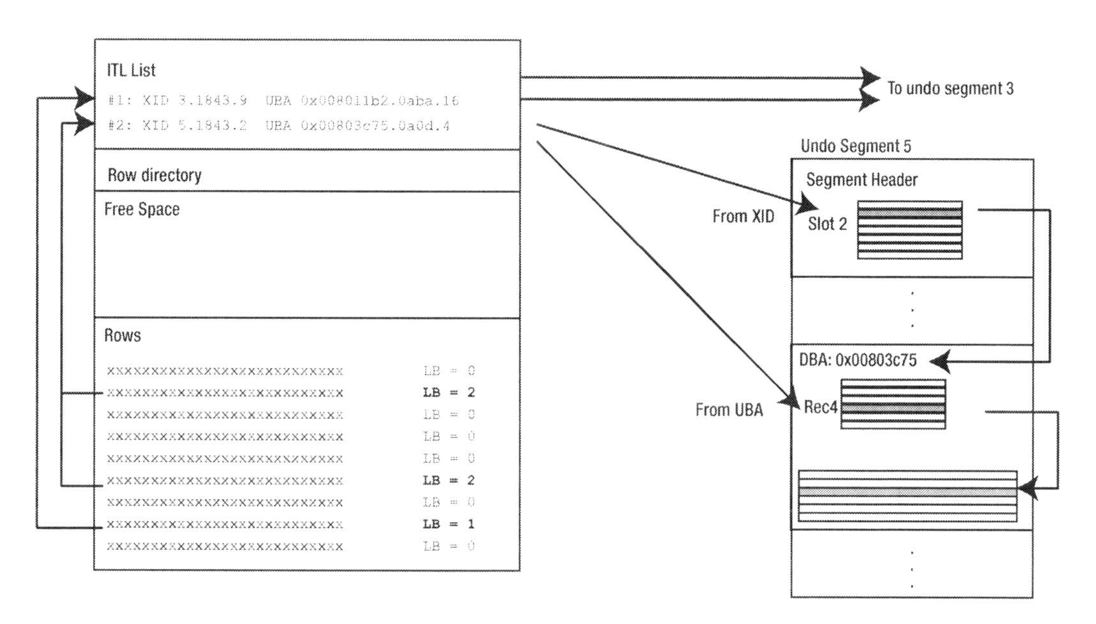

Figure 3-3. *Links between an ITL entry and the associated undo segment*

Creating Consistency

So what happens next? Oracle clones the block in memory and does a load of work to get from the current version to a version that (again, stripped to the minimum) looks like this:

```
Itl           Xid                  Uba                Flag  Lck        Scn/Fsc
0x01   0x0009.00d.00002100  0x018030ca.074c.11  C---     0  scn 0x0000.01731c7a
0x02   0x0000.000.00000000  0x00000000.0000.00  ----     0  fsc 0x0000.00000000

0x12:pri[0]    offs=0x1f68
0x14:pri[1]    offs=0x1f71
0x16:pri[2]    offs=0x1f85

tab 0, row 0, @0x1f68
tl: 9 fb: --H-FL-- lb: 0x0  cc: 2
col  0: [ 2]  c1 02
col  1: [ 2]  c1 02

tab 0, row 1, @0x1f71
tl: 10 fb: --H-FL-- lb: 0x0  cc: 2
col  0: [ 2]  c1 03
col  1: [ 3]  c2 02 03

tab 0, row 2, @0x1f85
tl: 9 fb: --H-FL-- lb: 0x0  cc: 2
col  0: [ 2]  c1 04
col  1: [ 2]  c1 04
```

Notice particularly that ITL entry 0x2 is back to the state "never been used" and that ITL entry 0x1 is reporting transaction ID 0x0009.00d.00002100 rather than transaction ID 0x000a.00e.00001b93. Moreover, this transaction is marked as committed and cleaned out (Flag = C---) with the lock count reset to zero. This transaction is the committed transaction from session 2 that we are supposed to see. The changes due to sessions 1 and 3—which hadn't yet committed—have disappeared completely from this version of the block.

Take a look at the data: the values in the three rows are (1,1), (2,102), and (3,3), and all three rows are showing a zero lock byte (i.e., none of the rows is locked). Here's another little point to note, though—check the address in the block of row 0: it's moved *again*, from 0x1f7b to 0x1f68. Oracle's algorithm has done the following:

1. Clone the block into another buffer, using the clone as the target for the next four steps.
2. Apply cleanout to any *committed* transactions that need it.
3. Reverse out the changes from any *uncommitted* transactions.
4. If there are any changes due to transactions with a commit SCN higher than the target SCN (i.e., the snapshot SCN at the start of the query, DML, or transaction), reverse out the changes for the transaction with the highest commit SCN.
5. Repeat step 4 as necessary.

In our case, this didn't take many steps. Here's the ITL for the current version of the block again, before any read-consistency work:

```
Itl           Xid                  Uba         Flag  Lck        Scn/Fsc
0x01   0x000a.00e.00001b93  0x01800518.04f5.34  --U-    1  fsc 0x0000.01731c83
0x02   0x0004.00c.00001964  0x018036ad.05ff.3a  ----    1  fsc 0x0000.00000000
```

Oracle's first step is to check (by looking at the state of slot 12 in the transaction table in undo segment header 4) that the transaction in ITL entry 0x02 is still active. Since it is, the changes it has made to this block have to be reversed out, so Oracle goes to undo block 0x018036ad, checks that its sequence (incarnation) number is 0x5ff, and then looks at record 0x3a, which tells it that "column 1 of row 0 of table 0 should be changed to value c1 02" (Oracle's internal representation of decimal 1). This change affects the length of the row, so Oracle copies the row into the block's free space and makes the change. The undo record also has the instruction to rewrite the ITL entry as "never been used." So the ITL in our clone now looks like this:

```
Itl           Xid                  Uba         Flag  Lck        Scn/Fsc
0x01   0x000a.00e.00001b93  0x01800518.04f5.34  --U-    1  fsc 0x0000.01731c83
0x02   0x0000.000.00000000  0x00000000.0000.00  ----    0  fsc 0x0000.00000000
```

There are no more uncommitted transactions, so Oracle checks the SCN it's supposed to reach and all the SCNs in the ITL and decides that 0x01731c83 is too high, and that it's the highest of the guilty SCNs. So Oracle starts the process of reversing out the changes due to transaction 0x000a.00e.00001b93 by reading undo record 0x01800518.04f5.34. This undo record tells it to change column 1 of row 2 of table 0 to c1 04 (decimal 3). Since this doesn't affect the size of the row, Oracle makes the change in place. The undo record also tells Oracle that it has just unwound the first change made to this block by this transaction and that it's also holding the previous version of this ITL entry, which should also be copied back. As explained in Chapter 2, the first change a transaction makes to a block is a special case—it's the need to select an ITL and preserve the current contents that makes it special (and, occasionally all the current ITL entries will be in use and the transaction will have to create a new one—if there's enough space). Specifically, the undo record contains some information that is clearly an ITL entry, which looks like this:

```
op: L  itl: xid:  0x0009.00d.00002100 uba: 0x018030ca.074c.11
                      flg: C---    lkc:  0     scn: 0x0000.01731c7a
```

So Oracle copies this back in place, leaving the ITL of our clone looking like this:

```
Itl           Xid                  Uba          Flag  Lck        Scn/Fsc
0x01   0x0009.00d.00002100  0x018030ca.074c.11  C---    0  scn 0x0000.01731c7a
0x02   0x0000.000.00000000  0x00000000.0000.00  ----    0  fsc 0x0000.00000000
```

Again Oracle checks to see if there are any SCNs in the ITL that are higher than the target SCN—and at this point there aren't. So this is the correct read-consistent (and very private) version of the block that this session needs to use.

■ **Note** When Oracle accesses a row through an indexed access path, it may be able to use the *RowCR* (row consistent read) mechanism when it gets to the table block. This means that Oracle has gone through the complex processing I've just described to get the *index leaf block* into a read-consistent state and has then been able to check that the row itself has not changed since the reconstructed commit SCN for the index entry.

Consistent Doesn't Mean Historic

An interesting little point to pick up here is that the thing that we've constructed is a version of the block that has *never actually existed.* We now have a block where the change from session 1 simply doesn't exist; but the change from session 2 is in place and visible. In the train of events up to the point where we started our query, this never happened.

In fact, the closest we came to the state of our read-consistent clone was probably the moment just before we started the update from session 3. At that moment the ITL for the block looked like this:

```
Itl           Xid                  Uba          Flag  Lck        Scn/Fsc
0x01   0x0009.00d.00002100  0x018030ca.074c.11  --U-    1  fsc 0x0000.01731c7a
0x02   0x0004.00c.00001964  0x018036ad.05ff.3a  ----    1  fsc 0x0000.00000000
```

Notice, by the way, that ITL `0x01` is showing the effects of a *commit cleanout* (`--U-, 1, fsc`) even though the undo record that we eventually retrieved from the next transaction to use this ITL entry stored (`C---,0,fsc`). This is an example of *delayed logging block cleanout.* The next transaction didn't copy the information that was in the ITL entry, but rather stored the information that *would* have been in the ITL entry if Oracle had cleaned it out properly the first time around.

Note There's a common (and reasonably valid) approximation that *read consistency* takes cloned blocks back into "the past." But it's actually more subtle than that because we may have to deal with a mix of committed and uncommitted transactions, as well as tidying up the side effects of *commit cleanout*. This is probably why RAC differentiates between the *CR* (consistent read) state and the *PI* (past image) state. The PI state identifies copies of the block that are versions of the block that *really did exist* at some point in the past, and could therefore be used as a basis for rolling forward if the instance holding the current version crashed.

There are variations on this theme that we could consider, but I think I've said enough about the mechanism and given you enough block dumps to deal with in one go. It's worth mentioning that things do get a little messier (particularly in 10*g*) because of the side effects of in-memory undo and private redo, but the differences are really just details of when changes actually become visible in block dumps (from memory and from disk). To make things a little easier to follow, I ran all my demonstrations with repeated calls to `alter system checkpoint` and `alter system flush buffer_cache` so that I could always pick up the latest state of a changed block from disk and avoid some of the timing oddities from private redo and in-memory undo; this does affect the way that Oracle works, of course, but I don't think the differences are material to the basic understanding of what's going on.

Work Done

There's one last little detail about read consistency that's worth taking special note of at this point: how to measure the work done. There are three significant statistics:

```
CR blocks created
data blocks consistent reads - undo records applied
consistent gets - examination
```

Every time you start to construct a read-consistent copy of a data block, you increment the first statistic, and every time you read an undo record from an undo block in the process of constructing a read-consistent copy, you increment the second statistic, and every time you visit an undo block to do this, you perform a type of block visit that requires you to acquire and hold the relevant *cache buffers chains* latch as you read the block—this "single latch hold" visit is recorded under the third statistic.

Note It's worth pointing out that whenever you do a *flashback query*, you're doing the same type of work that Oracle normally uses for read consistency—but you could be doing a lot more of it because you're trying to go read-consistent in the past.

Unfortunately there are other actions that visit blocks using the same "single latch hold" strategy—some accesses to index blocks, including index organized tables, and single table hash clusters, for example—and there are two other reasons for `undo records applied` (we'll see the third one soon), so these figures don't give you an immediate and perfect understanding of the impact of constructing read-consistent blocks; but they are quite helpful.

Another related statistic is the `consistent changes` figure, which has the same (or virtually the same) meaning as the `data blocks consistent reads - undo records applied` but is an older version of the statistic. Finally, you should be aware of the fact that you often find that you don't need to do any work at all to construct the correct version of a block, and many of your consistent reads may be recorded as `no work - consistent read gets`.

■ **Note** Statistics related to `consistent gets` record the work done getting the "right version" of the block. Unfortunately the statistics cover a multitude of sins. The basic statistic, for example, counts the number of blocks that have been reconstructed as well as the number of block visits you have made to undo blocks to do that reconstruction. Fortunately the visits to the undo blocks are also recorded under `consistent gets - examination`, and the reconstructed blocks are recorded under `CR blocks created`. Unfortunately both these statistics include counts from other tasks as well.

Commit SCN

Finally we come to the third linked list that runs through the undo records—the history of commit SCNs—and this is a topic that covers a lot of ground.

Earlier in this chapter I pointed out that when a transaction commits, it writes the current SCN into its transaction table slot, and that the redo change vector for this data block change constitutes the entirety of the so-called "commit record."

Historically this was the only block change your session would make when committing a transaction, after which it would post a message to the log writer to copy the log buffer to disk and wait for the log writer to confirm that it had completed the write. The benefit of this approach (combined with the fact that the log writer would sit in the background constantly writing the log buffer to disk anyway) was that a commit would take the same amount of time irrespective of how much work you had done modifying data in the course of the transaction. This strategy earned the name *fast commit.*

With the advent of Oracle 7.3, though, this strategy changed to address the "pinging" problem suffered by Oracle Parallel Server (OPS)—the precursor to RAC. If the only thing you've done to show that a transaction has committed is to update a transaction table slot, then it will be up to someone else to clear up the mess you've left behind in the data blocks—namely, clear the lock bytes, set the `Fsc/Scn` to the commit SCN, and set the commit flag to `C---`.

■ **Note** There are a few places in Oracle which "hide" work by sharing it out. The principle is simple: if I tidy up the 1,000 blocks that I've changed, it will take me a lot of extra time; if the next 200 sessions that visit those blocks tidy up a few each, no single session will notice the overhead. There are times when lazy is good.

This later action is the mechanism known as *delayed block cleanout*, and most of the time it works very well because it's an almost invisible overhead, especially in OLTP systems running on a single instance. But in RAC (OPS), if your session is the one that needs to do delayed block cleanout, you might have to send a request to another instance, asking for the relevant undo segment header blocks so that you can find out the commit SCN of any apparently uncommitted transactions in the block you're looking at. Under OPS, passing a block around meant one instance writing it down to disk—possibly flushing some of the redo log buffer to disk before doing so—and the other instance reading it back; this is what is meant by "pinging." The same thing can still happen with RAC (but only rarely, we hope) where writes of this type are recorded by the statistic `fusion writes`; in general, though, *cache fusion* means that we expect most blocks that move between instances to travel across the network.

Commit Cleanout

Because of the old OPS problem, Oracle changed the fast commit to be a little slower. While your session is changing data blocks, it is also building in its session memory a list (limited to 10 percent of the size of the cache) of those blocks, and on the commit it revisits any of those blocks that are still in the buffer, updates the `flag` in the relevant ITL entry with the value `-U--`, and sets the commit SCN, but doesn't bother to log those changes. This process is known as *commit cleanout*. It's just enough work to tell any session that subsequently views the block that the transaction has committed and exactly when it committed.

■ **Note** You might wonder why Oracle doesn't do a complete cleanout on commit. The reason is probably speed. If you know which ITL entry you've been using (and that's part of the information the session keeps in its list of modified blocks), you can calculate exactly where in the buffered block you have to apply your changes. Remember, ITL entries do not move; on the other hand, the location of a row in a block can change, so the only way to clear a row lock byte is by following pointers—which could take more time (especially in the bad old days when CPUs had very small caches). There's also the point that the full cleanout would have to be logged, but Oracle has a strategy to avoid logging the commit cleanout.

So the general strategy for dealing with commits is to make a *logged* change to the transaction table slot, and an *unlogged* change to some of the data blocks. In fact, the work done during a commit cleanout has amazingly low visibility—not only is the change to the ITL entry not logged, the action isn't even reported as any type of buffer visit that you would normally recognize. The script `cleanout.sql` (available in the Source Code/Download area of the Apress web site), for example, creates a table with 500 rows spread across 500 blocks and then updates every row. On the commit, the work done—according to a snapshot of `v$sesstat`—was as follows:

```
Name                                     Value
----                                     -----
session logical reads                       13
db block gets                                1
consistent gets                             12
db block changes                             1
redo synch writes                            1
```

```
commit cleanouts                           500
commit cleanouts successfully completed    500
redo entries                                 1
redo size                                   96
```

We have visited all 500 blocks on the commit (`commit cleanouts 500`), but we've done virtually no block visits of the type we would normally think about (that is, `session logical reads`, `db block gets`, `consistent gets`); moreover, despite changing those 500 blocks, we've recorded just one `db block change`—which is misleading—and a single, tiny redo entry—which is the change to the undo segment header as we updated the transaction table slot, and is truthfully recording the one thing we logged.

■ **Note** Technically the list of candidate buffers that a session keeps for a single commit cleanout is allowed to be 10 percent of the size of the buffer cache. So it is possible for a single commit to use quite a lot of CPU and cause quite a lot of latch activity on commit—without showing exactly what's going on, unless you know where to look.

An interesting variation on this test is to flush the buffer cache (`alter system flush buffer_cache;`) before issuing the commit—just to see what happens; the change in statistics is a little surprising:

```
Name                                     Value
----                                     -----
commit cleanout failures: block lost       100
commit cleanouts                           100
```

As you can see Oracle seemed to give up after 100 attempts at doing a commit cleanout, and didn't even look at the other 400 blocks. This is an interesting example of the type of "statistical guess" that Oracle makes about the best run-time strategy—the commit cleanout doesn't seem to be working very well here, so it has stopped trying.

In this variation of the test, of course, I now have 500 blocks on disk that have been changed by a committed transaction, but the relevant ITL entry in each block makes it appear as if the transaction has not yet committed. Interestingly, if I, or another session, read those blocks back into the cache before I commit, then I am still able to clean them out when I commit.

Before taking a closer look at what's going to happen to those blocks if they aren't in the cache, I'll just pick up one last point about how the fast commit affects the workload. Script `core_cleanout_2.sql` (available in the Source Code/Download area of the Apress web site) is a version of the original commit test that I've modified to execute the following statement three times, first after updating my 500 rows, then after a checkpoint (`alter system checkpoint;`), and finally after the commit:

```
select
        objd, count(*)
from
        v$bh
where
        dirty = 'Y'
```

```
group by
        objd
order by
        count(*)
;
```

The code simply counts the number of buffers in the cache which have their "dirty bit" set, grouping by data object ID to make it easy for me to pick out the blocks from my table. Ignoring some of the very small numbers that appeared because of background activity, I found the following:

- After the initial update, 504 blocks from the table and 212 undo blocks were dirty.
- After the checkpoint there were (as we would expect—see Chapter 6) no dirty blocks in memory. Remember that a checkpoint call makes Oracle copy any dirty blocks to disk; it *doesn't* make Oracle remove them from the buffer cache.
- After the commit cleanout, 500 blocks from the table and two undo blocks were dirty.

Because of the "pseudo-delay" I introduced between the update and commit, Oracle is going to end up writing those 500 table blocks a second time. Realistically this particular detail probably won't have any significant impact on most systems, but it's just a little hint to remind you not to let your code wait a long time between the update and the commit.

Note When the current version of a block in the buffer cache doesn't match the copy on disk, the buffer is said to be dirty (a dirty block). When dbwr copies the buffer to disk, the buffer becomes clean because once again it matches the block on disk.

Let's go back, now, to the case where we flushed the buffer cache and saw Oracle report 100 commit cleanout failures and then ignore the last 400 blocks. What's going to happen to the 500 blocks the next time anyone reads them?

Delayed Block Cleanout

We have 500 table blocks with committed changes, but the blocks weren't in memory when we issued the commit, so Oracle wasn't able to update their ITL entries to show that the transaction had committed. So how will anyone find out, when they query the blocks, that the transaction *is* committed and (if they need to know) exactly *when* it committed?

If at this point we run a query that does a tablescan on the table, we'll see statistics something like the following in 11*g*:

```
Name                                       Value
----                                       -----
db block gets                                  0
consistent gets                            1,012
consistent gets from cache (fastpath)        501
consistent gets - examination                506
```

```
physical reads                                  504
db block changes                                500
calls to kcmgrs                                 500
redo entries                                    500
redo size                                    36,000
cleanouts only - consistent read gets           500
immediate (CR) block cleanout applications      500
commit txn count during cleanout                500
cleanout - number of ktugct calls               500
table scan blocks gotten                        500
```

I have omitted various "small" values that aren't relevant to the discussion, and a few of the statistics that re-iterated the 500-block count of the table. The items I want to pick up particularly are the following:

- We looked at 500 table blocks in our tablescan but did 1,012 consistent gets: where did the extra 500 (and a bit) come from?
- Of the 1012 consistent gets, 506 are reported as `examinations`—and by now you know that one of the possible causes of examinations is looking at blocks from the undo tablespace.
- Oracle has reported no `db block gets`, but we have done 500 `db block changes` and generated 500 redo entries (averaging 72 bytes each). This is another example, like the one we saw with commit cleanouts, where the well-known statistics are not giving us the full picture.
- We have done 500 `calls to kcmgrs` (Kernel Cache Miscellaneous Get Recent SCN). As a side note on the way in which the code and instrumentation changes, this statistic wasn't incremented when I ran the test under 10*g*.
- We have a number of statistics relating to "cleanouts," including two that seem to be saying something about committed transactions: `commit txn count during cleanout` and `cleanout - number of ktugct calls` (Kernel Transaction Undo Get Commit Time).

What's happening is this: as we read a table block from disk, Oracle can see that there is an ITL that *seems* to hold an uncommitted transaction and can see the rows marked by that transaction, so it has to think about creating a read-consistent version of the block. Our session reads the correct undo segment header block (`consistent get - examination`) to check the state of the transaction (it's possible that it checks `v$transaction` before visiting the block, but that's only a conjecture), at which point it finds that the transaction has committed and can see the commit time (`kcmgrs`, `kcmgct`).

Having found the committed transaction, Oracle can copy the commit SCN back to the ITL entry, set the commit flag, and clear the lock bytes from the block—but that's a data block change to something that we know is the current version of the block (it's just come off disk, so it must be the current version even though we didn't report a `db block get`), and a data block change means we generate some redo.

This process happens for every single block of the tablescan—hence the frequent appearance of a value close to 500 in many of the statistics – and when the tablescan is complete, all the data blocks from the table are dirty and we've generated 500 redo records. You might note, by the way, that our session doesn't show any change in `redo synch write` (that's the counter the session increments to show that it needed the log writer to write the log buffer to disk), so the redo records won't be written to disk immediately, but they will get there in a few seconds, or when the next transaction commits, or when dbwr decides to write some of the dirty table blocks to disk and posts lgwr to write the redo protecting those blocks before it writes the blocks themselves (see Chapter 6).

■ **Note** Parallel queries—and serial direct path reads in 11*g*—have an interesting side effect on delayed block cleanout. When you do a direct path read of a block (i.e., into private memory, the PGA, rather than the public memory, the SGA), Oracle still has to go through the routine of creating the correct consistent read version of the block. If this means doing delayed block cleanout, the operation is carried out in private. In this case we don't generate the redo and we don't put a dirty copy of the block back into the buffer cache.
If I take the final tablescan from `core_cleanout_2.sql` and make it a parallel tablescan (see script `core_cleanout_3.sql`, available in the Source Code/Download area of the Apress web site) the extra 500 `consistent gets`, calls to `ktugct`, and so forth are performed *every single time* I repeat the tablescan. Similar behavior appears when you make tablespaces `read only` and the tablespaces hold objects that are in need of some delayed block cleanout—although 11*g* has introduced the concept of a *minimum active SCN*, which may have some impact on this behavior. 11*g* has also introduced the *read only table*, but when a table (rather than a tablespace) is declared read only, 11*g* will still apply and write back the changes due to delayed block cleanout.

We've seen that Oracle is able to recognize that a block is in need of delayed block cleanout, and has a mechanism for finding out the commit SCN of the relevant transactions and cleaning out the block properly, but all we've seen so far is the tip of the iceberg.

In the example we ran our tablescan moments after we had committed the data, so when Oracle saw the offending ITL entry, it could read the transaction ID (`xid:`) from the ITL entry and say "let's go to the correct undo segment header and transaction table slot and see what's happened."

Remember, though, there are only 34 (or 48, or 96, depending on version and option) transaction table slots per undo segment, and only a limited number of undo segments per undo tablespace. If I create a brand-new undo tablespace in my 11*g* database, switch into it, and drop the old tablespace, I'll have 10 undo segments available (to start with). So how will Oracle deal with delayed block cleanout if I execute 17,000 transactions (that's 50 × 10 × 34) somewhere else in the database before I reread the table? After all, with that much extra work happening before I look at the table again, the transaction table slot I used when updating the table is sure to have been overwritten. The answer, perhaps surprisingly, is that the resulting statistics look *no different* from the previous test (see `core_cleanout_4.sql`, available in the Source Code/Download area of the Apress web site) even though I must have overwritten every single transaction table slot in the entire database about 50 times.

So how did I find the information I need to tidy up the ITL entries? The answer (for this example) is that I don't need to know *when* my original transaction committed; I just need to know that it *has* committed. As usual a data block dump is very revealing; this is what the ITL looked like in one of the table blocks after the cleanout (the relevant transaction entry is `0x02`—notice the flag column reads, `C-U-`):

```
Itl           Xid                  Uba         Flag  Lck        Scn/Fsc
0x01   0x0001.007.00001e7b  0x01800381.0561.13  C---    0  scn 0x0000.0186e2e6
0x02   0x0003.005.000021a9  0x01800376.06fd.0c  C-U-    0  scn 0x0000.01877523
```

This is an example of the delayed block cleanout using *upper bound commit*. The significance of the `C` is that it marks the transaction as committed and shows that the lock bytes for the rows will be clear. The significance of the `U` is that the commit SCN is not guaranteed to be exactly correct—the transaction had committed by the time Oracle got to this SCN, but it may have committed earlier. The querying session has done just enough work to figure out that the transaction committed before the query started, and it's used the oldest SCN that it can find *cheaply* to determine this fact, and the work it has done is only just a tiny bit more than the previous example where it had to look for the right transaction table slot.

What's happening is similar to the previous case, to start with: Oracle looks at the block and sees that there is an ITL that seems to hold an uncommitted transaction and can see the rows marked by that transaction, so it has to think about creating a read-consistent version of the block. As before, it goes to read the correct undo segment header block (`consistent get - examination`) to check the state of the transaction. But in this case the `wrap#` of the transaction is higher than expected (the slot has been reused about 50 times since the original transaction ran).

Because the transaction slot has been overwritten, Oracle can infer that the transaction has committed, which (in this case) is all it cares about. But it needs to put something in as the commit SCN on the ITL, so what value should it use?

It could simply use the SCN it finds in the overwritten transaction slot, but—in much the same way that Oracle picks the oldest (least recently committed) entry when it has to reuse an ITL entry from a data block—Oracle also reuses the oldest (least recently committed) transaction table slot in the undo segment when it needs to start a new transaction, so a better approximation would simply be to use the oldest commit SCN it can find in the transaction table. In fact, Oracle can do just a little bit better than that, because each time Oracle reuses a transaction table slot, it copies the previous commit SCN from that slot into the *transaction control* mentioned at the start of this chapter. So, for the upper bound commit SCN, Oracle identifies the relevant undo segment, picks the SCN from its transaction control, and copies that into the ITL.

Transaction Table Rollback

There are cases where it's very cheap to get a "sufficiently accurate" commit SCN for blocks that require delayed block cleanout, but are there any circumstances that might require us to do more work to improve the accuracy of the "upper bound" estimate?

The first thought is that our test case used a single session, which makes it a bit special, so what happens if we use the two sessions shown in Table 3-3?

Table 3-3. *Failing to make an upper bound commit expensive*

Time	Session 1	Session 2
t1	Update table t1, flush buffer, commit	
t2		Execute a loop of 17,000 (committed) transactions against table t2
t3	Select from table t1	

It makes no difference to the results; again, session 1 need only check that its original transaction committed before the final select statement began. It doesn't need to know exactly when the transaction committed, so again it can use the SCN from the transaction control as a good-enough approximation to the commit SCN.

How about the sequence of events provided in Table 3-4, though?

Table 3-4. *Making an upper bound commit expensive*

Time	Session 1	Session 2
t1	Update table t1, flush buffer, commit	
t2	Issue a call to `set transaction read only;`	
t3		Execute a loop of 17,000 (committed) transactions against table t2
t4	Select from table t1	

By setting the transaction to read-only, I am, in effect, faking a long-running query. When the select statement runs at line 4, it has to see the database as it was at line 2. This produces some interesting results (the test case is a variation described in `core_cleanout_4.sql`) from which I've extracted some key figures:

```
session logical reads                                     2,407
consistent gets                                           2,407
consistent gets from cache                                2,407
consistent gets - examination                             1,900
CR blocks created                                             1
transaction tables consistent reads - undo records applied    1,395
transaction tables consistent read rollbacks                  1
```

Our first test showed roughly 1,000 `session logical reads` with 500 `consistent gets - examination`. This test shows (roughly) an increase of 1,400 on both these statistics, and the same count on a statistic called `transaction tables consistent reads - undo records applied`. We have done a lot of work to find a suitable commit SCN; we have applied 1,395 undo records to create a single read-consistent copy of the undo segment header so that we can see what the transaction table looked like at the moment of the original commit.

Transaction Control (TRN CTL::)

It's time to say a little more about the *transaction control* content and what happens at the start of a transaction. Here's an example of the transaction control just before a new transaction starts in the undo segment:

```
TRN CTL:: seq: 0x08f5 chd: 0x000d ctl: 0x0017 inc: 0x00000000 nfb: 0x0001
          mgc: 0xb000 xts: 0x0068 flg: 0x0001 opt: 2147483646 (0x7ffffffe)
          uba: 0x0180120f.08f5.21 scn: 0x0000.018bc704
```

You'll notice that there's an scn: recorded at the end of the transaction control, and just before it there's a thing labeled uba:, a label we've seen before as part of an ITL entry, meaning undo byte address but holding (as this uba also seems to) an undo *record* address. The obvious questions when we see these items are, "What's in that uba?" and "Where does that scn come from?"

You'll also notice the chd (chain head, perhaps) and ctl (chain tail). These are the ends of a linked list that tell us, respectively, the next transaction table slot to use and the last transaction table slot used in this undo segment.

Since the next (chd) slot is 0x0d, the following is what that slot looks like at this point (with a few details deleted to make the line fit the page):

```
index state cflags wrap#  uel         scn             dba        nub        cmt
-------------------------------------------------------------------------------
0x0d     9    0x00  0x6a60 0x000b 0x0000.018bc75e 0x0180120d 0x00000001 1305214727
```

If we now start a new transaction, the transaction control and transaction table slot change to become as follows:

```
  TRN CTL:: seq: 0x08f5 chd: 0x000b ctl: 0x0017 inc: 0x00000000 nfb: 0x0000
            mgc: 0xb000 xts: 0x0068 flg: 0x0001 opt: 2147483646 (0x7ffffffe)
            uba: 0x0180120f.08f5.24 scn: 0x0000.018bc75e

index state cflags wrap#  uel         scn             dba        nub        cmt
-------------------------------------------------------------------------------
0x0d    10    0x80  0x6a61 0x0017 0x0000.018bcd3e 0x0180120f 0x00000001          0
```

Then, as we commit (and assuming no other transactions have been using the same undo segment), they change to

```
  TRN CTL:: seq: 0x08f5 chd: 0x000b ctl: 0x000d inc: 0x00000000 nfb: 0x0001
            mgc: 0xb000 xts: 0x0068 flg: 0x0001 opt: 2147483646 (0x7ffffffe)
            uba: 0x0180120f.08f5.24 scn: 0x0000.018bc75e


index state cflags wrap#  uel         scn             dba        nub        cmt
-------------------------------------------------------------------------------
0x0d     9    0x00  0x6a61 0xffff 0x0000.018bcd92 0x0180120f 0x00000001 1305278699
```

We'll take a moment to look at the chd, ctl, and uel values first, because that part is straightforward. You will recall from table 3-1 that the uel column in the transaction table slot points to the slot that should be used next. Before we started the transaction, the transaction control was pointing to slot 0x000d, and slot 0x0d had a uel of slot 0x000b. As the transaction starts you can see that the chd value changes to 0x000b, and the uel value changes to 0x0017

■ **Note** In some versions of Oracle the uel will change to point back to "itself" when it's in use, while in other versions it will change to zero. This is probably an irrelevant change in detail because the state shows that the current slot is not available whatever the uel is pointing to.

Finally, after we commit, the `ctl` changes to `0x000d` and the `uel` changes to `0xffff` ("nothing after me"). So we pick a slot from the head of the list, use it, and return it to the tail of the list. Consequently, the slot we pick for a new transaction is always going to be the oldest committed (lowest SCN) slot in the transaction table.

Another little change you might spot is the `nfb` entry in the transaction control. This is the *number of free blocks* in the free block pool, a short list of blocks in this undo segment that still have space available for undo records. There was one block in this list before we started the transaction (`nfb: 0x0001`), but we took it off the list to use it (`nfb: 0x0000`), and when we committed there was still plenty of space in it so we put it back in the free pool (`nfb: 0x0001`). Here's a dump of the free block pool (limited to the first entry) just after we commit:

```
FREE BLOCK POOL::
  uba: 0x0180120f.08f5.24 ext: 0x17 spc: 0xe56
```

As you can see, the entry tells us how much space is still available in the block (`spc`), which extent (`ext`) the block is in, and the undo record address (`uba`) of the last undo record in that block. Because my transaction was a very small transaction using just one undo record, the `uba` here is the same as the `uba` I wrote to the transaction control—the `uba` in the transaction control is for the first record of my transaction, and the `uba` in the free pool is for the last record of my transaction, and in this case they're the same thing.

Let's get back to the transaction control, and its `scn` and `uba`.

The `scn` has been replaced by the commit SCN from the transaction table slot I've just reused. This is what gives Oracle the fast way of finding the "oldest SCN in the transaction table" very quickly in the simpler cases of the upper bound commit. It checks the slot it wants, sees that it is at the wrong `wrap#` for the transaction it is checking, and goes straight to the transaction control.

The `uba` has been replaced by the `uba` of the first undo record of the *new* transaction. Actually, although I've already claimed twice that `0x0180120f.08f5.24` is the first undo record of the new transaction, that's not immediately visible in the information I've printed so far. I had to dump the relevant undo block to confirm that fact—and here are the first few lines dumped for that specific record:

```
*-----------------------------
* Rec #0x24  slt: 0x0d  objn: 99692(0x0001856c)  objd: 99692  tblspc: 9(0x00000009)
*       Layer:  11 (Row)   opc: 1   rci 0x00
Undo type:  Regular undo    Begin trans    Last buffer split:  No
Temp Object:  No
Tablespace Undo:  No
rdba: 0x00000000Ext idx: 0
flg2: 0
*-----------------------------
uba: 0x0180120f.08f5.21 ctl max scn: 0x0000.018bc704 prv tx scn: 0x0000.018bc75e
txn start scn: scn: 0x0000.018bcd3e logon user: 86
 prev brb: 25170445 prev bcl: 0
```

I mentioned in Chapter 2 that the first undo record of a transaction is a special case—this is where we finally discover how special.

First Change

Before we started the transaction, the transaction control listed uba `0x0180120f.08f5.21` and scn `0x0000.018bc704`. These have appeared in the undo record (three lines from the bottom) with the labels `uba:` and `ctl max scn:`—the transaction control information has been copied to the first record of the next transaction and has then been updated with a pointer to tell us where that record can be found.

But there's more. The previous contents of the transaction table slot that we have picked for our new transaction have also been copied into the new undo record. The `scn` and `dba` values in our slot were `0x0000.018bc75e` and `0x0180120d`, and we can now see them in the undo record with the labels `prv tx scn:` and `brb` (although the `brb` has been dumped in decimal rather than hexadecimal). We've also saved the start scn (`0x0000.018bcd3e`) for the new transaction in the undo record with the (strangely repetitive) label `txn start scn: scn:`.

In summary, then, every time a new transaction starts, it saves the old transaction table slot information to its first undo record, updates the pointer in the transaction control to point to that record, saving the previous value of the pointer into the same undo record. This makes it possible for a process to walk a linked list of "first undo records" to reconstruct the transaction table back to any point in the past (until it runs out of undo records). Let's walk through the process to see how it works.

Imagine I visit a block at some time in the future and see from the ITL that there are some rows that appear to be locked by transaction `0006.00d.00006a5f` (that's undo segment 6, slot 13, `wrap#` 27231).

I look at undo segment 6, transaction slot 13, and find that its `wrap#` is currently at 27233 (`0x6a61`). Because the `wrap#` shows me the slot has been used a couple of times since the changes made by transaction `0006.00d.00006a5f`, I can conclude that the row changes have been committed but at a lower SCN than I can currently see in the slot.

Before I do any more work, I may decide that that SCN is a good enough approximation for an "upper bound commit," but if it isn't, I can look at the SCN in the transaction control because it's either the previous commit SCN from slot 13 (although statistically that's very unlikely) or the commit SCN from another transaction/slot that committed after the previous commit from slot 13. So the transaction control SCN is another possible "upper bound commit."

At this point all I've done is a quick visit to the undo segment header to get an approximate commit SCN. But if that small amount of work hasn't yet produced a good enough approximation, I now have to start working quite hard to create a read-consistent view of the transaction table that is sufficiently old that it gives me an even better, or possibly exact, commit SCN.

Transaction Table Consistent Read

The steps involved in creating a read-consistent copy of the transaction table are as follows:

1. I clone the undo segment header block in memory—that's the action that increments the statistic `transaction tables consistent read rollbacks`.
2. I use the `uba` from the transaction control to identify the first undo record of the transaction that last updated the transaction control. This was, as we have seen, the oldest transaction slot available in the transaction table at that moment.
3. The undo record tells me which transaction table slot its undo should be applied to (remember the `slt: 0xNN` entry on the record), and the commit SCN for that slot, so I can apply the undo to my clone—that's the action that increments the statistic `transaction tables consistent reads - undo records applied`. At the same time I read back the `uba` and `scn` values that need to be written to the transaction control and apply them.

4. At this point I have taken the transaction table and transaction control one step back into the past. It's possible that the commit SCN I've recovered is "good enough" (i.e., the first time I've seen an SCN lower than the exact value I'm interested in) for an upper bound commit. It's possible that this step actually took slot 13 (the one I was interested in) back to exactly the right `wrap#` and gave me the exact commit SCN. (In my case I said that I was starting with a `wrap#` of `0x6a61` and needed to get back to `wrap# 0x6a5f`, so I'm not going to be that lucky that soon; I'll have to get through `wrap# 0x6a60` first.)

5. If I haven't found a low enough SCN yet, I have at least managed to construct an older version of the transaction control, so I go back to step 2 and repeat until I reach a suitable value or run out of undo records and crash out with Oracle error "ORA-01555 snapshot too old" because I haven't kept enough history in the undo segment to look that far back into the past.

This, then, is the last chain that runs through the undo segment. The first undo record of each transaction points to the first undo record of the previous transaction that started in the same undo segment; the transaction control points to the *first* "first undo record"; and by following first undo records backward, we can reclaim critical details about the history of transaction table slots, and reconstruct old versions of the transaction table and identify the exact commit SCN of any transaction that took place at some time in the past and is now in need of an accurate delayed block cleanout.

ORA-01555

If you don't know that Oracle error 1555 translates into "snapshot too old," you can't be a real DBA. It is probably the most well known of error numbers in the Oracle world. It happens because we can't keep history indefinitely. (Anyone who's tried to create a full audit system for a database to hold seven years of history knows the problem—a complete history requires a lot of space, and after a while you hope that no one ever queries it because of the amount of I/O a single audit trail query can take.)

We define an undo tablespace (per instance) to hold history, but in the normal course of events we only want to hold enough history to make sure that our big, slow queries can find enough history for read consistency as they run. This is quite difficult to do, because we create multiple undo segments in the undo tablespace so that incoming transactions don't end up competing for too few transaction tables; and sometimes a few segments can grow very large, using up an "unfair" share of the space, which can make it hard for Oracle to use the undo tablespace effectively.

To improve the situation, Oracle Corp. introduced *automatic undo management*, allowing the instance to take undo segments offline and bring them online, to grow and shrink them, to move available extents from one segment to another, and even to allocate and drop undo segments (the latter is under the control of the background process `smon` and is only triggered once every 24 hours). The target driving automatic undo management is the parameter `undo_retention`, which the DBA uses to state how long history should be kept (the default is 15 minutes/900 seconds). It was the introduction of automatic undo management that demanded the presence of the retention table shown earlier in Figure 3-2. The table allows Oracle to decide when it is safe to remove an extent from an undo segment. In Oracle 11.2, the tracking has been enhanced by the internal introduction of the minimum active SCN, which is also used to avoid some of the work done in finding upper bound commit times.

LOBs

It's worth saying a few words about LOBs since Oracle has some special methods for handling undo and redo on LOBs, and these methods follow through to the handling of transactions and read consistency. If a LOB value has been stored in the row, it is in no way special; it's just another column. But if a LOB value was stored "out of row" (either because the specific value was too large or because the LOB has been declared with the `disable storage in row` option), then the LOB data itself is not subject to the normal undo handling and need not be subject to the normal redo handling.

There are variations on the basic theme, but the critical thing to remember with LOB values that have been stored out of row is that you have to access them through pointers stored in the row or through the LOBINDEX, which, although it's a slightly special variation of Oracle's standard B-tree index, *is* subject to the typical undo and redo processing and is therefore amenable to the normal transactional and read-consistency behavior.

When you update a LOB value that is stored out of row, Oracle creates a new copy of that value and leaves the old one in place—the old copy *is* the undo, and part of the LOB definition tells Oracle how long it can keep old copies of LOB values. But as we create the new copy, we update the LOBINDEX in two places: one to say where the new copy is, and the other to control the order in which old copies will be overwritten. The limit for history can be set by reference to space (percentage of LOB space used for old copies) or time (number of seconds to keep old LOBs). In either case, it is possible to cause massive space and performance problems if the nature of your LOB activity causes very frequent updates to occur.

To deal with LOBs, therefore, we need only worry about the transactional and read-consistent processing of the index. Once we have the correct version of an index block, we know that it will be pointing to the correct version of the LOB value we want. This does lead to one special case. In the course of a long-running query, Oracle may find enough undo information to be able to take a LOBINDEX block to the correct read-consistent version and then find that the LOB value it was pointing to has been overwritten. This scenario leads to the special "snapshot too old" message reserved for LOBs, Oracle error ORA-22924.

Summary

There are two key structures in the database that make it possible for Oracle to handle transaction processing and read consistency efficiently: the *interested transaction list* (ITL) that appears in each data block and lists recent transactions that affected that block, and the *transaction table* that appears in the segment header block of each undo segment and lists recent transactions that affected the database.

An ITL entry records a transaction ID (`xid:`), an undo record address (`uba:`), and a commit SCN. The commit SCN tells Oracle if (and when) the transaction committed. If the commit SCN is not available, then the transaction ID identifies a transaction table *slot* with sequence number, and this information allows Oracle to check the state of the transaction and when (if) it committed. If your session needs to hide the changes made by that transaction, it can use the undo record address to find the start of a chain of undo records that tells it how to reverse the changes made by that transaction to that data block.

A transaction table slot records the state of a transaction, the address of the last undo block that it wrote to, and (when committed) the commit SCN. Because there aren't many transaction table slots in a database, they are continuously reused, so the slot has a `wrap#` number counting the number of times it has been used, and this also becomes part of the transaction ID. If a transaction has to be rolled back, the pointer to the last undo block allows Oracle to find the last undo record created by the transaction, and each undo record points to the previous undo record for its transaction, so the undo records can be visited and applied in the opposite order to the order in which they were created.

Transaction table slots can be overwritten fairly quickly, which means the commit SCN for a transaction would be lost if Oracle didn't have a mechanism to preserve information from the transaction table slot before reusing it. Each undo segment header has a transaction control section summarizing the use of the transaction table. As a transaction table slot is overwritten, its commit SCN is written into the transaction control along with the address of the first undo record of the transaction that has just acquired the slot. The previous information in the transaction control is then written into the first undo record of the new transaction, and this effectively builds a linked list of undo records (the "first record" of each transaction) that can be used to roll the transaction table back to an earlier point in time.

Any time that Oracle is following a list of pointers through the undo segment and arrives at an undo block with the wrong `seq:` (i.e., incarnation) number, you will get an Oracle error ORA-01555, "snapshot too old," because the block you wanted to see has been reused.

Read consistency for LOBs is completely different. Essentially, Oracle doesn't update LOBs; it simply keeps old copies of LOBs for a while before overwriting them, but uses the standard read-consistency mechanism on the LOBINDEX to allow it to point to the correct old copy. There is a special "snapshot too old" error for LOBs (ORA-22924) that appears when the index has become read consistent but the LOB value has been overwritten.

CHAPTER 4

Locks and Latches

I would have included pins and mutexes in the title, but that would have made it too long and lose the alliteration. Oracle uses all four mechanisms to ensure that resources don't get damaged by conflicting requirements for access and modification. The mechanisms may slow down the rate at which you are allowed to work, to ensure that you can work safely, although, as we shall see in Chapter 7, some of the mechanisms can save you time when you keep repeating the same piece of work.

There are two significant differences between locks and latches. Locks and pins adopt a polite, queue-like strategy with a first-come, first-served approach, while latches and mutexes adopt a pushy strategy where everyone tries to grab the latch simultaneously. Secondly, locks, pins, and some mutexes tend to be held for a significant amount of time, while latches should be held only very briefly. The differences are, in many ways, a side effect of the difference in usage—locks tend to be used to protect objects, while latches tend to be used to protect shared memory, so the latch activity tends to be highly concurrent and very quick.

As you can see from these comments, mutexes (which started to appear in Oracle Database 10*g* most significantly as a replacement for pins in the *library cache*) fall somewhere between locks and latches: sessions fight over mutexes the way they fight over latches, but sessions can hold mutexes for long periods just as they can hold locks (and pins) for a long time.

First Things, First . . .

Before we can talk about what latches are and how they work, though, you need some idea of how Oracle uses arrays, pointers, linked lists, and hash tables when tracking information in memory, because those are the types of structure that need the most protection when they are shared by multiple users.

Arrays

An array is essentially a list of objects of the same shape and size, and since all the objects are the same size, it's easy to walk through the array looking at each object in turn. For example, `x$ksuse` (the structure for user sessions reported through `v$session`) is a fixed array with rows of 11,360 bytes in Oracle 11.2.0.2 on 32-bit Windows. Oracle need only record the starting position of the array, and the code can work out the starting position of any row in the array by simple arithmetic.

In some cases the array is a "segmented" array, which means Oracle allocates an initial chunk of memory for a fixed number of array items, but may allocate more chunks dynamically as needed. In this case Oracle needs to record the addresses of the starting point of each chunk—which might mean that it keeps a little list of the chunks, or that each chunk includes a little information about the next chunk in the list. The structure `x$ktatl` (the entry labeled `temporary_table_locks` in `v$resource_limit`) is such a case. In a little test I ran against a 10*g* instance, this started life as an array with 16 entries of 144 bytes each, but then added chunks of 16 rows at a time, with each chunk allocated fairly randomly in memory. In a similar fashion, although `x$ksqrs` and `x$ksqeq` start with a much larger array size they can grow by chunks of 32 rows at a time.

■ **Note** The entry for `enqueue locks` in the dynamic performance view `v$resource_limit` is broken. In my little test I pushed the allocation for `enqueues locks` up to 2,500 entries when the original `limit_value` was 1,130. At this point `v$resource_limit` still showed the `limit_value` as 1,130 and the value for the `current_allocation` had stuck at 1,129. It's by spotting little anomalies like this that I often learn what Oracle is doing. Perhaps this particular anomaly is a clue that entry 1,130 is being used to point to the next segment in a segmented array.

Pointers

This brings us briefly to the idea of pointers. A *pointer* is just a memory location holding the address of a more interesting piece of memory. For example, if I look in the *fixed SGA* variables array `x$ksmfsv`, I can find the following entry (numeric values will differ across versions):

```
ADDR           INDX    INST_ID KSMFSNAM     KSMFSTYP     KSMFSADR   KSMFSSIZ
-------- ---------- ---------- ------------ ------------ -------- ----------
035004B0       3923          1 kcbllsb_     ksqeq *      03D3C818          4
```

This tells me that location `0x035004b0` holds the value `0x0d3c818`, which is an item of data that is 4 bytes long, and it is a "pointer to something of type `ksqeq`." When I dump the contents of address `0x0d3c818` I find the value `0x21a33960`, which happens to be the address of the first row in the fixed array `x$ksqeq`. So I'm looking at a pointer to a pointer to a fixed-length array—this is another clue, perhaps that we have a segmented array where the last element of a segment is pointing to the first element of the next segment.

On the other hand, we might find for (some) segmented arrays that we have two entries in `x$ksmfsv`, one telling us how many segments there are, and the other pointing to an array of pointers, each of which points to one of the segments.

Linked Lists

Once you have the idea of pointing from one location to another, of course, you can think about getting away from the rather rigid "fixed structure" approach that characterizes arrays. You can create lists of associated data items of varying shapes and sizes simply by making sure that each item points to the next item in the list, and this approach is used quite frequently in Oracle. In fact, many of the lists used by Oracle are *doubly linked* lists, which means each item points forward to the next item of the list *and* backward to the previous item.

We don't even need to look at anything as transient as memory structures to find examples of linked lists, because we've already seen an example of Oracle using one in Chapter 3, in the transaction table (and transaction control) in the undo segment header. Here, stripped to a minimum, is a reminder of the structure:

```
  TRN CTL:: seq: 0x0b02 chd: 0x0011 ctl: 0x001c inc: 0x00000000 nfb: 0x0001

TRN TBL:
  index  state cflags  wrap#    uel         scn            dba
  ------------------------------------------------------------
...
   0x11    9    0x00  0x2d25  0x001b  0x0000.041c818a  0x00805805
...
   0x19    9    0x00  0x2d24  0x002e  0x0000.041c81d1  0x00805c0b
...
   0x1b    9    0x00  0x2d23  0x0019  0x0000.041c81ce  0x00805c09
   0x1c    9    0x00  0x2d24  0xffff  0x0000.041c907c  0x00805c0d
...
   0x27    9    0x00  0x2d25  0x001c  0x0000.041c9072  0x00805c0d
...
   0x2e    9    0x00  0x2d1f  0x001a  0x0000.041c81d2  0x00805806
```

In the transaction control we see that the head (`chd`) of the list is element `0x0011`, and the tail (`ctl`) is element `0x001c`. If we look at row `0x11` (using the `index` column) in the list, the `uel` column points us to row `0x001b`; row `0x1b` points us to `0x0019`, row `0x19` points us to `0x002e`, row `0x2e` points us to `0x001a` . . . at which point I've omitted the next 30 or so links . . . until something points us to row `0x27`, which points us to row `0x1c` (the `ctl`), which terminates the linked list by "pointing" to `0xffff`.

Note In the previous example you can see that the dump switches between one and two bytes for the `index`/`uel` entry. It's important to remember that you can't depend on the various dump files to tell you the truth, the whole truth, and nothing but the truth. If you want to know whether the item is stored as 1 or 2 bytes (or whether the `index` is actually stored at all—it isn't), then you need to check the raw data rather than relying on the dump file.

It is interesting to note that this is an example where we have an array (fixed size, fixed type of element) but still use a linked list so that we can pick the next item that we want to use (the head item) as quickly as possible and, by attaching an item to the current end (tail) of the list when we've finished with it, ensure that the previous item that we used won't get used again until every other item has also been used. This is a fairly convenient way of dealing with the need to allow *multiple* sessions to remove an entry from the list, hold it for a random amount of time, and then put it back on the list.

This is an example of a *singly linked* list—it's a one-way journey. If we pick an item, it's easy to find out which item we're going to use next because the item we're looking at currently points to it, but it's expensive to identify the previous item because we have to check every other item to see which one is pointing at the current item. (Notice, also, how Oracle has to keep a separate note of the tail of the list so that it can attach an item to the end of the list without having to walk the whole list first.) You could call this an example of a *FIFO* (first in, first out) linked list; in other circumstance (e.g., *freelist space management*) Oracle uses linked lists to represent stacks (or *LIFO*s—last in, first out).

Although the singly linked list works perfectly for our transaction table, there are many places in the code where Oracle needs to use doubly linked lists. Again, we don't need to go into memory structures to see this, as the principle is visible in a well-known data structure. Here's an extract from a dump of the header section of an index leaf block that demonstrates the point:

```
Leaf block dump
===============
header address 116564572=0x6f2a25c
kdxcolev 0
KDXCOLEV Flags = - - -
kdxcolok 1
kdxcoopc 0x80: opcode=0: iot flags=--- is converted=Y
kdxconco 1
kdxcosdc 2
kdxconro 571
kdxcofbo 1178=0x49a
kdxcofeo 1190=0x4a6
kdxcoavs 12
kdxlespl 0
kdxlende 0
kdxlenxt 4194525=0x4000dd
kdxleprv 4194523=0x4000db
kdxledsz 6
kdxlebksz 8036
```

Note the entries `kdxlenxt` (next leaf block) and `kdxleprv` (previous leaf block) near the end of the dump. If we want to do a large index range scan, it's clearly convenient to be able to move from one leaf block to the next without having to climb up and down the B-tree, so a forward pointer is a good idea; and since Oracle also allows descending index range scans, then a backward pointer is also a good idea.

Hash Tables

Arrays are fine if you have to deal with fixed structures, and linked lists can be very useful with a relatively small number of associated items; in both cases you may have to pay the cost of walking through the whole array or list to find something, but that's okay if the number of items involved is small.

How do you deal with a large number of items that are constantly appearing and disappearing when you need to find the right one quickly every time? Of course we're familiar with the idea of using B-tree indexes for rapid data access, but the concept might not work too efficiently when we are handling lots of very small in-memory structures concurrently. However the B-tree index isn't the only mechanism for locating data quickly. Some Oracle DBAs take advantage of *hash clusters*, and this mechanism translates very nicely into the most commonly used mechanism in the Oracle code for handling memory.

The hash concept is simple. You decide on a fixed number of buckets (powers of two are popular, as are prime numbers, for the number of buckets you choose because of the number of mathematical studies that have used them for investigating hashing functions). You then choose a *hashing algorithm*, a piece of arithmetic that you can apply to an object to produce a number between 1 and the number of buckets (or, if you think like a computer, zero and "number of buckets – 1"). For example, you might choose to distribute your friends across ten buckets using the algorithm "associate person with bucket *N*, where *N* is the last digit of their mobile phone number"; alternatively you might choose to distribute them across 16 buckets according to the algorithm "put person in bucket *N*, where *N* is the number of children they have mod 16."

There are details that need some thought, of course: hashing your friends on the last digit of their phone number will probably spread them fairly evenly across the ten buckets, but you won't be able to find a specific friend easily unless you already know the last digit of their phone number; moreover, you may have lots of friends, so scattering them over ten buckets could leave a lot of people in each bucket, which means you still have a lot of work to find a friend even after you've picked the right bucket. (So maybe you should have 100 buckets and hash on the last two digits, but that makes it even harder to remember which bucket to look in for a given friend.)

Hashing your friends by number of children is probably going to leave a lot of the higher-numbered buckets empty and place a lot of friends in each of the lower-numbered buckets—even though you may find it easier to remember which friend has how many children.

In both cases, of course, the hash value for a friend could change—they may get a new phone number, or they may produce another child.

These examples highlight a few important principles about hashing:

- Different input values (friends) may hash to the same hash value (bucket).
- You don't want to have lots of items hashing to the same bucket.
- Some hashing algorithms will spread the data more evenly than others.
- The hashing algorithm must put an object in the same bucket every time it sees it.
- You want the hashing algorithm to be applied to something useful.

Let's take the library cache as an example of Oracle using hashing. At the moment, logging on to an instance with a fairly small SGA and dumping the library cache at level 2 (see Appendix), I can see that I have 131,072 buckets for my library cache with 5,880 buckets in use; most buckets have one object in them, 136 buckets have two objects, and one bucket has three. (In passing, of the 6,000 current objects, around 800 are currently *child cursors*, which are the things that appear in `v$sql`.)

Note The number of hash buckets in the library cache seems to have a hard-coded upper limit of 131,072 in recent versions of Oracle. In earlier versions you could increase this by fiddling with a hidden parameter, but in later versions you can only reduce it.

When you pass an SQL statement to Oracle and say "find it" (or place it) in the library cache, Oracle treats the SQL statement as a stream of numbers and does some fancy arithmetic to it to create a bucket number—so the most memorable thing about the statement (its text) is the thing that tells Oracle where to find it—and the arithmetic does a good job of sharing different statements across a large number of different buckets (although some of the early implementations, around v7, weren't all that clever about their choice of algorithm).

So we have the "even spread," the "useful algorithm," and "not much in a bucket." But this still leaves two important questions: what, exactly, is a bucket, and how does Oracle deal with two statements ending up in the same bucket? The answers to these questions explain why I started this section with a discussion of arrays, pointers, and linked lists. A bucket is just an item in a segmented array, acting as the end point to a doubly linked list of objects. Figure 4-1 shows one (highly simplified) view of the library cache.

Note You will see the terms *hash bucket* and *hash chain* used interchangeably. There's no great point in splitting hairs about the way people use the two terms, but if you want to make a distinction, you can think of the bucket as being the fixed end point, and the chain as being the list attached to the end point.

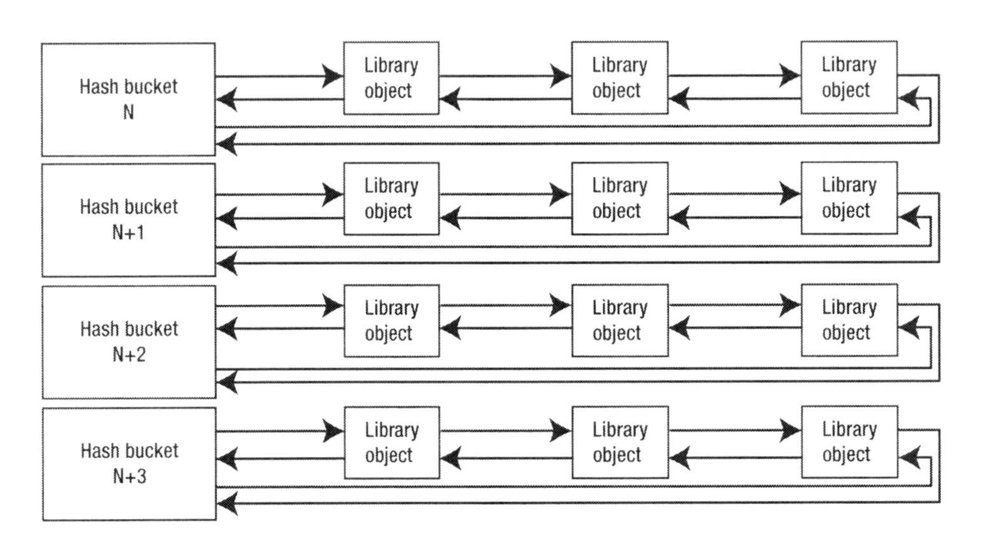

Figure 4-1. *First approximation to the structure of a very small library cache*

To load a new object into the library cache, Oracle does a bit of arithmetic to decide which bucket the object belongs to, and then it links the object into the appropriate list—which means picking two existing objects that currently point to each other, setting the forward and backward pointers in the new object to point to them, and then modifying the backward pointer on one object and the forward pointer on the other object to point to the new object. Adding a new object to a linked list forces me to interfere with two existing objects, as shown in Figure 4-2.

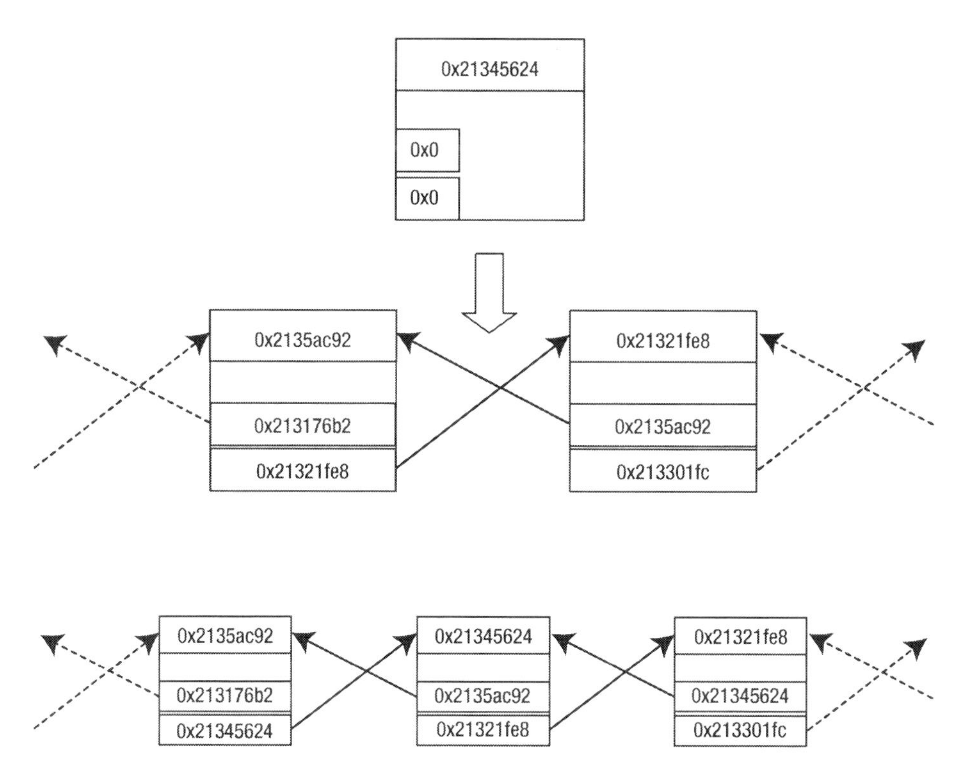

Figure 4-2. *Inserting an item into a (doubly) linked list*

Conversely, there will be times when there is not enough memory (no single chunk of free memory large enough) to create a new object in the library cache, in which case Oracle uses a least recently used (LRU) algorithm to pick a few "random" objects that can be detached from their hash chains so that their memory can be attached to the memory free lists for reuse. Again, I have to interfere with the two objects on either side of the one I am removing to make them point to each other once I've taken the target object out of the chain.

This is the point at which we finally realize that we need a high-speed mechanism to stop accidents from happening to complex memory structures. Imagine that your session decides that it needs to *use* an object in the first hash bucket in the diagram; unfortunately, at the same time, my session has decided that it needs to *free* some memory to use it somewhere else and has decided that there is an item in the same hash bucket that can be removed.

If we are both allowed to access the contents of the hash bucket at the same time, your session could end up following a pointer to an object that I've just discarded because I haven't yet had time to correct both pointers—and bear in mind, as you work through this scenario, that the operating system could preemptively stop my session running at any moment, so I could easily be in a position where I've got through half the work I need to do. Somehow we have to ensure that I can't restructure the linked list if you're walking along it, and you can't walk the linked list if I'm restructuring it.

A well-known mantra among Oracle users is "Readers don't block writers, and writers don't block readers"—but this is only true at the data level; when you get down to the *raw memory* level, there are moments when readers must block writers, and where a single write must block all other operations.

Note Oracle uses latches to eliminate problems that would appear if multiple processes were allowed to modify shared memory simultaneously; the patterns of use may vary but the intent is always the same. One pattern of use addresses the conflict between searching linked lists and modifying the contents of linked lists. Another, simpler pattern involves "isolating" a counter or pointer so that only one process can update it at a time (such as the control pointers for the redo log buffer).

Latches

Latches come in two flavors—*exclusive* and *shared read* (the shared read latches became relatively common in 9*i* but, as I learned very recently, there were a few in Oracle 8.0), and to make things a little more confusing, it is possible to acquire a shared read latch in exclusive mode—so from now on I'll refer to them as *shareable* latches.

There are also two ways of categorizing latch activity: the *willing to wait* gets (most of them) and the *immediate* gets. And again we have an area of overlap because some latch activity starts as immediate and then repeats as willing to wait, but we'll ignore this topic for the moment.

Essentially a latch is the combination of a memory location in the SGA and an *atomic* CPU operation that can be used to check and change the value of that location. (There are also between 100 and 200 bytes of infrastructure and instrumentation, varying quite dramatically with version of Oracle, which go with the latch.)

Note The significance of the word "atomic" is that on a multiuser system, most operations can be interrupted by the operating system scheduler, and on a multi-CPU system, different CPUs can be modifying memory at the same time. Ideally, the entire "check and change" operation needs to be a single CPU instruction so that it cannot be split into two pieces and descheduled in mid-change, but the key feature is that latching can work safely only if a single CPU can guarantee that the entire operation cannot be interrupted and, if you're running with multiple CPUs, that the same memory location cannot be modified by two CPUs at the same time. The latter requirement leads to special CPU instructions that do things like locking the memory bus to ensure that only one CPU at a time can access the critical location.

Logic Behind Latches

The fundamental logic of using latches is simple: "If I can set the latch memory location to some value *N*, then I can do something with the structure that the latch is protecting." (And when it has finished the protected operation, of course, it has to reverse the change to the latch). The basic *exclusive* latch get can be represented by the following pseudocode:

```
Set register X to point at latch address A
If value at address A is zero set it to 0xff ***
If the value at address A is set to 0xff then you "own" the latch
If not then go back to the top and try again—for a couple of thousand attempts
```

We'll postpone for a few pages the problem of what to do if you've still failed after a couple of thousand attempts. The line marked *** is the one that has to be atomic—our session has to be able to say, "if the latch bit was zero and is now 0xff, I must have set it." If this operation, which is commonly implemented as a "test and set" CPU instruction, could be interrupted, then you could end up with the following sequence of events:

1. Session A prepares the code loop.
2. Session B prepares the code loop.
3. Session A tests and finds zero and then gets interrupted.
4. Session B tests, finds zero, sets the value to 0xff, and then gets interrupted.
5. Session A resumes, sets the value (redundantly) to 0xff, and assumes it has acquired the latch.
6. Session B resumes, finds the value set to 0xff, and assumes it has acquired the latch.

Similarly, if we couldn't implement some form of memory locking in a system with multiple CPUs, we could change the last four steps to read as follows:

1. Session A running on CPU 1 tests and finds zero.
2. Session B running on CPU 2 tests and finds zero.
3. Session A sets the value to 0xff and assumes it has acquired the latch.
4. Session B sets the value to 0xff and assumes it has acquired the latch.

In either case, we now have two processes that could take some mutually destructive action, while happily assuming that they have sole access to some critical resource.

■ **Note** If you want to know more about the way in which multiple CPUs can interact, and the effects and costs of such activity, then the best book on the topic for the Oracle practitioner is still James Morle's *Scaling Oracle8i*, which is now available as a free download at www.scaleabilities.co.uk/index.php/Books/. (Ignore the 8i in the title—fundamental principles rarely change much.)

The drawback to the exclusive latch, of course, is that it is exclusive. Only one session can hold the latch at a time, which means only one session can access the protected resource at any one moment. This doesn't scale very well in a highly concurrent system if many sessions simply want to read the protected memory structure and don't want to change it. So in 9*i*, Oracle Corp. expanded its use of shareable latches into some of the busiest areas of code—perhaps aided by the appearance of the more subtle *compare and swap* operation appearing in common CPU architectures. There are variations in the CPU implementation, of course, but the basic pseudocode is typically something like this:

```
Set flag F to zero
Set register X to point to latch address L
Set register Y to hold the current value stored at L
Set register Z to hold a new value you want to see at L
If "value in Y" = "value in L" then set L to "value in Z" and set flag F to 1 ***
If flag F is set to 1 you have modified the latch value
```

Again, the line marked *** is the one that has to be uninterruptible. The advantage of this "word-sized" latch is that we can set up an algorithm that allows multiple readers to "count themselves on and off the latch" but also allows writers to block new readers (and other writers) by setting one bit of the word as an "exclusive write" bit. A *reader's* request might work as follows:

```
Loop (spin) a few thousand times
If write bit is set then go back to top of loop
Attempt to set latch value to value+1 (to acquire right to read)
If flag is set exit loop
```

Again, we'll postpone for a few more pages the question of what to do after a couple of thousand failures. As a reader process finishes with the object it is reading, it goes through a similar cycle to decrease the latch value by one—except that it doesn't need to check the write bit.

On the other hand, a *writer* (who must have exclusive access) might go through a set of steps like the following:

```
Loop (spin) a few thousand times
If write bit is set then go back to top of loop
Attempt to set latch value to "write bit + current value" (to acquire write bit)
If flag set then exit loop
Wait for reader value to drop to zero
```

As you can see, the effect of the two different strategies is to allow a writer to grab the "exclusive" bit while readers are using the resource, and then wait while the readers "count themselves off" the resource. At the same time, new readers are not allowed to count themselves onto the resource if a writer is holding the write bit, and only one writer at a time can hold the write bit. So we maximize shareability for readers while minimizing the delay involved with writers.

■ **Note** The details of how latches behave under concurrent activity have changed significantly over time, but the common understanding is still stuck around the version 8.0 timeline. If you want to learn more about the inner working of latches, the best online resource is probably the blog "Latch, Mutex and Beyond" published by Andrey Nikolaev at `http://andreynikolaev.wordpress.com/`, who I would like to make a particular point of thanking for reviewing this chapter, and especially my comments about latches and mutexes. (Any mistakes you might find, though, are mine—and some of them are deliberate simplifications.)

In fact, Oracle's read/write conflict resolution is a little more subtle than my original description. It is probably best explained with some examples of values, shown in Table 4-1, which I generated through various calls to `oradebug` (see Appendix for details).

Table 4-1. *Examples of Values Recorded in the Memory Location for a Latch*

Latch Value	Interpretation
`0x00000005`	There are five processes currently holding the latch as shared readers.
`0x40000003`	There are three processes currently holding the latch as shared readers, but an exclusive writer (we can't tell who it is) has set a blocking bit to stop new readers.
`0x20000014`	Process `0x14` (`v$process.pid`) is holding the latch exclusively as a writer.

As Table 4-1 suggests, if a writer has to compete with readers for a shareable latch, it goes through two steps to modify the latch, first using one bit to mark it as "blocked," and then, when all the readers have finally counted themselves off the latch, using a different bit to mark it as write-only and stamping it with its process id. The process actually starts by assuming that there are no competing readers, though, and its first action is to attempt to go straight to the holding value.

Latch Activity Statistics

Before talking about what happens if you attempt to get a latch and fail, I'll describe a few of the latch activity statistics. When you query `v$latch` (the basic latch statistics view, although you could be more particular and query `v$latch_parent` or `v$latch_children`), the most interesting statistics are those shown in Table 4-2.

Table 4-2. *Statistics Visible in the Latch-Related Dynamic Performance Views*

Statistic	Description
`gets`	The number of times a process has attempted to get a latch in *willing-to-wait* mode This statistic is incremented only after the latch has been acquired, no matter what pattern of `misses` and `sleeps` took place before the latch was finally acquired.
`Misses`	The number of times a process has tried to get a latch in willing-to-wait mode and failed on the *very first* "test and set"/"compare and swap." A miss usually ends up as a get when the latch acquisition is finally successful, so `misses` is effectively a subset of `gets`.
`spin_gets`	The number of times the attempt to get a latch in willing-to-wait mode missed on the first "test and set"/"compare and swap" but acquired the latch in the subsequent code loop . A large number of `misses` can mean a lot of CPU time lost even when they turn into `spin_gets`. `Spin_gets` is a subset of `misses`.

Continued

Statistic	Description
Sleeps	Number of times that a process has attempted to get a latch in willing-to-wait mode and failed even after spinning. Depending on version, Oracle may wake up after a sleep and try some more spinning, so a single miss may result in multiple sleeps. This pattern of multiple sleeps does not happen in newer versions of Oracle.
sleep1 ... sleep11	These columns exist so that Oracle can record how many times a process had to put itself to sleep while trying to acquire a willing-to-wait latch. From 8.0, Oracle never updated any of the sleepN columns past sleep3 (they didn't even exist in the physical memory structure); if a process slept more than three times, it would ultimately only populate the sleep3 column. From 10.2, even the first three sleepN columns (along with lots of other instrumentation columns) have disappeared.
Immediate_gets	The number of times a session has tried to acquire a latch in *immediate* mode and has got it on the first call to "test and set"/"compare and swap."
Immediate_misses	The number of times a session has tried to acquire a latch in immediate mode and has failed to get it on the first call to "test and set"/"compare and swap." Note, immediate_misses do *not* increment the immediate_gets counter. An example of this usage would be the redo allocation latch (in 10*g*, at least) where a session can try to acquire each of the private redo threads in turn, moving on to the next one immediately each time it fails to acquire the protecting latch.
Wait_time	The total time spent by sessions waiting for this latch. This applies only to willing-to-wait latches. The time is reported in microseconds, but (depending on version, platform, and bugs) it can appear to be in other units, so I always used to compare it with latch free wait times from v$system_event to check the units.

Latch Misses

My initial description of latch activity included the directive "loop a few thousand times." It's now time to consider what happens if you fail to acquire the latch even after running around this loop.

Historically the session would set an alarm to wake itself up after a short interval and take itself off the operating system run queue. When it was put back on the run queue by the operating system scheduler and got to the top of the queue, it would go into a loop again to try and acquire the latch, and put itself back to sleep if it failed again. The sleep time was designed to use an *exponential backoff* algorithm—meaning the more times the session went to sleep, the longer the sleep interval became—and this could, occasionally, lead to very long delays as a process tried to get a latch. Here's one of the extreme examples I once saw on an Oracle8i system when a session spent over 8 seconds trying to acquire one of the library cache latches:

```
WAIT #4: nam='latch free' ela= 1 p1=-1351741396 p2=62 p3=0
WAIT #4: nam='latch free' ela= 1 p1=-1351741396 p2=62 p3=1
WAIT #4: nam='latch free' ela= 1 p1=-1351741396 p2=62 p3=2
WAIT #4: nam='latch free' ela= 3 p1=-1351741396 p2=62 p3=3
WAIT #4: nam='latch free' ela= 3 p1=-1351741396 p2=62 p3=4
WAIT #4: nam='latch free' ela= 7 p1=-1351741396 p2=62 p3=5
WAIT #4: nam='latch free' ela= 9 p1=-1351741396 p2=62 p3=6
WAIT #4: nam='latch free' ela= 18 p1=-1351741396 p2=62 p3=7
WAIT #4: nam='latch free' ela= 15 p1=-1351741396 p2=62 p3=8
WAIT #4: nam='latch free' ela= 55 p1=-1351741396 p2=62 p3=9
WAIT #4: nam='latch free' ela= 33 p1=-1351741396 p2=62 p3=10
WAIT #4: nam='latch free' ela= 69 p1=-1351741396 p2=62 p3=11
WAIT #4: nam='latch free' ela= 100 p1=-1351741396 p2=62 p3=12
WAIT #4: nam='latch free' ela= 150 p1=-1351741396 p2=62 p3=13
WAIT #4: nam='latch free' ela= 151 p1=-1351741396 p2=62 p3=14
WAIT #4: nam='latch free' ela= 205 p1=-1351741396 p2=62 p3=15
```

In principle the elapsed time (`ela= nnnn`, reported here in hundredths of a second) should double *every other* wait until it hits the maximum of 2 seconds,[1] but the extreme CPU overload on the machine made the queue times very unstable in this case.

■ **Note** It is interesting to consider that the 1/100-second wait time was originally introduced in Oracle 6 (or earlier) at a time when "fast" CPUs were running at a few megahertz. Now that CPUs run at speeds of a few gigahertz, a wait time of 1/100 second is (relatively speaking) hundreds of times longer than it used to be.

It's important to note, though, that things *no longer work like this*: in outline, a process that doesn't acquire its target latch almost immediately will attach itself to a *latch wait list* and go to sleep until woken. There are variations in the amount of effort a session will use before doing this, and Andrey Nikolaev, mentioned in an earlier note, has used DTrace on a Solaris system to track down the details, which are summarized in Table 4-3.

[1] Steve Adams, *Oracle8*i *Internal Services for Waits, Latches, Locks and Memory* (Sebastopol, CA: O'Reilly Media, 1999).

Table 4-3. *Summary of Activity When a Latch Isn't Acquired on the First Attempt*

Required Latch Access	Method Used
Get exclusive latch	Attempt immediate get, go into spin cycle once (in this case the process spins 20,000 times), attach to wait list, attempt immediate get, go to sleep
Get shareable latch in exclusive mode when another process is holding it in some mode (whether shared, exclusive, or blocking)	Go into spin cycle (in this case the process spins 2,000 times each cycle), attach to wait list, repeat spin cycle, go to sleep if unsuccessful
Get shareable latch in shared mode when another process has got the latch in exclusive or blocking mode	Don't bother spinning—go straight to the wait list
Get shareable latch in shared mode when other processes have the latch in shared mode	Spin just `cpu_count` + 2 times before going to sleep

The key point here is that when a process fails to acquire a latch, it attaches itself into a list, and then waits to be woken up. The wakeup mechanism is the thing that has changed most in the newer versions of Oracle—a process that is currently holding the desired latch will post the process at the top of the list when it releases the latch, and this can have some interesting side effects.

■ **Note** The post/wait mechanism for latches was available in earlier versions of Oracle, but was not applied to many latches. The higher profile it enjoys in newer versions of Oracle depends on improvements in the available operating system features, and can (but shouldn't) be controlled by the hidden parameter `_enable_reliable_latch_waits`.

If it's not a very busy latch and no other processes are trying to acquire the latch, we can see that every process that is on the wait list is effectively in a queue, because when one process releases the latch it posts the next waiter.

Of course, if it's not a very busy latch, it's not very likely that a wait list will appear, but you have to ask what happens to a busy latch if a wait list appears and more processes are trying to acquire the latch. In this case it's possible for a new process to acquire the latch even though other processes are still waiting to be posted—the queuing mechanism isn't fair!

In the case of exclusive latches, the larger value for spin count may have been selected to minimize sleeping problems. You can assume that any code path a process follows while holding a latch should be as short as possible, so perhaps the 20,000 cycles around the loop is supposed to take longer than any code path protected by an exclusive latch. Nevertheless, we don't appear to have any statistics available that tell us about the following type of scenario:

1. Session 1 gets an exclusive latch.
2. Session 2 tries to get the exclusive latch and goes to sleep.
3. Session 1 releases the latch and posts session 2.
4. Session 3 gets the latch before session 2 manages to get started.
5. Session 2 wakes up, spins, and has to go to sleep again.

Perhaps there's some cunning piece of code that we can't see that stops this race condition from happening; perhaps it's supposed to be such a rare event (or such a low-cost event) that it doesn't really matter that it doesn't get recorded directly.

We can infer the number of "recurrent sleeps" by noting that *in principle* a latch miss must eventually turn into a spin_get or a sleep, so `misses = spin_gets + sleeps`, or to put it another way, `sleeps + spin_gets - misses = 0`. But if the preceding scenario does happen, then we will record extra sleeps and the excess should be `sleeps + spin_gets - misses`.

There seem to be opportunities for a single latch get to take a long time, and I'd like to know what happens when that occurs; in the preceding scenario, does session 2 go back to the head of the queue or drop to the end of the queue? We can only hope that this mechanism is generally more efficient and fairer than the earlier mechanism where processes simply set alarms to wake themselves up so that they could fight over the latch acquisition.

▒ **Note** Throughout this chapter I have been talking about *sessions* getting latches; technically it is a *process* that gets, or misses, or waits for a latch—and a *process* that eventually holds a latch (as can be seen in the dynamic performance view `v$latch_holder`, which is underpinned by the structure `x$ksuprlatch`).

We can hope that the exclusive latch access is relatively low frequency and therefore less likely to cause major time loss, but there are threats built into the wait-list approach for sharable latches that really could matter.

If a sharable latch is held exclusively, then a request you make to get the latch shared drops your process to the end of the queue immediately, and a request you make to get the latch exclusively drops you to the end of the queue after a short spin. So a single call to get a shareable latch in exclusive mode can result in a long queue appearing. When the latch is released, one process from the queue can acquire the latch, and any concurrent processes not queued can now get the latch. If most of the processes are after shared latches, the queue should empty rapidly (every process releasing the latch allows one more process to dequeue). But as soon as another exclusive get occurs, the processes trying to get the latch in shared mode start extending the queue again, and you could easily end up with a long queue of shared waiters interspersed with a few scattered exclusive waiters. In cases like this, a relatively small number of exclusive waits could end up seeing some very long wait times.

There isn't a lot you can do about long wait times for latches—it's a side effect of how Oracle's code handles the competition for critical memory. There are only three strategies for limiting the damage:

- As a designer/developer/coder, don't do things that generate lots of latch activity; avoid, for example, splitting a job into a very large number of very small steps.
- As a DBA, look for (legal) opportunities to increase the number of latches covering a particular type of activity. A classic defensive measure here is to identify a hot spot in the data and find a way to spread that data across more blocks. It's also a good idea to keep an eye open for the latest patches.
- As a designer/developer for Oracle Corp., create mechanisms that reduce our reliance on latch activity. (And this is what they've been doing with pins and mutexes.)

Figure 4-3 shows a (still very simplified) picture of the library cache; it simply expands Figure 4-1 to indicate the significance of one type of latch, the *library cache* latch.

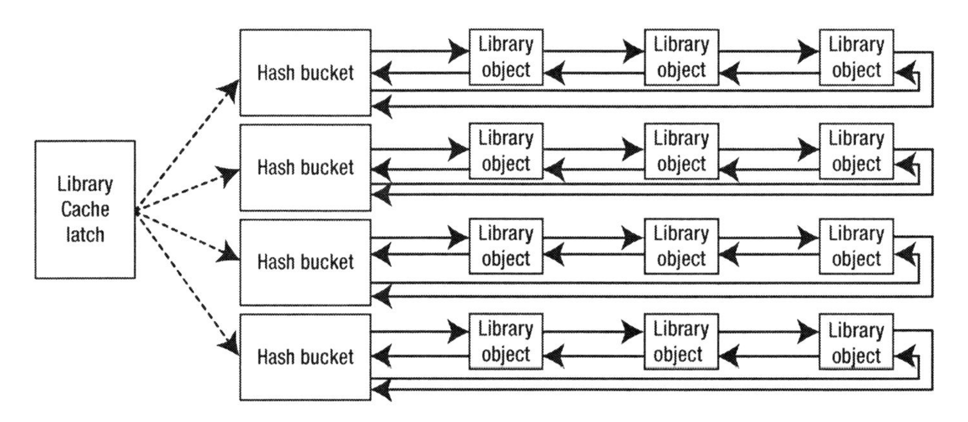

Figure 4-3. *Second approximation to a small library cache, including the library cache latch*

This picture, with minor variations, could be reused as a diagram of the library cache, the shared pool free lists, the data buffer cache, the dictionary (row) cache, locking, and many other patterns of memory management in Oracle.

We have created complex collections of memory structures and have set up known starting points for the structures so that we can either walk along linked lists or do arithmetic to find out where to jump to. We can find anything we need to find by doing arithmetic or following pointers—the latch mechanism ensures that it is safe to use those locations.

Note Oracle made dramatic changes in 11*g* to the way it handles the library cache. The descriptions in this chapter are mainly about versions of Oracle up to 10*g*. Comments on the 11*g* implementation will appear in Chapter 7: Parsing and Optimising

---

Latch Scalability

I mentioned earlier in this chapter that I happened to have 131,072 hash buckets in my library cache. If I want to execute an SQL statement from the SQL*Plus command line, one of the steps taken by the server process managing my session will be to search for that statement in the library cache. This means doing some arithmetic to create a hash value from the text of the statement to produce the bucket number, and then walking along the linked list (hash chain). Critically, there is another piece of arithmetic that allows Oracle to work out which latch is protecting each hash bucket, so the code will acquire that latch, walk the linked list, do whatever it needs to do with the object if it finds it, and then drop the latch.

There are three important aspects, then, of latch contention:

- How many different latches are covering the library cache—one for each bucket, one for the whole library cache, or something in between? The more latches there are, the less likely you are to collide with someone who needs to walk a linked list covered by the latch you want; on the other hand, the more latches you have, the more work you may have to do in some form of maintenance, reporting, or garbage collection.
- How often will you need to go through the process of acquiring a given latch—once or twice when you first optimize a statement, every time you execute a statement, or something in between? The more times you have to get the latch and walk the list, the more likely you are to collide with someone who wants the same latch.
- How long do you have to hold the latch? The longer everyone holds latches, the more likely they are to have problems with other people holding latches that they want to acquire. It should be fairly obvious that you're not going to hold a latch continuously while you execute a statement, but when is it safe to let go?

Until 10*g* the number of latches covering the library cache was remarkably small. On my little system I have three latches covering 131,072 buckets. The number is dependent on the number of CPUs (it's roughly the same as the `cpu_count` parameter) up to a maximum of 67 latches. That's a surprisingly small number, really, given the potential for collisions occurring on even a small number of frequently executed statements; and two processes don't have to be executing the same SQL, or even accessing the same hash bucket, to be colliding on the same latch—they need only be accessing two hash buckets covered by the same latch.

Given the small number of latches involved, you won't be surprised to learn that there are mechanisms in place to minimize the number of times we have to search the library cache for an object. We can attach a *KGL lock* to an object once we've found it so that we have a shortcut to it, and we can attach a *KGL pin* to it to show that we are actively using it. (Both these structures are the subject of changes due to the introduction of mutexes, which started to appear in 10*g* and have nearly taken over the library cache in 11*g*. I'll say more about KGL locks, KGL pins, and mutexes in Chapter 7.)

As far as the amount of time you hold a latch is concerned, Oracle Corp. seems to make endless changes to the code as we go through different versions, point releases, and patches to minimize the time that any one latch is held. Sometimes this meant breaking tasks into smaller pieces and introducing new types of latch to protect (each of) the shorter operations. There are (or were) several different latch types associated with the library cache. To demonstrate how things keep changing, Table 4-4 provides a list of the latches that exist in a few different versions of Oracle.

Table 4-4. *Latches Associated with the Library Cache by Oracle Database Version*

Latch Name	8.1.7.4	9.2.0.8	10.2.0.5	11.2.0.2
Library cache load lock	X	X	X	X
Library cache	X	X	X	
Library cache pin		X	X	
Library cache pin allocation		X	X	
Library cache lock			X	
Library cache lock allocation			X	
Library cache hash chain			X	

I'm not going to go into the details of what all these latches are for, and the structures they protect—especially since most of them have disappeared in 11*g*—but we will see similar mechanisms when we look at the buffer cache in Chapter 5.

MUTEXES, PART 1

A brief comment about mutexes is necessary at this point because a mutex is very similar to a latch in the way it is implemented and used.

Mutexes were introduced in the library cache processing in Oracle 10.2 as a step toward eliminating the use of pins (which I will discuss in conjunction with library cache locking toward the end of the following section). Essentially a mutex is a "private mini-latch" that is part of the library cache object. This means that instead of a small number of latches covering a large number of objects—with the associated risk of competition for latches—we now have individual mutexes for every single library cache hash bucket, and two mutexes (one to replace the KGL pin, the other related in some way to handling dependencies) on every parent and child cursor, which should improve the scalability of frequently executed statements.

The downside to this change is that we have less information if problems arise. The support code for latching contains a lot of information about who, what, where, when, why, how often, and how much contention appeared. The code path for operating mutexes is shorter, and captures less of this information. Nevertheless, once you've seen how (and why) Oracle operates locking and pinning in the library cache, you will recognize the performance benefits of mutexes.

Locks

We've seen latching as a mechanism for protecting memory while we search through, and possibly modify, lists, but I've pointed out that we ought to avoid holding latches for any length of time. This means that if we need to do something time-consuming when we've found the bit of memory we were searching for, we need to devise a different mechanism to protect that memory while we're using it so that we can release the latch. This is where library cache locking (and pinning) comes into play.

Before looking at library cache locks, though, we'll turn our attention to the better known and more easily observable form of locking—the activity we see in **v$lock**, which, broadly speaking, is a view over **x$ksqrs** (the enqueue resources) joined to a union of **x$ksqeq** (the enqueues) and various other structures.

■ **Note** If you're ever asked, "What's the difference between a lock and an enqueue?" the answer is "nothing." They are two terms for the same concept, even though, historically, the documentation tended to use the term "lock" while the internal structures were called "enqueues" and the instance activity stats referred to "enqueues"; for example, if you query the dynamic performance view v$lock, you are querying the structure defined by the parameter enqueues. To add to the confusion, there are structures called KGL locks, or *breakable parse locks*, which are never called enqueues and which people don't generally think of when you mention locks.

Infrastructure

There are many types of resources in Oracle—tables, files, tablespaces, parallel execution slaves, and redo threads, to name just a few—and there are many different reasons why we might want to protect a resource for a long time (and, to paraphrase former UK Prime Minister Harold Wilson, "7 milliseconds can be a long time in Oracle").

To create a standard method for handling different types of resources, Oracle keeps an array in the SGA (exposed as **x$ksqrs** and **v$resource**, with a size defined by hidden parameter _enqueue_resources) where each entry can be used to represent a resource. The critical columns in the array definition are

```
Name              Null?    Type
----------------- -------- ------------
KSQRSIDT                   VARCHAR2(2)
KSQRSID1                   NUMBER
KSQRSID2                   NUMBER
```

You will probably recognize hidden in these column names the **type**, **id1**, and **id2** that are revealed in view **v$lock**. To use an array entry as a representative of some resource, your session will simply fill in the columns; for example:

- ('PS', 1, 4) represents parallel execution slave P004 on instance 1.
- ('TM', 80942, 0) represents the table that has 80,942 as its object_id.
- ('TX', 65543, 11546) represents the transaction using slot 7 (mod(65543,65536)) in undo segment 1 (trunc(65543/65536)) for the 11,546th time.

Once we have an in-memory object representing a particular resource, we can start attaching things to it to show which sessions want to use that resource and how restrictive they want to be in their use. There are several arrays of structures that Oracle uses for this. The most frequently used are x$ksqeq (generic enqueues), x$ktadm (table/DML locks), and x$ktcxb (transactions). The others are x$kdnssf, x$ktatrfil, x$ktatrfsl, x$ktatl, x$ktstusc, x$ktstusg, and x$ktstuss. These arrays have a common core of elements that, with the exception of a couple of columns from x$ktcxb, follow a uniform naming convention. These columns are given different names when they are exposed through v$lock, but the original names from the x$ structures are as follows:

```
Name              Null?    Type
----------------- -------- ------
ADDR                       RAW(4)   -- ktcxbxba in x$ktcxb
KSQLKADR                   RAW(4)   -- ktcxblkp in x$ktcxb
KSQLKMOD                   NUMBER
KSQLKREQ                   NUMBER
KSQLKCTIM                  NUMBER
KSQLKLBLK                  NUMBER
```

It's just possible to recognize the last four columns as the lmode, request, ctime, and block of v$lock. The various structures also have a column ksqlkses, which is the session address of the locking session, exposed indirectly through v$lock through the sid (session id), and a column x$ksqlres, which is the address of the resource it's locking, exposed indirectly through the type, id1, and id2.

The basic idea, then, is very simple: if you wish to protect a resource, you acquire a row from x$ksqrs, label it to identify the resource, and then acquire a row from x$ksqeq (or equivalent), set the lock mode, and link it to the row from x$ksqrs. There are, of course, many subtleties to worry about:

- How do you find out (efficiently) whether or not someone else has already labeled a row in x$ksqrs to identify the same resource so that you don't create a duplicate?
- If someone else has already labeled a row from x$ksqrs, will you always be allowed to attach your row from x$ksqeq (or equivalent) to it? (What if their lmode denies you access to the resource?)
- If you are allowed to attach your row from x$ksqeq (or equivalent), does that mean you will be able to use the resource? If not, how do you find out when you can use the resource?

A Graphic Image of v$lock

Before doing anything else, let's extract some rows from v$lock and draw a picture of what those rows look like in the SGA:

```
select
        sid, type, id1, id2, lmode, request, ctime, block
from    v$lock
where
        type = 'TM'
and     id1 =  82772
;
```

```
     SID TY        ID1        ID2      LMODE    REQUEST      CTIME      BLOCK
-------- -- ---------- ---------- ---------- ---------- ---------- ----------
      37 TM      82772          0          3          5         66          1
      36 TM      82772          0          3          0         42          1
      39 TM      82772          0          0          6         27          0
      35 TM      82772          0          0          3          3          0
```

I have four sessions here handling a table that is the child table of a parent/child link—and there is no supporting index on the child table for the foreign key constraint. To get into this state, I took the four sessions through the following steps:

1. Session 37: The only child of parent 1.
2. Session 36: The only child of parent 2.
3. Session 39: Attempt to lock the child table in exclusive mode (and start to wait).
4. Session 37: Attempt to delete parent 1 (and start to wait due to missing FK index).
5. Session 35: Attempt to delete the only child of parent 3 (and start to wait).

I contrived this unlikely sequence of actions because I wanted to demonstrate the range of possibilities with locking. Without the history I've given you, you might find it a little hard to determine the sequence of steps that led to this set of rows in `v$lock` even though all the necessary clues are available in the output. Figure 4-4 converts the text to a picture.

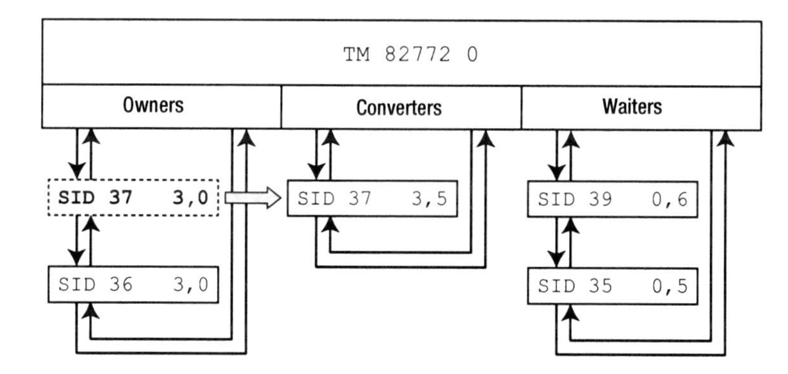

Figure 4-4. *A graphic image of a few rows from v$lock*

A single row from `x$ksqrs` (`v$resource`) holds the end points of three doubly linked lists (often referred to as queues in this case). The three lists are made up of rows from one of the enqueue structures, the choice of structure being dependent on what the resource represents. In our case the enqueues will come from `x$ktadm` because the resource represents a table (resource type is TM).

The three lists are for owners (sometimes called holders), converters, and waiters, and the process of "locking" an object requires you to join the end of the waiters queue until there is no one ahead of you in the waiters queue or the converters queue, and only then can you attach yourself to the owners queue—provided the lock mode you want is compatible with the modes held by everyone currently on the owners queue.

■ **Note** There are a few places in the Oracle code where a process may take a lock in one mode to start doing some work, and then find that it needs a more aggressive level of locking as the work proceeds. This results in *lock conversion*. This is not the same as *lock escalation*—a mechanism Oracle does not need to implement—which involves (for example) changing from a set of row locks to a single table lock to minimize the number of locks acquired from a lock resource by a session.

The most common example of lock conversion appears in the *foreign key locking* problem. If you declare a foreign key constraint on a table but don't create a supporting index for the constraint, then a session that tries to delete or update a parent key value will try to lock the child table with a share lock (mode 4); however, if the session had deleted some rows from the child table before modifying the parent table, then it would already be holding a subexclusive lock (mode 3), which means it has to *up-convert* the lock mode. In fact, the rules of lock modes dictate it would have to convert to a mode 5—not just a mode 4—which is what we see in our example.

So in Figure 4-4 we see that SID 35 is sitting at the end of the waiters queue because SID 39 was already stuck there. SID 39 has to wait because SID 37 is in the way in the converters queue. SID 37 is stuck in the converters queue because it wants to convert a mode 3 lock to mode 5 and SID 36 is in the owners queue holding a lock in mode 3—and no one else is allowed to hold a mode 5 if anyone is holding a mode 3.

As processes commit (or roll back), the queue will shuffle forward as follows:

1. When SID 36 commits, the owners queue will become empty, which will allow SID 37 to move from the converters queue to the owners queue, acquiring its mode 5 lock and setting its `ctime` back to 0. Sessions 39 and 35 will still be stuck on the waiters queue.
2. When SID 37 commits, the owners queue will again become empty and SID 39 will be able to move to the owners queue, acquire its mode 6 lock, and set its `ctime` to 0. SID 35 will now be at the front of the waiters queue, but can't join the owners queue because you can't get any lock on a table if any other session is already holding an exclusive (mode 6) lock.
3. When SID 39 commits, the owners queue will again become empty and SID 35 will be able to move to the owners queue, acquire its mode 3 lock, and set its `ctime` to 0.

If you compare this picture with the extract I've shown from `v$lock`, you might realize that you can't normally get the whole picture unless you're a little lucky (or have a helpful author). In our case we can see that session 36 is holding mode 3 and that it is blocking something (block = 1). Since we know that converters take precedence over waiters, we can deduce that session 37 is the thing blocked by session 36 and that it too is blocking something. We can see that sessions 35 and 39 are blocked, but we can't necessarily tell which one is at the top of the queue—fortunately I waited several seconds after each step of the demonstration so we can look at the `ctime` column and see that session 29 started waiting roughly 24 seconds before session 35. The `ctime` column, however, is only updated each time the lock times out, which usually means every 3 seconds, so it won't always help—and this generally is where we have a little bit of an information gap: if several sessions are blocked somewhere in the converters or waiters queue, we can't always tell which one will be released first.

■ **Note** If you're waiting to acquire a lock, the `ctime` column tells you how long you've waited, and if you're holding a lock, it tells you how long you've been holding it. But if you're converting from one mode to another, does it tell you how long you've been waiting to convert to the new mode, or how long you've been holding the old mode? Both pieces of information are useful, but the one you get is how long you've been holding the old mode. It would be nice if Oracle Corp. could enhance the view (and underlying code) to give us both times.

If you really need to pick the details apart, when you're jammed in a complex locking pattern, you could dump an enqueue trace. It will look a little messy, and you'll have to do some decoding and formatting, but it will give you a completely sequenced picture. The command is

```
alter session set events 'immediate trace name enqueues level 3'
```

Here's an extract from the trace file I dumped after I had got all my locks in place:

```
res      identification         NUL SS  SX  S   SSX X   md link
         owners               converters          waiters
-------------------------------------------------------------------------
21A4CD90 TM-00014354-00000000 U   0   0   2   0   0   0  8 [21a5534c,21a5534c]
         [212d1190,212d1190] [212d1008,212d1008] [212d1254,212d13dc]

   lock     que owner    session       hold wait ser link
   ----------------------------------------------------------------------
   212D1188 OWN 2198C2C4 2198C2C4 (036)   SX NLCK  12 [21a4cd98,21a4cd98]

   212D1000 CON 2198D5AC 2198D5AC (037)   SX  SSX  65 [21a4cda8,21a4cda8]

   212D124C WAT 2198FB7C 2198FB7C (039) NLCK    X  17 [212d13dc,21a4cda0]
   212D13D4 WAT 2198AFDC 2198AFDC (035) NLCK   SX   6 [21a4cda0,212d1254]
```

There are two lines of data about each resource, starting with its address in `x$ksqrs` and then listing the resource's identity (`type, id1, id2`).

The second line of information identifies the three linked lists using a format that appears very frequently in all sorts of trace files: two addresses in square brackets, the first address acting as a "forward pointer" and the second address acting as a "backward pointer." In this case the first address points to the first item of the linked list of enqueues and the second address points to the last—but just to confuse the issue, there's an 8-byte offset in the figures. Take a look at the pair of pointers for the waiters queue: the forward pointer (`212d1254`) minus 8 is the value that appears at the start of the third line of the locks, and the backward pointer (`212d13dc`) minus 8 is the value that appears at the start of the fourth line of the locks. We see the same pattern in the pointer pairs for the owners and converters queues, but the forward and backward pointers are the same as each other because there is only one item in each queue.

The same linked list format appears in the locks information in the `link` column. Again the waiters (`que = WAT`) are the easier to follow. Note how the forward pointer (`212d13dc`) minus 8 in line 3 points to the lock address in line 4, while the backward pointer (`212d1254`) minus 8 in line 4 corresponds to the lock address in line 3.

Finally, we can see that the backward pointer in line 3 and the forward pointer in line 4 are both (`21a4cda0`) pointing back to the resource address (`21A4CD90`), although the offset is 32 rather than 8. (The same logic applies to the converters and owners, but the offset for owners is 8 bytes and the offset for converters is 24 bytes—this may seem like an error, but it's probably just a case of pointing to the specific field rather than pointing to the start of the whole record.)

Deadlock

Looking back as the original picture, you might wonder what would happen if session 36 decided to delete the parent row for the child row it has successfully deleted. Because of the missing foreign key index, it would have to convert its mode 3 lock to a mode 5 lock, which means it would have to join the converters queue behind session 37—you always join a queue at the tail end.

When I drew my picture, I left a "ghost" of session 37 on the owners queue; if you look at the trace file it's not really there, of course, but as a visualization of the way the code works, it's quite helpful to think of it as still sitting in the owners queue while also being in the converters queue.

So at this point we have session 37 in the converters queue waiting for the owners queue to empty, and session 36 sitting "behind" session 37. But session 36 (or its "ghost") is at the end of the owners queue, so session 36 is also "in front of" session 37—we have constructed a simple deadlock, where both sessions are waiting for the other session to get out of the way.

Within 3 seconds, one of the sessions will do a statement level rollback and raise Oracle error ORA-00060, "deadlock detected," dumping a deadlock trace into the session's trace file at the same time. Although the manuals say that a session will be chosen at random, I have found that it's always the session that has been waiting the longest that gets the deadlock error. In this case it would be the session at the front of the converters queue, session 37. The explanation for this behavior is that TM enqueues (and many other types of enqueue) have a timeout interval of 3 seconds—so every 3 seconds a session waiting for a TM lock will wake up, check the state of all the locks on the table, and (typically) go into another 3-second wait. It's this check on timeout, though, that allows a session to realize it's in a deadlock and raise the error.

So what should session 37 do when it raises the error? Many applications will respond to the error by simply terminating the session (which usually clears up the locking problem automatically, eventually, because of the implicit rollback). Some application will issue an explicit `rollback;`, which will also clear out the problem but may need a lot of time to roll back the work done up to that point. Some applications, unfortunately, will simply retry the last step—which in our case would put session 37 in the waiters queue behind session 36, resulting in session 36 reporting a deadlock error within 3 seconds, and if the application is consistent, it will make session 36 try again, leading to session 37 reporting a deadlock error within 3 seconds, and so on.

There is no perfect solution for handling deadlocks. Rolling back the transaction is a safe but possibly expensive option; terminating the session with extreme prejudice so that it doesn't do an implicit commit of the work done so far is an alternative. Ideally, though, you could consider coding your application so that any *long-running* jobs (which are the ones where it really matters) that receive a deadlock error are coded to identify the other session involved and either page a DBA to resolve the problem or check which session will have to roll back the smaller amount of work—with the option, then, to terminate the other session. However it's done, applications shouldn't be allowed to respond to deadlocks with an arbitrary failure.

Note Although I've said that it's always the session that has been waiting the longest that gets the deadlock error, I have to point out that I managed to construct a very specific and totally repeatable sequence of steps in 9.2.0.1 where both sessions got a deadlock error simultaneously. I couldn't reproduce this behavior in any other version of Oracle, so it may have been a temporary side effect (or bug) due to some of the changes that were working their way through the enqueue manager in 9.2.

Technically it's also possible (at least in theory) that your O/S scheduler could break this pattern. Even if the two waiting sessions are restarted in the right order, this only means they are put on the CPU run queue in the right order. If your hardware implements multiple run queues, it's possible for the second process that goes onto a run queue to be the first process that actually runs.

I've used table locking to demonstrate the structures involved and highlight one of the classic examples of locking and deadlocking. *Foreign key deadlocking* is relatively common, but you are probably more likely to see transaction deadlocking or (to give it another name) data deadlocking.

As you saw in Chapter 3, a transaction table slot is the "focal point" for all the work done by a single transaction, and every data (and index) block modified by a transaction will hold a reference to that transaction table slot in its interested transaction list (ITL). The session executing the transaction will lock the transaction table slot by creating an enqueue resource for it (type TX, `id1` representing the undo segment number and slot number, and `id2` representing the slot's sequence number) and attaching an enqueue to it—specifically, a row from `x$ktcxb` rather than `x$ksqeq`—at lock mode 6 (exclusive).

If a second session wants to update a row that has been modified but not committed by the first session, then it will attach an enqueue to the first session's TX resource requesting an exclusive lock—and this enqueue will be attached to the waiters queue. If, at this point, the first session decides to modify a row that has been modified but not committed by the second session, it will attach an enqueue to the second session's TX resource—again, this enqueue will have to go into the waiters queue.

So we have the first session in the waiters queue on the second session's TX resource, and the second session in the waiters queue on the first session's TX resource—the classic transaction (or data) deadlock. Within 3 seconds, one of the sessions will raise an Oracle error ORA-00060 and its last statement will be rolled back; if the deadlock occurs inside a PL/SQL block and you don't have an exception handler for it, then all the uncommitted SQL statements inside the block will be rolled back.

Note When a data deadlock occurs and dumps a trace file, the most important lines in the trace file (from the perspective of Oracle Corp., at least) will say

```
DEADLOCK DETECTED ( ORA-00060 )
[Transaction Deadlock]
The following deadlock is not an ORACLE error. It is a deadlock due to user error in the
design of an application or from issuing incorrect ad-hoc SQL.
```

The ORA-00060 error is (almost always) a program error, although, unfortunately, there have been some recent changes in 11*g* that have introduced some very strange locking anomalies

---

When deadlocks happen, the session that gets the error will dump a trace file. There's a lot of information in it, but the starting point is the *deadlock graph*, which, in the simple case I've described, would look like this:

```
Deadlock graph:
                       ---------Blocker(s)--------  ---------Waiter(s)---------
Resource Name          process session holds waits  process session holds waits
TX-00030026-000040d6        13      38     X              12      50           X
TX-00060002-00004113        12      50     X              13      38           X
```

In this graph you can see that session 38, process 13, was holding TX lock (undo segment 3, slot 38 (`0x26`), sequence 16,598) in mode 6, and session 50, process 12 was waiting to acquire it. Conversely, session 50 was holding TX lock (undo segment 6, slot 2, sequence 16,659), which session 38 was waiting for.

The rest of the trace file will tell you the SQL statements the sessions were executing when they got stuck, may give you the `rowid` for problem rows, and will give you the entire process state dump for the session that got the error.

It's worth highlighting a couple of important concepts. First, of course, it's possible for several sessions to get into a ring; a deadlock doesn't have to be limited to two sessions, although the commonest ones are. Secondly, although TX locks crossing over in mode 6 are the most common form of deadlock, any time that it's possible to wait for a lock, it's also possible to engineer a scenario where you can get into a deadlock (as we saw with the discussion of table deadlock from the earlier example).

■ **Note** When a transaction deadlock occurs, one of the sessions involved will have to `commit;` or `rollback;` to resolve the problem. Even though you can set savepoints in a transaction, it is important to remember that a `rollback to savepoint` is not sufficient to clear the deadlock as it does *not* release the TX resource; all it does is apply any undo records created since the savepoint was declared.

There are a few variations on TX deadlocks that are worth mentioning. If one of the tables is an index organized table (IOT), one of the waits will be for mode S (share). An IOT is an index, and if you're waiting to modify an IOT, you wait in mode 4 (share) rather than mode 6 (exclusive).

This leads to several other possibilities relating to indexes—and bear in mind my earlier comment that if there are circumstances that make you wait for a lock, there will be a variation on those circumstances that will result in a deadlock. Various coding errors can lead to waits because of conflict over indexes; for example:

- Two sessions try to insert the same primary key value
- One session inserts a row into a child table as another session deletes the parent
- One session inserts a parent row and another inserts child rows before the parent row has been committed
- Two sessions try to delete rows that are covered by the same bitmap index chunk

Essentially, if you're waiting for another session to commit because of a conflict over indexes (or possibly the constraint enforced by those indexes), then you will see a TX wait in mode 4. There's even an index case where the problem isn't a coding problem—which appears when you have to wait for another session to complete a leaf block split

There are, however, a few other causes for TX/4 waits. The most common (though still rare) appears when a transaction wants to modify a block whose ITL is full of active transactions and there is no free space to grow the ITL. If this happens frequently, then you need to decide whether it's worth tracking down the problem object and changing its definition (typically the `initrans` value). Conveniently, 10*g* displays ITL waits as a specific type of TX wait (`enq: TX - allocate ITL entry`), and captures information about the specific objects in the Statspack and AWR reports as `Segments by ITL Waits`.

Distributed transaction can also result in TX/4 waits and, surprisingly, these waits can appear on select statements. In recent versions of Oracle (9.2.0.6 and later), this can only happen if you are using database links; in earlier versions it could happen through XA-compliant transaction-processing monitors (TPMs). The problem comes from the *two-phase commit* (2PC)—if a remote database has modified some of your data and has sent you the prepare step but not yet sent the commit step of a two-phase commit, your database doesn't know whether to view the changes as committed or rolled back, so anyone who queries the modified data has to wait until the commit (or rollback) arrives. (If you're using an XA- complant TPM, Oracle will simply create a read-consistent version of the data, which, theoretically, could lead to inconsistent results across a distributed system.)

There are a few other exotic reasons for TX/4. One of them relates to starvation of free lists (but it's a very extreme edge case, and most systems have stopped using free lists anyway). Another relates to waits for a data file to finish growing, so watch out what you set your `autoextend` values to. Yet another is when you switch a tablespace to read-only mode and have to wait for all current transactions to complete before the tablespace switch can occur, and that's a necessity and not something you should be doing often anyway.

Lock Modes

I always have trouble remembering the names of the different locking levels (or modes) that Oracle allows. I tend to think in numbers, and Oracle doesn't make it easier by having two different names for some of the lock modes. So I've produced Table 4-5 to show a list of the lock modes with a brief note of how they apply to tables. It's probably easiest to understand the purpose of the different modes in the context of tables, but, in principle, any resource could be subject to locks in any of the lock modes.

Table 4-5. Lock Modes, by Name and Number

Mode	Name(s)	Application to Table
1	Null Lock (NL)	Not relevant to tables. Held by the PX slaves during some parallel DML operations (e.g., update) while the QC is holding an exclusive lock
2	Sub Share (SS)	select for update until 9.2.0.5
	Row Share (RS)	Lock table in row share mode
		Lock table in share update mode
		Appears at the opposite end of a referential integrity constraint during DML since 9.2.0.1
3	Sub Exclusive (SX)	Update (also select for update since 9.2.0.5)
	Row Exclusive (RX)	Lock table in row exclusive mode
		Appears at the opposite end of a referential integrity constraint during DML from 11.1
4	Share (S)	Lock table in share mode
		Can appear during parallel DML in the PX slave sessions, except it has `id2` = 1 so it's not the same as the normal table resource
		Common symptom of foreign key locking (missing index) problem
5	Share Sub Exclusive (SSX)	Lock table in share row exclusive mode
	Share Row Exclusive (SRX)	Less common symptom of foreign key locking but likely to be more frequent if the foreign key constraint is defined with `on delete cascade`
6	Exclusive (X)	Lock table in exclusive mode

Unless you've done something unusual with your application, and ignoring the lock-related bugs that have appeared in 11g, the only significant thing you need to remember about table locks is that if you see a mode 4 or mode 5, you probably need to create an index on a foreign key constraint.

In fact, for many applications, the only table locks that will ever appear will be mode 3 as the code updates tables, and (for versions in the 9.2 range) mode 2 locks associated with foreign key constraints.

Latches for Locks

We haven't yet answered the question of how efficiently we can find out whether we need to set up a new row in `x$ksqrs` (`v$resource`) to represent a new resource or whether there's a row in use already that we should attach our enqueue to. We also have an outstanding question about the apparently random "link" values we saw in the enqueue trace file.

There are two more parts of the infrastructure we need to know to be able to answer these questions—and we're back to arrays, pointers, linked lists, and hash tables, which inevitably bring in latching.

We've already seen that **x$ksqrs** and **x$ksqeq** (which I'll use as representative of all the rest of the enqueue structures) are arrays—each row is a fixed size, and it's easy to get the *N*th row if we know where the array starts and how long each row is. But we know that each of the rows in the underlying structures holds lots of pointers—we saw them in the fragment of the enqueue trace, even though they're not visible in the x$ itself—and by playing with pointers, Oracle can "rearrange" the arrays to make them look like something completely different.

We've already seen that there are three doubly linked lists attached to the resources array (**x$ksqrs**), and that these link together chains from the enqueue arrays (**x$ksqeq**, et al.). What we haven't yet seen is how Oracle makes it possible to use these structures efficiently—and the answer is a picture very similar to the earlier picture of the library cache, shown in Figure 4-5.

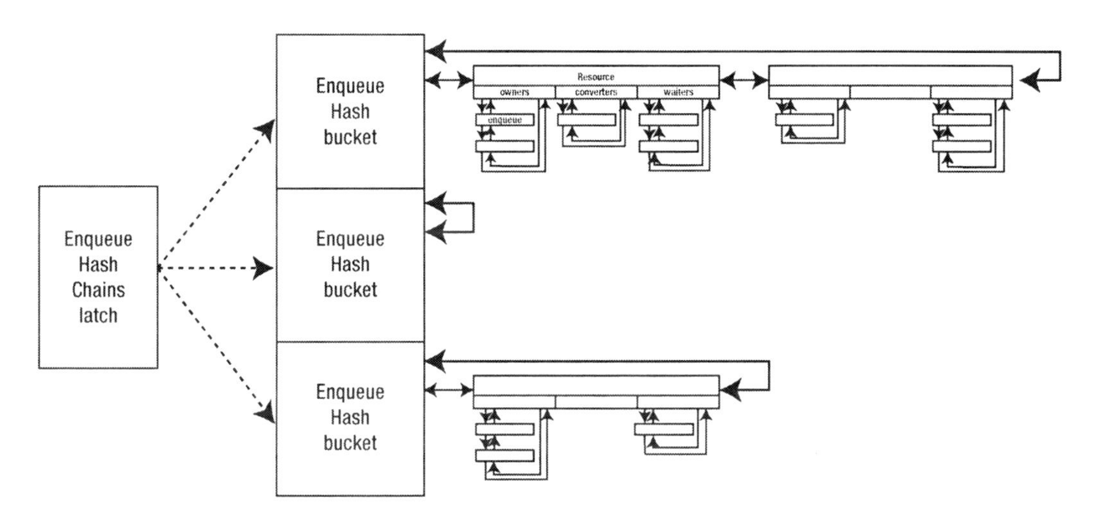

Figure 4-5. *Enqueues and enqueue resources in use—the bigger picture*

The resource in Figure 4-5 labeled "Resource" is a miniature copy of the resource from Figure 4-4, but now it's shown as one link in an enqueue hash chain. The whole picture can best be explained by describing the process of acquiring a lock:

- Use the resource identifier (**type, id1, id2**) to generate a hash value. The size of the hash table seems to be 2 * **sessions** + 35, so doesn't fall into either of the common patterns of "prime number" or "power of 2"!

- The hash buckets are protected by latches known as the *enqueue hash chains* latches. The number of latches matches the number of CPUs, and the hash buckets are shared "round-robin" across the latches. So get the latch and search the bucket (i.e., walk along the chain) to see if a row from **x$ksqrs** has already been linked to that hash chain to represent the resource you want to lock.

- If the enqueue resource is in place already, then pick a row from the relevant enqueue structure (`x$ksqeq`, et al.), but to do this you have to get the associated enqueue latch to stop other people from picking the same enqueue row at the same time. The latch you need to acquire depends on the specific type of enqueue you are using; for example, if you want a row from `x$ksqeq` you need to get the *enqueue* latch but for a row from `x$ktadm` you need to get the *dml allocation* latch. Drop this latch as soon as you have made the enqueue row safe.
- If the enqueue resource is not in place, then (still holding the enqueue hash chains latch) pick a row from `x$ksqrs`, label it to represent your resource, link it in to the hash chain, and then get an enqueue row to link to it.
- Once all this is done, you can drop the enqueue hash chains latch.

There are two places where we might have to worry about efficiency, and both of them involve the same type of work: if you need to pick a row from the enqueue resources or the enqueues, how do you avoid walking through the array looking for an unused item? In a large, busy system with lots of resources and enqueues, you may have to walk through a large section of the array before finding a free element.

To my surprise, it looks as if Oracle does *exactly that* when looking for an enqueue row (whether it's looking at `x$ktadm`, `x$ksqeq`, or [I assume] any of the other shorter arrays).

On the other hand, something completely different happens with the `x$ksqrs` array. I'm not sure of all the details, and there may be two or three variations in strategies that make it hard to work out what's going on, but, firstly, when Oracle takes enqueue resources off the hash chains, I think it has a mechanism that uses another set of "linked list" pointers in the structure to emulate a stack (LIFO) so that it always has a pointer to the first available row in `x$ksqrs` and doesn't have to search the array.

I think there's also a lovely example of Oracle's "lazy cleanup" strategy. When the last enqueue is detached from an enqueue resource, I think Oracle leaves the enqueue resource in the hash chain, simply marking it as "available for reuse." The benefit of this is that, over time, all the hash chains will end up with a few "empty" resources linked to them, so if you don't find the resource you want when walking a hash chain, you will already have an empty one there waiting to be used and you won't have to scan the `x$ksqrs` array. If this hypothesis is correct, there will also have to be code to handle the case when there are no free enqueue resources on the hash chain you are searching, and you find that your only available option is to transfer a resource from another hash chain.

If you're trying to get to grips with the complexities of how Oracle works, one of the best places to start is with the enqueue mechanisms. The methods and structures are typical of the behavior that appears all through the Oracle code, but enqueues have a wonderful benefit for the early student—they happen quite slowly and are easy to control, so it's much easier to observe the activity and work out what's going on.

KGL Locks (and Pins)

After all the groundwork we've put in on enqueues, there isn't really very much to say about library cache locks (and pins and mutexes) at this point; we've covered the key points of why we need to protect areas of memory in a multiuser system, and we've talked about the need to be able to find the right bit of memory as efficiently as possible.

We used an initial picture (figure 4-1) of the library cache to demonstrate the concept of hash buckets with linked lists attached as a mechanism for finding (or placing) an object efficiently. Then we saw a picture (Figure 4-4) of an enqueue resource with a number of enqueue chains linked to it—and that's a pattern that reappears in the library cache (although the things we attach to a library cache object come from different x$ structures). Finally, we used a picture (figure 4-5) showing the enqueue hash chains latch and the collection of hash buckets it protects—and the association of latches and hash buckets in the library cache is exactly the same, until we get to 10g, and by the time we reach 11.2 it's completely different. We'll stick with the older library cache mechanisms to start with, because they are still repeated in the buffer cache, even in 11g.

Every object in the library cache belongs in a library cache hash bucket, and the bucket number is derived from the object's name (and the term "name" is interpreted very freely in this context). The hash buckets are shared evenly around a number of library cache latches, and the number of latches is similar to the number of CPUs, up to a maximum of 67 latches (and, like me, you might think that seems to be a rather small number of latches). The most significant difference between the locks we attach to library cache objects and the locks we attach to enqueue resources is that there are two sets of locking structures involved with the library cache objects—the KGL locks and the KGL pins—and I don't think Oracle creates three queues for each type, so there may only be two, the owners and waiters. (The picture that I've described so far doesn't look very different from the enqueues picture shown in Figure 4-5, so I won't provide another one in this chapter.)

Locks and Pins

If you're wondering why we have two types of locking structure on the library cache objects, it's because they express two different intentions. (I have to say that I've never quite managed to convince myself that two structures are absolutely necessary, but that probably means I haven't thought through the requirements properly—it may simply have been a scalability decision.)

The most important task of the KGL lock (which is exposed in `x$kgllk` and becomes `v$open_cursor`) is to improve concurrency. If your session has a KGL lock on an object—and for an SQL statement, that means a lock on the parent cursor and on the relevant child cursor—then the Oracle code has a mechanism that allows it to go directly to the address it has for the object rather than having to grab the library cache hash chain latch and search the hash chain.

There are three major ways in which you can make sure that this little saving in work takes place:

- You can write your front-end code to "hold" cursors that you know you are going to use frequently.
- You can set the `session_cached_cursors` parameter so that Oracle library code will automatically start holding a cursor if it sees you using a statement more than two or three times.
- You can benefit from the semiautomatic way in which PL/SQL will hold cursors that have been opened (explicitly or implicitly) from within a PL/SQL call—from Oracle 9.2.0.5 onward, setting the `session_cached_cursors` parameter will also control this feature.

Note The `session_cached_cursors` parameter dictates how many cursors can be held when your code does not explicitly hold cursors. It also controls the number of cursors that can be held open by PL/SQL code being run by the session. Historically (pre-9.2.0.5) the size of the PL/SQL cursor cache was set as a secondary feature of `open_cursors`. The value people use for `open_cursors` is often quite high (sometimes too high), but many people leave `session_cached_cursors` to its default, and the default value is often too low.

The KGL pin comes into play when you actually use an object. Although a KGL lock will hold an object in memory, there are parts of the object that are dynamically re-creatable (the execution plan for an SQL statement, for example), and these can still be discarded if there is a heavy demand for memory even if you have a KGL lock in place.

However, when you are actually using an object (running an SQL statement, say), you need to ensure that the re-creatable bits can't be pushed out of memory, so you pin the object to protect them.

The KGL locks and KGL pins themselves are simply little packets of memory that, at one time, were individually created and discarded on demand by making calls to allocate memory from the shared pool. Since a KGL lock is about 200 bytes and a KGL pin is about 40 bytes, you can imagine that between them the constant allocation and freeing of memory could cause the free memory in the shared pool to end up in a "honey-combed" state—i.e., lots of free memory in total, but not many large pieces of contiguous memory. The KGL pins were particularly nasty because they would come and go very quickly; the KGL locks weren't quite so bad because they could stay attached to an object for some time.

Another issue with the KGL locks and KGL pins was that, to use them, you had to constantly manipulate linked lists, attaching and detaching chunks of memory, and you had to do this while holding a latch exclusively (and, as I've pointed out, there are surprisingly few latches for the library cache). So for very busy systems, the whole lock/pin issue could become a significant scalability threat. In 10g, though, Oracle Corp. introduced the *library cache lock* latch and the *library cache pin* latch, which allowed some concurrent activity to be done on different hash buckets covered by the same library cache latch (you could pin a cursor in one bucket while I locked a cursor in another bucket because we wouldn't both need to hold the same library cache latch at the same time).

However, as we moved through 10g to 11g, the whole KGL lock/KGL pin mechanism was gradually replaced by the mutex mechanism.

MUTEXES, PART 2

The mechanisms of locking and pinning in the library cache allowed two problems to creep in. First, there aren't many latches covering all the work that has to be done; second, it's quite a lot of work to create a packet of memory, label it properly, and insert it into a linked list (or, conversely, to remove a link from a linked list and put it back in the shared pool). So 11.2 got rid of all the little packets of memory and the linked lists—in fact, it even got rid of the latches used to protect the hash chains, and replaced them all with mutexes.

A mutex is a "micro-latch" and its usage involves a very short code path. Like a latch, it's just a counter that can safely be incremented to show "one more person is interested" or can be modified with a similar "high-bit" approach to say "I'm waiting for exclusive access" followed by a different bit saying "I've got exclusive access" when everyone else has counted themselves off the mutex. There are a number of differences when you start to look closely at the details of operation, but from the high-level view there is a great deal of similarity.

If you have mutexes on hash buckets, you have one micro-latch per bucket instead of a maximum of 67 latches covering (in my case) 131,072. If you have a mutex on each library cache object to represent the KGL locks and another to represent the KGL pins, then you don't have to do all that memory allocation and deallocation and don't have to run code to connect things to linked lists. (In fact, both locks and pins still exist as structures in 11.2, but Oracle Corp. has rewritten the code for allocating and freeing them; it is, however, possible that they will eventually disappear completely.)

Of course, you do have to rewrite all the code for manipulating the hash chains and for locking, pinning, queuing, unpinning, and unlocking library cache objects, but once you've done that, you have a system that is potentially far more scalable because you have spread the contention over far more points.

There is, inevitably, a threat to cover. The structure of KGL locks and KGL pins includes the information about which session owned the lock or pin. Mutexes are small, and don't have lists associated with them, we now have information pointing one way, the session knows which mutexes it is holding, but the mutex doesn't know which sessions are holding it. If the code for mutex handling is not perfect, a session could "lose" a mutex and fail to decrement it—and the overhead of having a house-keeping task that has to check for lost mutexes could be significant.

There is one particularly interesting difference between latches and mutexes: latches are held by *processes*, while mutexes are held by *sessions*—and a process can operate on behalf of several sessions (think shared server or connection pooling). Technically this means that two sessions operating within the same process could end up deadlocking each other on mutexes. I haven't yet investigated the circumstances that could cause this to happen, though.

We'll be coming back to the library cache and its memory management in Chapter 7, but before that we'll see in Chapter 5 how the same pattern of latches, hash buckets, and linked lists runs through the buffer cache, and how the buffer cache still makes use of pins even in 11.2

Summary

In a multiuser system where shared memory is used to maximize scalability, you need mechanisms to make it impossible for two processes to modify the same piece of memory simultaneously. Oracle has four mechanisms to do this: locks, pins, latches, and mutexes. Table 4-6 outlines the key features of the different mechanisms.

Table 4-6. *Simple Categorization of the Four Serialization Mechanisms*

Type	Duration	Behavior	Levels
Latch	Short	Compete, then queue (10g+)	Shared or exclusive
Lock	Long	Join queue	Enqueues: various, complex KGL locks: shared or exclusive
Pin	Long (relatively)	Join queue	Shared or exclusive
Mutex	Long when acting as a pin, short when acting as a latch	Compete, then queue	Shared or exclusive

At the lowest level Oracle uses the latch, or its new "little brother" the mutex, as a way of blocking processes that might interfere destructively. There are certain operations that a session can perform only if it can first acquire a latch or mutex in the appropriate way. The latch and the mutex basically depend on an *atomic* "compare and swap" operation, which says, "If I can change the value of a word from X to Y, then I can do my work."

Some of the tasks that need the protection of a latch or mutex can run concurrently, provided they still shut out destructive operations. This led Oracle Corp. to introduce the *shared read* mechanism, which allows readers to count themselves on and off the latch or mutex, while writers can still acquire the latch or mutex in exclusive mode by using a couple of the high bits to introduce a two-phase "want it/got it" strategy for modifying the value.

For requirements where a resource may be held for a (relatively) long time and a queuing mechanism needs to be in place, Oracle has a generic locking mechanism that involves attaching linked lists (queues) of memory elements representing the sessions that want to use a resource to a memory structure that represents that resource. There are two main areas where this locking is made visible: in `v$lock`, where we see enqueues attached to enqueue resources, and in `v$open_cursor`, where we see KGL locks attached to library cache objects (we also have KGL pins attached to library cache objects, but they are not exposed in any dynamic performance views). The two variants on locking use very similar mechanisms, but there are, inevitably, some critical differences between them. Over the course of the last two versions of Oracle, the mechanisms relating to KGL locks and KGL pins have been re-engineered to take advantage of mutexes.

CHAPTER 5

Caches and Copies

Caching means keeping copies of things that we expect to use soon, and keeping them close by so that we can access them quickly. Chapter 2 described how Oracle changes various types of data blocks (including undo blocks) and showed you a few of the structures that you can see stored in blocks, but it didn't say anything about how Oracle manages to keep a selection of recently used or popular blocks in memory. Chapter 2 simply assumed that whenever we needed a block, the correct version of that block would be available.

In Chapter 4, you saw a simplified diagram of the library cache and learned how you can use hash chains (or buckets) to ensure that you can find an object quickly, provided that you can work out a sensible way of turning an object's identity into a "magic number" that you can use as the number of the bucket it belongs to.

In this chapter, you will see how this pattern echoes through the structures in the data cache as Oracle copies data blocks into memory, accesses those blocks rapidly when it needs them, and juggles multiple copies of the same block as the data is changed by multiple concurrent processes.

Before we get down to blocks and buffers, though, we'll take a look at the large-scale structures, starting with granules and then considering how granules are linked to create buffer pools.

Following a brief discussion on the different buffer pools we can create—and why we might not want to create them—we'll start to slice the buffer pools into the working data sets that Oracle uses to handle the problems of freeing buffers for reuse and reading data into memory.

Working data sets give us only one of the chains running through the buffer cache, though, and don't give us a method for finding specific data blocks quickly, so we will also spend time looking at the much shorter hash chains that Oracle uses in its strategy for locating data in memory quickly.

Memory Management

There are so many different chains running through the data cache that it's hard to know where to begin, so I'm going to step backward and start with the easiest bit. For the purposes of this discussion, I am ignoring any version of Oracle prior to version 9*i* because I want to talk about granules—the large-scale unit of memory that Oracle uses for shared memory areas.

Granules

Oracle Corp. introduced *automatic system memory management* (ASMM) in 10*g* with the intention of eliminating the question, "How much memory should I set for the **db_cache_size** (data cache) and how much should I put into the **shared_pool_size** (code cache)?" The official (though not always appropriate) answer to this question from 10*g* onward is, "Don't ask." In 9*i* you can move memory between the key areas while the database is running, but in 10*g* you're simply expected to tell the instance how much memory should go into the system global area (SGA) and let the instance itself work out the best way to use it—which (crudely speaking) it does by estimating the time that it could save on disc I/O if it increased the data cache (`db_cache_size`), compared with the time it would save on optimization if it increased the code cache (`shared_pool_size`).

To make it easy to move memory efficiently between the `db_cache_size` and the `shared_pool_size`, Oracle re-engineered the SGA in 9*i* to use fixed-size memory chunks called *granules*. The granule size varies with the operating system, the version of Oracle, and the size of the SGA; for "small" SGAs the unit is 4MB, while for larger SGAs the unit is 8MB if you are running Oracle on Windows and 16MB or 64MB if you are running Oracle on Unix. (In this context, "small" currently means up to 1GB—for earlier versions of Oracle the breakpoint was 128MB, and it's possible that there are other variations on limits and granule sizes that I haven't yet come across.)

If you want to check the granule size for your current instance, then you can query **`v$sgainfo`** as follows:

```
select bytes from v$sgainfo where name = 'Granule Size';
```

It's possible that this query may become obsolete in future versions of Oracle, though, as the presence of the column **`granule_size`** in the view **`v$sga_dynamic_components`** may be a clue that Oracle will move to multiple granule sizes at some point.

Oracle doesn't supply a dynamic performance view to give us details about individual granules, but if you have SYS privileges, the object **`x$ksmge`** will give you a list of all the granules—the **`grantype`** tells you what the granule is being used for, and the **`granstate`** tells you if it is allocated, free, or invalid. In 9.2 you can join on **`grantype`** to **`x$ksmgv`** to translate the **`grantype`** for allocated granules into a description of use; in 11.2 you join to **`x$kmgsct`**. For example, the following query shows us which granules belong to which components of the SGA, and the order in which they are linked:

```
select
        ge.grantype, ct.component,
        ge.granprev, ge.grannum, ge.grannext
from
        x$ksmge         ge,
        x$kmgsct        ct
where
        ge.grantype != 6
and     ct.grantype = ge.grantype
order by
        ge.grantype,
        ct.component
;
```

■ **Note** In 9*i* Oracle introduced granules and the option for DBAs to reallocate memory manually across a limited subset of the parts of the SGA while the instance was running. In 10*g* you could configure Oracle with the `sga_target` parameter to allow it to reallocate memory automatically, and more of the subpools of the SGA could be modified. In 11*g* Oracle took one more step, replacing ASMM with AMM (automatic memory management) by allowing a single parameter, `memory_target`, to define the sum of the SGA and the PGA (the process memory limit, formerly set by parameter `pga_aggregate_target`). For large, complex, systems you need to exercise some caution before committing yourself to either automatic option.

Granules and Buffers

If we examine only the granules relating to the data cache, the next level of refinement is to consider what goes into a granule. There are three components: the largest part is the array of *buffers* used for holding copies of data blocks; next is the array of *buffer headers* (made visible through the structure `x$bh`); and finally there is a small amount of management overhead.

Depending on the version of Oracle, and whether it is running on a 32-bit system or a 64-bit system, a row in `x$bh` can be anywhere between 150 bytes and 250 bytes (apart from changes in content, it includes a lot of pointers, which change from 4 bytes each to 8 bytes each as you move from 32-bit to 64-bit Oracle).

■ **Note** Buffer headers are tied very closely to buffers. There is a permanent one-to-one link between a row in the array of buffers and the corresponding row in the array of buffer headers. Don't be fooled into thinking, though, that the buffer headers are the same thing as the block headers—they're not; buffer headers hold some data about the block, some data about the state of the buffer, and lots of pointers to other buffer headers.

At first sight it seems strange that Oracle uses two separate arrays for the buffers and buffer headers, and you might wonder why the two arrays aren't combined into a single array with a larger row size. I can think of two possible reasons. By isolating the buffers, the start of each buffer is on a very regular boundary address, and this may offer some performance benefits when data is loaded from disc to memory. Secondly, there is a lot of history to Oracle: granules only appear in 9*i*, and before that the buffer header array was allocated in a totally separate part of the SGA from the data buffers themselves, potentially in a separate shared memory segment; keeping the buffer headers separate when changing to memory granules may simply have been the lower-risk option during recoding.

When you consider a single 8MB granule with an 8KB block size, you might initially assume that you should get 1,024 buffers per granule; but when you remember that each buffer needs a few hundred bytes of buffer headers, you realize that an 8MB granule is more likely to hold closer to 1,000 buffers. As an indication of the variation, following are the results from a pair of queries run against a 32-bit 9.2.0.8

(where the **x$bh** row size is 186 bytes) and then repeated against 11.1.0.7 (where the **x$bh** row size is 208 bytes), both running under Windows XP. First from 9*i*:

```
SQL> select  current_size, granule_size
  2  from    v$sga_dynamic_components
  3  where   component = 'buffer cache';

CURRENT_SIZE GRANULE_SIZE
------------ ------------
    50331648      8388608

SQL> select block_size, buffers from v$buffer_pool;

BLOCK_SIZE    BUFFERS
---------- ----------
      8192       6006
```

Then the results from 11*g*:

```
CURRENT_SIZE GRANULE_SIZE
------------ ------------
    50331648      8388608

BLOCK_SIZE    BUFFERS
---------- ----------
      8192       5982
```

In both cases I have set the default buffer cache to 48MB with an SGA large enough to make Oracle use 8MB granules. As you can see I have 6,006 buffers in the 9.2.0.8 buffer cache, but only 5,982 in the 11.1.0.7 buffer cache. That's 1,001 buffers per granule and 997 buffers per granule, respectively. Figure 5-1 is a simplified picture of a single granule showing its header, the array of buffer headers, and the array of data buffers.

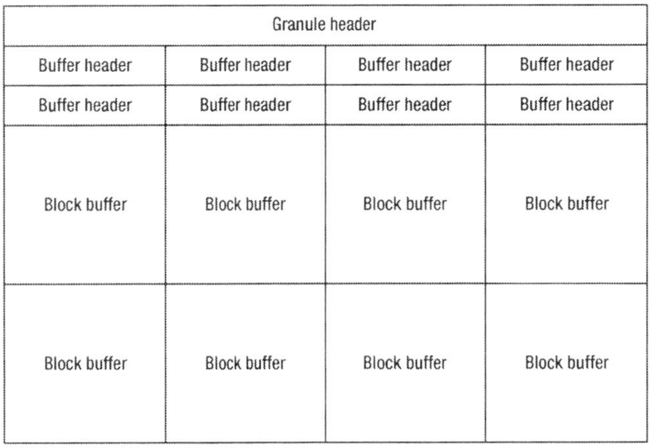

Granule header			
Buffer header	Buffer header	Buffer header	Buffer header
Buffer header	Buffer header	Buffer header	Buffer header
Block buffer	Block buffer	Block buffer	Block buffer
Block buffer	Block buffer	Block buffer	Block buffer

Figure 5-1. *Schematic of a granule allocated to a db_cache*

■ **Note** Oracle makes enormous use of pointers, and a lot of the code path in Oracle is all about following pointers. When you migrate from 32-bit to 64-bit Oracle, pointers are twice the size, which means you need more memory to manipulate the same amount of data. If you want to check the number of buffers per granule directly, the information is available in column `bp_bufpergran` of `x$kcbwbpd`, the structure behind `v$buffer_pool`.

There is another layer of detail we can look at before things start to get complicated—the option to have multiple data caches.

Multiple Data Caches

Oracle allows for a total of eight different data caches: five to allow for different block sizes, three to allow (at least nominally) for variations in behavior. Table 5-1 lists the eight parameters, with comments, that define these caches.

Table 5-1. *Parameters Defining Data Caches*

Parameter	Description
`db_cache_size`	Default cache for blocks of the size used in the `create database` statement. The `system`, `sysaux`, and `temporary` tablespaces have to use this block size.
`db_keep_cache_size`	Objects that have been defined with a storage clause of `(buffer_pool keep)` will use this cache. In principle you would consider using this cache for objects that you really want to keep cached at all times. In practice (because of the mechanics of read consistency) it usually has to be much larger than the sizes of the object(s) that you want to keep cached (between 1.5 and 6 times)—although a recycle cache size of a few percent of the keep cache size may take care of most of the read-consistent clones—and you probably won't beat the default LRU (least recently used) caching algorithm that Oracle uses anyway.
`db_recycle_cache_size`	Objects that have been defined with a storage clause of `(buffer_pool recycle)` will use this cache. You could consider using this cache for objects whose blocks tend to see very little reuse; consequently you would tend to make this a relatively small cache. It is particularly useful for caching LOBs. If you have defined a keep cache, most of the read-consistent clones of blocks from the keep cache will be created in the recycle cache, which might mean you have to make the recycle cache larger than you expected, to reduce time spent on event `free buffer waits`. In the past I have found that the recycle pool may be more useful than the keep pool, as it gives you an option for limiting the damage a large, randomly accessed object can do to your ability to keep useful data cached.

Continued

Parameter	Description
db_2k_cache_size	You are allowed to create tablespaces with block sizes other than the default (database) size. You will need to set up this cache if you have created a tablespace using a 2KB block size when the default block size is not 2KB.
db_4k_cache_size	As for db_2k_cache_size, but catering for a 4KB block size.
db_8k_cache_size	As for db_2k_cache_size, but catering for an 8B block size. However, 8KB tends to be the default block size offered by the Database Configuration Assistant (DBCA) on most platforms and is probably the commonest block size used in the world—and you can't set up the db_Nk_cache_size if your default block size is *N*KB.
db_16k_cache_size	As for db_2k_cache_size, but catering for a 16KB block size. There are a few interesting anomalies (bugs) that can appear if you use 16KB blocks, typically relating to counters reaching their legal limit before the block is full.
db_32k_cache_size	As for db_2k_cache_size, but catering for a 32KB block size. The option for a 32KB block size is restricted to a limited number of platforms, and the comments relating to 16KB blocks are equally valid for 32KB blocks.
db_Nk_cache_size	The option for adding caches for blocks of different sizes was originally introduced to allow people to transport tablespaces between databases that had been built with different defaults. Although it is possible to use multiple block sizes in a single database, it is a feature rarely (and probably inappropriately) used. I have had a few occasions when it made sense for a couple of specific IOTs or LOB segments to be isolated in this way—a larger block size in the case of the IOTs happened to allow related rows to fit into a single block; a smaller block size for the (small, out of row) LOBs happened to avoid wasting a huge amount of space.

Although it's not stated explicitly in the manuals, there is a common assumption that the default block size has to be one of the values 2KB, 4KB, 8KB, 16KB, or (when available) 32KB, but technically it is possible to use other sizes. I have created databases with default block sizes of 12KB, 5KB, and even 4.5KB in the past, but only to see if they would work. (On one occasion I actually did have a rationale for the 12KB block, but there was absolutely no way I was going to give an Oracle support analyst the opportunity to say "not supported.")

In my experience most databases have nothing but an 8KB block size as their default block size and no nonstandard block sizes; a few try to take advantage of the keep cache and/or recycle caches; and a few use 4KB or 16KB as their default block size. Personally I prefer to see 8KB as the size for the default as this is the size that sees most testing in the field and is generally the option least likely to result in odd problems, with 4KB a good second bet on some of the Linux platforms.

BUFFER POOLS AND HISTORY

You will have spotted the expression `buffer_pool` in the definitions of `db_recycle_cache_size` and `db_keep_cache_size` in Table 5-1. This is an example of the inexorable pressure of history. In earlier versions of Oracle we specified the size of the data cache through a parameter called `db_block_buffers`, which defined the number of buffers to allocate and had no options for keep or recycle caches (let alone block sizes other than the database default).

When Oracle introduced the keep and recycle caches, the first implementation used two parameters called `buffer_pool_keep` and `buffer_pool_recycle`—hence the storage clause, and the names of dynamic performance views `v$buffer_pool` and `v$buffer_pool_statistics`. And it is still very common for people to talk about *buffer pools* when making comments about the data cache—I'll be doing it in the rest of the chapter.

These parameters aren't entirely obsolete, in fact. If you are running Oracle on 32-bit Windows, there are features built into the operating system that allow you to use a "memory windowing" or "memory paging" mechanism to address memory beyond the typical 32-bit limit of 4GB. Oracle can use this extra memory space for the data cache, but only if you specify the cache sizes using the older parameters.

Granules and Buffer Pools

The only important point I want to make about the different buffer pools in relation to the use of granules is that each granule is allocated to a specific buffer pool. This means that any one granule will contain buffers of just one size, which makes the positioning of buffers in the granule nice and tidy. As a minor detail, it's also worth noting that, as with so many memory structures in Oracle, granules show us an example of mixing arrays and linked lists: there is an array of granules, but elements of the array point forward and backward to other elements in the array to link together the granules that make up each of the different components of the SGA. We can see this from the results of the sample query provided earlier if we restrict it to just the keep cache:

```
  GRANTYPE COMPONENT            GRANPREV    GRANNUM   GRANNEXT
---------- ------------------ ---------- ---------- ----------
         8 KEEP buffer cache          26         27          0
                                      25         26         27
                                      24         25         26
                                      23         24         25
                                      22         23         24
                                      17         22         23
                                      16         17         22
                                      12         16         17
                                       0         15         14
                                      15         14         13
                                      14         13         12
                                      13         12         16
```

The second column of figures is the granule number, the first column of figures is the previous granule, and the last column of figures is the next granule in the component. The first line shows us that granule 27 has no next granule—it's the last granule in the list, but the previous granule was number 26.

We can follow 26 back to 25, 25 back to 24, and so on very tidily for a while, but then we get to granule 22, which points back to 17; 17 points back to 16, but then 16 shows another gap as it points to 12. The gaps in the linked lists indicate that various resize operations have occurred where granules have been added to and removed from the keep cache over time. (We could confirm this by querying `v$sga_resize_ops` in 10*g* or, if we have the `memory_target` configured, `v$memory_resize_ops` in 11*g*.)

As we have done in previous chapters, we can take a diagram, shrink it, clone it several times, and then link the clones together to see a bigger picture of how Oracle works. Figure 5-2 is an indication of how this works with granules.

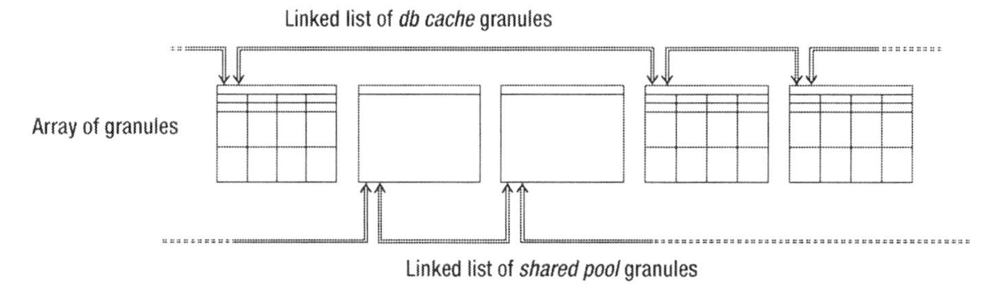

Figure 5-2. *Schematic of granules in an array and on linked lists*

Buffer Pools

Granules break a large volume of memory into smaller chunks for basic administrative reasons. By handling memory in equal-sized chunks, it is easier to reallocate a chunk of memory from one function (e.g., data cache) to another (e.g., shared pool). But long before Oracle Corp. introduced granules, it had already used another strategy to break a large data cache into smaller pieces, in this case for scalability reasons rather than simple administration.

The mechanism has changed in many ways over the years, both at the high level and in the detail, and no doubt there is still room for change in the future. In its most commonly cited form, it is known as the *least recently used list* (LRU list), but it is more appropriate to talk about the *working data set*.

Each of the different buffer pools can be split into several slices, simply to reduce the number of buffers that have to be handled as a unit. These slices cut across the granules, so if a buffer pool consists of four working data sets, a single slice would hold one-quarter of the buffers from each of the granules. Every buffer pool has the same number of working data sets (even if some of those sets are actually empty—i.e., they don't have any allocated granules), and since there are eight buffer pools, the number of working data sets in an instance is always a multiple of eight.

The structure describing the working data sets is `x$kcbwds`; the structure isn't exposed directly in a dynamic performance view, but some of its workload statistics are summarized in the view `v$buffer_pool_statistics`. If you describe `x$kcbwds`, one of the first columns you see is called `dbwr_num`—each working data set is associated with a single database writer, and each database writer may be responsible for multiple working data sets. Figure 5-3 is a diagram of one buffer pool showing you the relationship between granules, working data sets, and database writers. The pattern is then repeated for each of the buffer pools owned by the instance, the only variation being the number of granules in each buffer pool.

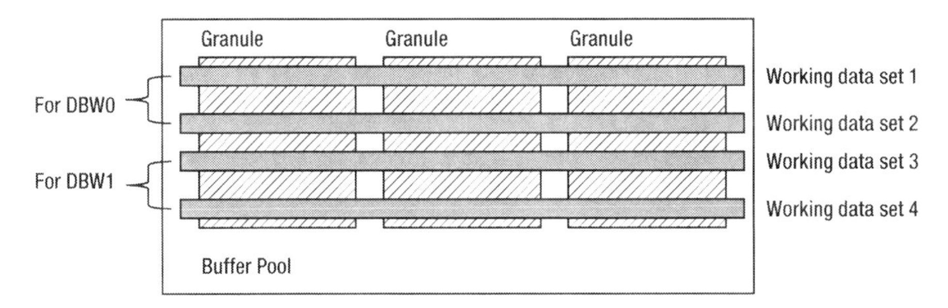

Figure 5-3. *Schematic of granules, working data sets, and database writers*

The intention behind working data sets is twofold. First, they allow the write I/O workload to be shared more evenly between multiple database writers; second, they help to minimize competition between processes trying to read data blocks into a buffer pool by allowing concurrent readers to pick buffers from different working data sets. The fact that you don't really need many writer processes (especially in a system that implements asynchronous I/O) explains why Oracle allows each database writer to handle multiple working data sets from each buffer pool.

The algorithms for deciding the number of database writers and working data sets (per buffer pool) are dependent on the Oracle version and the number of CPUs recognized by the instance—with some extra complexity introduced if your hardware uses NUMA technology. In a non-NUMA 10.2.0.5 system, the number of working data sets per buffer pool is set as `cpu_count / 2`, but in 11.2.0.2 it matches `cpu_count`; in both versions the number of database writers is ceiling(`cpu_count / 8`). To give you a feeling for what this means, if you are running 10.2.0.5 with 32 CPUs, then you will have 16 working data sets per buffer pool, 4 database writers, and each database writer will be responsible for 4 working data set per buffer pool. For experimental purposes you can also modify the number of database writers by setting another parameter (`db_writer_processes`), but, contrary to frequent comments on the Internet, this is a parameter that rarely needs to be adjusted on a production system.

■ **Note** If you want to see how memory allocations change with the number of CPUs, you can adjust parameter `cpu_count` and restart the instance; however, in 11.2 you also need to set parameter `_disable_cpu_check` to `false`.

Working Data Sets

So we've reached an important unit of memory, a collection of buffers that underpins the *physical* I/O behavior in Oracle. I emphasize the word *physical* because the mechanisms for finding and visiting buffered data (i.e., the so-called "logical" I/O) introduce a whole new pattern that cuts right across the buffer pools and working data sets . . . but we'll come to that in a while.

■ **Note** In all the discussion to date, I have been ignoring the options for *direct path* reads and writes—I/O that goes to and from private process memory rather than the shared memory area. Actions that take place in private are not particularly complex, although they may cause various overheads, such as reads and block cleanout, to take place repeatedly. It's public activity, where there's a risk of conflict, that leads to complicated implementation details.

For the purposes of thinking about physical I/O, we need only consider a single working data set as representative of the entire cache, and I'd like to start with a quick look at part of **x$kcbwds**, the structure that defines a working data set. The number of columns varies significantly with version of Oracle, but I only want to highlight eight of them at present:

```
Name                             Null?    Type
 ------------------------------ -------- --------------------
 CNUM_SET                                  NUMBER
 SET_LATCH                                 RAW(4)
 NXT_REPL                                  RAW(4)
 PRV_REPL                                  RAW(4)
 NXT_REPLAX                                RAW(4)
 PRV_REPLAX                                RAW(4)
 CNUM_REPL                                 NUMBER
 ANUM_REPL                                 NUMBER
```

The `cnum_set` is the number of buffers in the working data set, and the `set_latch` is the address of the cache buffers lru chain latch covering the set. The next six columns listed include the text REPL; these are columns that describe the *replacement* list—often referred to (not quite correctly) as "the" LRU chain. There are several other groups of six columns in the rest of the structure, but they relate to writing rather than reading, so I'll ignore them until we get to Chapter 6.

Two important clues about the nature of the replacement list are visible in the column definitions. The first clue is that it comes in two parts, REPL (the main replacement list) and REPLAX (the auxiliary replacement list). Second, it is yet another example of the doubly linked list approach that appears so often in Oracle: we can see this in the "next" and "previous" prefixes in the column names and in the `raw(4)` column types (which would be `raw(8)` in a 64-bit system).

We know that a working data set slices across several granules, and each granule holds an array of buffer headers, as depicted earlier in Figure 5-2; but we now see the end points of a pair of linked lists in **x$kcbwds**, and if we check **x$bh** (the buffer headers themselves) we will find another pair of columns (`nxt_repl` and `prv_repl`) that tell us how that linked list works. This lets us superimpose all the forward and backward pointers on an image of the buffer header arrays from a couple of granules then, unraveling the tangle to produce an image of two simple lists, view the results from a different perspective, as in Figure 5-4.

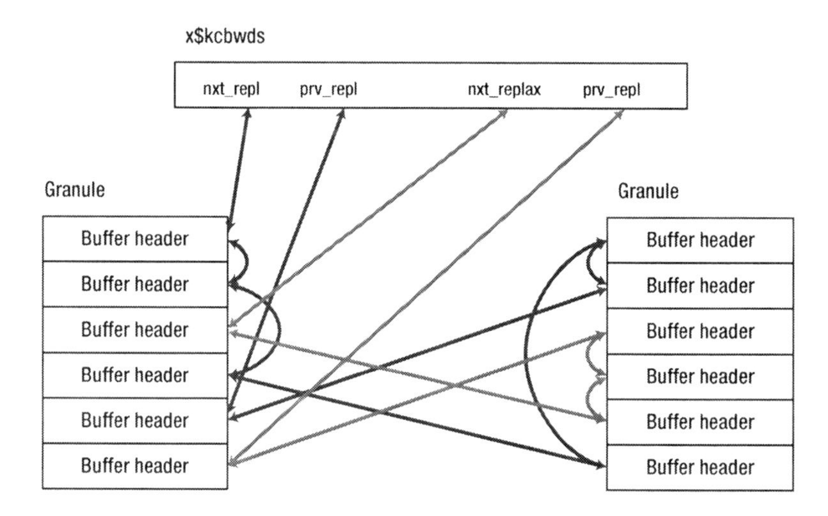

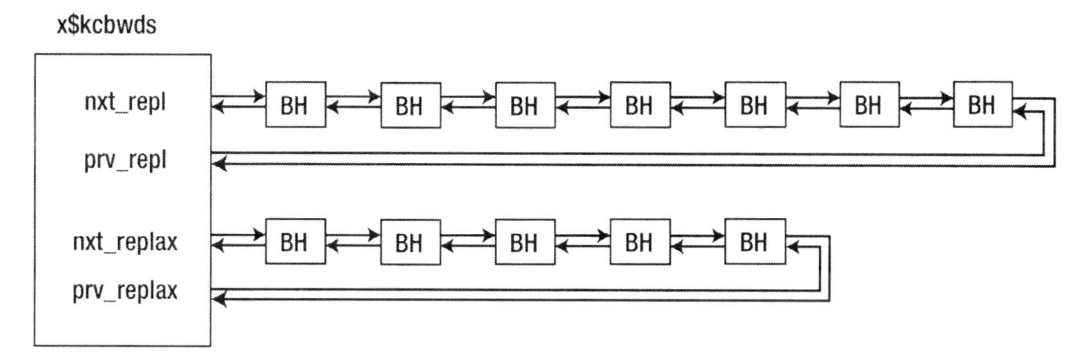

Figure 5-4. *Turning tangled pointers into tidy lists*

When you look at the final image in Figure 5-4, the top set of linked buffer headers is the picture you will see labeled as "the LRU list" in most of the literature, with the **nxt_repl** column pointing to the MRU (most recently used) end of the list and the **prv_repl** column pointing to the LRU end.

Before examining the workings of the LRU list, I'll just mention that the final two columns I've listed from **x$kcbwds** tell you the number of buffers attached to the lists—**cnum_repl** is the total number of buffers in the two lists, and **anum_repl** is the number of buffers currently linked to the auxiliary replacement list (REPL_AUX).

The LRU/TCH Algorithm

So we have linked lists of buffer headers, and each buffer header points to a buffer, and each buffer holds a copy of a block. What we need now is an algorithm for deciding which buffer to over-write if we need to read a new block into memory. The algorithm that Oracle uses is a modified LRU (least recently used) with touch count (TCH).

Note In the following pages, I really ought to talk about things like ". . . the block held by the buffer pointed to by the buffer header that . . ." but this would make the wording very clumsy. A common practice, and one I shall adopt, is to say "the buffer" when you really mean "the buffer header pointing at the buffer."

The LRU/TCH algorithm appeared in 8*i* as a mechanism to reduce the latch activity that typified the earlier "pure LRU" algorithm. Typical LRU algorithms move an object to the top of a list every time the object is used; but for something like a buffer cache, which will see a lot of object use, the cost of moving things all the time will be high and result in a lot of contention. To circumvent the problems of extreme usage, Oracle Corp. added a counter (and a timestamp—called `tim`) to the buffer header, and every time someone visits the buffer, they increment the touch count and update the timestamp—provided that at least 3 seconds has passed since the last update; they *don't* move the buffer header.

If all the algorithm does is update a touch count, though, where does the LRU bit come into play? The answer is, "at the last possible moment"—in other words, just at the moment when you have to make a decision about discarding the contents of the buffer. Let's walk through a couple of examples to explain the principle.

Note There is a commonly held theory that you can identify which block is causing latch contention on a given cache buffers chains latch by checking for very high touch counts (TCH) on all the buffers covered by that latch. Unfortunately this is not a very sound method. A buffer that is visited an average of once per second for half an hour will have a touch count around 600; a buffer that has been visited 10 million times in the last 5 minutes will have a touch count of around 100. The touch count can give you a clue, but it is not the final answer. (If you're really desperate, Oracle has a facility for tracking hot block problems, enabled by setting the hidden parameter `_db_hot_block_tracking`, but you might do better by taking advantage of the latchprofx tool created by Tanel Poder and available as a download from his blog at `http://blog.tanelpoder.com`.)

LRU/TCH in action

We're going to start with an image that is fairly typical of the diagrams commonly used to explain how Oracle reads data into the data cache. The diagram (Figure 5-5) contains just one working data set (which is a reasonable simplification) but fails to make any reference to the *auxiliary replacement list* (which is an over-simplification – and we will be talking about that in a little while).

▒ **Note** You don't really have to worry about drawing a diagram that involves multiple working data sets when thinking about reading data from disc. Each time your session needs to read a block, it will pick one of the working data sets to supply a free buffer. Its choice starts with a pseudorandom selection of an appropriate set (i.e., one from the relevant buffer pool) and an attempt to acquire that set's cache buffers lru chain latch with an immediate get. If the latch acquisition succeeds, the session uses that set; otherwise, it works around each set in turn until it has acquired a latch.

The working set in Figure 5-5 consists of just six buffers, and introduces a couple of new columns: on `x$bh` we have the touch count column `tch`, and on `x$kcbwds` we have the "midpoint" pointer `cold_hd`. I've used a single figure to represent two consecutive events: scenario (a), where we read a new block into the working data set, and scenario (b), which is the first stage of attempting to load a second block into the set.

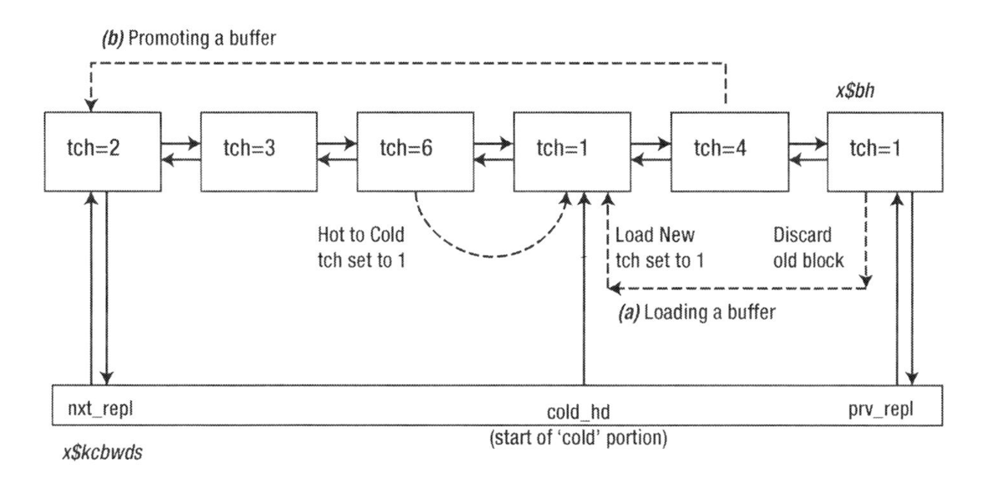

Figure 5-5. *Schematic of the LRU/TCH algorithm, ignoring REPL_AUX*

In scenario (a), if I want to load a new block into the working data set, I first have to find a free buffer to copy it into. I start my search at the LRU end of the replacement list (except that there's an error in that statement that I shall come back to shortly). Luckily for me the buffer at that end of the list has a touch count of 1 (it's not a very popular block and the buffer hasn't seen much activity). I have to check that the buffer isn't currently *pinned* (we'll discuss that concept in a while) and that it isn't in need of writing back to disc. Assuming all the checks are okay, I pin the buffer exclusively (to make sure no one else can do anything with it), read the block I want into the buffer, update the buffer header in various ways, unlink the buffer header from the end of the list, relink it at the midpoint (i.e., the link in the chain pointed at by `x$kcbwds.cold_hd`), and then unpin the buffer.

That's already quite a lot of work, but I haven't told you the whole story yet; I have several other links to the buffer header that need to be adjusted at the same time

Relinking a Buffer

Since we're reading a different block into memory, I have to detach the buffer from the cache buffers chain that it was connected to and connect it to the new cache buffers chain—which means acquiring two cache buffers chains latches at some point—and then I have to update two object queues, detaching the buffer from one and attaching it to another. (I'll discuss the cache buffers chains later in this chapter, and the object queue in Chapter 6.)

Here's a summary, not necessarily in exactly the right order, of all the changes that Oracle makes:

- Change `x$kcbwds.prv_repl` to point to the next buffer header along the list.
- Change the next buffer header along the list to point back to `x$kcbwds`.
- Modify the two buffer headers currently at the midpoint to point to my buffer header rather than to each other.
- Change `x$kcbwds.cold_hd` to point to my buffer header.
- Detach the buffer header from its old cache buffers chain (hitting one of the cache buffers chains latches at some point) and attach it to its new one (hitting another cache buffers chain latch).
- Detach the buffer from its old object queue and attach it to its new one.

This brings us to scenario (b). Assume that the buffer with `tch = 1` has been loaded with a new block and moved to the midpoint of the list so that the buffer with `tch = 4` is now at the end of the list. What difference does that value for the touch count make as we try to read another block into the working data set?

The buffer holds a "popular" block; the buffer has been visited several times since the block was loaded into it, so we shouldn't be in too much of a hurry to wipe the buffer clean and use it for another block. Oracle detaches the buffer from the LRU end of the list and reattaches it at the MRU end—*halving* the touch count as it does so—and moves on to check the next block in the list. So a popular block is moved to the MRU end of the list only at the last possible moment just as it is about to "fall off" the LRU end of the cache, not every time someone uses it, and this is a huge improvement in scalability.

Oracle's treatment of the touch count does seem to be a little odd at this point. Clearly there has to be strategy to ensure that a block keeps earning the right to stay in the cache, and that justifies Oracle halving the touch count as it moves a buffer to the MRU end of the list. But when you look at all the hidden parameters, you discover that Oracle has lots of ways of fine-tuning the algorithm. One of the strangest things about the possible variations is the behavior when more buffers are moved to the MRU end of our list and the buffer that we just moved there (with the touch count reduced from 4 to 2) is inexorably pushed down the list toward the LRU end. As the buffer crosses the midpoint and becomes the target of the `cold_hd` pointer, its touch count drops to 1, which means that if no one visits it again before it gets to the LRU end of the list, it will be eliminated.

Note I've never seen any discussion of exactly how Oracle can detect that a buffer is "crossing the midpoint" even though I've seen plenty of documents saying that it happens. My best guess is that after Oracle has linked a block to the MRU end of the LRU list, it uses the `cold_hd` pointer to get to the midpoint buffer, follows the link to the next buffer, changes the touch count on that buffer to zero, and then modifies `cold_hd` to point to that buffer.

You might ask why there are two strategies for reducing the touch count, especially since one of them seems to make the other totally redundant. I don't know the answer. It's possible that it's just a side effect of the Oracle developers giving themselves lots of options to experiment with, but perhaps there are some important exceptions to the general pattern.

There are several more options that could appear when we examine the last buffer on the LRU list. It might be *pinned*, which means you have to skip over it and examine the next buffer along, or it could be *dirty*, which means you have to link it to the *write list* (which we'll be looking at in Chapter 6) before you skip over it. The problem with the LRU end of the LRU list is that we really want to pick a buffer from it very quickly—and there are various reasons why we might have to do a lot of "irrelevant" work before we get to a buffer that we can use. Ideally we would like the first buffer we look at to be a "perfect" candidate for reuse every time we need a buffer, and that's where the REPL_AUX list comes into play.

REPL_AUX

The description I've given so far of Oracle's use of the replacement list is incomplete. It's not seriously wrong, and if you didn't look closely at what's going on you could easily think it was correct and complete, but it's not quite right. When your session needs to find a buffer to read in a new block, Oracle *doesn't* start by looking at the LRU end of the REPL_MAIN list (which is what I have been saying), but rather starts by looking at the REPL_AUX list (the auxiliary replacement list), which exists as a source of buffers that are almost certain to be immediately reusable. Because of this guarantee, your session gets a little performance benefit when it's searching for a buffer—it won't have to waste resources dealing with dirty buffers, pinned buffers, and other complications.

Note As I pointed out earlier on, the standard picture of the LRU/TCH mechanism that I presented in Figure 5-5 is actually incomplete. It's not unreasonable as a first approximation but the "end of the LRU list" is actually the whole of the REPL_AUX list, which is essentially a list of buffers that—with the exception of some tablescan processing, discussed later in this chapter—can (probably) be discarded instantly without causing performance problems. By maintaining a separate list of discardable buffers, Oracle has a better chance of finding a buffer very rapidly when it needs a buffer to load a new block from disc or clone a current buffer.

When the instance is started, all the buffers are linked in to REPL_AUX, and there are no buffers linked in to REPL_MAIN (you can re-create this situation by issuing `alter system flush buffer_cache`, which sets the `state` on each buffer header to free [state 0] before moving them to REPL_AUX). When a session needs a buffer to load a block from disc, it scans REPL_AUX from the LRU end (though it's not entirely meaningful to talk about the "LRU" end when there is no LRU algorithm in place) to find a candidate buffer, detaches the selected buffer from REPL_AUX, and attaches it to REPL_MAIN. So buffers migrate into REPL_MAIN as time passes.

At this point you may be wondering why REPL_AUX isn't empty within 5 minutes of starting the instance. If we transfer a buffer from REPL_AUX to REPL_MAIN every time we read a block into a buffer, it won't be long before every buffer has been transferred. (If REPL_AUX did become empty, of course, the earlier description of how Oracle finds a buffer would become a complete description of the action taken.) So there has to be some mechanism that moves buffers from REPL_MAIN back to REPL_AUX.

I have seen a couple of notes explaining that the database writer (dbwr) moves buffers onto REPL_AUX after writing their contents to disc (and you'll learn more about that mechanism, and the relevance of the WRITE_MAIN and WRITE_AUX lists, in Chapter 6), but I know that that's an incomplete answer as it's easy to set up a demonstration where blocks are constantly being reattached to the REPL_AUX even when there are no dirty buffers left for the dbwr to write; and I can create cases where the number of buffers on REPL_AUX increases even after I've suspended the dbwr. (The first observation could be due to a different code path in dbwr as it checks to see if there are any dirty buffers, but the second has to be due to some other process.)

By default, REPL_AUX seems to have a target size of 25 percent of the working data set; `anum_repl` will drift downward as you run queries but will keep climbing back up to that limit. And you can change the limit, which gives me some confidence that the constant reloading of REPL_AUX is part of a deliberate strategy and not just a side effect of some other action. There is a parameter called `_db_percent_hot_default` that dictates the percentage of the default buffer pool reserved to hold popular (or "hot") data; in other words, it changes the arithmetic Oracle does to choose the target for the `cold_hd` pointer. By default, this parameter has the value 50, but if you *decrease* the value (and restart the instance), you'll find that the target value for `anum_repl` also decreases, maintaining itself at half the parameter value, so a setting of 40 for `_db_percent_hot_default` results in a target of 20 percent of the working data set for `anum_repl`.

■ **Note** If my hypothesis about the REPL_AUX list is correct, then Oracle is doing some "redundant" work to relink buffer headers at some point in its processing. This means there has to be a savings somewhere else in the work cycle that makes this overhead worthwhile.

The other thing I've noticed is that when I run code that keeps a steady trickle of reads happening, I can see that the auxiliary replacement list keeps shrinking as I do the reads, but grows back to its target level almost immediately—and this makes me wonder whether there is a piece of code that runs as part of the disc read activity that scans REPL_MAIN from the LRU end and transfers some buffers to the "MRU" end of the REPL_AUX.

If this is correct, then there are probably some strict rules about which buffers may be transferred, how many can go at a time, and how much work is acceptable in moving them. Clearly buffers that are dirty should not be moved, nor should buffers that are pinned or buffers that have a touch count greater than 1. It would also be reasonable to guess that read-consistent copies of blocks—especially when the number exceeds the limit of six set by parameter `_db_block_max_cr_dba`—were good candidates for moving. I would also assume that a buffer will only be transferred if the reader can get the relevant cache buffers chains latch in immediate mode; and perhaps there is a rule that limits the transfer to a single linked section of the REPL_MAIN list, thus minimizing the number of links between buffers that have to be broken and re-created.

But once you start thinking about the type of work that Oracle has to do if it wants to keep replenishing REPL_AUX, you have to ask yourself where the benefit is. It takes resources to unlink buffers from REPL_MAIN and relink them to REPL_AUX, so where does the benefit come from? The answer may simply be in scheduling.

Remember that most systems do a lot more work creating clones of blocks that are already in memory, so they need to find buffers for clones much more frequently than they need buffers for reads—and when you're busy doing lots of memory operations and cloning lots of blocks, it's good to minimize the time you spend walking along linked lists, skipping over pinned or dirty blocks. Perhaps Oracle uses extra resources to populate REPL_AUX during slow disc operations (when a little extra work will have low visibility) so that it can reap the benefit when it's trying to do fast buffer operations.

Finding Data

So far we've been looking at the mechanics of copying a block from disc into memory. Now, working round and round in circles as you have to when learning Oracle, we have to address the question, "How did you know that you needed to read that block from disc, and how did you decide, quickly and efficiently, that it wasn't already in memory?"

We've been looking at the replacement list, which lets us decide which buffer to reuse for new data, but we don't want to search through the replacement list one buffer at a time to see which one (if any) holds the block we're interested in. We now need a different way of viewing those buffers so that we can find the one we want as quickly as possible.

We've already seen the answer to this problem, twice, in Chapter 4: the first time when looking at a picture of the library cache, and the second time when looking at the mechanism Oracle uses to manage enqueues.

We use a hash table with a very large number of buckets; we attach a very short linked list of buffer headers to each bucket; and we group the buckets into small groups, protecting each small group with a separate latch—the infamous cache buffers chains latch. Figure 5-6 shows a miniature Oracle buffer cache, with 4 hash latches, 16 hash buckets, and just 23 buffer headers.

▒ **Note** Figure 5-4 showed how I could take a very neat diagram of arrays of buffer headers and make it look very messy by adding lots of pointers between different items, and then make the diagram look tidy again by rearranging the buffer headers to turn the tangled pointers into nice straight lines.

Once we have a collection of buffer headers, we can impose any pattern we like onto that collection by defining suitable pointers that link together interesting subsets of buffer headers. The cache buffers chains pattern is just another pattern produced through pointers that acts completely independently of the granules, buffer pools, working data sets, and replacement lists. (And we still have a few more patterns waiting for us in Chapter 6.)

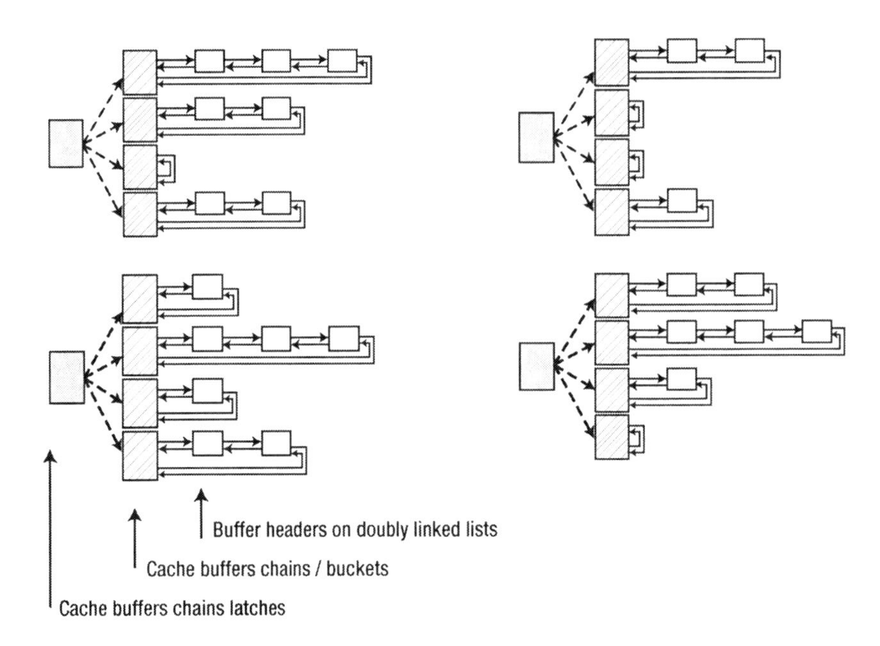

Figure 5-6. *A very small Oracle buffer cache*

Figure 5-6 is (I hope) neat and tidy and is, in some ways, representative of the truth. Remember, though, that this specific picture is simply one way of representing the complex web of pointers that runs through the data cache.

If I wanted to superimpose the replacement lists on Figure 5-6, they would appear as two tangled lines weaving their way randomly through the buffer headers, obeying only the rules that (a) every buffer header would be on one of the lines and (b) no buffer header would be on both lines. Conversely, if I go back to Figure 5-4, which shows us two nice, tidy replacement lists, and try to superimpose the cache buffers chains on top of that, I would have lots of tiny lines, each connecting two or three buffers scattered all over the replacement lists.

You can get a simple insight into the overall complexity of pointers by dumping the buffers at level 1. Here's a single buffer header from such a dump:

```
BH (66BEAF5C) file#: 1 rdba: 0x004096b0 (1/38576) class: 1 ba: 668D8000
  set: 3 blksize: 8192 bsi: 0 set-flg: 0 pwbcnt: 0
  dbwrid: 0 obj: 18 objn: 18 tsn: 0 afn: 1
  hash: [6ffa0870,6ffa0870] lru: [66bfab94,66bed2f0]
  lru-flags: moved_to_tail on_auxiliary_list
  ckptq: [NULL] fileq: [NULL] objq: [66bed348,66bfabec]
  st: XCURRENT md: NULL tch: 0
  flags: only_sequential_access
  LRBA: [0x0.0.0] HSCN: [0xffff.ffffffff] HSUB: [65535]
```

There are two lines in this dump that report some type of linked list: the fourth line shows the pointers for the cache buffers chains (`hash`) and the replacement lists (`lru`), and the sixth lines shows the pointers for the *checkpoint queue* (`ckptq`), *file queue* (`fileq`), and *object queue* (`objq`). The block isn't dirty, so it's not yet on a checkpoint or file queue, but we'll be examining those queues and the object queue in Chapter 6. In this example, the fact that the forward and backward pointers for the hash chain are the same tells you that this is the only buffer header on that hash chain—and this is the way that Oracle likes it. The fewer buffer headers you have in any hash bucket, the faster you can check the contents, and if Oracle is searching a hash bucket to see if a particular block is already in memory, it wants to find it (or discover it's not there) as quickly as possible.

Figure 5-6 shows only four cache buffers chains latches, each covering a few buckets, with a tiny scattering of buffer headers per bucker. The number of buffer headers per bucket is probably fairly representative of a production system, while the number of latches and buckets is not. Oracle creates a huge number of hash buckets (see side bar), and then covers many buckets with each latch (typically 32 buckets per latch in recent versions).

DB CACHE HASH BUCKETS

In early versions of Oracle (including 8.0) the number of hash buckets was roughly `db_block_buffers/4` (adjusted to a prime number) with a separate latch for each hash bucket.

As the sizes of databases grew, with data cache sizes growing to match, Oracle changed the algorithm so that the number of buckets was roughly twice the number of buffers and each latch covered many buckets—typically between 32 and 128 buckets per latch. The number of buckets was still rounded up to a prime number (though the hidden parameter `_db_block_hash_buckets` didn't necessarily report this fact—I have an 8.1.7.4 in front of me now, and the parameter reports 16,384 buckets, but checking the sga variable `kcbnhb` (see Appendix for method) the actual value is the prime number 16,411).

In the latest versions (10g and 11g) the number of buckets is a power of two, and the number of buckets per latch seems to be fixed at 32. It's possible that the presence of the powers of two may be there to allow for dynamic adjustment if the number of buffers changes dramatically under automatic resizing (using the same strategy that Oracle has for merging and splitting the partitions of a hash-partitioned table); perhaps it simply allows the code to right-shift five times to convert a hash bucket number into a latch number.

As we saw in Chapter 4, when Oracle needs to locate an SQL statement in the library cache, it applies a hash function to the text to generate a meaningless number that it uses to identify a library cache hash bucket. This means there is a quick, and relevant, way of connecting an object with the location where it should be found.

The same strategy applies to the data cache. Oracle applies a hash function to the absolute file number and block number of a block (and possibly some other attribute of the block, such as the tablespace number) to produce a number that identifies which hash bucket the block should be placed in. Note that we are talking about blocks at this point, not buffers. When we copy a block into memory, it might end up in any one of the available buffers, but the link between the buffer and the hash bucket is identified by the *block*, not by any attribute of the buffer.

Pinning Buffers

Once we can associate a block with a hash bucket, there are just a few operations we need to worry about: putting a buffer into the right bucket as we read the block from disc; removing a buffer from a bucket when we want to use it for a different block; visiting the current version of a buffered block; modifying a buffered block; and cloning a block that is already in the buffer so that we can build a read-consistent version from the clone. All these operations require us to read the linked list that is the cache buffers chain, possibly breaking the chain to insert or delete a link. This means that we can expect to go through something like the following sequence of operations:

1. Work out the correct hash bucket from the block address.
2. Get the relevant cache buffers chains latch.
3. Start walking the pointers from the hash bucket to find the buffer.
4. Do something with the buffer content.
5. Release the cache buffers chains latch.

This overview highlights an important threat. Although we may be able to walk a single linked list very quickly, we will be holding a latch while we "do something"—so whatever we do, we need to do it very quickly because accessing buffered data is a popular pastime in an Oracle system, and lots of sessions could be trying to get the same latch at the same time.

■ **Note** You may be wondering why Oracle uses a single latch to cover 32 or more hash buckets. The answer comes from two different directions: we want a lot of hash buckets so that we can keep the hash chains very short; on the other hand, a latch is a fairly large structure with a long code path, so we'd like to keep the number of latches to a minimum. With the current setup, the *average* chain length will be no more than one buffer, so even though a latch may address 32 buckets, when you grab a latch, you don't have to do much work to check every buffer in the bucket you're interested in.

Since "doing something" with the buffer content can take a relatively long time, Oracle often adopts a two-step strategy to latching so that it doesn't have to hold a latch while working. There are some operations that can be completed while holding the latch, but Oracle often uses the following strategy:

1. Get the latch.
2. Find and *pin* the buffer.
3. Drop the latch.
4. do something with the buffer content.
5. Get the latch.
6. *Unpin* the buffer.
7. Drop the latch.

This means we need to add more detail to our picture of the buffer cache. Figure 5-7 shows a single hash chain with two buffer headers and a few *buffer pins* attached.

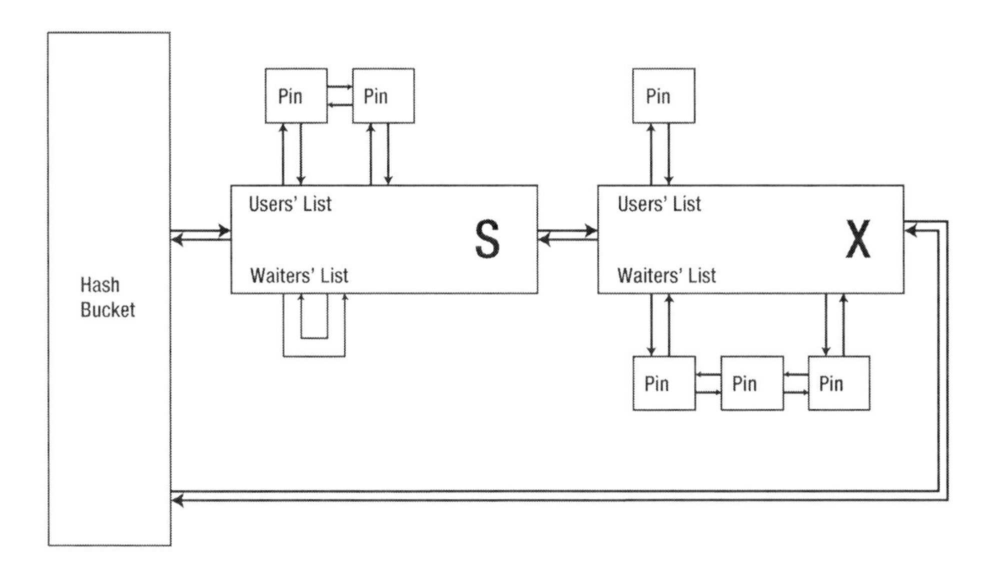

Figure 5-7. *A single hash chain with a pair of pinned buffers*

You'll see that each buffer header has a *waiters' list* and a *users' list*, and when we look at the `x$bh` structure, we will see a now-familiar pattern in pairs of columns—NXT and PRV warning us that we are looking at yet more linked lists, in this case the users' (US) and the waiters' (WA):

```
Name                          Null?    Type
----------------------------- -------- ---------
US_NXT                                 RAW(4)
US_PRV                                 RAW(4)
WA_NXT                                 RAW(4)
WA_PRV                                 RAW(4)
```

You'll notice that one of the buffer headers in Figure 5-7 is labeled with an S, and the other is labeled with an X. When you pin a buffer, you can pin it in shared (S) mode or exclusive (X) mode. If the buffer is not currently pinned, or is pinned in a *compatible* mode, then you can attach a pin (exposed in the structure `x$kcbbf`) to the users' list. If the buffer is already pinned in an incompatible mode, you have to attach your pin to the waiters' list—and then go into a wait state until the buffer becomes available. The wait state is the infamous `buffer busy waits` event, although, in a special variant introduced in 10g, if the session you're waiting for is currently reading the block from disc into the buffer, the event is `read by other session`.

The structure of a pin includes the address of the session holding, or waiting, on the pin. So when a blocking holder removes their pin from the buffer header, they can post the waiter at the head of the waiters' list. There is a timeout on the buffer busy wait of 1 second (configurable with hidden parameter `_buffer_busy_wait_timeout`), so if a waiter isn't posted inside this time limit, the session wakes up, assumes that a deadlock has occurred between the holder and waiter, reports a `buffer deadlock` wait event (though it doesn't actually wait), and tries to resolve the problem by releasing any pins it is holding and trying to reacquire them. One second seems a rather long time to wait for an individual buffer, but unless you see unreasonable amounts of time lost on buffer busy waits, I wouldn't try playing with the hidden parameter.

Note Things you can do while holding a cache buffers chains latch: add or remove a buffer header from the chain; add or remove a pin from a pin list, updating the pin mode. Things you can't or don't usually do while holding the cache buffers chains latch: modify the content of a buffer. You do this only if you are holding an exclusive pin on the block, and at that point you don't need to be holding the latch. (The *commit cleanout* is an exception to this rule.)

The final thing to note about buffer pins is that once you have attached a pin to a buffer header, you don't have to unpin that buffer header immediately. If the query engine thinks that you will revisit the buffer in the near future, it will keep the buffer header pinned right up until the end of the database call if necessary. This is where the statistic `buffer is pinned count` comes from—Oracle has pinned a buffer early on in the query and revisited it without unpinning it between visits: it's the cheapest buffer visit that Oracle can do.

Logical I/O

All physical reads start with a logical read, so we're going to leave physical I/O to last as we work through the ways in which Oracle handles blocks. We'll start with the simplest example: looking at the contents of a block that is sitting in the data cache and hasn't been modified for ages (not that we know that it's there before we start, of course).

We do the arithmetic that tells us which cache buffers hash chain the block ought to be linked to. This lets us work out which latch we need to get, so we get it and walk the hash chain and find the block.

At this point we might be able to examine the block and drop the latch immediately. This action is reported in the instance statistics as a `consistent get - examination`; it's cheaper than a normal buffer get, hitting the latch only once. The candidates for this type of "half-price" or "single-get" visit are index root and branch blocks, index leaf blocks of unique indexes, table blocks accessed by unique scan of a unique index, and undo blocks.

If the block is in memory but isn't a candidate for examination, then we might see the more traditional "two-latch get" action. This means that having got the latch, we will attach a *shared* pin to the buffer header, drop the latch, view the contents of the block, get the latch, remove the pin, and drop the latch.

It's possible in this case, though, for Oracle to assume that it's going to revisit the buffer in the next few microseconds, so it might decide to keep the buffer pinned for a while, and it may decide to keep it pinned until the end of the current database call.

■ **Note** Buffer pins are also referred to as *buffer handles*. There are a few parameters relating to the number and use of pins: `_db_handles` is the size of the array of pin structures defined, and `_db_handles_cached` is the number of pins that can be "reserved" by a session. The default value for `_db_handles_cached` is 5, but parameter `_cursor_db_buffers_pinned` specifies the total number of buffers a session can pin at any one moment. The statistic `buffer is pinned count` tells us how many times a session has been able to take advantage of pinning to revisit buffers.

Even if the block is in memory, though, someone else may have modified it since we started our query, so we may have to go through the process of creating a read-consistent copy. But we won't look at that process just yet because it requires us to move a buffer from REPL_AUX onto the hash chain, and we also have to do that when we do a physical read, so we'll cover both options together in a moment.

Updates

The next thing we'll look at is a simple update, and the first one we'll try is by primary key—and we'll find that there's virtually no difference between reading a block and updating the block: we get the latch, walk the chain, attach an *exclusive* pin to the buffer, drop the latch, modify the buffer, get the latch, and detach the pin from the buffer. Of course, there's a lot more work going on because we will have to get an undo segment header and undo block to record the undo, so there are two other hash chains and cache buffers chains latches involved—but that doesn't change the basic mechanism of handling the table buffer.

A key word here, though, is *exclusive*. If anyone else has pinned the buffer in any way, then we can't pin it and we might have to attach our pin to the waiters' list and post a `buffer busy wait`.

There are alternative code paths, though. For example, if I update the block through a tablescan, Oracle will `switch current to new buffer` rather than update the block in place. This means yet another mechanism where buffers can go on and off the replacement list and on and off the hash chains. When the current goes into a new buffer, the previous version becomes a read-consistent copy, of course, so if you update the block five times in a row, you will have reached the limit of six clones set by parameter `_db_block_max_cr_dba`. So, to avoid getting too much garbage into the cache, and to keep the length of the hash chain short, Oracle will start switching the older clones on to the replacement list if you continue updating the block.

Loading a Hash Chain

Since physical I/Os, creation of read-consistent clones, and switching current blocks to new buffers all require you to take a buffer off the replacement list and add it to the hash chain, this seems to be the moment to discuss how it's done.

There is an interesting problem here. As I commented in Chapter 4, a process is not allowed to request a latch in willing-to-wait mode if it is already holding a lower-level latch. So what are the levels of our two latches?

```
SQL> select     name, level#
  2  from       v$latch
  3  where      name in ('cache buffers lru chain','cache buffers chains')
  4  /

NAME                              LEVEL#
------------------------------ ----------
cache buffers lru chain                2
cache buffers chains                   1

2 rows selected.
```

The cache buffers chains latch has a lower level than the cache buffers lru chain latch, so we can't request the cache buffers lru chain latch in willing-to-wait mode if we're already holding the cache buffers chains latch. Think about what this means: we're holding the cache buffers chains latch (which I will call the *hash latch* for the rest of this subsection) because we've just searched the hash chain for a buffer and discovered that, for whatever reason, we need to add another buffer to the chain. So we have to acquire the cache buffers lru chain latch (which I will call the *lru latch* for the rest of this subsection) to move a buffer from the REPL_AUX list to the midpoint of the REPL_MAIN list; but we can't request it in willing-to-wait mode because we're already holding a lower-level latch.

Now, we may be able to get the lru latch in immediate mode if we're lucky, or if we have multiple working data sets per buffer pool (which means lots of CPUs or manually declaring multiple database writers)—and you will see that Oracle makes more use of immediate gets for this task if you do have multiple working data sets. But if you can't get the lru latch with an immediate get, you have to drop the hash latch, get the lru latch, and then get the hash latch again. I'm not going to pretend that I know exactly how Oracle juggles this activity, but I do know that the amount of latch activity that takes place in these circumstances is more than you would expect to see for something that appears (at first sight) to be a fairly simply action.

■ **Note** There is an important difference in the available choice of buffer pools when creating clones. If you `switch current to new buffer`, the new buffer has to come from the same buffer pool; if you have `CR blocks created`, Oracle knows that it is producing a transient copy of a block and will try to minimize the impact of that block on the rest of the cache management. For example, if you create a CR copy of a block that belongs in the *keep* pool, it will be created in the *recycle* pool (if one exists), hence minimizing the damage to the keep pool. This strategy is still evolving. As a consequence, in recent versions of Oracle you may even find buffers in the *default* pool that you expected to see in the keep pool.

Read-Consistent Copies

Having got through the basic complexity of attaching a new buffer to a hash chain, I don't really have much more to say about creating read-consistent copies. At this point we have the correct latch and start walking the linked list. We find that the CUR (current) version of the block is in memory, but the SCN is higher than the start SCN for our query, so we may need to create a read-consistent copy of the block.

Before we start on the work of creating a copy, though, we can carry on walking down the hash chain because it's possible that an appropriate read-consistent copy already exists. There is a tiny optimization built into the hash chain at this point—the CUR version of a block is always the first one you will find as you walk the hash chain. I also recall seeing a note many years ago suggesting that any CR copies will appear in SCN order on the chain, most recent SCN first, but the first test I ran didn't seem to agree with the hypothesis.

If we don't find a copy that matches our needs exactly, we will either clone the CUR copy or be lucky and find that we can use one of the CR copies as a starting point, which will save us a little effort because it will be nearer to our target point in time. This, of course, is when we may have to do our little juggling act—we have to pick a block from REPL_AUX and link it in to REPL_MAIN, attaching it at the same time to the hash chain; and since we don't want anyone to read it or change it by accident, we have to attach an exclusive pin to it. It's at this point that the benefit of having REPL_AUX as a separate source of available buffers becomes obvious: we need to be able to find a buffer very quickly at this point because any delay in these memory operations will become very obvious if the system gets very busy.

Once we've made it that far we can release any latches we are still holding and start taking the block backward in time. This, of course, means we will have to start locating and applying undo records, which means getting cache buffers chains latches and searching hash buckets for undo blocks—possibly even reading older undo blocks from disc into memory.

Physical I/O

Assume, then, that we find that a block we want isn't in memory (it's not attached to the hash bucket we expect it to be in) and we have to read it into a buffer from disc. We don't want to hold the latch while we're reading the block because that would result in a very long hold, and we want to avoid holding any latch for a long time. On the other hand, if we just drop the latch and start worrying about getting the block into a buffer, then no one else will know that we're trying to load that block, and another session may try to read the same block. So we need get a buffer header from REPL_AUX, label it with the data block address, attach it to the correct hash chain, and pin it in exclusive mode so that everyone can see that the block is (nominally) in memory but not yet physically available for access. At this point it's safe to drop any latches we're still holding and start the work of loading the block into the buffer.

■ **Note** We can read blocks into buffers using methods that report waits for `db file sequential read` (single block reads), `db file parallel read` (multiple blocks from random locations; e.g., reading several index leaf blocks identified a single branch block), or `db file scattered read` (several blocks that are logically adjacent in a file). It is worth noting that the maximum size of the scattered read is set by parameter `db_file_multiblock_read_count` but Oracle probes the cache for each target in turn before doing a scattered read to see if any of the blocks are already in cache—and it only reads up to the first cached block.

Tablescans

When anyone says "tablescans," you should usually add the phrase "and index fast full scans." A tablescan can be one of the most labor-intensive tasks in Oracle, especially if the whole table has to be read from disc. If you scan a large object, you could flush a huge amount of useful data from the cache, data that you may then have to reread very promptly. Tablescans shouldn't really happen often in OLTP systems, and when they do happen, you need to ensure that they don't cause problems. The potential for performance problems relating to tablescans resulted in Oracle Corp. writing code to distinguish between "short" and "long" tables (and, recently, "medium" tables, although there are no statistics collected to record that particular option).

Note Oracle introduced the option to do direct path reads for serial tablescans (and index fast full scans) in 11*g*—and then introduced the option to do buffered reads for parallel tablescans (and index fast full scans). This gives you some idea of the difficulty of working out the best way to use the available resources when you're running a data-warehouse or decision-support system. When is caching good? When does caching cause problems?

The idea of the "long" table is that if you're going to scan a really big object, you don't want its blocks to wipe everything else from the data cache as you read it, so you need a damage limitation algorithm. Historically (which in this context means 8*i* and 9*i*) Oracle had a simple strategy: if the runtime engine believed the table was less than 2 percent of the size of the data cache, then the tablescan reads would be treated pretty much like any other read except, whether by accident or design, the touch count (TCH) of the buffers used would not be incremented, so the object would fall off the end of the LRU list the moment it got there and never get promoted to the hot portion no matter how much you visited it—even if some of the subsequent visits weren't by tablescan.

If the optimizer thought the table was larger than the 2 percent limit, then the buffers used to read the table were immediately dropped to the end of the LRU list as the blocks were read, which generally meant that you kept reusing the same small number of buffers to read the table. If you check the instance statistics (`v$sysstat`), you will find that two of them reflect the different tablescan activity (although there are no equivalent "long vs. short" statistics for index fast full scans):

```
table scans (short tables)
table scans (long tables)
```

The strategy changed in 10g, with three different conditions to consider. There is still a 2 percent limit (dictated by the hidden parameter `_small_table_threshold`) and the blocks are still loaded into the data cache in the normal way, but the touch count *is* incremented for these buffers.

The second case has a 10 percent limit (though I don't know how it's set) where the tablescan is initially considered to be a long tablescan, so touch counts will not be incremented as the blocks are read into buffers and (most of) the buffers will immediately be moved to REPL_AUX; however, if you repeat the tablescan while the blocks are still in the data cache, the touch count on the buffers *will* be incremented at that point and the tablescan will be reported as a *short* tablescan. This has a potentially nasty side effect: most of the blocks will be in buffers that were moved to REPL_AUX as the blocks were read, but you're now incrementing the touch count, and there doesn't seem to be a mechanism to move these buffers back to REPL_MAIN until they hit the end of the LRU list and get promoted to the hot portion of REPL_MAIN. This means that at some point in the future one session is likely to request a single buffer and stall while it promotes all those buffers (possibly as much as 10 percent of the cache) into REPL_MAIN.

The final case has a limit of 25 percent where the touch count is never incremented and the buffers are cycled to REPL_AUX very quickly—basically you do a multiblock read pulling a few buffers from REPL_AUX, you do the next multiblock read pulling more buffers from REPL_AUX but pushing the first batch of tablescanned buffers into REPL_AUX, and keep repeating this cycle. For a very large table you will end up with the entire REPL_AUX loaded with blocks from that table, and a small number of blocks from the table in REPL_MAIN. Thus, Oracle protects a very large fraction of your data cache from overaggressive tablescans.

■ **Note** I've said that Oracle's behavior depends on what it "thinks" the size of the table might be. Recent versions of Oracle base their decision on the object statistics, so if the statistics are misleading, Oracle may do something totally inappropriate (like trying to cache an enormous table that has statistics that make it look very small). This only works once, though, as Oracle checks the actual size against the predicted size, and uses the corrected information for future scans, until the information is flushed from the SGA.

Summary

The data cache can be split into multiple *buffer pools*, either by block size or (with the keep and recycle pools) by usage. Many sites, though, stick to a single buffer pool using the default block size offered by the Database Configuration Assistant (DBCA) for their platform—and this is generally the most sensible strategy.

The data cache is also split into *granules* of a fixed size—4MB, 8MB, or 16MB, depending on platform version and the size of the SGA. The granular approach makes it possible to reallocate memory dynamically between the data cache and other key parts of the SGA. Each buffer pool is made up of many discrete granules, and each individual granule is owned by a single buffer pool. A granule that belongs to the data cache holds an array of buffers and a matching array of buffer headers, as well as a little management overhead.

Each buffer pool may be split into several *working data sets*, which are constructed as linked lists of buffer headers and hence, implicitly, the buffers pointed to by the buffer headers. The working data set is an important "unit of complexity" in Oracle; each one is protected by its own cache buffers LRU chain latch and is kept "clean" by a single database writer (dbwr) process. A single database writer, though, may be responsible for many working data sets. The numbers of working data sets (per buffer pool) and database writers are dependent on the `cpu_count`.

Each working data set is split into a pair of linked lists, the main *replacement list* (REPL_MAIN) and the *auxiliary replacement list* (REPL_AUX), with buffers moving constantly between the two. (There are other linked lists that connect small subsets of the working data set intermittently, but these relate to writing and will be addressed in Chapter 6). The function of the REPL_AUX list is to hold buffers that are believed to be instantly reusable if a session needs a buffer to read a block from disc or clone a block that is already in memory. The purpose of REPL_MAIN is to keep track of recently used (buffered) blocks, ensuring that "popular" blocks stay buffered while allowing "unpopular" blocks to fall out of memory as rapidly as possible.

There is a second structure imposed on the content of the data cache, again employing linked lists (but very short ones), that uses the data block address of the buffered blocks to scatter the buffers across a very large hash table. This means that if we want to find a block in the data cache, we can work out very rapidly where it should be in the hash table structure and check a small linked list to see if it is currently in memory.

A combination of latches (when we want to manipulate or examine the contents of the linked lists) and pins (when we want to protect or modify the contents of a buffer) allows us to move a buffer from one hash bucket to another as we replace a copy of one block with a copy of another; at the same time, further latch activity allows us to relocate the buffer or, strictly speaking, its header in the replacement lists.

Because the choice of hash bucket depends on the data block address, consistent read copies of a given block will be attached to the same hash bucket. If we have a large number of copies of a block, the hash chain for that bucket will become very long, and the time taken to find the correct copy of a block in the bucket will become a performance threat. For this reason Oracle tries to impose a limit of six on the number of copies that you can have of a block.

CHAPTER 6

Writing and Recovery

The Moving Finger Writes; and Having Writ, Moves On

(*The Rubaiyat of Omar Khayyam*)

In previous chapters you've seen how Oracle changes the content of data blocks (including undo blocks) and generates streams of redo information as it does so. You've seen the mechanisms that combine changes into transactions and ensure that those transactions appear to be atomic, consistent, and isolated, the first three requirements of ACID, but the questions remains, how does Oracle satisfy the *D* of ACID and make transactions durable?

So far we've been looking at change without making any comments about whether the data we are changing is in memory or on disc. In this chapter we start to take notice of the fact that while most of the work we do starts out in memory, it has to end up on disk at the right time, in the right order, and as efficiently as possible. This means examining the roles of the database writer (dbwr) and the log writer (lgwr), the processes responsible for copying information from memory to disk.

I will also make a few comments about the issue of being able to apply an "infinite" (i.e., arbitrarily large) amount of change and how you avoid the need to create infinitely large files for redo and undo.

Targets

A few years ago I would have said quite happily that there weren't many databases small enough to fit completely in memory, but that's no longer true given the very large memories that computers can manage these days. Even so, most of the Oracle databases I see aren't memory-resident, and even if the database can fit in memory, its owners probably don't feel safe unless they have a fairly recent snapshot of the data copied to disk. Whatever we do with memory to make our databases go faster, we have to recognize that for most databases the software has to have a good strategy for copying changed memory to disk.

In the case of Oracle we have two types of content to think about, the (buffered) data blocks and the redo log (buffer), and two different but interlinked strategies for writing that content to disk. Of the two sets of content, the redo log buffer is the more important because it is the one that gives us durability with scalability, by minimizing the disk I/O we have to do to secure our database changes. But we need to be sure that the strategies we use for writing both sets of content will always leave us in a position where instantaneous failure of an instance will allow us to restart without losing any committed transactions (which is the durability requirement).

As we have seen, the log file holds a description of all changes we make to the data blocks, so if we can find an old copy of the database somewhere, and all the redo log files that have been written since that copy was made, then we can work through the log files and apply the change records they contain to the database copy to bring the copy up to date.

Through a simple mechanical process we can bring an old copy of the database up to the state it was in just before the instance failed. In particular, if our "old copy" is just a few seconds or a few minutes old because it's the live production copy of the database that's on disk and being kept up to date in near real time, then we can recover from instance failure very quickly.

The difficult bit, for Oracle Corp.'s developers, is designing an infrastructure that allows this recovery phase to complete as rapidly as possible while ensuring that any work done in anticipation of recovery is kept to a minimum during normal operation.

The key to being able to recover is writing the *redo log* to disk in a "timely" fashion; but the key to minimizing recovery time is to keep writing *database blocks* to disk, and the key to minimizing the work you do writing database blocks is to batch them up and write them in the correct order—which (in the case of Oracle) means oldest first.

So we're going to look at the activity of the log writer (lgwr) and I'll explain what I mean by "timely," and we'll look at the database writer (dbwr) and I'll explain the significance of "oldest first" and why that strategy on its own doesn't quite work.

The problem I have, though, is deciding where to start. Which should come first, lgwr or dbwr? You could argue for the log writer because it *must* write a change description to disk before the database writer writes the block that has been changed. On the other hand, the database writer sometimes calls the log writer to write, and also generates redo records as it writes data blocks, so there's a good argument for talking about the database writer first.

Note One of the most important features of the Oracle code is that the database writer will not write a changed block to disk before the log writer has written the redo that describes how the block was changed. This *write-ahead logging* strategy is critical to the whole recovery mechanism. In effect the redo log files (including the archived ones) form the definitive version of the database; the data files themselves are simply a recent, approximate snapshot. (Any nologging operations invalidate this viewpoint, of course.)

So here we are, going round and round in circles again. I'm going to start with the log writer, then handle the database writer, and then fill in a few of the gaps I left on the first pass through the log writer by describing, in particular, the interactions between the two.

Log Writer

The log writer has one critical task: copy the contents of the log buffer from memory to disk. The activity surrounding this task has, however, increased over the years to cope with increased volumes of change and higher levels of concurrency. (The requirement has also expanded to allow for the possibility of writing to a remote standby database by way of calls to RFS [remote file server] processes from LNS [network server] processes in 10g and NSS or NSA [redo transport sync/async] processes in 11g.

In earlier versions of Oracle there was just a single contiguous area of memory called the *log buffer*, and, to a very large extent, the appearance of multiple public and private buffers hasn't changed the mechanics that Oracle used on that single buffer, so we'll start by talking as if there is still only a single buffer and cover the differences later.

■ **Note** Recently disk manufacturers have started to produce disks with a 4KB sector size. For reasons we will see later, a larger block size for the log file can make lgwr waste more space in the log file; on the other hand, a smaller block size can make log file writes less efficient (because of the need for a read/write) cycle. From 11.2 Oracle lets the DBA choose which is the lesser of two evils by allowing you to specify the block size for the log file as 512 bytes, 1KB, or 4KB.

The log files are automatically formatted in blocks matching the disk sector size (typically 512 bytes), and the log buffer itself is mapped as a "rolling window" onto the current log file, with a 16-byte header labeling each block. Figure 6-1 uses a log buffer sized at 8 blocks to demonstrate the principle.

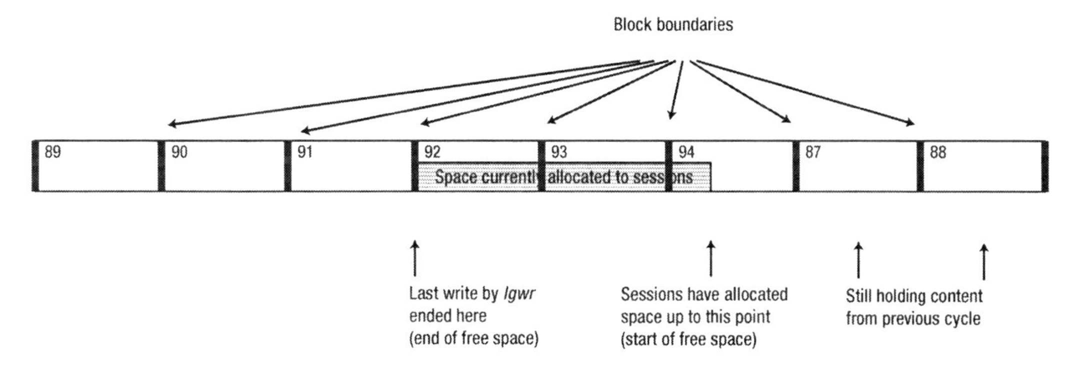

Figure 6-1. *Simple schematic of log buffer*

In Figure 6-1, the log buffer has filled and wrapped 11 times since the last log file switch (the first time around the separate block buffers were formatted to match blocks 1 to 8 of the file). At the moment we are on the 12th cycle through the buffer, which is why the last position in the buffer is formatted for block 88 (i.e., 8 blocks × 11 cycles). The log writer has just written blocks 89 to 91, and will shortly be writing blocks 92 to 94, and relabeling block 87 to become block 95.

■ **Note** There are many notes on the Internet about sizing the log files, but many of them are out of date. Essentially, you shouldn't need to set the `log_buffer` parameter from 10*g* and later; it's automatically set by the instance at startup, typically allowing each public log buffer to be a few megabytes. In very special cases you may need to set the parameter to a value such as 16MB or 32MB to extend the memory allocation to multiple granules, but only if you are seeing significant time lost on `log buffer space` waits.

Since the log buffer is public, and subject to modification by multiple concurrent processes, you might expect it to be protected by latches. It is, but not directly. There are three (public) memory locations affecting the use of the log buffer, and it is these locations that are protected by latches. Two locations hold *pointers*, one identifying the start of *free space* in the buffer and the other identifying the end of free space. The third location is a flag showing whether or not lgwr is busy writing. With multiple public log buffers, there are two pointers per buffer, but there is just one write flag covering all the buffers—because there is just one lgwr. The mechanics of pointer manipulation are fairly straightforward, and Figure 6-2 gives an idea of the actions required.

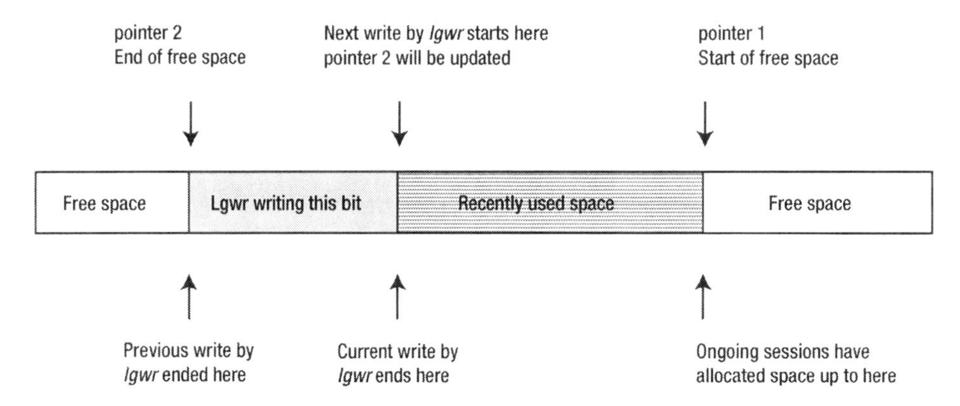

Figure 6-2. *Key points in the log buffer*

In Figure 6-2 we see that lgwr is currently writing, and some sessions have allocated (and possibly filled) some space beyond the end of the write. Over the next few moments the following sequence of actions (with minor variations) will take place:

- lgwr will complete its write, at which point it will also move the "End of free space" marker (pointer 2) up to the point labeled "Current write by lgwr ends here"/"Next write by lgwr starts here."
- lgwr will be triggered (we'll see how and why in a moment) into writing more of the buffer to disk. Its target will be to copy out any of the log buffer currently allocated (and we'll consider what that means and the possible side effects in a moment).
- Other sessions will be generating more redo for copying into the buffer, so they will be allocating space for themselves by moving pointer 1 ("Start of free space") forward to leave space behind the pointer that they can use. Eventually pointer 1 will fall off the end of the buffer, which means it will cycle back to the beginning of the buffer.

The description is simple, but the questions it raises are significant. What triggers lgwr? How do sessions avoid overwriting each other's redo? What happens when a session wants more space than is free? What risks are there of destructive interference between lgwr and the other sessions? Let's start with an easy one—what triggers lgwr.

Log Writer Writes

Traditionally there have been four reasons given for lgwr to start writing:

- On a wake-up alarm call that lgwr sets itself every 3 seconds
- When the (public) log buffer is one-third full
- When the (public) log buffer holds more than 1MB of change records
- When a session issues a `commit;` or `rollback;` (see note)

■ **Note** As stated in Chapter 3, when a session issues a commit, it generates the redo describing how to update its transaction table slot in the undo segment header block, puts this redo into the log buffer, applies it to the undo segment header block, calls the log writer to flush the log buffer to disk, and then goes into a `log file sync` wait until the log writer lets it know that its entry in the log buffer has been copied to disk. A call to roll back ends in a similar fashion: after applying the undo change vectors (and logging the changes they make), the last steps taken by a rollback also update the transaction table slot and call the log writer. This commit/rollback mechanism is the fourth item in our list, and it's the mechanism that makes transactions *durable*.

The first option is easy to observe, especially if you're prepared to enable tracing for wait states on lgwr. Every 3 seconds you will see that lgwr is waiting on event `rdbms ipc message` (waiting for *interprocess communication*) with a timeout of 300 centiseconds. So, if nothing happens for a few seconds, lgwr will wake up, do a little tidying up, and write any outstanding log buffer to disk.

If you want to check the next two options (1MB or one-third full), you can do so by setting up carefully sized array updates from a single session and checking three statistics: `messages sent` and `redo size` in the user session, and `messages received` in the lgwr session. With the `log_buffer` set to a value less than 3MB, you can see a message going from the user session to lgwr when the `redo size` is one-third of the log buffer size (as reported by `x$kcrfstrand` rather than the `log_buffer` parameter); but when the log buffer is larger than 3MB, you can see that the messages start appearing when the `redo size` is about 1MB.

Of course, the idea of a space limit raises more questions. The log writer sleeps for 3 seconds at a time, so how does it know how much of the buffer has been used? The answer is that each session checks the total allocated space (i.e., the size of the gap between the "End of free space" and the "Start of free space") every time it does an allocation. If the total space used exceeds the limit, then the session sends a message to lgwr immediately after it has copied its redo into the buffer.

But that raises another question: in a busy system where lots of sessions are generating bits of redo very quickly, won't there be lots of redundant messages sent to lgwr the moment the amount of redo in the buffer exceeds the limit? This doesn't happen, thanks to the *write flag* that I mentioned earlier.

When the log writer starts to write, it sets the write flag, and when it finishes writing, it clears the write flag; so any session that thinks it needs to send a message to the log writer checks this flag to see if lgwr is already writing, and if lgwr is writing, the session doesn't send the message. This is where latching comes in: lgwr gets the redo writing latch to set and clear the flag (which means two gets for every write), and each session has to get the latch to read the flag so that it doesn't read the flag while it's in flux. In both cases the gets on the latch are in willing-to-wait mode.

MESSAGES

In Chapter 3 I made the comment that the statistic `redo synch writes` counts the number of times a session has sent a message (statistic `messages sent`) to lgwr on a commit. This is an approximation; in fact, "sending a message" may not involve a real message.

Although there may be cases where two processes pass data to each other through shared memory locations, it's quite possible that there is no message content moving between the foreground sessions and lgwr. The key feature of `messages sent` is that the recipient is currently off the operating system run queue, and the sender calls an operating system function (typically relating to operating system semaphores) to get the recipient put back on the run queue. It's then up to the recipient to figure out what to do next.

In the case of a session "sending a message" to lgwr, if lgwr is not writing it will be off the run queue showing a wait for `rdbms ipc message`, so the session simply calls the operating system to put lgwr back on the run queue. When lgwr gets to the top of the run queue and starts to run, it doesn't need to know who caused it to wake up or how much log buffer to write; it just writes as much log buffer as it can and then looks to see which sessions are currently off the run queue, waiting on `log file sync`, with their `buffer#` ([parameter 1 of the event) lower than the last buffer written by lgwr.

Conversely, when a session wakes up after a `log file sync` wait, it checks to see if its write request has been satisfied before continuing. (There is a timeout on `log file sync`—hard-coded at 1 second until 11.1, but 10 centiseconds and configurable from 11.2.0.1—so it's possible that the session was woken by its own alarm call rather than lgwr.) It's easy for the session to check, of course, because it knows where lgwr had to get to to satisfy its write (the session's `buffer#`) and it can see where the current start of free space is—and it doesn't even need to get the `redo allocation` latch to do this check.

So the fourth cause of lgwr writing (a session issuing a `commit;`) is true—if we ignore for the moment an enhancement in 10*g* that I shall discuss shortly. However, as we have just seen, if lgwr is already writing, the foreground session will not send a message; it will simply increment `redo synch writes` and go into a `log file sync` wait. This leads to one more cause for lgwr writing.

When lgwr completes a write it can scan the list of active sessions to see which of them is waiting on a `log file sync` and post them to allow them to resume. (In earlier versions of Oracle, I think it used to scan the structure underlying `v$session`, but as systems got larger, later versions of Oracle may have introduced a secondary structure that listed just those sessions that were waiting for lgwr). When lgwr scans for sessions, it can see where in the log buffer their commit record was (`parameter1` of `v$session_wait` is their target `buffer#`) so it can post the sessions that have been satisfied by the write and, if there are any sessions still outstanding, start a new write immediately. So a final trigger that makes lgwr write is that it has just finished writing and can see that there are already more commit records in the log buffer that need to be written.

PL/SQL Optimization

We have seen that after putting a commit record into the log buffer, a session will wait on a `log file sync` wait until lgwr posts the session to allow it to continue processing, and this is how Oracle ensures the durability of transactions. But this isn't always the way things work. There is a little-known PL/SQL optimization (and you may argue with that choice of label) that means PL/SQL *doesn't always wait* for the write to complete.

Consider, first, a simple PL/SQL block (see script core_commit_01.sql, available in the Source Code/Download area of the Apress web site [www.apress.com]):

```
begin

        for r in (
                select  id from t1
                where   mod(id,20) = 0
        ) loop
                update  t1
                set     small_no = small_no + .1
                where   id = r.id;

                commit;

        end loop;

end;
/
```

This simple piece of code updates every 20th row in a table I've created that holds 500 rows, for a total of 25 updates and 25 commits. If we run this code in isolation (so that other sessions don't confuse the issue with concurrent redo generation and commits) and examine the session activity, we might expect to see the following statistics and wait events:

```
user commits (session statistic)            25
messages sent (session statistic)           25
redo synch writes (session statistic)       25
log file sync (session events)              25

messages received (lgwr statistic)          25
redo writes (lgwr statistic)                25
log file parallel write (lgwr events)       25
```

If we saw this output we could interpret it as 25 cycles of the following sequence:

- User session issues a commit
- User session posts lgwr and increments redo synch writes
- User session goes into a wait (log file sync) waiting to be posted by lgwr
- Lgwr gets woken up
- Lgwr writes the log buffer to disk, waiting a short time on each write

However, when I first ran this test (some 12 years ago on Oracle8*i*), I got results more like the following:

```
user commits (session statistic)              25
messages sent (session statistic)              6
redo synch writes(session statistic)           1
log file sync (session events)                 1

messages received (lgwr statistic)             6
redo writes (lgwr statistic)                   6
log file parallel write (lgwr events)          6
```

Clearly the user session is not behaving as expected—it has posted lgwr to write a few times, but it has only incremented `redo synch writes` once, which suggests it didn't stop and wait for lgwr to wake it up again. The user's session is breaching the durability requirement; if the instance crashed somewhere in the middle of this loop, it's entirely possible that a transaction that had been committed would not be recovered.

There is a rationale for this behavior: until the entire PL/SQL block has finished running, you (the end user) don't know how many of the transactions have committed, so Oracle doesn't try to make them recoverable until the moment before the PL/SQL block ends and control returns to the calling program; that's the one point at which the session increments `redo synch writes` and goes into a `log file sync` wait. In fact, you might not see a `log file sync` at all; you could, for example, insert a call to `dbms_lock.sleep()` as the last statement in the block and make the session pause for a few seconds, giving lgwr time to do one of its 3-second timeouts and clear the buffer. With a long enough pause in place, the session would wake up, check the state of lgwr, and find that it had already written all the necessary redo log. In this case you would see `redo synch writes` incremented, but no `messages sent` and no `log file sync` wait.

■ **Note** Generally speaking, if you issue commits inside a *single database call*, your session will not go to sleep and wait for lgwr to wake it up on each commit. Instead, it will go into a `log file sync` wait (incrementing `redo synch writes`) just once as the call is about to end. The commonest example of this is probably the case of commits inside a PL/SQL loop, which could, in principle, leave you in a position where some committed transactions will not be recovered after instance failure. Having made this point, though, it's worth mentioning that the window of opportunity for things to go wrong is (typically) less than a few hundredths of a second. This strategy does not get used if the code is doing updates across database links, so there have been occasions in the past where I've used a totally redundant *loopback database link* to ensure that some PL/SQL code would wait for a `log file sync` on every commit.

There is a flaw with the rationale. Although you can't *normally* tell exactly how many transaction have committed (because the moment you query the data to find out, you're too late because some more have committed by the time you get the result), Oracle gives you various mechanisms (such as pipes, external procedures, or `utl_file`) to push a message out from the PL/SQL block—and this means you have a mechanism for seeing the discrepancy.

Consider, for example, a banking application that uses a PL/SQL block to loop through a table one row at a time, calling an external procedure to transmit funds across the world, updating each row to say the funds have been sent, and then committing for each row. With a little bad luck you could find, after recovering from an instance failure, that you have a table showing rows where funds were (apparently) still due to be sent even though they had already been sent. Technically an application like this has a design flaw—it's trying to do a distributed transaction without using two-phase commit, and that can always lead to inconsistent data. If your loop involves a database link, which means Oracle is using two-phase commit internally, this commit optimization is disabled.

It's worth taking a few moments to look a little more closely at the results from the simple PL/SQL code. We can see six messages from the user session to lgwr; this might prompt you to ask if there is some special algorithm in the loop telling Oracle how often to send messages. In fact, we've already seen the answer to that question. Every time the code issues a commit, your session checks to see what lgwr is doing; if lgwr is writing, it would be a waste of resources to send a write message; if lgwr isn't writing, then your session sends a message. So if you try to repeat my little test, the number of messages you see will depend on the speed of your CPU (how fast can you go round the loop) compared with the speed of your disks (how long will it take lgwr to complete a write).

■ **Note** You will have seen that the statistic `redo synch writes` is tied up very closely with the event `log file sync`; they are nearly measuring the same thing. In fact, it gets better than that because the statistic `redo synch write time` (in hundredths of a second) is a match—with rounding errors—for the time spent in `log file sync` waits. 11.2.0.2 takes this a little further with two new statistics: `redo synch write time (usec)`, which is the time in microseconds, and a very useful indicator named `redo synch long waits`, which tells you how many times a session had to wait for a `log file sync` that was a little slow to complete (I can't find a statement of the limit but, at the moment, my best estimate is something between 13 and 17 milliseconds).

ACID Anomaly

If you look back at Chapter 3, or at the note in the section "Log Writer Writes" a few pages back, and think about my description of how the `commit;` works, you may notice a problem with durability in Oracle. The steps are as follows:

1. Create a change vector to update the transaction table.
2. Copy the change vector into the log buffer.
3. Apply the change vector to the undo segment header.
4. Post lgwr to write.

Between steps 3 and 4, another session will be able to see the transaction changes even though the commit record hasn't been written to disk. If the instance crashes between steps 3 and 4, then you could have a report (or a remote database) showing the results of a committed transaction that won't be recovered when the instance restarts. It's easy to demonstrate this effect:

1. Session 1: Use `oradebug` to suspend lgwr.
2. Session 2: Update some data and commit—the session will hang.
3. Session 1: Query the data, and notice that the update is visible.
4. Session 1: Crash the instance (shutdown abort).

When the instance restarts, the change in step 2 will not be visible and, as I said, this change might have been observed and recorded in another database, resulting in global inconsistency. On the plus side, lgwr doesn't crash often, and the window of opportunity is extremely short.

The most astonishing thing about this anomaly (to me, at least) is that I've described how the mechanism works many times over the last 12 years, and didn't notice the consequences of what I was saying until Tony Hasler (`http://tonyhasler.wordpress.com`) wrote a little blog item that raised the issue.

Commit Enhancements

It's time to look at a change that appeared in 10*g* when Oracle moved from a "secret" optimization on commits to a published option for controlling the behavior of commits through parameter `commit_write` that appeared in 10.2 and then turned into the two parameters `commit_logging` and `commit_wait` in 11g. In its simplest form you can address the durability issue of the PL/SQL loop by changing a `commit` into `commit write batch wait`.

Note The `commit` command allows for four new combinations: `commit write [batch|immediate] [wait|nowait]`. In 11*g* the `batch/immediate` choice can be set with the parameter `commit_logging` and the `wait/nowait` choice can be set with the parameter `commit_wait`. In 10*g* the single `commit_write` parameter is used to set both choices.

The quickest and simplest way to demonstrate the effects of the new `commit` options is to show the variations in a few critical statistics when I run my little PL/SQL loop test (on its own) with the original `commit` and then with the four different combinations offered by the new feature. Table 6-1 shows the results for an instance of Oracle 11.2.0.2.

Table 6-1. *Effects of* `commit_logging` *and* `commit_wait`

Statistic Name	Simple commit	Immediate wait	Immediate nowait	Batch wait	Batch nowait
`messages sent`	7	25	7	25	0
`redo entries`	25	50	50	25	25
`redo size`	11,500	12,752	11,876	12,068	11,012
`redo synch writes`	1	25	0	25	0
`redo wastage` (lgwr)	820	12,048	1,468	3,804	0
`redo blocks written` (lgwr)	25	50	27	32	0

The most important points to note in these results are as follows. If you specify the `wait` option, then your session will increment `redo synch writes` on every commit and wait on a `log file sync`. This generally results in a larger number of smaller writes and an increase in `redo wastage` (which we will examine shortly), `redo size` (because each write has its own little packet of management information when using multiple log buffers), and `redo blocks written` (the number of redo log blocks written to disk). You'll notice, of course, that the value of `redo entries` is 25 compared to 50; the smaller number is the one we expected; it's the standard 10*g* redo optimization (which we saw in Chapter 2) collecting redo change vectors for a small transaction into a single redo record.

If you specify `immediate` rather than `batch`, then two key changes appear: the *commit change vector* becomes a separate redo record (I can't think why; perhaps it's to minimize the time window on the ACID anomaly I previously mentioned), which gives you a small increase in the `redo size`, and—provided you haven't specified `wait`—your session doesn't send a message to lgwr *at all*; it simply assumes that something else will trigger a write in the near future.

The bottom line with the new `commit` options is simple: if you really need to ensure that every commit is guaranteed to be recoverable (e.g., in a banking system or medical system), then you should use the `wait` option, and the `batch wait` combination ought to give you a little edge of efficiency if the transactions are all small. If you don't mind risking a few committed transactions disappearing in the event of an instance crash (e.g., a social network), then `batch nowait` is clearly worth looking at for the reduction in redo, redo wastage, and session waits.

Mechanics

In the last few pages I've managed to throw out teasers about lgwr writing as much of the log buffer as possible, redo wastage, and contention with or between user sessions. It's time now to take a closer look at how the log buffer is used. We'll look at some log writer mechanics first, followed by redo wastage, and then examine *private redo*, which is Oracle's latest strategy for reducing contention.

Figure 6-3 shows the log buffer at a moment in time when several sessions have committed transactions, other sessions have been busy generating more redo, and the log writer is writing. It's a very busy picture with lots of components and illustrating a number of different points.

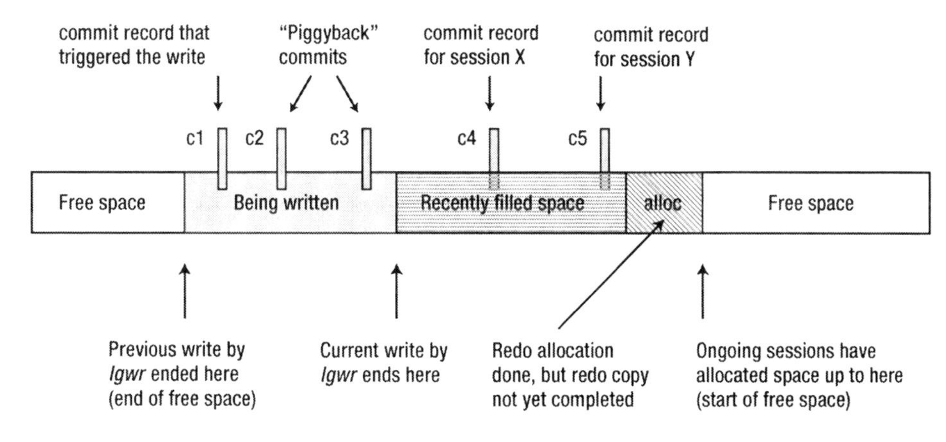

Figure 6-3. *A busy log buffer*

In the moments before we got to the state in Figure 6-3, the log writer was woken up by a `redo write` message arriving from the session that generated the commit record labeled c1. Before lgwr could swing into action, various other sessions managed to get more redo records into the log buffer, including two sessions that created commit records c2 and c3, respectively, and posted further `redo write` messages to lgwr, so at this point there are three sessions waiting on `log file sync` waits. Note that it's possible for there to be a delay between a session posting lgwr and the moment that lgwr actually starts running—it's this time lag that allows the extra sessions time to post lgwr (redundantly) despite the fact that the Oracle code tries to avoid redundant calls by using the write flag.

At the moment it woke up, lgwr would have acquired the `redo writing` latch, set the write flag, and dropped the latch, thus ensuring that all future sessions could tell that it was busy writing. Then it would have acquired the `redo allocation` latch to identify the highest point allocated in the log buffer at that moment (i.e., the start of free space), moved the pointer up to the end of the block—this is the point labeled "Current write by lgwr ends here" (I'll explain the significance of allocating to the end of the block in the next section, "Redo Wastage")—dropped the latch, and started copying the log buffer to disk. Note that although c1 was the commit record that triggered the write, lgwr is going to write all the way through commit records c2 and c3 as well, earning c2 and c3 the title of *group* or *piggyback* commits.

So Figure 6-3 shows lgwr in the act of writing, but as it writes, more redo arrives, including a few more commit records (c4, c5). The sessions that supplied these commit records will have acquired the `redo writing` latch and discovered that lgwr was writing, so they won't have posted lgwr (`messages sent` will not change) although they will have incremented `redo synch writes` and they will be waiting on `log file sync` waits. We can also see that some space has been allocated by a session that has not yet copied in the redo record it has prepared.

As lgwr completes its write, it will clear the write flag (getting and releasing the `redo writing` latch to do so), move the "End of free space" pointer up to the point it has just written (getting and releasing the `redo allocation` latch to do so), and run through the list of sessions waiting on `log file sync` waits, signaling the operating system to put back on the run queue any session whose commit record has just been written. (I may have the exact order of activity wrong here, but these are the steps that have to take place.)

■ **Note** If there are a lot of processes waiting on lgwr, and they all wake up at the same time, this can lead to a peculiar *priority inversion* problem where lgwr is pushed off the run queue by the sessions it has woken—lgwr has been working hard up to this point and the sessions haven't, so they get a higher priority than lgwr when they get back on the run queue. As a result you can sometimes see the system slowing down because lgwr isn't allowed to work. In rare cases this means you might be justified in raising the priority of the lgwr process or preventing the operating system from applying its normal rules to lgwr for reducing the priority of tasks using too much CPU.

The next thing that lgwr does is notice that there are some sessions waiting on `log file sync` that were not cleared by its write, so it goes through the cycle again (set the write flag, move the "Start of free space" pointer, and start writing), except this time around it discovers that there's a hole in the log buffer; a session has allocated space but not copied into it. You might ask how it can tell, and to answer that question we have to switch briefly to the foreground sessions at this point to see what steps they take to copy their redo into the log buffer. It works like this:

1. Get a `redo copy` latch. Since the number of latches is 2 × `cpu_count`, we can try each in turn in immediate mode, only going to willing-to wait-mode if they are all busy. The latch we pick first is randomized so that different sessions won't all end up waiting on the same latch.
2. Get the `redo allocation` latch. (With multiple public redo threads, the copy latch will dictate which buffer, which dictates which allocation latch; I'll make a few more comments on the effects of multiple log buffers a bit later in the chapter.)
3. Move the start of free space pointer.
4. Drop the redo allocation latch.
5. Make the copy.
6. Drop the redo copy latch.
7. If the allocation has taken the used space over one-third of the log buffer or 1MB, or if the redo record was a commit record, then post lgwr to write (but get the `redo writing` latch first to check if lgwr is already writing).
8. If the redo record was a commit record, increment `redo synch writes`, set up a `log file sync` wait, set up a 1-second (10*g*) or 10-centisecond alarm (11.2), and take self off run queue.

■ **Note** When a session gets the `redo allocation` latch to allocate some space in the log buffer, it may find that there isn't enough space available. In this case it will drop the latch and get the `redo writing` latch to check whether lgwr is writing, posting it to write if it isn't already doing so. The session will then drop this latch and put itself into a wait for `log buffer space`. So another check that lgwr has to make when it completes a write is a check for sessions waiting on `log buffer space` so that it can post them to continue processing. If lgwr was already writing when the session checks, the session simply goes back to the `redo allocation` latch and has another go at allocating space because the current write from lgwr should free up some space in the log buffer.

So a session allocates space in the log buffer and then copies into that space while holding the `redo copy` latch. In theory this means that lgwr need only get (and then release) all the `redo copy` latches as a check for holes before it starts to write, because once it is holding all of them, any holes in the log buffer must have been filled. According to a note by Steve Adams, though (see `www.ixora.com.au/tips/tuning/redo_latches.htm`), Oracle stopped doing this after 8.0; instead, it has a mechanism for seeing who is currently holding the redo copy latches without obtaining the latch (using the internal equivalent of `v$latchholder`), and if there are any holders, it starts waiting on `LGWR wait for redo copy` until posted that the latch has been released.

By watching the latch activity, we can see that something like this must be happening, but I don't know for certain what process posts lgwr (presumably it has to be the session holding the latch) and I don't know how it knows it has to post lgwr. However, since `parameter1` of the `LGWR wait for redo copy` wait is the `copy latch #`, and since each session will know which `redo copy` child latch it is holding, it's not hard to imagine that there is some code a session always calls just before it drops the latch to check if it has been holding the latch that lgwr has been waiting for, and posting lgwr if it was.

LOG FILE SYNC

It's common for people to worry about the speed of writes to the log file when they see `log file sync` waits ("we're waiting for the log writer!"). If you do this, though, you will be attributing the whole of the foreground `log file sync` wait to the background `log file parallel write`.

Look back at Figure 6-3 and the session that copied commit record c4 into the log buffer and you will see a lot of activity that *isn't* about that specific record appearing between the moment the session started waiting on `log file sync` and the moment the session started running again.

If lgwr is currently writing, it will have to complete its current write and wait to get back onto the CPU, do some work with some latches, and then post a number of foreground sessions (which may push lgwr off the CPU—see the earlier note following Figure 6-3). If lgwr is not currently writing, there may still be a time lag between the foreground posting it and the moment it starts running.

Lgwr then has to check that there are commit records pending, do some work with latches, and possibly wait for some redo to be copied into the buffer, before it can finally start to write, after which it does a little more work with latches and posts the relevant foreground processes.

Once the foreground has been posted, that doesn't mean it's running, only that it's back on the run queue, and there may still be a time lag before it runs, especially if there are a lot of other processes on the system.

So if your `log file sync` times seem to be long, it's not necessarily a problem with the time it takes to write to the log files, but rather may be a problem with load on the system.

Redo Wastage

I pointed out earlier that one of the first things that lgwr does in response to a write request is to get the `redo allocation` latch and move the start of free space to the end of the current block. Figure 6-4 zooms in on Figure 6-3 as we move on from one write to the next.

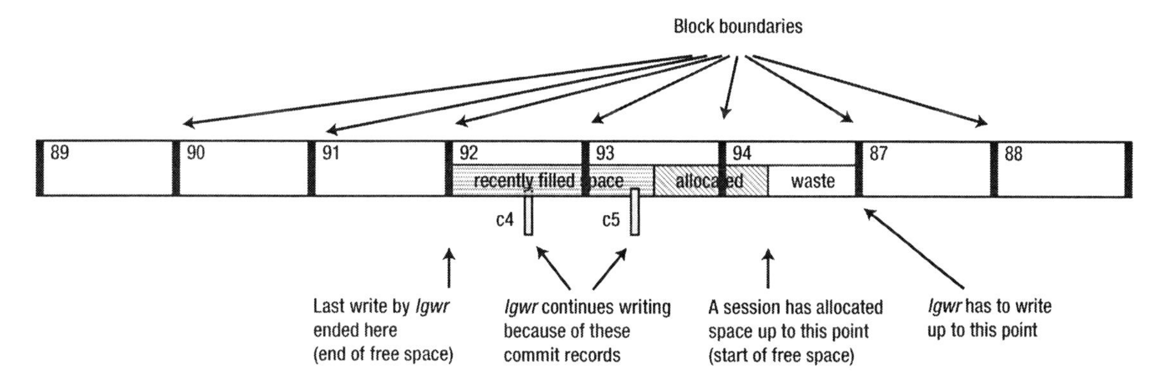

***Figure 6-4.** Block boundaries and redo wastage*

In Figure 6-4 I'm back to showing my tiny log buffer, with space for just eight blocks. The log writer has moved on from the write that cleared commit records c1, c2, and c3, and has noticed that a couple of sessions still have outstanding commit records in the buffer.

In this diagram, though, I have included the block boundaries, and you can see that the most recent space allocation doesn't reach the end of a block. So why does lgwr get the `redo allocation` latch and move the start of free space forward, wasting some space in that last block?

Writes to disk have to operate at the granularity of the *disk sector*, which is typically 512 bytes—the commonest block size for the redo log (and that's not an accident). If lgwr didn't move the start of free space to the end of the block, it would have to write part of a sector to disk, which would require a pre-read and fill to take place. Moments later another session would fill in the rest of the space in that last block, and lgwr would have to either copy the same block from the buffer again or read the sector back from disk, fill just the extra redo, and write it out again. The idea of reading the sector back and writing it again was seen as a nasty performance threat (especially in the days of Oracle 6 when the redo log concept was introduced); and the idea of keeping track of a block that had already been partly written was, presumably, seen as an undesirable complication in the code.

So Oracle's strategy is simple: move the pointer to the end of the block, write the block, never read, and never look back. The aim is to keep the code as simple as possible and keep streaming the log to disk without interruptions.

The space wasted by moving the pointer forward is reported as `redo wastage`. Since lgwr is the only session that deals with writing the log buffer, it's the only thing that moves the pointer in this way, and hence is the only session that will show a non-zero value for `redo wastage`. Statistically the average volume of redo wastage per write is likely to be about half a block unless all your transactions are virtually the same size. One of the worst cases of "same size" transactions, though, appears in applications that do a very large number of very small data changes—the killer "row by row" applications that aren't taking advantage of the features of the database.

In fact, in the example I used for Table 6-1, I've accidentally demonstrated the problem. Looking at the column for the stats for `commit write immediate wait` you can see that I've generated just over 12.5KB in `redo size` and a further 12KB in `redo wastage`. Each of my transactions needed just a few bytes more than a block (if you're doing the arithmetic, don't forget that there's a 16-byte header that you can't use in each block), so we lost most of the rest of the second block on each write.

This brings me back, of course, to my comments about newer disks and 4KB sector sizes. On one of the new disks my demo would have generated 12KB for the `redo size`, and about 89KB of `redo wastage`—that's about 510 bytes of `redo size` for each of the 25 transactions and 3.5KB to get to the end of the block. There will be some applications where you will want to look carefully at what your `redo wastage` is likely to be, and make a choice between 512 or 1,024 bytes for the redo log block size to minimize the `redo wastage` but paying the penalty of rereading blocks, or using 4KB blocks to minimize the overheads of rereading and updating blocks but paying the penalty of increased `redo wastage` with the associated increase in the volume of redo written.

Private Redo

It's about time I said something about the impact of the 10*g* enhancements on redo handling, and this basically means dealing with the role and use of private log buffers (usually called private redo threads) and multiple public log buffers. Fortunately there isn't a lot of new stuff to add.

The first point to note is that the number of threads in use, both private and public, is dynamic and Oracle tries to keep the number to a minimum, only using more if the `redo allocation` latches come under pressure and start showing sleep time. So, for example, when I had a system with 4 public threads and 20 private threads and started running six very busy sessions for half an hour, I found that most of the time only 1 of the public threads and only 6 of the private threads had been used. (I had a tiny amount of work done in the second public thread and, thanks to various background jobs, a seventh private thread had reported a little work.)

■ **Note** Although Oracle will dynamically modify the number of public and private redo threads in use, the memory is allocated and fixed at instance startup.

The second point is that the basic handling of the public threads doesn't change. When a session wants to copy something into a public thread, the method is just the same as always. The significant difference is that sessions are usually copying the content of a private thread into the public thread so, instead of a small allocation for a redo record holding a couple of change vectors, a session might allocate 80KB for a redo record holding 120 change vectors. (See Chapter 2.)

A key difference, of course, is that when a session starts a transaction, it's going to try to acquire a private redo thread. The initial (and maximum) number of private threads defined is `transactions / 10`, which means that for many systems the session will often find an available private thread; if there are no private threads available, the session will use one of the public threads in the traditional (pre-10*g*) fashion.

Each private thread has its own `redo allocation` latch, and to acquire a private thread a session will first get the associated latch. I had assumed that Oracle would use an `immediate get` to do this, on the basis that there are multiple private threads, each with its own private latch, so if it failed on the first thread/latch it could immediately try the next one (in much the same way that Oracle deals with the `redo copy` latches), only using a willing-to-wait get on the latch for the last thread. On a simple test, though, it looked as if the sessions were always getting the latches in willing-to-wait mode, leading me to believe that a session walks through the private redo structures without taking any latches, looking for the first thread that is not in use, and only gets the latch to mark that thread as in use. (This still leaves a window of opportunity for two sessions to try to get the same latch for the same private thread at the same time, of course, but generally reduces the work done trying.)

The final difference I want to mention relates to the write activity. When lgwr is posted to write, it has to go through every single (active) public redo thread in turn. This means it may have to go through all the activity of acquiring allocation latches and waiting for redo several times in the course of a single post. In part this explains why Oracle adjusts the number of active buffers dynamically to keep it to a minimum.

Database Writer

Oracle uses the redo log and lgwr to make transactions durable, so we don't need to copy changed database buffers from memory to disk the instant we change them; but it's nice (and in almost all cases necessary) to copy changed buffers to disk at some time. It feels somehow more "natural" and safe if we have a copy of the "real" data on disk, and most systems only have limited memory anyway, so with a DB cache capable of holding *N* blocks, they've got to start copying something to disk if they want to change block *N*+1.

Once we know that we have to copy blocks to disk, we can start asking interesting questions such as "when do we do it?" and "how do we pick which blocks to copy?" These questions take us straight back to lgwr.

In principle, because of the way that redo works, you could pick any data block off disk at any time, check its SCN (one of the many SCNs you can find on a block is the *last change SCN*, the SCN at which a change was last made to a block), go to the redo log that holds that SCN, and read forward from that point, finding and applying all the change vectors for that block until you run out of redo log. At that point you will have constructed a logical match for the current in-memory block.

■ **Note** It is a little-known feature of Oracle that when a session finds a corrupted data block in the DB cache, it will automatically go through the process I have just described—limited to just the online redo logs—to create a corrected, up-to-date, in-memory copy of the block. It has to pin the buffer exclusively while this is going on, but otherwise the process is transparent. The `block recover` feature of RMAN extended this to allow the DBA to instruct Oracle to read archived redo logs; and 11.2 introduced *automatic block media recovery* (see hidden parameters like `_auto_bmr%`) to allow the automatic use of archived logs (a feature I first saw in action when it caused a massive performance problem as three sessions all tried to recover the same index root block by scanning all the archived redo from the last few days). If there is a physical standby available, the code will even start by visiting the standby to see if it can find a recent copy of the block as a starting point for the recovery.

In practice we don't really want to keep doing this reconstruction; and if we find that we do have to do it, we don't want to walk through an enormous amount of redo; and we probably don't have an unlimited amount of disk to play with, anyway, so we won't want to keep an indefinite volume of redo logs online. Consequently, the strategy dbwr uses is basically one that minimizes the amount of work we have to do if we need to recover data blocks. The core of this strategy is to keep a record of how long ago a block was first changed in memory, and copy buffers out "oldest first."

Buffer Headers

We're back, once again, to linked lists and working data sets. So let's take a look at a dump of the buffer header of a dirty buffer:

```
BH (11BFA4A4) file#: 3 rdba: 0x00c067cc (3/26572) class: 1 ba: 11B74000
  set: 3 blksize: 8192 bsi: 0 set-flg: 0 pwbcnt: 0
  dbwrid: 0 obj: 8966 objn: 8966 tsn: 2 afn: 3
  hash: [217b55d0,10bf2a00] lru: [15be9774,11bf6748]
  lru-flags: hot_buffer
  obj-flags: object_ckpt_list
  ckptq: [147eaec8,11beab1c] fileq: [147eaed0,11beab24] objq: [1e5ae154,147ed7b0]
  st: XCURRENT md: NULL tch: 9
  flags: buffer_dirty gotten_in_current_mode block_written_once
         redo_since_read
  LRBA: [0x294.539f.0] HSCN: [0x0.4864bf4] HSUB: [57]
```

I discussed the cache buffers lru chain(s) and the cache buffers chains (represented here by the pairs of pointers labeled `hash:` and `lru:` on the fourth line of the dump) in Chapter 5. In this chapter we will be looking at the checkpoint queue (`ckptq:`), file queue (`fileq:`), and object queue (`objq:`), of which the checkpoint queue is most significant and the one I will address first.

In this case you can see that `flags:` shows the buffer is dirty, and it's on the checkpoint queue and (necessarily) a file queue. Interestingly, `obj-flags:` is set to `object_ckpt_list`, which may simply be a shorthand description for being on both the object and checkpoint queues but (for reasons I will mention later) may be giving us a clue that there is yet another set of concealed queues we should know about, a set where each queue links together all the dirty blocks for a given object.

Checkpoint Queues

Let's just focus on the checkpoint queue first. Each working data set has two checkpoint queues associated with it, which you can infer from the latches exposed in `x$kcbwds`:

```
SQL> desc x$kcbwds
 Name                          Null?    Type
 ----------------------------- -------- --------
...
 CKPT_LATCH                             RAW(4)
 CKPT_LATCH1                            RAW(4)
 SET_LATCH                              RAW(4)
 NXT_REPL                               RAW(4)
 PRV_REPL                               RAW(4)
...
```

Although these latches are highly visible, appearing in `v$latch` with the name `checkpoint queue latch` and matching the `addr` columns of `v$latch_children`, it's not possible to see the end points of the two queues in the structure because there are no `nxt_ckpt`, `prv_ckpt` columns to match the `nxt_repl`, `prv_repl` columns. When I ran a quick test to generate some dirty blocks and dump all the buffer headers, it was fairly easy to run some PL/SQL to read the trace file and rebuild the linked lists: there were two of them with roughly the same number of buffers per chain and their end-point addresses were fairly close to some of the other pointers listed in `x$kcbwds`. (A similar analysis of the `fileq:` pointers showed that there was one file queue for each data file—again with values similar to the other pointers listed in `x$kcbwds`.)

When a session first makes a buffer dirty, it will get one of the `checkpoint queue latch` latches (irritatingly the word "latch" really does appear in the latch name) for the working data set that the buffer belongs to and link the buffer to the "recent" end of that checkpoint queue, at the same time setting the `LRBA:` (low redo block address of the associated redo record in the form `log file seq# . log file block#`); this means that the buffers are actually linked in order of redo block address—which means they can't go onto the checkpoint queue if they're subject to private redo that hasn't yet been flushed to the log buffer. The latch get is generally in immediate mode (there's no point in using willing-to-wait mode initially because there are two latches, and one of them is likely to be free) and the buffer is linked while the session holds the latch. My guess is that the session uses a randomizing mechanism to decide which latch to pick first—possibly based on the block address—and then uses a willing-to-wait get on the second latch if both latches fail to succumb to an immediate get.

Note In the redo block address (RBA), the reference to file number is the constantly increasing `seq#` from `v$log_history`, not the `group#` from `v$log`, which simply numbers the active redo log files in the instance. This means the RBA is constantly increasing and is a reasonable choice as a sequencing mechanism.

Although this linking process takes place only when the buffer first becomes dirty, there is a special case to consider due to block cloning. When you update a table through a tablescan (and perhaps on other occasions), your session will clone the current block to create a new current copy (statistic `switch current to new buffer`; see Chapter 5). This means the buffer that is linked into the checkpoint queue is no longer the latest version of the block, so it has to be detached and the new buffer has to be attached instead. The new buffer doesn't go to the end of the queue, of course, because it has to go to the same place as the previous copy so that the buffers stay in the right order. The session knows where to find that copy because the header of the buffer it has just cloned was pointing to the two buffers on either side of the target that has to be relinked (see Figure 6-5). In this more complex case the session gets the necessary latch in willing-to-wait mode.

Note The `LRBA:` on the header won't change as a clone buffer is exchanged onto the checkpoint queue, but the `HSCN:` (high SCN) together with the `HSUB:` (high Sub-SCN, a fine-tuning value introduced in 9*i* for log buffer parallelism) will be adjusted to the current SCN. For reasons we shall see soon, it's important that dbwr can tell when the most recent change was made to the buffer. (Oracle also makes use of this value during in-memory recovery of a block, as it tells the code that's scanning through the redo logs where to stop.)

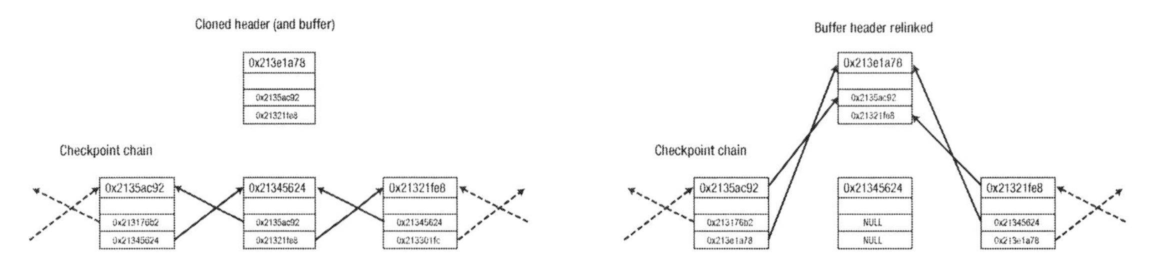

Figure 6-5. *Exchanging a cloned buffer (header) in the checkpoint queue*

The whole link/unlink mechanism has to be protected by latches because there could be multiple sessions doing the same thing at the same time—but there's one very special process that's attaching the checkpoint queues at the same time as the user sessions, and that's dbwr. Every 3 seconds dbwr wakes up, does any work it's supposed to, and then sets an alarm for itself before going to sleep again for the next 3 seconds.

Incremental Checkpointing

When dbwr wakes up, it gets each checkpoint queue latch latch in turn (using a willing-to-wait get) to see if there are any buffers in the queue, and then it walks the `LRBA:` queue from the low end collecting buffers and copying them to disk and detaching them from the checkpoint queue (marking the buffer as clean and clearing the `LRBA:` at the same time) until it reaches a buffer that is more recent than the target that it was aiming for. Sometimes, of course, dbwr will wake up, check the aged end of each checkpoint queue, find that there are no buffers to be copied, and go straight back to sleep.

The concept of "more recent" is very variable—there are five different parameters to think about as we move through different versions of Oracle, and some of those parameters changed their meaning across versions: `fast_start_mttr_target`, `fast_start_io_target`, `log_checkpoint_timeout`, `log_checkpoint_interval`, and `_target_rba_max_lag_percentage`. Then, on top of all these parameters is the self-tuning mechanism that came in with 10*g*. All these options translate to the same simple intent, though: every time dbwr wakes up it works out a target redo byte address and copies out any buffer with an `LRBA:` lower than that target. The `log_checkpoint_interval` is probably the simplest example to understand. It specifies a number of log file blocks, and dbwr simply subtracts that number from the redo block address that lgwr last wrote to (allowing for crossing file boundaries), and then copies out buffers with a lower `LRBA:` than the result. The other parameters simply use different algorithms to derive their targets.

■ **Note** You can appreciate why each working data set has two checkpoint queues when you understand the work done by dbwr. While dbwr is walking along one queue, all the sessions that want to put buffers onto a queue are likely to end up using the other queue thanks to their strategy of using immediate gets on the latches compared with the willing-to-wait gets used by dbwr. (There is a latch named `active checkpoint queue latch`—might we guess that dbwr updates a public variable to show which queue it is walking so that foreground sessions don't even try to attach new buffers to it unnecessarily?) Even when dbwr is walking a specific queue, there will be some occasions when a session will have to exchange a buffer on that queue, so dbwr has to keep getting and dropping the `checkpoint queue latch` latch as it walks the queue.

Inevitably there's more to copying out data buffers than this. The mechanism I've been describing so far is known as *incremental checkpointing*, and it's just one of several mechanisms that involve the word "checkpoint." It is, however, probably the most important because it gives us a guarantee that the data files are a reasonably accurate, fairly recent snapshot of the current state of our data. Moreover, it puts an upper bound on the amount of work that is needed if the instance crashes and we have to use the information in the redo logs to bring the database forward to the moment the crash occurred.

In fact, because of the way that the incremental checkpoint is constantly targeting the `LRBA:` and moving that target forward as time passes, we know that we can eventually throw away (or rather, overwrite) older online redo logs. Once we've got a database running at a steady state, the combination of a fixed number of online redo log files with the data files gives us a guaranteed perfect copy of our data even if the instance itself crashes. Getting the number and sizes of online redo logs right can take a little trial and error, but since you can't really make your log files too large, it's only difficult if you're under pressure to minimize your use of disk space.

If lgwr manages to fill all the available online redo logs too quickly, then it won't be able to overwrite the first one, which means it won't be able to write any redo changes to disk, which means your database can't change—which tends to mean the database stops. Typically this means your redo log files are too small, or you don't have enough of them to deal with peak levels of processing; sometimes it means you have a coding problem that is generating huge volumes of redundant redo; occasionally it means you need a faster device for your redo logs.

So what else is there to worry about? Two key points: first, I've pointed out that lgwr always writes out the changes made to a data block before dbwr writes the data block; second, there are other occasions when dbwr is required to write data blocks before they reach the aged end of the checkpoint queue, and one of those occasions is critical to performance (and a common point of confusion).

Database Writer Interactions

The database writer doesn't operate in a vacuum, and given its intent to protect the data "eventually" some time after the log writer has copied the log buffer to disk, it won't come as a surprise to learn that dbwr has to co-operate with other processes on the system. We'll start our examination of how dbwr behaves by looking at its interaction with lgwr, and then we'll move on to the way it has to share the LRU lists with other processes, and take a close look at the checkpointing mechanism that aims to copy a steady stream of dirty buffers to disk.

Database Writer Meets Log Writer

Lgwr always writes changes before dbwr writes data blocks. This means a data block that's on disk can always be moved "to the future" by applying records from the redo log, and it never needs to be moved "to the past" after a crash. This results in a very robust recovery mechanism; however, dbwr typically writes blocks by checking their `LRBA:`—the earliest moment at which they changed—so what happens if a buffer that is about to be written has also been changed in the last few microseconds before dbwr got to it? It's quite likely that dbwr will sometimes find a block that has been changed so recently that the redo log for the latest change has not yet been written.

During an incremental checkpoint, dbwr will simply post lgwr to write (with the usual proviso that it will take the redo writing latch beforehand to check if lgwr is already writing anyway and doesn't need to be told again) before writing the problem data block. Since it doesn't seem to wait for lgwr to complete its write (I've never noticed dbwr reporting a `log file sync` wait), I assume it must skip over the problem block and carry on along the checkpoint queue, coming back once it has got to the end to check again whether the relevant log buffer entries have been written. Short of tracing everything dbwr does (and I'm not keen to do that), I can't think of any way to infer from the information available in the various stats, events, and latch activity exactly what goes on at this point, but there has to be a final step that dbwr takes to bypass the problems of a very slow log write at this point—perhaps it simply ignores the block, pretends it has missed a checkpoint, and allows the problem to resolve itself 3 seconds later.

I'll just mention at this point that this posting to lgwr isn't the only interaction between dbwr and lgwr. It's worth noting that when dbwr writes data blocks to disk, it creates a redo record called a *block written record* for each batch of blocks it has written, puts it into the log buffer (using the usual copy and allocation latches), and posts lgwr to write—again without waiting for a `log file sync`, but taking the usual step of checking the `redo writing` latch beforehand. The following is a dump showing what goes into a block written record:

```
REDO RECORD - Thread:1 RBA: 0x0002a7.00000003.013c LEN: 0x0074 VLD: 0x02
SCN: 0x0000.049e100b SUBSCN:  1 08/08/2011 21:15:04
CHANGE #1 MEDIA RECOVERY MARKER SCN:0x0000.00000000 SEQ:  0 OP:23.1
 Block Written - afn: 5 rdba: 0x01805b0d BFT:(1024,25189133) non-BFT:(6,23309)
                   scn: 0x0000.049e0fa9 seq: 0x02 flg:0x06
 Block Written - afn: 5 rdba: 0x01805b13 BFT:(1024,25189139) non-BFT:(6,23315)
                   scn: 0x0000.049e0fd3 seq: 0x02 flg:0x06
 Block Written - afn: 5 rdba: 0x01805b18 BFT:(1024,25189144) non-BFT:(6,23320)
                   scn: 0x0000.049e0fd1 seq: 0x02 flg:0x06
 Block Written - afn: 5 rdba: 0x01805b19 BFT:(1024,25189145) non-BFT:(6,23321)
                   scn: 0x0000.049e0fb3 seq: 0x02 flg:0x06
```

As you can see, a block written record is simply a list of block addresses together with the *last change SCN* for that block. I'll explain what these records are for when we look at recovery later in the chapter. You'll notice in this example that the record covers four blocks in absolute file (`afn:`) 5, relative file 6. The code to create the symbolic dump doesn't know whether the block came from a *bigfile tablespace* or not, which is why there are two possible interpretations offered for the `rdba:`, one as a `BFT:` and one as a `non-BFT`.

Note There are many pieces of user-facing code in Oracle that use a file number as an input, but sometimes you can't tell whether that should be a relative or absolute file number, and it can be hard to test because by default Oracle will make the relative file number match the absolute file number until you have 1,024 files in the database. For testing purposes you can set event 10120 before adding a data file to the database—this makes Oracle create a file with different absolute and relative numbers.

You will have to take my word for it that these blocks were updated by a small collection of random updates to a large table (there were several more batches of blocks from the same table in other `BWRs`), and that they were not updated in the order they have been reported. Clearly dbwr sorted the list of blocks before starting to write them in the hope of getting a little improvement in the write throughput.

Database Writer and LRU

As I pointed out earlier, there are times when dbwr has to copy a buffer to disk before it has reached the aged end of the checkpoint queue. To introduce the most important (and perhaps most complex) reason, we have to go back to the LRU (or REPL) lists of Chapter 5. In Figure 6-6 we have an image of a single, small, working data set showing the slightly more accurate image of how Oracle's LRU/TCH algorithm works.

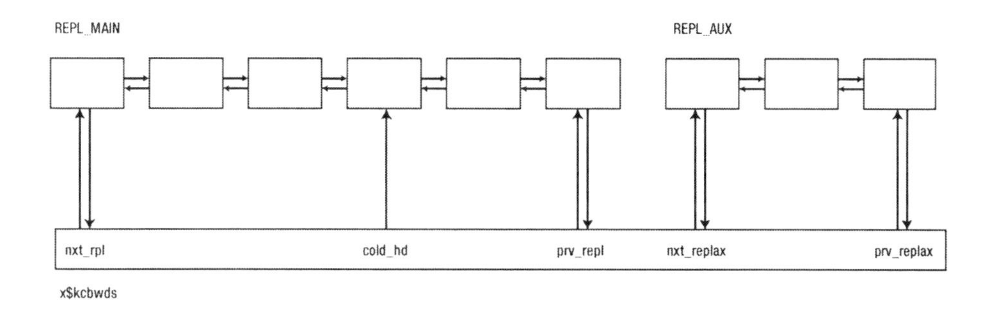

Figure 6-6. *REPL_MAIN and REPL_AUX*

As we saw in Chapter 5, Oracle tries, by default, to keep about 25 percent of the buffers of the working data set in REPL_AUX, and the intention is that buffers in that list are most likely to contain blocks that can be discarded so that the buffer can be relinked to the `cold_hd` location in REPL_MAIN and used to read a new block into memory. So, *usually*, the contents of REPL_AUX are read-consistent clones, or blocks that have been visited only once (i.e., won't need to be promoted to the hot end of REPL_MAIN), and blocks that won't need to be written to disk. But things don't always work perfectly. There are always boundary conditions that cause anomalies to appear; moreover, when the system is under pressure, it's possible for REPL_AUX to become empty, and that, too, is likely to cause some anomalies.

Consider, then, an extremely intense period of very random reads. As lots of blocks are read, REPL_AUX empties out, its buffers are attached to REPL_MAIN, and gradually all those buffers migrate down REPL_MAIN to the end of the chain. Remember, then, how a session finds a buffer for reuse: it scans REPL_AUX looking for a suitable candidate, which means a buffer that isn't pinned doesn't need to be written and has a touch count less than 2 (because a session will relink buffers with a higher touch count to the hot end of REPL_MAIN), and, if it doesn't find one, it starts to scan REPL_MAIN. Ultimately there is a limit (set by parameter `_db_block_max_scan_pct` at 40 percent of the working data set) to how much scanning the session will do before it gives up, posts dbwr (to tell it to write some blocks to disk to free up some buffer space), and goes into a `free buffer waits`, waiting to be told that dbwr has cleaned and freed some dirty buffers by copying their contents to disk.

This is where things get messy because we introduce another pair of linked lists to the working data set, WRITE_MAIN and WRITE_AUX (which, as a pair, are often called LRU-W). Here are the relevant entries from `x$kcbwds`:

```
SQL> desc x$kcbwds
 Name                          Null?    Type
 ----------------------------- -------- --------------------
...
 NXT_WRITE                              RAW(4)
 PRV_WRITE                              RAW(4)
 NXT_WRITEAX                            RAW(4)
 PRV_WRITEAX                            RAW(4)
 CNUM_WRITE                             NUMBER
 ANUM_WRITE                             NUMBER
...
```

The columns echo the pattern of the replacement lists: we have pairs of (`nxt_write`, `prv_write`) for the pointers to the main and auxiliary lists, `cnum_write` for the total number of buffers on the two lists, and `anum_write` for the number of buffers on the auxiliary list.

As the foreground session was scanning for a free buffer, it would have *unlinked* dirty buffers (that were not pinned) from whichever replacement list it was scanning and linked them to WRITE_MAIN. When the session gives up and posts dbwr, dbwr knows why it has been posted and is going to see those buffers on WRITE_MAIN and copy them to disk before posting any session that is waiting on event `free buffer waits`.

So, although there may be dirty buffers in the hot portion of REPL_MAIN that were first changed minutes ago, we have just put buffers on the write list that came into the cache and were changed just moments ago. Chasing the tail of the checkpoint queue isn't enough. Because of the way the LRU/TCH algorithm works, *unpopular*, dirty buffers may have to be copied to disk long before they reach the aged end of the checkpoint queue.

■ **Note** I have occasionally heard people suggest that dbwr *flushes* blocks from the data cache, implying that the blocks disappear from the buffers and have to be reread after dbwr has written them. This is wrong; all that dbwr does is copy the content to disk. It's possible that a slightly mangled description of how buffers are moved to the write list (and onward) *when a session needs to find a free buffer* has resulted in this misunderstanding.

Figure 6-7 outlines the basic flow of activity from the moment a session starts to search for a free buffer. The shaded blocks are ones that are not pinned but cannot be used because they are dirty. The rest of the blocks between the start and end of the scan are either pinned (and possibly dirty as well) or have a touch count that gets them promoted to the hot end of REPL_MAIN.

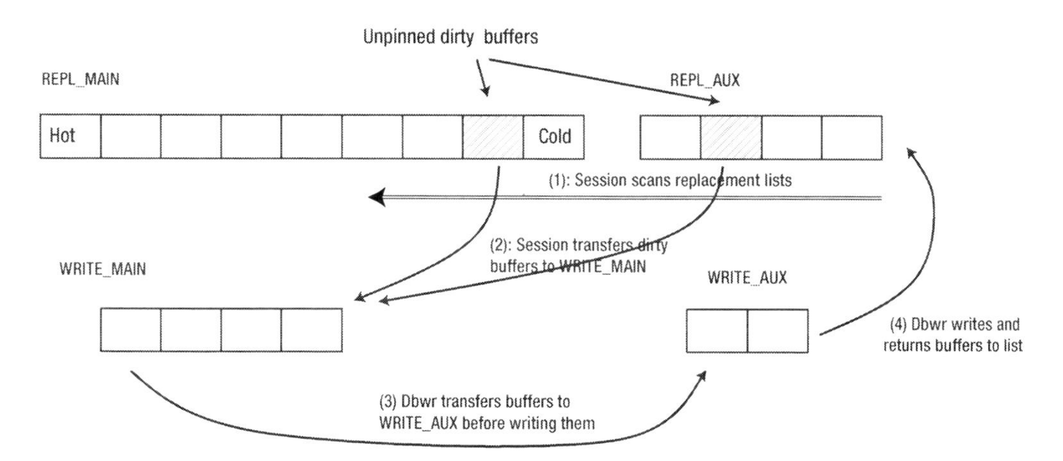

Figure 6-7. *The cycle through the write lists*

As the dirty, unpinned buffers are found, they are unlinked from REPL_*xxx* and linked to WRITE_MAIN. Note how different this is from the treatment of the checkpoint queue—a buffer does not get unlinked from the replacement queue to go onto the checkpoint queue, so it can be "in two places at once," but a buffer can only be on one of the four sublists WRITE/REPL/MAIN/AUX. When the session panics (or when the write list reaches a critical size), it stops scanning the replacement lists and posts dbwr. Dbwr wakes up and scans through WRITE_MAIN, unlinking buffers from WRITE_MAIN and relinking them to WRITE_AUX. Remember that a changed buffer can't be copied to disk until the related redo has been written to disk—it's at this point that dbwr can compare RBAs, decide that a buffer shouldn't go from WRITE_MAIN to WRITE_AUX, and post lgwr to write the redo. Once dbwr has finished its scan, it pins the blocks on WRITE_AUX exclusively and initiates the write to disk, and once the write has completed and the buffers are clean, it can unlink them from WRITE_AUX, relink them to REPL_MAIN, and (because the buffers are now clean) detach them from the checkpoint queue. Then dbwr can go back for another scan of WRITE_MAIN for any blocks it skipped the first time around.

Checkpoints and Queues

Incremental checkpointing is something that appeared quite late in the life of Oracle, showing up in Oracle8*i* at the same time as the LRU/TCH algorithm. Prior to that the only well-known checkpoint was the checkpoint at log file switch. Whenever lgwr has filled an online log file, it wants to make the contents redundant because in a short time it's going to run out of online log files and will need to start reusing them. This requirement introduces the need for a checkpoint.

A *checkpoint* used to be a simple moment of synchronization, a moment when Oracle could say "if a data block was changed before this moment in time, that data block, with the change made to it, is now on disk." Oracle would simply post dbwr telling it to copy every dirty block to disk, and then make a note of the moment it *sent* the instruction. That moment (recorded as an SCN, but only after dbwr had confirmed that it had copied all the data) became a marker that said "any redo generated before this point is redundant because we've brought the data files up to date to that point."

Historically, these moments appeared as each log file was filled. Suddenly dbwr would go into a frenzy writing data blocks to disks, and when it had finished (and that might be some time later), Oracle would update each data file header block with the SCN to show that that file was "complete" up to that point in time. When databases were small (and in Oracle 6 you were limited to 63 files), it was dbwr that handled the file header update, but as databases got bigger and Oracle added more functionally, a dedicated process called *ckpt* (checkpoint process) was added to deal with all aspects of checkpointing. Apart from updating data file headers, ckpt is also responsible for updating the control file every 3 seconds with the low RBA (or possibly SCN, or both) as it was at the start of the incremental checkpoint.

CONTROL FILE

So far I've discussed only data files and redo log files, but there are other files that make up an active Oracle database. The control file (which is usually duplicated, sometimes triplicated) is a file that describes the rest of the database. It lists all the data files, log files (both online and archived), backup pieces, and various bits of information about the state of the files. If you want to get an idea of the information stored in the control file, you can query `v$controlfile_record_section`.

Updates to the control file (such as the 3-second incremental checkpoint SCN) are serialized by the `CF enqueue`. The control file doesn't usually see much activity, but if you do a large number of unrecoverable operations (which could happen in a system handling lots of nonlogged LOBs, for example), you can see contention for the `CF enqueue` because of the number of updates you are doing to the control file.

The log switch checkpoint (also known as the *media recovery checkpoint*) used to cause a few problems, largely due to the sudden spike in the I/O load and the time it would take to complete. This is why the incremental checkpoint appeared—it reduced I/O spikes by keeping dbwr a little busy all the time and, as a byproduct, reduced the time it took for a session to find a free buffer when it needed one.

Note I have seen documents suggesting that ckpt works out the `LRBA` that dbwr should be using for the incremental checkpoint. This certainly sounds sensible, as ckpt is the process that updates the control file. However, there is no sign of messages being sent and received between ckpt and dbwr every 3 seconds, so it is not obvious how ckpt would know that the writes had been completed. Possibly dbwr calculates the `LRBA` and writes it to a shared memory location once the writes are complete (protected by a latch, of course—perhaps my earlier guess about the function of the latch called `active checkpoint queue latch` was wrong) and ckpt simply wakes up to check the latch and memory location.

The media recovery checkpoint and incremental checkpoints are not the only types of checkpoint, and the issues of the time it takes to write large numbers of blocks to disk are not restricted to log file switches. So dbwr has mechanisms to prioritize writes, and has several different linked lists to deal with other types of checkpoints. We can see these linked lists in `x$kcbwds`, each echoing the same group of six columns (I've only printed the first column of each group of six below) that we saw for the write list:

```
SQL> desc x$kcbwds
 Name                          Null?    Type
 ----------------------------- -------- --------------------
...
 NXT_WRITE                              RAW(4)
 PRV_WRITE                              RAW(4)
 NXT_WRITEAX                            RAW(4)
 PRV_WRITEAX                            RAW(4)
 CNUM_WRITE                             NUMBER
 ANUM_WRITE                             NUMBER
...
 NXT_XOBJ                               RAW(4)
 NXT_XRNG                               RAW(4)
 NXT_REQ                                RAW(4)
 NXT_PNG                                RAW(4)    --      8.1
 NXT_L2W                                RAW(4)    --     11.2
 NXT_L2R                                RAW(4)    --     11.2
 NXT_L2K                                RAW(4)    --     11.2
...
```

The lists are all about buffers that need to be copied to disk for different reasons, and the variation in reason dictates a different priority for the writes. Table 6-2 gives a list of names and functions for the lists.

Table 6-2. *Functions of the Different Write Lists*

Short Code	Description
XOBJ	Linked list of buffers that need to be written at high priority due to specific object-level requests such as truncate or drop You may find it hard to observe anything in this list because it will be clear very quickly.
XRNG	Described as the reuse range list, this is another list for buffers that need to be written at high priority—in this case for actions such as `alter tablespace read only`.
REQ	Unknown—possibly the list of buffers for which cache fusion write requests have been made (in which case it corresponds to the list formerly known as the `ping` list, and would require the blocks to be written most urgently).
PNG	Disappeared in 9*i*. Linked list of buffers that were due to be written to disk because another instance had requested the block (or a block covered by the same lock element).
L2W	11.2: DB Flash Cache Write list (?)—function unknown at present
L2R	11.2: DB Flash Cache Read list (?)—function unknown at present
L2K	11.2: DB Flash Cache Keep list (?)—function unknown at present

---

■ **Note** I don't have anything to say about the various L2 lists, which, I am guessing, are related to the *database flash cache* that appeared in Oracle 11.2. The same version also introduced a second *cache buffers lru chain* latch for each working data set, though it doesn't expose it in `x$kcbwds`. I haven't seen the new latch in action yet, and my initial guess is that it may be related to the three L2 lists.

When you read the descriptions of the various lists, you can appreciate that there are bulk operations that could require a lot of buffers to be copied to disk very quickly; and each of these activities is a form of checkpointing. So (lurking in the Oracle executable itself) we can see signs of the following types of checkpoint—I've extracted the names from the Oracle executable with a call to `strings -a oracle` and reproduced the results in table 6-3, with my understanding of when or why each type of checkpoint takes place.

Table 6-3. *Checkpoint names and triggering events.*

Checkpoint Name	**When triggered:**
Instance recovery checkpoint	After completion of instance recovery
Media recovery checkpoint	Following a redo log file switch
Thread checkpoint	Following a redo log file switch – although in recent versions of Oracle the checkpoint activity may start quite a long time after the switch.
Interval checkpoint	At moments dictated by the setting of parameter `log_checkpoint_interval` or parameter `log_checkpoint_timeout`

Tablespace checkpoint	In response to one of the commands:
	`alter tablespace begin backup;`
	`alter tablespace offline;`

PQ tablespace checkpoint	Before a session can invoke direct path reads. Prior to 11g this could only be for parallel query, but in 11g it may happen for serial queries.
Close database checkpoint	In response to either of the commands `alter database close;` `shutdown [normal	immediate	transactional]`
Incremental checkpoint	Every 3 seconds, due to a timeout mechanism built into the checkpoint process (ckpt).

Checkpoint Name	When triggered:
Local database checkpoint	In response to the comman: `alter system checkpoint local`
Global database checkpoint	In response to the command: `alter system checkpoint global`
Object reuse checkpoint	In response to a command to truncate an object
Object checkpoint	In response to a command to drop an object
RBR checkpoint	This is a recent addition to the full list of checkpoints. Its full name is the reuse block range checkpoint, and I have seen it appear as an index rebuild completes. So perhaps it is a type of object checkpoint for objects that have just been created.
Multiple object checkpoint	This is another recent addition. As its name suggests, it is probably triggered when an action requires multiple objects to be checkpointed at the same time. e.g. dropping partitioned object.

I have to say that I'm not sure what the difference could be between a local database checkpoint and a thread checkpoint. Since a thread seems to be synonymous with an instance, and a "local" database is, presumably, just a single instance, they seem to suggest the same result—but perhaps there are different ways of invoking them.

There are a couple of checkpoints here that are worth a brief mention. Parallel query often results in direct path reads (full tablescan or index fast full scan). This means that blocks are read from disk straight into the session's private memory, bypassing the data cache; but that means if there are dirty buffers in the data cache, the session won't see the most recent versions of the blocks unless they are copied to disk before the query starts—so parallel queries start with a type of checkpoint. Be warned, by the way, that 11*g* allows for serial direct path scans, and these will also require a preceding checkpoint.

Strangely, the first thing your session does when dropping or truncating an object is to initiate an object checkpoint, telling dbwr to copy any dirty buffers for that object to disk—and then you throw them away. (The state of each buffer is also changed to `free`, although Oracle doesn't bother to clear the information about the previous occupant of the buffer from the buffer header.)

■ **Note** It seems strange to copy dirty buffers to disk just before you drop an object, but there is a rationale. Since 8*i*, Oracle has been able to do *cross-DDL read consistency*: if you drop a partition of a partitioned table while another session is querying that table, the other session can still see where that partition is (even though the tablespace is now showing it as free space). By copying out dirty buffers before dropping the object, Oracle allows the other session to reread the blocks they need—at least until someone else manages to allocate the space to a new object. I can't think of a good reason for doing this on a `truncate`, though.

Finally, when you put a tablespace into backup mode (if you are still doing manually managed backups from the operating system), or take it offline, Oracle writes all the dirty blocks from the tablespace to disk before changing the state of the tablespace.

When you compare the three examples I've given, you can appreciate that there is an argument for different checkpoints having different write priorities—if you drop an object, you might not be too worried about how long it takes the buffers to disappear from the cache, but if you're running a parallel query, you'd like it to start right away. And if you implement several different write lists, it becomes a lot easier to associate functionality—hence priority—with the lists.

My main problem with the various write lists is that I can't see them being populated. I assume that they are supposed to behave like WRITE_MAIN and WRITE_AUX, in that buffers are unlinked from the replacement list and linked to the relevant MAIN by the session, then unlinked from the MAIN list and linked to the associated AUX list by dbwr, and then written to disk, unlinked from the AUX list and put on the auxiliary replacement list by dbwr. But if this is happening, the columns in `x$kcbwds` don't seem to be updated to reflect the use of the lists. I even tried suspending dbwr (on a 10.2.0.3 instance) so that any blocks that got onto any write lists would get stuck on the MAIN sublist, but I didn't see parallel queries, truncates, or drops populating any write lists, though the commands did get stuck on waits for `enq: KO - fast object checkpoint` (PQ) and `enq: RO - fast object reuse` (truncate/drop).

Buffer Header Queues

It is worth taking a quick look back at the buffer header dump when we see the enqueue waits because there is some significance to the "fast" label. Here's a copy of the buffer header dump presented earlier in the chapter, in the section "Buffer Headers":

```
BH (11BFA4A4) file#: 3 rdba: 0x00c067cc (3/26572) class: 1 ba: 11B74000
  set: 3 blksize: 8192 bsi: 0 set-flg: 0 pwbcnt: 0
  dbwrid: 0 obj: 8966 objn: 8966 tsn: 2 afn: 3
  hash: [217b55d0,10bf2a00] lru: [15be9774,11bf6748]
  lru-flags: hot_buffer
  obj-flags: object_ckpt_list
  ckptq: [147eaec8,11beab1c] fileq: [147eaed0,11beab24] objq: [1e5ae154,147ed7b0]
  st: XCURRENT md: NULL tch: 9
  flags: buffer_dirty gotten_in_current_mode block_written_once
         redo_since_read
  LRBA: [0x294.539f.0] HSCN: [0x0.4864bf4] HSUB: [57]
```

I made a very brief reference to `fileq:` and `objq:` earlier in the chapter and wondered whether the value of `object_ckpt_list` for the `obj-flags` was hinting at the existence of another set of object queues. Whether or not there is another set of object queues, the queues shown in the dump tell us something about object-based and tablespace-based checkpoints.

If I want to drop or truncate an object, I need to write all the dirty blocks from that object to disk and set the status of each buffer to `free`. But as I loaded each block into memory, I linked it to the relevant object queue so I have a direct route to every single relevant buffer.

Similarly, if I want to run (say) a parallel tablescan against an object, I need to write the dirty blocks from that object to disk; again, I could just follow the object queue and deal with just the dirty blocks, but if there was also an object queue list for just the dirty blocks, I could be a little more efficient.

Note You can see the object queue headers exposed in `x$kcboqh` (kernel cache buffers object queue header) and the individual buffers in `x$kcbobh` (kernel cache buffers object buffer headers). Since these structures are maintained in shared memory and could be modified by concurrent processes, they have to be protected by a latch, in this case the `object queue header operation` latch. Each working data set has its own object queue, which means you can find multiple rows for a single object in `x$kcboqh`, and each set of object queues has its own latch; so the number of `object queue header operation` latches is the same as the number of working data sets.

Again, for `tablespace begin backup` or `tablespace read only` I need to write all the dirty blocks from the tablespace to disk, which means writing all the dirty blocks from each file in the tablespace, and I have the `fileq` to help (but there isn't an externalized x$ for that one). However, if I want to offline, or drop, a tablespace, then I need to mark the status of all the buffers as `free`—and blocks only go on the `fileq` when they become dirty, so there seems to be a little gap in the implementation.

Checkpoints and Log Files

After all the diversions into linked lists and write queues, we come back to the impact of checkpoints—and particularly the media recovery checkpoint—on the log buffers. The basic purpose of any type of checkpoint is to say "the data files (or some part of them) are up to date to point in time *X*." The purpose of the media recovery checkpoint specifically is to say "the data files are up to date as far as the end of a given redo log file." When this type of checkpoint is complete, ckpt updates every data file with the starting SCN of the next log file—which is enough to tell Oracle that the previous redo log file is now surplus to requirements—and updates the control file with the same information on each file entry.

Think about this scenario, though. A session updates a couple of rows in a table—acquiring a private redo thread to do so—and then goes idle for a while. A few minutes later the current log file becomes full and a log file switch takes place, which means Oracle wants to use the current SCN as the starting SCN of the next log file. But in that case, what's going to happen to the private redo that was produced a few minutes ago? Unless Oracle takes some special action, we're going to end up with that private redo going into the next log file, which means some of the redo in the file will have a lower SCN than the starting SCN of the file.

You won't be surprised to learn that the developers at Oracle Corp. thought about this problem and handled it, but it leads to an interesting side effect. The Oracle code assumes the worst-case scenario for a log file switch—i.e., that every *active* public and private thread is full—so it triggers the log file switch prematurely, at the moment when the amount of space at the end of the log file is large enough to hold all the redo that might still be in the buffers. For example, if you had 2 active public threads of 5MB each, and 12 active private threads of 128KB each (adding the redo and IMU parts), then the switch would be triggered when you had 11.5MB of space (2 × 5MB + 12 × 128KB) still free in the log file. If there happened to be virtually no outstanding entries in the log buffers at that time, then that space won't be used—this is why Oracle dynamically adjusts the number of threads to keep it to a minimum. If you constantly see that your archived redo logs are a few megabytes smaller than the online redo logs, then (from 10*g* and later) this may explain why.

■ **Note** When Oracle archives an online redo log file, it only copies the used portion of the file. There are several reasons why the resulting archive may be smaller than the original file, and the allowance for private redo is just one of them. The commonest reason, perhaps, is that DBAs often set the `archive_lag_target`, or define `cron` jobs to ensure that a log switch takes place at regular intervals.

The previous paragraph explains how Oracle makes sure it has space available in the current log file for all the outstanding redo at the moment of a media recovery checkpoint, but how does all the "extra" redo get into the file? The database writer gets it there. I mentioned in Chapter 2 the concept of the *IMU flush*, a moment when the private redo is copied into the public buffer prematurely. One of the causes of IMU flushes is the media recovery checkpoint. In fact, any time dbwr needs to copy a buffer to disk and finds that the buffer is subject to private redo, the same effect appears. In an action reported in `x$ktiff` under statistic `Contention flushes`, dbwr will get and drop the `redo allocation` latch for the relevant private redo thread so that it can change the state of the private thread to `being flushed`, and then copy (all) the redo from that thread into the public redo thread, apply it to the data blocks, and mark the thread as `flushed` (again getting and dropping the latch) before carrying on with copying out data buffers.

If the foreground session tries to generate more redo while dbwr is doing this, then it runs into a problem—it can't use the private redo thread because dbwr has taken control of it, and it can't use the public redo thread because otherwise its newest redo change vectors might get into the buffer ahead of its older redo change vectors. So the session has to suspend itself until dbwr has finished the transfer. This is the source of the `log file switch (private strand flush incomplete)` wait that you will see reported in the alert log occasionally.

When dbwr has finished flushing the private redo into the public buffer, it posts the waiting session to continue processing, and from this point onward any further redo generated by the session goes into the public redo thread in the traditional way, although the private thread is still bound to the session and can't be used by any other transaction until the session commits. It is an interesting little quirk that the redo initially created by the foreground session up to this point gets recorded against the `redo entries` and `redo size` statistics of *dbwr*, but the undo generated is recorded against the `undo change vector size` of the *foreground session.*

Recovery

Having spent so much time on how dbwr and lgwr work, it's about time we looked at one of the most important tasks the DBA has to succeed at—recovery. When everything breaks, the DBA has to be able to recover the database. I've already mentioned instance recovery (i.e., what happens if the instance crashes): in principle we just start it again and Oracle simply replays *all* the entries from the redo log to bring the database up to the moment it crashed. The clever bit is how Oracle minimizes the amount of work it needs to do—and this is where the media recovery checkpoint, incremental checkpoint, and block written records come into play.

On a media recovery checkpoint, Oracle updates every data file header to hold the SCN at which the checkpoint started (or, depending on how you count, you might call it the one after the checkpoint started); in the case of a media recovery checkpoint initiated by a log file switch, this means the SCN recorded in the data file header is the first SCN of the new log file.

■ **Note** The connection between log file switches and the media recovery checkpoints is just a little messier than I've described, and 11*g* has introduced two new parameters, `_defer_log_boundary_ckpt` (defer media recovery checkpoint at log boundary) and `_defer_log_count` (number of log boundaries media recovery checkpoint lags behind), defining this behavior. Effectively these parameters allow Oracle to be lazy about copying buffers to disk on media recovery checkpoints until a few extra log files switches have taken place. This type of mechanism has been in place since 9*i*—but with no visible controls—presumably in the hope that a little extra delay at peak processing periods would allow incremental checkpointing to spread the write load that an immediate media recovery checkpoint would cause.

So when the instance restarts it can check for the lowest SCN recorded in the data file headers. (There are a number of complications here, such as offline events, read-only tablespaces, etc., but if you want the complete breakdown of how recovery works, there are entire books written on just that one topic, and they get updated for every version of Oracle.) Each redo log file holds in its header the lowest SCN it has recorded. This means that Oracle can immediately identify which log file is the earliest one it needs to start scanning. But it's more precise than that because the control file also holds the last incremental SCN and RBA, so (provided it doesn't contradict the decision from the data file headers and redo log file headers) Oracle can go the most precise place possible to start reapplying the redo.

But there is a two-phase approach to applying redo. Oracle starts by scanning all the relevant redo looking for block written records. Since each block written record tells Oracle the last change SCN at which various blocks were written to disk, Oracle can build a list of each block that appears, capturing only the highest change SCN for the block that is known to be on disk. Then, on the second pass, Oracle can ignore the change vectors for any block on the list unless the SCN on the change vector is higher than the last change SCN recorded for the block, thus avoiding the cost of reading a block from disk that isn't going to need any change vectors applied until a later point in the recovery.

So the three mechanism work together to minimize the work done on recovery, but the real stroke of genius is this: *no special code is needed to apply the change vectors on recovery!* Compare run-time activity with recovery. At run-time we have code that creates redo vectors, puts them into the log buffer, and applies them to data blocks. On recovery we read redo change vectors from a file and apply them to data blocks. The only difference between recovery and run-time activity is the *source* of the change vectors—but what Oracle does with them is identical.

The final point of recovery often seems to cause confusion. People often ask the question "but what happens about transactions that weren't committed?" The simplest way to answer this question is to propose a thought experiment: imagine that instead of witnessing a system crash you simply shouted (very loudly) "Everyone stop working now!" On crash recovery, that's exactly the point you recover to (technically it's usually called the *roll-forward*)—every (logged) block in the database has been recovered perfectly, including the undo blocks and undo segment header blocks with their transaction tables; the database looks as if everyone has just stopped. So at this point if you want to emulate the last stage of recovery, you just tell everyone to issue a `rollback`. In a real recovery this is the point where the *smon* process (possibly assisted by, and sometimes hindered by, parallel execution slaves) takes over and rolls back any uncommitted transactions it finds in the transaction tables in the undo segment header blocks.

Media Recovery

So what's the difference between *instance* recovery and *media* recovery? Virtually nothing, provided you've been taking copies of your data files from time to time, and have been archiving the online redo log files (and if you're using *RMAN* Oracle makes it easy to do this, provided you've got enough storage space). The critical thing is that you need all the archived redo logs from the moment you started the data file backups. In principle you could take a backup of the database the moment after the `create database` statement had finished running and apply all the archived redo log files from that moment to bring a completely empty database up to the last committed transaction. This might take a long time, of course—and, depending on version, you would have to play around with adding nonexistent files. However, the principles and mechanisms are the same: if you can start with a valid block and a (archived) redo log that brackets the last change SCN of that block, you can just keep finding and applying redo change vectors until you've brought that block far enough forward in time. Everything else about recovery is just housekeeping and storage.

It's worth mentioning the archive processes (arc*N*), though, because they can do a lot of writing, and this chapter is about writing. Essentially the archive processes copy an online redo log to another location once the log switch is complete. Historically the other location was somewhere else on the same set of disk drives the database was using, and this is still a common implementation. The archive process or processes do their work very efficiently, using large reads and writes, but they are doing I/O, and sometimes people forget that that's just another I/O load on the system that might be part of a performance problem.

Occasionally an archive destination can get full, at which point the archiver has to stop, which means it's no longer copying the online redo logs, and lgwr won't overwrite an online redo log if you're archiving (i.e., in archivelog mode) and haven't managed to make a copy of that log; so a full archive destination (in fact, if you're unlucky, even an archive destination that slows down, such as an overloaded network) can stop your database temporarily. Once you start taking advantage of the more subtle things that redo allows you to do, you need to think more carefully about the volume of redo that's moving about and the rate at which it has to move.

Standby Databases

Of course, once you can do instance recovery you can do media recovery; and once you've done media recovery you realize you can recover the database to a different machine; and once you've recovered the database to a different machine while the original database is still running you realize you can keep two (or more) copies of the database going, one doing real-time processing, the other in permanent recovery mode. Suddenly you have a high-availability option because of redo—if your live system fails you run the last bit of redo log into the recovering copy, finish the recovery, and you're live again.

Then Oracle Corp. wrote the official wrapping to this technology and followed up with a few clever things that required internal access, so now you can fail the primary to the standby and back again almost invisibly. Then they did a really clever thing and (for a license fee) fiddled with the code so that you can apply redo to a recovering database and have it open for query at the same time. That's the point at which I start to worry, mainly because I tend to take a pessimistic view of software when it comes to complex software. As I pointed out, the truly brilliant thing about recovery is that the live code for applying redo is the same as the recovery code—but is that still true if you can now have the database open for query while applying redo? I can imagine a couple of reasons, relating to side effects of block cleanout, why it *might* not be, and if it isn't, then the most important piece of code in Oracle has changed in some very subtle ways and I'm worried that that might have introduced some very subtle bugs.

Another feature of standby databases that worries me a little is the idea of lgwr being responsible for the first stage in getting the redo transferred to a remote system in real time in the *maximum protection* mode for Data Guard. The implementation of how this works keeps changing, though, so we can hope that Oracle keeps finding and fixing any threats with the mechanism.

Flashback Database

Redo is about going forward, and Flashback Database is about going backward, so at first sight they don't seem to be related; but without redo and recovery, database flashback can't work. Flashback logging is also another source of high-volume I/O, which is another good reason for including it in this chapter.

If you enable database flashback, you start generating flashback log, and the flashback log is a remarkable echo of the before-image (BI) file of Oracle 5—it holds entire blocks. Roughly speaking, before changing a data block Oracle checks to see if it has written that block into the current flashback log file, and if it hasn't it copies it (by way of the flashback log buffer) before changing it. Contrary to popular opinion, the copy doesn't happen on every change, so the flashback log ends up holding a very sparse history of blocks as they used to be in the database, nothing that, of itself, could be used to reconstruct a self-consistent database. However, the flashback log contains enough information to re-create an approximation of an older version of the database, and once you've got that you can use the archived redo to recover (roll forward) from there to an exact copy of the version you want.

To show how flashback logging works, Figure 6-8 represents the evolution of a single block in the database. Over time it goes through ten different versions, and as it changes a few of those versions are copied into the flashback logs. The lower half of the diagram shows the blocks that have been captured and the labeling of the flashback log files they appear in. Note that each file is characterized by the SCN at which it was first written to.

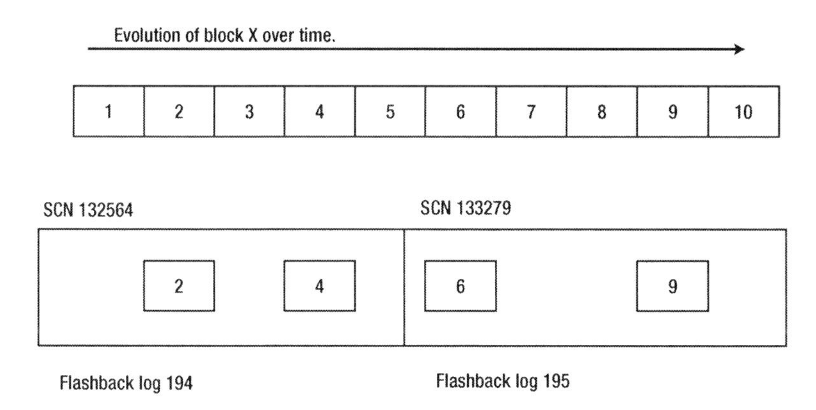

Figure 6-8. *Outline of flashback logging*

Imagine now that we flash back the database to SCN 132867, and assume that this is the SCN that should show the block at version 3, a version that was never captured in the flashback log. The flashback is a two-stage process: first we flash back to something that is approximately correct and that guarantees that no blocks are newer than they should be. Any block logged in file 195 will be a version with a last change SCN less than 133279—but it won't necessarily be a version with a last SCN that matches our target; any block logged in file 194 will be a version with a last change SCN less than 132564, so that's the file we need to aim at. So Oracle reads the list of flashback logs backward (starting from the newest), overwriting existing blocks with flashback log blocks only if the flashback log block shows a last change SCN less than the one we want to see.

When this pass is finished there will be no blocks in the reconstructed database that are newer than they should be. Unfortunately, there will be a lot of blocks that are older than they ought to be; our block, for example, will be version 2, though we were aiming to flash back to a point where version 3 was current. So we have a slightly smashed database. But that's not a problem if we have the archived redo log files. Oracle now starts to recover the database, starting from the archived *redo* log file that holds SCN 132564, stopping when it gets to the change that occurred at our target SCN—and then, as with any other recovery, it performs a rollback of any uncommitted transactions it finds in the transaction tables of the undo segment header blocks.

Side Effects

Apart from the I/O load introduced by the flashback log itself, you will also see an increase in I/O due to a change in the way the undo tablespace is handled when flashback logging is enabled. When Oracle wants to overwrite an undo block (other than a segment header) and increment its sequence number, it simply creates a new version of the block in memory (or, to use the jargon, it *news* it in memory), but if you have enabled flashback logging, the old version of the block will be read from disk and written to the flashback log—an event recorded under the statistic `physical reads for flashback new`. And if you have frequent housekeeping activities such as `create table` and `rebuild index`, you may find that on random occasions a task takes longer than usual and does a lot more I/O than usual because Oracle has decided that the space that an object is going into has to be copied into the flashback log before it can be reused.

Finally, although flashback logging avoids copying every before image every time you change a block, if your application does a lot of random access to update blocks (the sort of application where you may have defined a recycle cache to minimize damage to the rest of the cache), then you may find that some parts of your application really do end up copying a block into the flashback log for every update.

On the whole, you need a very good reason for running a production system with flashback logging enabled. Don't do it just in case it might be useful; do it only if you can justify bearing the overhead. On the other hand, if you can enable flashback on a physical standby, you can take it out of standby mode, do some work on it, flash it back to where it was before you started work, and put it back into standby mode. The opportunities offered by inventive use of the redo logs are wonderful.

Summary

Oracle uses a *write-ahead logging* strategy, which means a changed data block cannot be copied to a data file until the description of that change has been written to a log file.

With the exception of a hidden optimization in PL/SQL, and a documented commit option in 10*g*, transactions are made durable by the rule that the log buffer is written to disk when a transaction commits. The process that does the writing is the log writer (lgwr), and each time a session issues a commit it will post lgwr to write any outstanding log buffer to disk (if lgwr it not already writing), and then go into a wait state until lgwr sends a post to allow it to resume running.

Database blocks are copied to disk in a lazy fashion. There are two key strategies to the algorithm Oracle uses to select the next blocks to copy. One strategy is simply to copy the changed blocks that have been dirty for the longest time; the other is to copy dirty blocks that are on the point of being pushed out of the cache by the LRU/TCH algorithm.

The aging algorithm relies on a separate linked list (the *checkpoint* queue) running through the cache, and buffers being linked to the end of this list the first time they are made dirty. As sessions link buffers to one end of the list, dbwr can (effectively) unlink buffers from the other end and copy them to disk. To reduce contention between dbwr and the foreground sessions, there are two linked lists (in each working data set) so that foreground sessions can link buffers to one while dbwr is unlinking them from the other.

The LRU/TCH strategy requires a second pair of linked lists to complete the entire *LRU chain* in Oracle. In all there are four separate subchains: REPL_MAIN, REPL_AUX, WRITE_MAIN, and WRITE_AUX. The first pair is known as the *replacement list*, and the second is known as the *write list* (or LRU-W). When a session wants to find a free buffer, it scans the replacement list, starting with REPL_AUX, and transfers any dirty, unpinned buffers to WRITE_MAIN. One of dbwr's tasks when it wakes up (which it does every 3 seconds, or when posted by a foreground in a panic) is to check WRITE_MAIN for buffers that need to be copied to disk, which it does by first moving them to WRITE_AUX, copying them to disk, and then moving them to REPL_AUX—marking them as clean.

From time to time Oracle initiates a *media recovery checkpoint* to bring the database files up to date with the log files (although the log files continue gaining more redo, so the data files are already out of date the moment they've caught up to the point where the checkpoint was initiated). The trigger for this event, with some variation in implementation depending on version of Oracle, is when a log file is full and Oracle switches to the next log file. When the checkpoint is complete, all the data blocks changed by the redo in the filled log file will have been written to disk, which means that the log file is redundant. (Many systems, however, will have set up the archive processes, arc*N*, to copy log files to an archive location, or to a standby database, to keep them for some time for recovery purposes.)

Because of the write-ahead logging, the database can be stopped abruptly and recover any committed transactions on recovery thanks to Oracle's ability to bring the database up to date by applying the changes from the redo logs against an out-of-date copy of the database. Because of the constant trickle of writes from the checkpoint queue, the data files are kept nearly up to date in an efficient fashion, so if the instance does crash, it won't take much time for recovery to occur. Because of the media recovery checkpoints, we need only keep a (relatively) small number of online redo log files with the data file to ensure that the system can survive an instance crash; and if we take copies of the data files from time to time and keep archived log files, the media recovery checkpoints allow Oracle to use the minimum number of archived redo logs to take an old copy of the database, replay the archived redo, and move the copy forward in time to the most recent transaction commit point. Once you can deal with basic media recovery, all the other clever features relating to redo log files are just details around the edges.

CHAPTER 7

Parsing and Optimizing

Do You Come Here Often?

After spending time with the data cache in Chapters 5 and 6, we can come back to the code cache—more specifically the *library cache* although we'll also spend time looking at the *dictionary cache*. Both these caches are part of the *shared pool* (or SGA heap to give a more appropriate name) so, inevitably, we will have to look at some of the generic mechanisms that affect the shared pool at the same time.

Since the library cache is the place where your SQL (or PL/SQL) text ends up in a form that can be executed we're going to start our journey to the library cache at the point where an end-user program sends Oracle a piece of text and expects something to be done with it.

Once we've examined what Oracle does with a previously unseen piece of text, we'll examine the different ways in which we can re-execute a given piece of text, and see how, and understand why, Oracle's workload varies with the method we choose

Understanding SQL

Let's take a look at the process by which Oracle parses and optimizes SQL. Take the following simple SQL statement:

```
update
        t1
set
        small_no = small_no + 0.1
where
        id = 3
and     small_no = 1
;
```

How much work does Oracle have to do to understand what this statement means, and to work out the best way to run it? Strictly speaking, the first part of the question is about *parsing*, and the second is about *optimizing*; unfortunately many people tend to combine the two operations under the single title of "parsing."

Parsing

The first step, of course, is for Oracle to decide if the text looks like a valid SQL statement—this step is known as *syntactic* analysis; if it does look like a valid statement, Oracle then has to answer all sorts of questions about the statement, such as the following:

- What type of object is `t1`? A table, a view, a synonym, etc.
- Are `id` and `small_no` columns in object `t1`—(maybe `id` is a function returning a number)?
- Are there any constraints on column `small_no` that need checking on update?
- Are there any triggers on the object that might have to fire on update?
- Are there any indexes that have to be maintained as the object is updated?
- Does this user have the privileges to update the object?

This stage in the examination is the *semantic* analysis- the combination of syntactic and semantic analysis is what we mean by *parsing*.

Optimizing

After deciding that the statement is legal and that the user is allowed to run it Oracle then has to start *optimizing* it, an activity that requires answers to more questions, such as

- Are there any indexes on columns id or small_no (or both) that might help?
- What statistics are available for the columns, tables, and indexes?

After this the optimizer has to collect a few more numbers about the system (various parameter values—some dynamically variable—and system statistics) and start running a lot of complicated code to decide on an execution path. But we'll worry about that stage of the activity later on in the chapter. At present I want to stick with basic parsing.

To demonstrate the amount of work involved in parsing even a simple statement in 11g (11.2.0.2 in this case) I flushed the shared pool (for reasons that I will explain shortly) with a call to `alter system flush shared_pool;` enabled `sql_trace`, executed the query above, and ran *tkprof* against the resulting trace file. The closing section of the tkprof output file held the following summary information:

```
  1  session in tracefile.
  2  user  SQL statements in trace file.
 15  internal SQL statements in trace file.
 17  SQL statements in trace file.
 17  unique SQL statements in trace file.
737  lines in trace file.
  0  elapsed seconds in trace file.
```

There were two "user" SQL statements in the trace file—the first was the `alter session set sql_trace true;` that I had used to enable `sql_trace`, and the second was my update statement. However, there were also 15 *internal* SQL statements—statements run by Oracle to help it gather all the information it needed to understand (parse) and optimize my test statement; statements of this type are generally called *sys-recursive* statements. If you're thinking that 15 extra statements is a lot, bear in mind that you haven't seen the whole picture yet—the following are the activity statistics for those 15 statements:

```
OVERALL TOTALS FOR ALL RECURSIVE STATEMENTS
call     count       cpu    elapsed       disk      query    current        rows
------- ------  -------- ---------- ---------- ---------- ----------  ----------
Parse       15      0.01       0.00          0          0          0           0
Execute     99      0.06       0.05          0          0          0           0
Fetch      189      0.03       0.01          0        388          0         633
------- ------  -------- ---------- ---------- ---------- ----------  ----------
total      303      0.10       0.07          0        388          0         633

Misses in library cache during parse: 15
Misses in library cache during execute: 15
```

In the `Parse` line you can see the number of parse calls made to pass the 15 internal statements to the Oracle engine—but then the total number of `execute` calls across all those statements is 99, fetching a total of 633 rows of information in 189 `fetch` calls. The volume of work is surprising.

Actually this demonstration isn't a completely fair example of the workload involved, and I can highlight the bias I've introduced if I take advantage of another table I have in the same schema. The second table is called `t1a` and it is an exact copy of `t1`—right down to the definition of the primary key—and if I now run the same update statement substituting `t1a` as the table name I get the following results in the tkprof output file.

```
OVERALL TOTALS FOR ALL RECURSIVE STATEMENTS

call     count       cpu    elapsed       disk      query    current        rows
------- ------  -------- ---------- ---------- ---------- ----------  ----------
Parse       15      0.00       0.00          0          0          0           0
Execute     43      0.00       0.00          0          0          0           0
Fetch       51      0.00       0.00          0        135          0         526
------- ------  -------- ---------- ---------- ---------- ----------  ----------
total      109      0.00       0.00          0        135          0         526

Misses in library cache during parse: 0
```

Although the number of `parse` calls is the same, there's an interesting difference in the number of `execute` and `fetch` calls. There's also a significant difference in the number of `Misses in library cache`. This last detail, by itself, tells us a lot about the way Oracle tries to be efficient when handling SQL statements, and gives us some clues about the caching that goes on for the code we run—if we know how to interpret the output correctly.

Interpreting the tkprof Summaries

Before I ran the first statement, I flushed the shared pool. The reason for doing this was to ensure that any pre-existing versions of the statements were removed from the library cache along with privilege and dependency information for the objects, and all the object definitions had been removed from the dictionary cache.

When I tried to execute my first test statement Oracle had to query the database (or, to be specific, the set of tables known as the *data dictionary*) to find the definitions of all the objects referenced in the query—so in the trace file we end up with statements like the following:

```
select
        obj#, type#, ctime, mtime, stime, status,
        dataobj#, flags, oid$, spare1, spare2
from
        obj$
where
        owner#=:1
and     name=:2
and     namespace=:3
and     remoteowner is null
and     linkname is null
and     subname is null
;
```

This particular statement tries to check the existence of an object in a given namespace, with a certain name, belonging to a certain schema in the local database; other queries look at tables like **tab$** for table information, **col$** for column information, **ind$** for index information, **icol$** for index column information and so on. The reason I've picked this particular query as an example, though, is that it ran five times for the first test run, but only twice on the second test run.

In both tests the query ran twice to find some information about the table (t1 / t1a) and its primary key index (t1_pk / t1a_pk)—but in the first test it then ran a total of three more times to find information about a pair of indexes called **i_objauth2** and **i_objauth1** and a table called **trigger$**. Oracle needed to learn more about its internal tables and indexes so that it could work out how to run some of the recursive SQL it was using to find out more information about my tables and indexes. This explains why the work done for the first test was higher than the second test. The first test included a lot of "bootstrap" activity, while the second test took advantage of cached information from the first test.

When I say "cached," I don't mean data caching, though. In this case we're caching *metadata* (information about the data) and code—and that's what the dictionary cache and library cache respectively are for. The dictionary cache (also known as the *row cache*) holds information about objects—such as tables, indexes, columns, histograms, triggers, and so forth—the library cache holds information about statements (SQL and PL/SQL), their *cursors*, and lots of information about object dependencies and privileges.

CURSORS

The term *cursor* is one of the many vague and multi-valued terms that float around the Oracle world.

In end-user programs the term is often used to mean a result set—in fact it is little more than an index into an array that references the "executable" version of a statement as stored in the library cache, and links some local (end-user program) data with the remote (library cache) information.

Inside the Oracle instance the term has two (or even three) more commonly used interpretations. In its first meaning it is (transient) data—holding information about state, a subset of the results, etc.—stored in the session's process memory as the statement executes; in its second meaning it is the executable version of the SQL statement, stored publicly in the library cache.

The potential third interpretation arises because a single statement can end up with many different execution plans (together with details of their working environment) that are grouped together under a common place-holder in the library cache—as a consequence we tend to speak of a *parent cursor* (the place-holder) and its *child cursors* (the individual execution plans).

Note, particularly, that the *execution plan* is part of the child cursor information, and it is possible for different child cursors to end up holding identical execution plans. They are different child cursors for reasons relating to differences in environment, or name resolution—the fact that the execution plans they hold happen to be the same should just be treated as a coincidence.

The change in the number of executions in the second test run was a demonstration of Oracle taking advantage of the dictionary cache. There was no need to run any SQL to find information about the index `i_objauth1`, for example, because that information had already been read from the data dictionary and copied into the dictionary cache during the first test run.

Similarly, the change in the number of *library cache misses* in the second test run was a demonstration of Oracle taking advantage of the library cache. Take a look at the closing lines of the two summaries I have dumped. The first one reports as follows:

```
Misses in library cache during parse: 15
Misses in library cache during execute: 15
```

The second one reports as follows:

```
Misses in library cache during parse: 0
```

A *miss* in the library cache tells us that Oracle went to the library cache to check for an existing (legal and valid) child cursor, failed to find one, and had to optimize a statement before it could use it. On the first test all 15 of the recursive SQL statements had to be optimized on their first parse call. On the second test run none of the 15 statements had to be optimized, the appropriate cursors were available in the library cache. The first test is showing a miss on every parse *and* every execute. Missing on execution is possible, but in this case I think 11g is showing a bug (see following note) as a 10053 trace showed that it only optimized the statements once in the course of the test.

■ **Note** In the `tkprof` output, each statement reported should be followed by (up to) two lines stating the number of misses in the library cache during parse calls and execute calls. Between them these lines should tell you the total number of times the statement had to be optimized during the lifetime of the trace file. Unfortunately 11g seems to report a miss during execute immediately after the miss during parse—and I think (but obviously cannot prove) that this is a bug. In earlier versions of Oracle a quick check of the tkprof statistic `Misses in library cache during execute` was a useful way of spotting that optimized statements for held cursors were being lost because of demand for memory—in 11g I think you have to subtract the parse misses from the execute misses to get a true figure for the misses during execute.

We'll carry on using this example to take a closer look at the both the library cache and the dictionary cache, both in terms of structure and the way that Oracle uses them. We'll start with the dictionary cache.

The Dictionary Cache

The dictionary cache—also called the row cache because, effectively, it is used to cache individual rows of data from the data dictionary rather than data blocks—is the place where Oracle stores details of object definitions. We can view a summary of the content of this cache with a query against view v$rowcache. The results below come from an instance running 10g.

If you run the sample query against v$rowcache in 11g, you will see a couple of anomalies. One of the caches (cache# 11: dc_object_ids) has disappeared from v$rowcache, although it is still visible in v$rowcache_parent as cache# 11 but renamed to dc_objects; and cache# 7 has lost its parent entry, which seems to have migrated into cache# 10. Whether these are accidents or deliberate I don't know, but there are clear indications that at least some of the code to expose the dictionary cache structures has gone wrong in 11g (x$kqrpd, as a particular case, is a total mess—not that you're supposed to look at it anyway).

If you run the query against Oracle 9i you may find each item appearing multiple times—in the 9.2.0.8 instance I'm looking at currently there are eight rows for each combination of parameter, type, and subordinate#. This is affected by the (9.2.0.8 only) parameter _more_rowcache_latches, which defaults to true.

```
select
        cache#, parameter, type, subordinate#, count, usage, fixed, gets, getmisses
from
        v$rowcache
order by
        cache#, type, subordinate#
;

CACHE# PARAMETER              TYPE         SUB  COUNT  USAGE  FIXED    GETS GETMISSES
------ --------------------- ------------ ---- ------ ------ ------ ------- ---------
     0 dc_tablespaces         PARENT                8      8      0   62439        28
...
     7 dc_users               PARENT               10     10      0  157958        52
     7 dc_users               SUBORDINATE    0      0      0      0       0         0
     7 dc_users               SUBORDINATE    1      5      5      0    2600        31
     7 dc_users               SUBORDINATE    2      0      0      0       0         0
     8 dc_objects             PARENT              917    917     55   37716      3200
     8 dc_object_grants       SUBORDINATE    0     30     30      0    2079       196
     9 dc_qmc_cache_entries   PARENT                0      0      0       0         0
    10 dc_usernames           PARENT               11     11      0    4075        42
    11 dc_object_ids          PARENT             1225   1225     55  171218      2886
    12 dc_constraints         PARENT                1      1      0     362       131
...
```

This reports a list of lists. For example, we have a cache named dc_objects, which currently holds 917 items, all of which are currently valid; we have searched the list to find an item 37,716 times (gets) and failed to find that item 3,200 times (getmisses—that would require us to run the relevant recursive SQL statement to copy something from the data dictionary to the dictionary cache). The dc_objects cache also holds 55 fixed objects.

■ **Note** As we have seen Oracle may have to run some recursive SQL to find the information that tells it how to run your SQL. But how does it get started—surely it can't run *any* SQL until after it has run *some* SQL. The answer, as so often, is that Oracle cheats. There is some "bootstrap" code that knows the physical location of the first few objects in the database, and contains enough information to allow the optimizer to query them for further information. It is these bootstrap objects that appear as the fixed objects in `v$rowcache`.

If you want to know what the bootstrap objects are, read `$ORACLE_HOME/rdbms/admin/sql.bsq` up to the line holding "`//`". You can also see the SQL to recreate the bootstrap objects in the table `sys.bootstrap$` .At database creation time Oracle writes this information into the database and records the physical location of the start of `sys.bootstrap$` in the header block of the first file in the system and uses this back door into the database to read the table and learn about the base data dictionary at startup time. You can see this address if you dump the file header at level 3 (`oradebug dump file_hdrs 3`), and search for the entry `root dba`.

You'll notice that the rows reported fall into two groups—`Parent` and `Subordinate`. This relates to the way that Oracle will collate information in the cache—take `cache#` 8 as an example: it has a parent of `dc_objects` and a subordinate of `dc_object_grants`; this suggests that Oracle may be taking the (intuitively sensible) step of storing information about grants on `TableX` (say) together with the information about `TableX` itself.

As its name implies, this particular `cache#` holds the list of all objects currently known to the instance; roughly speaking it is a copy of all the rows from `dba_objects` (or, more specifically, the table `obj$`) that have been read by Oracle in its attempt to interpret SQL or PL/SQL statements. In fact, the list is somewhat longer than that because it will also record *non-existent* objects—a comment I can best explain by running the following SQL from my personal schema:

```
select count(*) from all_objects;
```

After I've run the query, there will be at least three items in the `dc_objects` cache named `all_objects`. One of them will be the definition of a *view* owned by *sys*, another will be a *synonym* owned by *public*, and the third will be a *non-existent* owned by my schema. This last item is an entry in the dictionary cache that doesn't exist in the data dictionary but allows Oracle to note that when I run a statement referencing (unqualified) *all_objects* it's not a statement about an object in my schema. In the absence of this entry in the dictionary cache Oracle would have to keep checking the data dictionary by running a query against `obj$` whenever I ran a query against (unqualified) *all_objects*. The presence of such objects of type non-existent in the cache is just a small argument in favor of making sure that your code uses fully qualified object names—but there are arguments against, and there are more important things you should do before you worry too much about this detail.

You can see a similar strategy in the data dictionary itself in the view *dba_dependencies* (and its subordinates) when you create objects that are dependent on public synonyms; for example, the following:

```
SQL> create or replace view my_objects as select * from user_objects;

View created

SQL> select
  2     referenced_owner, referenced_name, referenced_type
  3  from
  4     user_dependencies
  5  where
  6     name = 'MY_OBJECTS'
  7  ;

REFERENCED_OWNER   REFERENCED_NAME   REFERENCED_TYPE
------------------ ----------------- -----------------
PUBLIC             USER_OBJECTS      SYNONYM
TEST_USER          USER_OBJECTS      NON-EXISTENT
```

The correct interpretation of the view `my_objects` depends on the fact that my schema doesn't currently hold a real object called `user_objects`, so Oracle creates a real entry in the data dictionary to express this fact. If I now create a real object called `user_objects`, Oracle would delete the dependency on the non-existent one, hence recognizing that it has to invalidate the definition of the view `my_objects`.

So if Oracle is keeping a list of objects (and various other lists) in memory this raises two questions—how does Oracle maintain the list, and how does it search the list efficiently. The answers for the dictionary cache are the same as the answers we've already seen in Chapter 4 for the buffer cache, the library cache and enqueues. We have a collection of hash chain latches, hash chains and linked lists.

We can infer the presence of the hash buckets by switching our attention from the summary view (`v$rowcache`) to the two detail views of the row cache—`v$rowcache_parent` and `v$rowcache_subordinate`, both of which have a `hash` column showing values between zero and 65,535. To see the hash chain latches we need only query `v$latch_children` (in this case on an instance running 11.2.0.2), as follows:

```
SQL> select
  2     name, count(*)
  3  from
  4     V$latch_children
  5  where
  6     name like '%row%cache%'
  7  group by
  8     name
  9  ;

NAME                             COUNT(*)
------------------------------ ----------
row cache objects                      51
```

Having seen that we have multiple latches related to the dictionary cache we can go one step further. There are 51 latches, but a `count(*)` from `v$rowcache` (again on 11.2.0.2) reports 61 rows. If we check `x$qrst` (the X$ structure underlying `v$rowcache`), we find that it contains an interesting column, as follows:

```
SQL> desc x$kqrst
 Name                                    Null?    Type
 ----------------------------------------- -------- ----------------------------
...
 KQRSTCLN                                           NUMBER
...
```

This turns out to the *Child Latch Number* (*CLN*) for that part of the row cache, so we can write a simple query to associate each part of the row cache with its latch, and then do things like compare *dictionary cache* gets with *latch* gets, for example:

```
select
        dc.kqrstcid                                         cache#,
        dc.kqrsttxt                                         parameter,
        decode(dc.kqrsttyp,1,'PARENT','SUBORDINATE')        type,
        decode(dc.kqrsttyp,2,kqrstsno,null)                 subordinate#,
        dc.kqrstgrq                                         gets,
        dc.kqrstgmi                                         misses,
        dc.kqrstmrq                                         modifications,
        dc.kqrstmfl                                         flushes,
        dc.kqrstcln                                         child_no,
        la.gets,
        la.misses,
        la.immediate_gets
from
        x$kqrst                 dc,
        v$latch_children        la
where
        dc.inst_id = userenv('instance')
and     la.child# = dc.kqrstcln
and     la.name = 'row cache objects'
order by
        1,2,3,4
;
```

To my surprise (and I can't explain this to my satisfaction, yet) there was a common pattern indicating three latch gets for each dictionary cache get. I was expecting two, rather than three, and still have to spend some time thinking about why the third one appears.

The Structure

Having established that the dictionary cache is very similar in structure to the library cache and buffer cache, it's worth drawing a picture of one row from **v$rowcache** and the associated items from **v$rowcache_parent** and **v$rowcache_subordinate**, as shown in Figure 7-1.

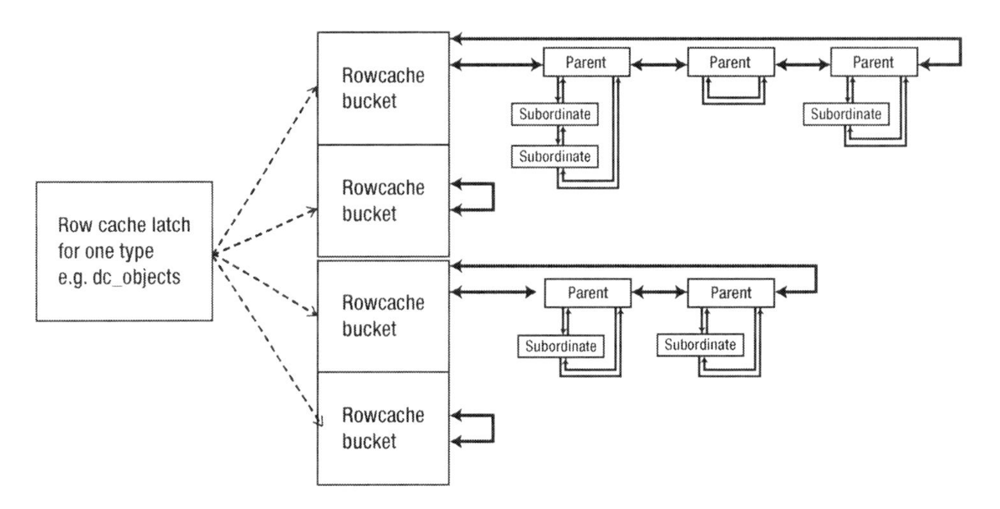

Figure 7-1. *A subset of the dictionary cache*

There are several assumptions built into this picture.

- I've assumed that each latch covers one parent type and all its subordinate types, and linked them together. On the other hand the structures `x$kqrpd` and `x$kqrsd` may be the *rowcache hash buckets* for the parent and subordinate types respectively and the existence of these structures suggest that parents and subordinates have been kept apart even though each set of parent and subordinate caches is covered by a single latch.

- I've assumed (though it's not obvious from the figure) that every latch covers 65,536 buckets so that any bucket is likely to hold only a small number of items. It's possible there's another layer between the hash value and the hash bucket that reduces the number of buckets per latch. We know, for example, that there are things called *row cache enqueues* (and/or *locks*)—so there may be an intermediate level before the individual hash buckets at which the latches operate.

- I've assumed that there are doubly linked lists between parent items in a bucket, and between a parent item and the subordinate items for that parent. Although `x$kqrpd` and `x$kqrsd` look as if they might represent the hash buckets, they expose nothing but counts and sizes—however their record lengths (as derived from the `addr` column of each object) are too long for the exposed information and, by using `oradebug peek` (see appendix) to dump the full record length, we can see lots of things that look like pointers in the hidden areas of the record.

Although I've suggested that each dictionary cache hash bucket is likely to hold only a very small number of items, it's worth pausing briefly to consider histograms. When we collect *column statistics* we have the option for collecting a histogram of up to 254 buckets (each of which could hold a 32 byte `endpoint_actual_value` among other things). Histogram data (`dc_histogram_data`) is subordinate to histogram definitions (`dc_histogram_defs`) though, so we might worry that a single dictionary cache hash bucket holding the data about a histogram might need to hold 254 items—in fact I think Oracle constructs a single (possibly large) item from the histogram data before transferring it to the dictionary cache—nevertheless histograms in the dictionary cache could use quite a lot of memory.

If you want to see the impact the dictionary cache has on memory you can run the following query against `v$sgastat`:

```
SQL> select * from V$sgastat where name like '%KQR%' order by name;

POOL         NAME                            BYTES
------------ -------------------------- ----------
shared pool  KQR ENQ                         82080
shared pool  KQR L SO                        65540
shared pool  KQR M PO                      1874488
shared pool  KQR M SO                       455312
shared pool  KQR S PO                       147288
shared pool  KQR S SO                        19456
shared pool  KQR X PO                         8016
```

I think we can probably decode the name as follows:

- KQR relates to the rowcache
- ENQ is presumably for row cache enqueues
- X / L / M / S for extra large / large / medium / small
- PO / SO for parent object / subordinate object

If you've ever seen your session crash with the error message `>>> WAITED TOO LONG FOR A ROW CACHE ENQUEUE LOCK! <<<` you'll appreciate that KQR ENQ is probably about rowcache enqueues; but apart from a couple of wait events (e.g. `row cache lock`) there is very little visibility to *row cache enqueues*. In fact, the sample output above came from an instance of 10.2.0.3 but when I ran the same query against an instance of 11.2.0.2 there was no entry for `KQR ENQ`—this may mean that Oracle has changed the code handling the dictionary cache, it may simply mean that the memory used for row cache enqueues has acquired a new label.

If we want more information about the memory allocation we could query `x$kqrpd` and `x$kqrsd`—the former will produce results like the following (curtailed) list:

```
SQL> select * from x$kqrpd where kqrpdnmk != 0;

ADDR           INDX    INST_ID   KQRPDCID   KQRPDOSZ   KQRPDNMK   KQRPDTSZ
-------- ---------- ---------- ---------- ---------- ---------- ----------
1FE45394          0          1          0        260          7       3584
1FE45474          2          1          2        208        406     103936
1FE454E4          3          1          3        216         68      17408
1FE456A4          7          1          7        284          9       4608
1FE45714          8          1          8        432        510     261120
1FE457F4         10          1         10        176          4       1024
...
```

Checking this against `v$rowcache`, we can see that `x$kqrpd.kqrpdnmk` corresponds to the `v$rowcache.count`; a quick check confirms that `kqrpdtsz` is `kqrpdnmk` times "`kqrpdosz` rounded up to one of 256 (S), 512 (M) or 1,024(L)" (with the exception of the largest (X) values for `kqrpdosz` that may simply be increased by 8 (or 16 in 64-bit Oracle)). Summing `kqrpdtsz` according to these rounding rules results in numbers that are close (but not perfect) matches for the stats from `v$sgastat`—and we'll explain the difference when we address memory allocation from the shared pool later on in the chapter. Notice, however, that this rounding means Oracle is prepared to waste memory in order to reduce the risk of memory fragmentation in the shared pool as dictionary cache entries are allocated and de-allocated. Strangely, if you do a heapdump (level 2 will be sufficient—but don't do it on a production system) of the SGA heap (shared pool) you will find the memory allocations in the heap are usually 28 bytes larger than the values listed earlier, viz: 284, 540, and 1,052.

Dictionary Cache Activity

Having seen the structure of the dictionary cache and its similarity to some aspects of the buffer cache, library cache and enqueue structures you won't be surprised to hear that the way in which Oracle uses the dictionary cache is fairly similar.

To find an item in the dictionary cache we have to protect the hash chains from being modified while we search them (and vice versa, to modify a chain we have to stop other sessions from reading it). Since the dictionary cache is broken into discrete sections based on the type of object, Oracle can easily work out the correct latch for that object type; but from this point onwards I have to start waving my hands about the strategies involved.

I can see that a dictionary cache get involves three latch gets—but I can't work out a strategy that makes this necessary and sufficient. It's possible, *for example*, that there is one more structure between the latch and the final hash bucket (after all, 65,536 buckets per latch does seem like a lot), forcing us to do two latch gets to pin and unpin that structure in shared mode and one more latch get while we read the hash bucket itself.

Whatever the specific order of events on reading (or modifying) the dictionary cache, the bottom line on the activity is that it's based on the same pattern of hash buckets and hash chains as so much of Oracle is—and chains have to be protected from read/write collisions.

We can see the effect this has with a simple example (see core_dc_activity_01.sql in the code library at www.apress.com) that involves running a large number of very similar statements through a simple PL/SQL loop and watching the dictionary cache activity, along with the related latch activity. The core of the test looks like the following:

```
execute snap_rowcache.start_snap
execute snap_latch_child.start_snap('row cache objects')

declare
        m_n     number;
        m_v     varchar2(10);
begin
        for i in 1..1000 loop
                execute immediate
                        'select n1 from t1 where id = ' || i
                        into m_n;
        end loop;
end;
/

execute snap_latch_child.end_snap('row cache objects')
execute snap_rowcache.end_snap
```

The two snap_xxx procedures take snapshots of v$latch_children and v$rowcache and report the change caused by the PL/SQL. The PL/SQL constructs 1,000 slightly different queries by concatenating a value to the end of a template, and the resulting query accesses one row in the table by primary key index. The following results come from 10.2.0.3 (the script in the code library includes the results from 11.2.0.2, which show some interesting differences):

```
----------------
Dictionary Cache
----------------
Parameter                 Usage Fixed    Gets  Misses
---------                 ----- -----    ----  ------
dc_segments                   0     0   2,000       0
dc_tablespaces                0     0       2       0
dc_users                      0     0   1,014       0
dc_objects                    0     0   1,000       0
dc_global_oids                0     0      12       0
dc_object_ids                 0     0   3,012       0
dc_histogram_defs             0     0   2,000       0

-----------------------------
row cache objects latch waits
-----------------------------
Address                      Gets      Misses
-------                      ----      ------
1FE4846C                    6,000           0
1FEC84D4                        3           0
1FEC910C                    3,021           0
1FF495DC                    3,000           0
1FFC9644                       18           0
1FFCAF14                    9,018           0
1F8B4E48                    6,000           0
Latches reported: 7
```

As you can see, allowing for tiny variations, the pattern of activity reflects the link between each part of the dictionary cache and the associated latch and each get on the dictionary cache results in three gets on the corresponding latch.

We have accessed `dc_segments` twice per query because we accessed the table and its index. We have accessed `dc_users` once per query—possibly for reasons of authentication. We have accessed `dc_objects` and `dc_object_ids` a total of 4,000 times—with a 1,000 / 3,000 split rather than the 2,000 / 2,000 you might expect for the table and its index; there is an anomaly with this that disappears in 11g when the `dc_object_ids` cache merges into the `dc_objects` cache. Finally we have accessed `dc_histogram_defs` 2,000 times—once for each query for each column referenced in the query; if we had selected two columns and used two columns in the predicate there would have been 4,000 gets from the dictionary cache. (If you needed an argument why you should select only the columns you need in a query, rather than using `select *`, the extra cost of accessing `dc_histogram_defs` should be enough to convince you.)

You can appreciate that a busy system generating a lot of lightweight SQL statements will cause a lot of latch activity on the row cache objects latches—particular the ones related to the column definitions—and could easily run into latch contention issues. This is (in part) why you will see so much fuss made about using bind variables for OLTP systems rather than constructing SQL by building values into literal strings.

Modify the test (see `core_dc_activity_02.sql`) to use a slightly different approach and the results change dramatically, as shown by the following—which lists the fragment of code that had to change and the resulting dictionary cache stats:

```
                execute immediate
                        'select n1 from t1 where id = :n'
                        into m_n using i;

---------------------------------
Dictionary Cache
---------------------------------
Parameter                  Usage Fixed    Gets  Misses
---------                  ----- -----    ----  ------
dc_segments                    0     0       2       0
dc_tablespaces                 0     0       2       0
dc_users                       0     0      15       0
dc_objects                     0     0       1       0
dc_global_oids                 0     0      12       0
dc_object_ids                  0     0      15       0
dc_histogram_defs              0     0       2       0
```

The number of gets (and the associated latch activity) has virtually disappeared; so much so that the "random noise" effects from background database activity could actually appear as a noticeable distraction on the complete result set. We have changed the text of the SQL statement so that it remains constant; but we have included a placeholder (`:n`)—which we typically refer to as a *bind variable*—in the text and added a `using` clause to the code so that each call to execute the text can pass in a different value with the text.

CURSOR_SHARING

Historically, many applications used to take the easy coding option of constructing SQL statements by concatenating user inputs with template statements. Because of the contention problems this caused—and we shall see more problems when we look at the library cache—Oracle introduced the `cursor_sharing` parameter in 8i and enhanced its use in 9i.

The parameter could be set to `exact` (the default), `force`, or (in 9i) `similar`. If the parameter were set to `force` the optimizer would copy the literals from an SQL statement to private memory and replace them with system-generated bind variables with names like `:"SYS_B_99"` before optimizing the statement. This would have the effect of making the 1,000 different statements in my first test look the same, and give me the performance of the bind variable version of the code. (In passing, this also means I'm not filling my shared pool with lots of little bits of text that aren't going to be used again, and are just waiting to be dumped from memory the next time there's a shortage of free memory.)

If the parameter were set to `similar` the same copy and edit would take place—but the optimizer might still re-optimize the statement if (according to a couple of rules) different values might require a different execution plan. The rules were as follows: if there is a range-based predicate, if there is a predicate on a column with a histogram, or if there is a predicate on a column that is a partition key of a partitioned table.

The combination of histograms and the `similar` option often resulted in sites running into contention problems that we will examine further in the section on the library cache, so that option has been deprecated in 11g with the arrival of *adaptive cursor sharing*, and people are now advised to use only `exact` or `force`.

To understand why bind variables have such an impact on the dictionary cache activity we need to know more about the difference between *parsing* and *parse calls*, and how the *library cache* works.

What Is a Parse Call?

There are two key concepts that need to be kept separate when we speak of parsing—one is the action of *parsing*, the other is a program subroutine called a *parse call*. It may come as a surprise, but

- a parse call may not happen in your code when you think it ought to
- a parse call does not necessarily result in any optimization taking place
- a parse call does not necessarily result in any parsing taking place
- parsing and optimization can occur on an execute call, not just on a parse call

If we go back to our simple loop program and check the session statistics for the two variants of the SQL statement we have constructed (see `core_dc_activitiy_03.sql` in the code library), we will see the following results about parse calls:

```
Name  (literal string test)           Value
----                                  -----
parse count (total)                   1,004
parse count (hard)                    1,001

Name  (bind variable test)            Value
----                                  -----
parse count (total)                       5
parse count (hard)                        2
```

`Parse count (total)` is a count of the number of parse calls made to the Oracle kernel; and the second set of results shows that your code doesn't always make a parse call when you might expect it to—the source code is only slight different from the literal string test, but the behavior is totally different. This is the effect of the *PL/SQL cursor cache* coming into play—the PL/SQL interpreter recognized that we were really re-executing a single statement inside a loop and used an internal mechanism to create a local *cursor variable* for our statement and held that cursor open—which means it didn't issue a *parse call* every time round the loop, it simply issued an *execute call* after the first pass through the loop. This was an optimization that didn't apply to the `execute immediate` mechanism until 10g, and if we run the test on Oracle 9i we can see the difference it has made to the statistics for the bind variable case, where we see a parse call on every cycle of the loop, as follows:

```
Name  (bind variable test 9i)         Value
---------------------------           -----
parse count (total)                   1,004
parse count (hard)                        2
```

`Parse count (hard)` is a count of the number of times Oracle optimized the statement, and in the first example—where every statement was different—Oracle had to optimize every single one of the 1,000 statements we sent it because it had never seen them before. As we saw earlier on in the chapter a "hard" parse will also show up as a `Miss in library cache during parse` in the tkprof output. (The difference of 3 between `total` and `hard` is a little bit of noise introduced by the test mechanism itself.)

But in the third example Oracle doesn't actually optimize the statement every time it arrives—it's possible to issue a parse call (`parse count(total)`) that Oracle can handle without optimizing (`parse count(hard)`) the statement—and that's where the *library cache* comes into the picture. The first time around the loop Oracle parses and optimizes the statement and loads it into the library cache; the second time around the loop Oracle searches the library cache for a match before starting the full work of parsing and optimizing the statement. If it finds the statement then it reuses it and your session doesn't have to pay the cost of optimizing it again—so doesn't need to record a hard parse.

■ **Note** The sequence of activity in parsing is a little more complicated than my original suggestion. When you pass a piece of text to Oracle it will do a syntax check to decide if it is legal, then it will search the library cache for a matching text (using a hash value computed from the text). If it finds a textual match Oracle starts the semantic check—checking to see if the new text actually means the same as the existing text (same objects, same privileges, etc.); this is known as *cursor authentication*. If everything matches, then the session need not optimize the statement again.

Cursor Caching

We haven't quite finished with the variation in the consequences of parse calls, though. To demonstrate this, the following is another version of the code loop (see `core_dc_activity_04.sql` in the code library) that uses explicit parse and execute calls from the `dbms_sql` package to make a point:

```
for i in 1..1000 loop

        m_cursor := dbms_sql.open_cursor;
        dbms_sql.parse(
                m_cursor,
                'select n1 from t1 where id = :n',
                dbms_sql.native
        );
        dbms_sql.define_column(m_cursor,1,m_n);

        dbms_sql.bind_variable(m_cursor, ':n', i);
        m_rows_processed := dbms_sql.execute(m_cursor);
```

```
            if dbms_sql.fetch_rows(m_cursor) > 0 then
                    dbms_sql.column_value(m_cursor, 1, m_n);
            end if;

            dbms_sql.close_cursor(m_cursor);

        end loop;
```

In this script I've captured the session statistics and the latch activity from `v$latch`, and I've run the above loop twice, making a critical change to the session environment between runs. On the second run I've reduced the parameter `session_cache_cursors` from its default value to zero with the command: `alter session set session_cache_cursors=0;` (the defaults are 20 in 10g and 50 in 11g). Tables 7-1 (session stats) and 7-2 (latch gets) show us the key consequences of this change.

■ **Note** These figures are from 10.2. The results are very different in 11g because of the way that Oracle now uses *mutexes* for the relevant operations.

Table 7-1. *Comparison of Session Stats for Different Session Cursor Cache Sizes*

Statistic Name	Session_cached_cursors Set to Default (50)	Session_cached_cursors = 0
Parse count (total)	1,064	1,077
Parse count (hard)	6	6
Session cursor cache hits	1,050	0

Table 7-2. *Comparison of Latch Gets for Different Session Cursor Cache Sizes*

Latch Name	Session_cached_cursors Set to Default (50)	Session_cached_cursors = 0
Library cache	6,393	10,549
Library cache lock	6.174	10.392

At first sight, the session statistics seem to tell us that the work we've done on parse calls is the same in both cases, and we note particularly that even though we've included 1,000 explicit parse calls (`dbms_sql.parse`) in our code the number of hard parses is tiny—which means we've only optimized a handful of different statements, so we must be re-using the statement that appears in our loop. However, there is a difference in the way we are accessing the cursor for that statement, and this changes the amount of work involved and the scope for contention.

By default we have the *session cursor cache* enabled, which means that if we call a statement often enough Oracle (10g) will attach a *KGL lock* to that statement's cursor to hold it open, and create a *state object* in our session memory that links to the cursor so that we have a short cut to the cursor and don't need to search the library cache for it every time we use it. You will often see comments that cursor caching occurs on the third call to the statement—this isn't quite correct; technically it's on the call after *cursor authentication*.

If you run a statement that has not previously been run, and then repeat the call a few times, you will see the statistic `cursor authentications` increment on the second call, and the statistics `session cursor cache hits` and `session cursor cache count` increment on the fourth call—the sequence of events is as follows:

1. Optimize on first call
2. Authenticate on second call
3. Cache *after* third call completes
4. Use cache thereafter

This sequence of events is consistent with the commonly held view that you have to run a statement three times to cache it. However, if someone else has *already* run the statement, your first call to run the statement will be an *authentication* against an existing cursor, so the statement will go into your session cursor cache after the *second* call. It is the existence of the session cursor cache that means a parse call may result in no parsing at all.

One of the surprising things about the session cursor cache is the default size—it's really rather small. There are probably a number of sites that could benefit from increasing the `session_cache_cursor` parameter, and it's probably appropriate to do so if they keep seeing the statistic `session cursor cache hits` much smaller than the difference between `parse count (total)` and `parse count (hard)`.

There is a great deal of overlap between the session cursor cache and the PL/SQL cache—in fact, since 9.2.0.5 the sizes of the two caches have both been set by the parameter `session_cached_cursors` (prior to that, the size of the PL/SQL cursor cache was set to match the value of parameter `open_cursors`). You might even ask, if you go back to the results of my second test loop (`core_dc_activity_02.sql`) how could I tell whether the SQL statement was being held in the PL/SQL cursor cache or the session cursor cache—the answer is that the number of `session cursor cache hits` for that test was zero, so the cursor must have been held in the PL/SQL cursor cache.

Note There is an important difference between the PL/SQL cursor cache and the session cursor cache that becomes visible only in 11g with the advent of *adaptive cursor sharing*. If you run a query that is currently held in the *session cursor cache* it will be subject to adaptive cursor sharing so it could be re-optimized; if it's held in the *PL/SQL cursor cache* it will bypass adaptive cursor sharing completely.

Holding Cursors

There is one more demonstration I can squeeze out of my test script, and that's the effect of holding cursors. The Oracle pre-compilers allow you to generate code that holds cursors without having to do any special coding, simply by using a precompiler directive; but sometimes you have to code explicitly for held cursors. If you look at the code in the loop for `core_dc_activity_04.sql` you'll notice that it has calls to open and close cursors inside the loop. This really isn't necessary. If I know that I'm going to be reusing a statement fairly frequently I can declare a cursor variable with a much wider scope, and keep the cursor open for as long as I like; then all I have to do is re-execute the cursor whenever I want. The following is the modified code (see core_dc_activity_05.sql in the code library) to demonstrate this:

```
begin
        m_cursor := dbms_sql.open_cursor;
        dbms_sql.parse(
                m_cursor,
                'select n1 from t1 where id = :n',
                dbms_sql.native
        );
        dbms_sql.define_column(m_cursor,1,m_n);

        for i in 1..1000 loop

                dbms_sql.bind_variable(m_cursor, ':n', i);
                m_rows_processed := dbms_sql.execute(m_cursor);

                if dbms_sql.fetch_rows(m_cursor) > 0 then
                        dbms_sql.column_value(m_cursor, 1, m_n);
                end if;

        end loop;

        dbms_sql.close_cursor(m_cursor);
end;
```

Running this code, the number of latch gets on the various library cache latches (in 10g) is in the hundreds, rather than the thousands we saw in the test where the open and close were inside the loop. As far as efficiency is concerned for high-frequency, commonly used, lightweight SQL statements, this strategy is the most cost-effective, and causes least risk of contention.

You do have to be a bit careful with this code strategy, though. I have come across two key errors where people have used it incorrectly—both, as it happens, only in Java environments. The first error appears when people do in Java the equivalent of my PL/SQL code with the open and close inside the loop—they adopt the strategy, but they have a class that opens and closes the cursor, but only executes the statement once; this is a large overhead with no offsetting benefits if you don't execute the statement frequently before closing the cursor. (I believe the latest JDBC drivers can circumvent this issue by keeping the cursor open in a library code layer below the program code—in much the same way that the Oracle session uses the session cursor cache.)

The second error is to forget to close the cursor—possibly in an exception handler rather than in the program body— and then discard the class. As far as the Java program (or programmer) is concerned the cursor must be closed; as far as Oracle is concerned the session still has the cursor open, and the library cache cursor won't close until the session ends. When this happens the program usually ends up crashing with Oracle error `ORA-01000: maximum open cursors exceeded`.

A few pages back I pointed out in a list of "surprises" that parsing and optimization can occur on an execute call, this is a side effect of holding cursors whether through explicit coding or because of the hidden PL/SQL optimizations. When you hold a cursor the user code is only handling a simple numeric variable—but internally this identifies various structures that, eventually, lead to a child cursor and its parent cursor in the library cache. If there is a demand from other sessions for free memory Oracle is allowed to clear almost everything about that child cursor from memory—even when it's a held cursor—leaving only enough information for your session to be able to recreate the execution plan. When this happens, the next time you execute the statement you will record a `Miss in library cache during execute` and increment the `parse count (hard)` value even though you *won't* increment the `parse count (total)` value. Counter-intuitively, it is possible to get see a value of `parse count (hard)` that is higher than the `parse count (total)`.

To get a better idea of why, and how, cursor content can be flushed out of the library cache (even when held), it's time to switch our attention to the library cache and the shared pool that it belongs to.

The Library Cache

If you look back to Chapter 5, Figure 5-6, the picture of a very small buffer cache with just four *cache buffers chains latches*, and compare it with Chapter 4, Figure 4-3, the second approximation to a picture of the library cache, you will see that there is some similarity between the two. The text associated with those figures points out that the number of *library cache hash buckets* per latch is amazingly high (thousands, if not tens of thousands), while the number of *cache buffers chains* per latch is relatively low (typically in the range 32–128). The problems of finding, filling, reading and emptying data buffers are the same as the problems of handling the library cache (and the other components that sit in the shared pool)—so it's not surprising that some of the solutions look remarkably similar.

The cache buffers chains and library cache chains serve essentially the same purpose—they allow Oracle to find the place where a particular item ought to be very quickly; but what about the issue of finding available memory when you want to load a new item into the cache? The buffer cache has the cache buffers LRU chains and the REPL_AUX list to deal with the problems of freeing and re-using the most appropriate areas of memory in an efficient fashion—is there a similar mechanism for the library cache? The answer is yes, but to see it you have to look above the library cache to the *shared pool* that holds it. The shared pool—under the protection of the shared pool latch—deals with keeping track of free memory, acquiring memory when free memory is in short supply, and supplying free memory to any of the areas that need it.

Provided we don't try and push the analogy too far, it's possible to draw a pair of pictures that highlight the similarity—and some of the differences—between the shared pool and the buffer cache. Figure 7-2 is such a picture.

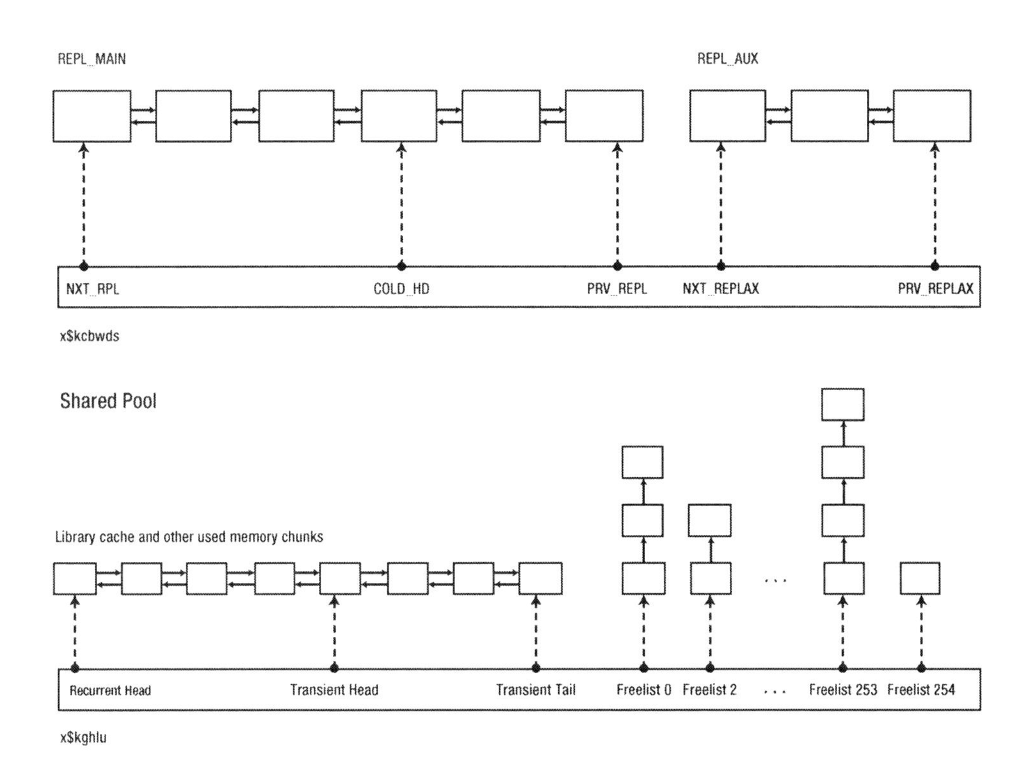

Figure 7-2. *Simple schematic comparing buffer cache and shared pool*

The top half of Figure 7-2 is a copy of the central LRU list in the buffer cache, showing just the REPL_MAIN and REPL_AUX linked lists of buffers. Broadly speaking *repl_main* is the set of buffers currently of interest, and *repl_aux*, whilst it isn't a collection of *empty* buffers, is the set of buffers that we are most likely to be happy to re-use when we want to read a block from disc or create a CR clone.

The bottom half of Figure 7-2 is a simplified image of the shared pool, showing the LRU list (holding such things as the library cache and dictionary cache) and the memory *free lists*. I have omitted the *reserved free lists* (that identify chunks of free memory in the parts of the shared pool known as the reserved pool—as specified by the parameter `shared_pool_reserved_size` and hidden parameter `_shared_pool_reserved_pct`). I have drawn the picture in a way that emphasizes the similarities.

- The buffer cache is split into *working data sets*—and the picture shows one working data set. In the same way the shared pool can be split into multiple non-overlapping *sub heaps*—though this feature was a bit buggy in 9i, and often had to be disabled by setting a hidden parameter—and this will happen automatically if your memory allocation is large enough (and the limit keeps increasing with version of Oracle) and the number of CPUs high enough.
- Each working data set is defined in a row from `x$kcbwds`—each sub heap is defined in a row from `x$kghlu`.
- The buffer cache is split into the MAIN (definitely used) and AUX (nearly free) lists, the shared pool is split into the LRU list and the free lists (that really are holding free memory).
- The buffer cache (MAIN) has an LRU (least recently used) list running through it, and uses a midpoint insertion algorithm to accept new items. The shared pool has an LRU list running through it, and an insertion point that splits the list into *recurrent* and *transient* parts. We'll be taking a closer look at that in a little while.
- Although it's not visible in the diagram the buffer cache (for the default block size) can be split into three areas—*keep*, *recycle*, and *default*. From 11g (and available through a hidden parameter in 10g) the shared pool is split into four separate sections for content of different "durations." In effect both mechanisms allow some isolation of different patterns of usage. In the case of the buffer cache it's controlled (sometimes successfully) by the DBA, in the case of the shared pool it's an internal mechanism—which we will be looking at in a little while.

Then there are the differences. Most significantly the buffer cache (or any one working data set) consists of chunks of memory that are all the same size—the block size defined for that part of the cache. This reduces the complexity of handling free memory—if you need a chunk of memory it will be the same size as any other chunk, you kick out a copy of one block and load in a copy of another block. Conversely the things that go into the shared pool can be all sorts of different sizes, and it's not just the library cache that makes demands on the shared pool (see Figure 7-3), so finding a piece of memory of the right size is much harder—and this explains why there are so many different free lists, and a reserved area, in the shared pool. So let's take a look at the structure of the shared pool, its reserved area, and the free lists.

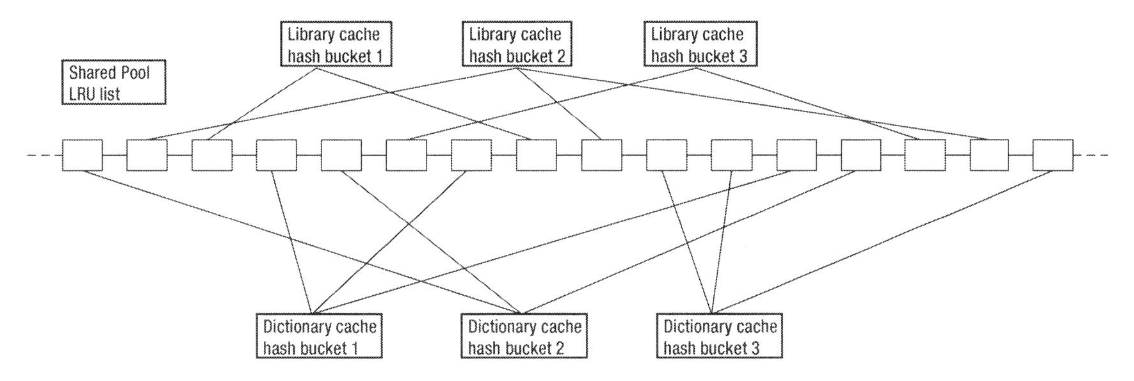

Figure 7-3. *One shared pool LRU list, many functions*

Shared Pool Structures

As a starting point the shared pool is made up of a number of *granules*, in exactly the same way that the buffer pool uses granules. It is this granularity that allows the automatic memory management mechanisms to move memory between the different parts of the SGA. The shared pool may then be split into sub-pools if you have a large enough SGA, and each sub-pool consists of a number of non-overlapping granules (which will be labeled as extents in the heap dump). If you are running 11g each sub-pool may also be split into four "sub-sub-pools" known as *durations*, and again each sub-sub-pool is a set of non-overlapping granules.

We can see this two-stage breakdown by doing a heap dump at level 2 (`oradebug dump heapdump 2`—the file is likely to be quite large, take a long time to dump, and you shouldn't do it on a production system) and extracting all lines with the text "sga heap" in them. The following is a sample output from a system with three sub-pools, showing the four durations. (I don't know why Oracle starts from 1 to count sub-pools and from zero to count durations.)

```
HEAP DUMP heap name="sga heap"  desc=072CA0E8
HEAP DUMP heap name="sga heap(1,0)"  desc=0AF66884
HEAP DUMP heap name="sga heap(1,1)"  desc=0AF674BC
HEAP DUMP heap name="sga heap(1,2)"  desc=0AF680F4
HEAP DUMP heap name="sga heap(1,3)"  desc=0AF68D2C
HEAP DUMP heap name="sga heap(2,0)"  desc=0AF6BDC4
HEAP DUMP heap name="sga heap(2,1)"  desc=0AF6C9FC
HEAP DUMP heap name="sga heap(2,2)"  desc=0AF6D634
HEAP DUMP heap name="sga heap(2,3)"  desc=0AF6E26C
HEAP DUMP heap name="sga heap(3,0)"  desc=0AF71304
HEAP DUMP heap name="sga heap(3,1)"  desc=0AF71F3C
HEAP DUMP heap name="sga heap(3,2)"  desc=0AF72B74
HEAP DUMP heap name="sga heap(3,3)"  desc=0AF737AC
```

If we simultaneously search the file for lines containing the text "EXTENT," we will be able to see how many granules have been allocated to each sub-pool—and Figure 7-4 is a picture of the result I got for the trace file that gave me the previous list of sub-sub-pools.

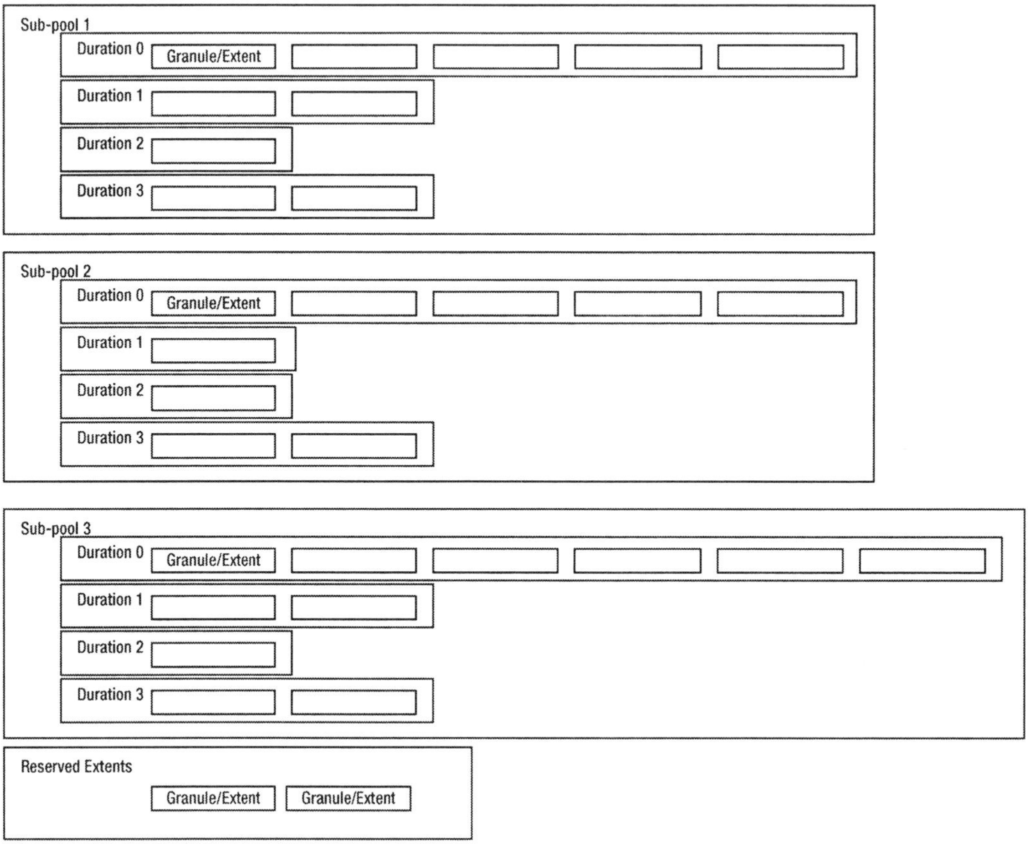

Figure 7-4. *Shared pool with sub-pools, durations, and reserved granules*

As you can see, the sub-pools can be different sizes from each other, as can the sub-sub-pools, although (and this may be a coincidence) the "duration 0" sub-sub-pools all seem to start out as significantly larger than the other durations. You will also note that I have some granules (or extents) still available for use but not yet allocated to any sub-sub-pool—the database has just started up, and Oracle has distributed enough extents to meet my starting requirements and will dynamically allocate the rest as time passes.

■ **Note** When an Oracle instance starts up it doesn't build the entire shared pool immediately—it prepares a few extents to get started, and then gradually adds more to the list. If you do a heap dump immediately after startup you will probably find the amount of memory reported in the dump is much less than you would expect. It's not until 11.2 that the heapdump will actually tell you that some extents are "reserved." It's only as the workload increases and memory gets allocated that the remaining extents will be brought into use.

The reason for splitting the shared pool is twofold. First, by introducing sub-pools (a feature that first appeared in 9i) we now have multiple shared pool latches active—one for each sub-pool. In early versions of the code, though, there was a side effect to this split—when allocating a memory chunk, a process will request memory from just one sub-pool, and it was possible for that process to find that there wasn't enough contiguous free memory in the sub-pool of its choice; this could result in a process raising error `ORA-04031: unable to allocate %n bytes of memory(%s, %s, %s, %s)` when there were suitable chunks of memory in the other sub-pools.

Ironically, the second reason for introducing sub-pools was to combat ORA-04031. To a great extent, `ORA-04031` is a side effect of memory fragmentation—it's possible to have lots of free memory in the shared pool, but find that it's all in little chunks that can't be coalesced to form a large enough contiguous free chunk. Unfortunately the work that Oracle does requires lots of variation in the size of memory chunks, and can result in lots of requests to acquire and free different sized chunks at different times, leading to a state where you could have literally tens of thousands of chunks of memory, none of which is larger than a couple of hundred bytes. If you want a single contiguous chunk of 4 KB, then there's no benefit in having 100 MB of free memory if the largest piece is only 280 bytes. Over time this problem led to three damage limitation strategies, of which the most recent is the sub-sub-pool (or duration) strategy. In order of appearance the strategies are as follows:

- *Reserved pool*: At database startup, Oracle isolates a chunk from each extent in the shared pool and labels it as "R-free" (reserved free). To protect it from accidentally being coalesced into adjacent free space Oracle also allocates two 24-byte chunks either side of it and labels them as "reserved stopper." These chunks make up the shared pool reserve, defined by two parameters: `_shared_pool_reserved_pct`, which defaults to 5 percent and the derived `shared_pool_reserved_size`). When a process needs a "large" chunk of memory (as defined by the hidden parameter `_shared_pool_reserved_min_alloc`, default 4,400 bytes), it first checks the rest of the free space, then calls back to the reserve. If there isn't a large enough chunk in the reserve, the process moves to the LRU list and starts kicking objects out of memory. (We will be examining this process quite soon.)

- *Standardization*: As we saw when looking at the dictionary cache, Oracle tries to allocate three basic sizes of memory chunks for dictionary cache data, even though there are many different sizes for the different types of cache entry. By "wasting" memory in this way Oracle hopes to increase the chances that chunks will be more readily re-usable and therefore lead to fewer cases of very small chunks being split off a chunk of free space that is just a little larger than needed. At the opposite end of the scale, Oracle also re-engineered much of the code that used to demand large chunks of memory so that the demand could be presented as a request for a collection of smaller, standard sized, chunks; 1,072 bytes and 4,096 bytes are very popular sizes.
- *Duration*: Different tasks require different sizes of allocation and patterns of usage. By splitting the shared pool by function we can isolate tasks that cause fragmentation from tasks that have a high probability of re-using a recently freed chunk of memory. If we take a close look at a heap dump we will see that the data for the memory for the dictionary cache (usually 284, 540, or 1,052 bytes) all comes from duration 1; we will see that the cursor "Heap 0" data (typically one 4 KB allocation per cursor) is in duration 2; and the cursor "SQLArea" allocations—the executable part—is in duration 3, again 4 KB allocations but potentially many more allocated at once for a single cursor, and less stable since they are liable to be flushed from memory more rapidly that the Heap 0 allocations.

Ignoring any other strategies for dealing with conflicting memory requirements for different functions, the shared pool mechanism for handling free memory is also completely different from the mechanisms in the buffer cache. Of course, unless you run the command `alter system flush buffer_cache`, or truncate, shrink or drop some objects, you don't really see empty buffers very often in the buffer cache, so it's a slight stretch of the imagination to equate the auxiliary list used by the buffer cache with free lists used by the shared pool. If you're prepared to accept the analogy, however, you can then recognize the most significant difference between the two, namely that the shared pool has to do something clever to supply the "best" chunk of memory as quickly as possible in response to a request. In the buffer cache, the response to a request is simply "kick a block out of a buffer at the end of the auxiliary list, and there's a buffer that will do for you." In the shared pool, the problem is "how do I find a piece of contiguous memory that's just the right size—if one exists at all—and how do I create one if I can't find one." So, let's take a closer look at the structure of the shared pool to see how this is done efficiently.

The Fine Structure of the Shared Pool

To understand what goes on in the shared pool, we're going to start by stepping through various fragments of the SGA heapdump, starting with the extent dump, then the free lists, then the LRU list(s). Once we've done this we will be in a position to understand more easily how memory moves back and fore between the various free lists and the LRU list.

Extent Listing

This listing basically reports each extent (granule) in turn, reporting one memory chunk per line, in address order. It doesn't really matter whether I show you the output from an instance using a single monolithic shared pool, or a sub-sub-pool from an instance using sub-pools and durations, the general principles don't really change. The following example happens to come from 11.1.0.7:

```
EXTENT 0 addr=1A800000
  Chunk 1a800038 sz=       24  R-freeable  "reserved stoppe"
  Chunk 1a800050 sz=   212888  R-free      "               "
  Chunk 1a833fe8 sz=       24  R-freeable  "reserved stoppe"
  Chunk 1a834000 sz=   969800    perm      "perm           "  alo=35876
  Chunk 1a920c48 sz=    16068    free      "               "
  Chunk 1a924b0c sz=     1072    recreate  "Heap0: KGL     "  latch=00000000
     ds 1b3e5d60 sz=     1072 ct=        1
  Chunk 1a924f3c sz=     2056    freeable  "parameter handl"
  Chunk 1a925744 sz=     4096    freeable  "sql area       "  ds=1A93000C
  Chunk 1a926744 sz=     4096    freeable  "sql area       "  ds=1A93000C
  Chunk 1a927744 sz=     1072    freeable  "CCursor        "  ds=1A9B9E44
  Chunk 1a927b74 sz=     4096    recreate  "sql area       "  latch=00000000
     ds 1a93000c sz=    12288 ct=        3
        1a925744 sz=     4096
        1a926744 sz=     4096
  Chunk 1a928b74 sz=     1072    freeable  "CCursor        "  ds=1A9B9E44
```

The granule size (which is the unit of the EXTENT) in this instance is 4 MB, and this is the first extent of the shared pool. The lines staring *Chunk* identify chunks of memory in the extent, and each chunk shows its starting address and size in bytes. Each chunk then has a class that will be one of (free, freeable, recreate, perm, R-free, R-freeable, R-recreate, R-perm), and most chunks will have a comment in double quotes.

Chunks of class *free* are on one of the shared pool free lists, chunks of class *R-free* are on one of the shared pool reserved free lists. You will notice that there is an R-free chunk of 212,288 bytes at the top of the list—this is the 5 percent (approximately) that is allocated from each extent as the extent is allocated to the shared pool. This instance has only been running for a short time, and it hasn't yet had to resort to allocating space from the reserve.

■ **Note** Although Oracle has been using the strategy of reserving 5 percent of each extent for many years you will find that 11.2 can allocate an entire extent to the reserve, although in this case the class seems to be *R-perm* (a class I don't think I've seen in earlier versions of Oracle) rather than *R-free*.

You can see a pair of 24 byte *R-freeable* chunks flanking the R-free chunk. These are the "stoppers," placed there to stop the R-free chunk from being accidentally merged into the wrong list if the adjacent chunks of memory become free. The significance of the *R-* in the class is that it is memory for the Reserve, the significance of *freeable* is that this is memory that could in principle be freed, but only if its "parent" calls the routine to free it—and we'll see the significance of that in just a moment.

If you look a little further down the list you will see that there are some *freeable* chunks and some *recreate* (recreatable) chunks. The naming is a little confusing—both types of chunk are recreatable and freeable but different bits of the Oracle code are in control of creating and freeing them. The code that maintains the shared pool (the *heap manager*) can issue a call to destroy a recreatable chunk and make it free—and that call will go to the owner of the chunk (e.g. the library cache manager). But there is no direct call the heap manager can make to destroy a freeable chunk; each freeable chunk will be linked to a recreatable chunk and the owner of a recreatable chunk is responsible for freeing the linked freeable chunks when it frees the recreatable chunk.

The dump demonstrates the principle quite well. Take a closer look at the addresses: chunk `1a927b74` is recreatable, but chunks `1a925744` and `1a926744` are freeable. If you look immediately below chunk `1a927b74` you will see a *ds* (data segment) label reporting a size of 12,288 and a count of 3. This tells us that chunk `1a927b74` is the first chunk of three, totaling 12,288 bytes, and the other two chunks are `1a925744` and `1a926744` (the two above, that were freeable); so the heap manager can issue a call to have chunk `1a927b74` destroyed and the memory put on the free list but, as a consequence of `1a927b74` being destroyed, the two freeable chunks will be freed at the same time and also go onto the free list. The address given by the `ds` line is in the middle of a freeable chunk commented as `PCursor` (parent cursor) further down the heap dump and this parent cursor will have to be told that it's lost its SQL Area. It's a coincidence, by the way, dependent on the fact that the instance has just started up, that all the related chunks happen to be in the same extent.

■ **Note** I don't think I've noticed R-recreate as a class in the past—possibly that's just a statistical anomaly since there's no obvious reason why it shouldn't happen. But while checking a recent 11.2 instance, I came across a 4 MB chunk in that class with the comment "KSFD SGA I/O b." As with R-freeable, the only significance is that the memory is in the reserve pool. It is interesting to note, though, that this allocation was (based on a matching comment) in the recreate class in the next 10.2 instance that I checked.

We haven't quite finished with this extract, as we still have the *perm* (permanent) chunk to explain. Such chunks aren't necessarily as permanent as their name suggests. Some really are, and were allocated as the instance started up; but some chunks may be allocated by dynamic processes to fix some memory that should not be discarded until the process terminates. Quite often the perm chunks are general purpose buckets that are allocated to hold lots of other bits and pieces—10.2, for example, will report in a library cache dump that it is allocating permanent space for such things as arrays of KGL locks and KGL pins.

The Free Lists

The previous extract simply shows the memory chunks of each extent in order, which means the free chunks were scattered randomly through the report. The next section of the heapdump shows the free lists, where we can see that Oracle has collected and collated (through a set of linked lists) all those free chunks. I indicated the presence of 255 free memory lists in Figure 7-2 and pointed out that I hadn't even tried to include the reserved free lists (of which there are 14). Clearly, I'm not going to dump all the free lists—let alone show the content of the free lists—but in the following, I will choose the bits I dump quite carefully:

```
FREE LISTS:
 Bucket 0 size=16
 Bucket 1 size=20
  Chunk 1b49f330 sz=       20    free      "               "
  Chunk 1b0fb8d8 sz=       20    free      "               "
  Chunk 1b492fe4 sz=       20    free      "               "
```

```
Bucket 2 size=24
  Chunk 1b4796dc sz=       24    free      "                 "
  Chunk 1ae6c930 sz=       24    free      "                 "
  Chunk 1b041994 sz=       24    free      "                 "
...
 Bucket 67 size=284
 Bucket 68 size=288
 Bucket 69 size=292
 Bucket 70 size=296
 Bucket 71 size=300
...
Bucket 187 size=812
  Chunk 1a9a02d0 sz=      872    free      "                 "
 Bucket 188 size=876
  Chunk 1a9a27c0 sz=      880    free      "                 "
...
 Bucket 251 size=12324
  Chunk 1a9293d4 sz=    14672    free      "                 "
  Chunk 1a920c48 sz=    16068    free      "                 "
 Bucket 252 size=16396
  Chunk 1a930374 sz=    18864    free      "                 "
 Bucket 253 size=32780
 Bucket 254 size=65548
Total free space   =    92620
RESERVED FREE LISTS:
 Reserved bucket 0 size=16
 Reserved bucket 1 size=4400
 Reserved bucket 2 size=8204
...
 Reserved bucket 13 size=65548
  Chunk 1a800050 sz=   212888  R-free      "                 "
  Chunk 1ac00050 sz=   212888  R-free      "                 "
...
Total reserved free space   =  5747976
```

We have a lot of free lists because we could have a lot of different sized memory chunks, and if I'm in a hurry to find a free chunk of (say) 64 bytes, I don't want to have to hunt through a long list of free chunks to find a match—conversely I don't want to grab the first chunk that's big enough, carve 64 bytes off it, and put the rest back on the list as this would end up producing a very long list of very small pieces. So Oracle reserves lists for specific sized chunks.

The first 176 (0 to 175) increment the chunk size by 4 bytes at a time; the next few increment by 12 bytes at a time, then there are about 60 buckets where the increment is 64 bytes (there are a couple of odd glitches on the way), and the last few buckets allow for increasingly large ranges. The reserved list is similar, but starts very small and climbs to a few thousand bytes very abruptly—there is a reason for this, which we will get to soon.

So, if I want a chunk of memory of 80 bytes I can do the arithmetic and work out that I will need to look at bucket 16. If I free up a chunk of 184 bytes I know I have to attach it to bucket 42. Things don't always work perfectly, of course, I don't have a free list for every size—you'll notice that bucket 187 is labeled as size = 812, but the chunks in that bucket are reported at 872 bytes. Once you get past the increments of four bytes, the size is a lower bound for the bucket.

You may wonder why I've included buckets 67 to 71 (size 284 to 300) in my example when there are no chunks in them. Think back to the rowcache—one of the allocation sizes for the row cache is 284 bytes; but what is Oracle supposed to do when there are no free chunks of exactly the right size? It checks the next size up, and the next, and the next, until it finds a suitable chunk; in some cases it will use that chunk, in others it will carve exactly the right amount from the chunk and put the rest back into the appropriate bucket. You recall that I said earlier on that when I calculated the space requirement for the rowcache the numbers weren't quite right; that was because some of my 284 bytes requirements had actually acquired 288, 292, 296, or 300 bytes of memory rather than a perfect 284; none of them had acquired 304 bytes or more though because 304 – 298 = 16, so if Oracle had to go to a larger chunk than 300 it would have taken 284 bytes exactly and put the rest back into one of the smaller buckets.

There is one crucial detail we haven't yet covered. Somewhere in memory, Oracle has—or can create—an ordered list of every chunk in each extent so every time a memory chunk is freed, Oracle can check the map to see if either of the chunks either side is already free; if so the Oracle can coalesce the adjacent chunks (removing them from their current free lists) before putting the resulting chunk on to the correct free list.

Note The structure `x$ksmsp` is, in principle a list of all the chunks in the shared pool and could, again in principle, could be the outward display of the mechanism that Oracle uses to detect the adjacency in free chunks. Don't try querying this object in a production system, though, not even with the query published on My Oracle Support, the side effects of the latch holds that take place are catastrophic.

I've spent the last couple of pages talking about the free lists; the same mechanisms and logic apply to the reserved free lists; the only differences are the size of the chunks and the tag that identify memory as being part of the reserved shared pool.

It's time now to move on to the LRU list(s), but before going on, you might like to check back to the extent dump and compare it with the free list dump—I chose my buckets to make sure that the free and R-free chunks in the extent dump appeared in the free list dump.

The LRU List(s)

I keep putting that final S in parentheses because it's a moot point whether you should think of the LRU as one list or two—the following extract from the same heap dump may show you why. Look at the *separator* line—it's possible that there are two lists and the separator is a construct of the code to dump the LRU. On the other hand, it's possible that (like REPL_MAIN in the buffer cache) a single linked list runs through these chunks with a pointer in `x$kghlu` to show where the break is, as follows:

```
      :
UNPINNED RECREATABLE CHUNKS (lru first):
  Chunk 203fffd4 sz=       44    recreate  "fixed allocatio"  latch=05987BB8
  Chunk 1ef5b480 sz=     1072    recreate  "PCursor        "  latch=00000000
...
  Chunk 1a927b74 sz=     4096    recreate  "sql area       "  latch=00000000
  Chunk 1ee5fddc sz=      284    recreate  "KGL handles    "  latch=00000000
```

```
SEPARATOR
  Chunk 1ef0ac28 sz=      540    recreate  "KQR PO         "  latch=1FDFD814
...
  Chunk 1af9545c sz=     4096    recreate  "PL/SQL MPCODE  "  latch=00000000
  Chunk 1a924b0c sz=     1072    recreate  "Heap0: KGL     "  latch=00000000
Unpinned space     = 10827744  rcr=3921 trn=8164
```

Although we have permanent, recreatable, and freeable chunks in the shared pool, it's only the recreatable ones that get onto the LRU list(s)—and even they are taken off the LRU temporarily when they are in use (i.e. pinned); permanent chunks cannot be re-used (unless a session frees them explicitly), and freeable chunks are only made free as a side effect of their associated recreatable chunk being re-used. At the bottom of this list you can see that we have about 10.8 MB of space—this is rather deceptive, if we freed all the recreatable memory we'd get back far more than that because all (or most of) the freeable memory would end up being freed at the same time.

▒ **Note** The heapdump lists unpinned objects—I don't know whether this means that objects are disconnected from the list as they are pinned (and then, perhaps, reconnected at the head of the LRU when the last pin is released) or whether the code to do the dump simply skips over the items on the list that are pinned. To a large extent, I think this would depend on whether Oracle is maintaining the LRU with a pure LRU algorithm or with a combined LRU and touch count algorithm, like the one employed for the buffer cache.

The other notation at the bottom of the list is significant, we have a total of 12,085 recreatable chunks, of these 3,921 are recurrent (*rcr*) and 8,164 are transient (*trn*)—the transient ones appear before the separator, the recurrent after the separator. This split is vaguely similar in concept to the mid-point (or *cold_head*) for the buffer cache—when a new item is inserted into the LRU list it is attached to the head of the transient list; if it is used more than once then it will be moved to the head of the recurrent list—so the transient list ends up with all the objects that aren't interesting and aren't used much, and all the interesting stuff that is potentially more interesting ends up in recurrent list.

In fact, although there are counters on all the objects, I don't know whether Oracle uses a touch count algorithm on the recurrent list to decide when to promote objects to the head of the list or whether it simply uses an old-style LRU approach (i.e. move something to the head of the queue as you finish using it). We'll see in a moment how movement through the list, and the presence of the two queues, affects the way objects are discarded and memory is made free.

If you want to see the numbers of transient and recurrent items, and watch the size of the list change over time, without doing a (slow and dangerous) heapdump, you can query `x$kghlu`, for example:

```
select kghluidx, kghlurcr, kghlutrn from x$kghlu order by 1;

  KGHLUIDX   KGHLURCR   KGHLUTRN
---------- ---------- ----------
         1       1593       2138
         2        645       1263
         3       1084       1150
```

This query (and the heapdump itself) exposes an important detail about the LRU lists when you are using sub-sub-pools (durations). This result came from a system with durations enabled, and three sub-pools, but there are only three rows in the result, not twelve—the LRU lists are associated with sub-pools, not with sub-sub-pools. This is going to raise an interesting question when we look at the action that goes on in the LRU list.

… and Action!

So far, we have a static picture of the LRU list(s). Now it's time to put a few pieces together and see what activity takes place as we try to use some memory in the shared pool. We will consider three scenarios.

Scenario 1: A Lucky Case

Assume we need exactly 1 KB (1,024 bytes) of memory—bucket 190 is defined to hold free chunks of 1,004 to 1,064 bytes, so we get the shared pool latch and check that bucket; if it holds a chunk that is the right size we can detach the chunk from the list and attach it to the head of the transient list, pin the chunk (because we're going to do something with it) and drop the shared pool latch. (Depending on what we're going to do with the chunk we will probably have acquired some other latch—such as a library cache latch or a dictionary cache latch—to attach the chunk to a hash bucket as well.

If we can't find an exact match for size, we may find a chunk in the bucket that is larger than we need. If it's less than 16 bytes too big we will simply use it and ignore the waste space, if it's 16 or more bytes too big we will "cut" the excess off the chunk and attach the excess to the appropriate free list bucket before continuing as above.

If we can't find a suitable chunk in this bucket, we go to the next bucket up and repeat the search until we do find a large enough chunk.

Scenario 2: Running Out of Luck

If we go through scenario 1 and don't find a large enough chunk in any of the free list buckets we have to free some memory, so we go to the tail end of the LRU list and detach some objects and mark them as free. We then attach these objects to the appropriate free lists; except we first check if any of the newly freed chunks have existing adjacent free chunks, in which case we can coalesce some chunks before we attach them to free lists.

Then we can check the free list buckets again to see if we've created a large enough chunk—if so, proceed as scenario 1, if not then repeat the exercise of freeing some items from the LRU list.

At this point, I am a little vague about exactly what happens. Several years ago I attended a presentation by well-known Oracle consultant Steve Adams, at which he described an algorithm where Oracle would free items on the LRU list in batches of eight, switching back and forth from the transient list to the recurrent list, taking (if I recall correctly) two batches from the transient list for each batch from the recurrent list. I have also seen a comment in an Oracle whitepaper that says we will scan the LRU list five times, freeing chunks. I am certainly aware that one nasty statement or pl/sql block can cause a huge volume of material to move from the library cache to the free lists—ultimately ending in an Oracle error `ORA-04031: unable to allocate %n bytes` if we are unlucky.

By watching `x$kghlu` (see above) very closely while hitting a carefully loaded system with a nasty PL/SQL block, I can see the number of transient and recurrent chunks dropping in a way that agrees with Steve's comments—and by modifying the test it is reasonably clear that Oracle is removing a few chunks at a time before repeating its checks for a large enough chunk of free space. If you really need to work out an exact sequence of events you will probably have to make use of a tool like *dtrace* or *SystemTap* to list the calls that take place.

The idea of walking the LRU list, freeing unpinned chunks as you go, raises some questions. I mentioned the problem of Oracle error ORA-04031. If your system has multiple sub-pools, your session will try to allocate memory from one of the sub-pools and start walking one of the LRU lists. It's entirely possible that you could end up raising Oracle error ORA-04031 because that sub-pool is badly fragmented, even when another sub-pool as plenty of free space.

A variant on this problem may appear for sub-sub-pools. We know (or, at least, believe) that different sub-sub-pools are used for different categories of information, but the LRU list operates at the level of the sub-pool. So, if you want to allocate some memory for a Heap 0 (say) that uses memory with duration 2, is there any chance that you will walk along the LRU list freeing up lots of rowcache entries, which use memory from duration 1 and therefore can't possibly help. (It seems likely that the Oracle developers would have thought of that one—but it's a question worth asking.)

Scenario 3: Allocating a Large Chunk

There is one more variant to consider—requesting a memory chunk that is larger than the `_shared_pool_reserved_min_alloc value` of 4,400 bytes. The first thing Oracle does in this case is exactly as scenario 1, it checks the standard free list buckets to see if they can supply a large enough chunk. If they can't then Oracle checks the reserved free list buckets. Then, if the reserved free lists don't help, we're back to freeing items on the LRU list and coalescing free memory. Bear in mind that it is technically possible for some chunks to be on the free list in the class *R-recreate* so each time Oracle pauses in its walk along the LRU it probably checks both the normal and the reserve free list buckets.

ORA-04031: Unable to Allocate %n Bytes

There is a wealth of information on My Oracle Support (Metalink) about the ORA-04031 error and how to determine why it's happening. As you have seen from scenarios 2 and 3, it arises when we are trying to allocate a free chunk and can't find, or create, a large enough chunk after walking the LRU list (five times according to the Oracle note) and freeing memory. There are various causes but generally it is likely an application design flaw, sending too many distinct SQL statements or PL/SQL blocks to the database; this can result in lots of activity that ends up fragmenting memory into lots of tiny chunks that can't be coalesced when we need a large chunk. Typical workarounds include

- Enabling cursor sharing to reduce the number of distinct statements. This can work, but will cause different problems if you're unlucky.
- Using `dbms_pool.keep()` to pin large objects in the library cache as the instance starts up, so that you avoid the worst cases of needing large memory chunks.

Ultimately the solution is to fix the application so that it doesn't generate so many distinct SQL statement, or, in very rare cases, make sure that you have actually given Oracle enough memory for the shared pool.

Parsing and Optimizing

Having spent so much time looking at how the bits and pieces of the shared pool are used to handle the library cache content, we can now take a little time to think about the sequence of activity as we make a parse call for a statement that hasn't previously been optimized.

We do the syntactic check and determine that it's legal SQL.

We hash the string to get a hash value, work out the relevant *library cache hash bucket*, and check the bucket to see if we can find a matching string.

We don't, so we start the semantic analysis of the string, checking object names, and so forth, in the string against dictionary cache—which means we have to keep hitting dictionary cache latches to check dictionary cache entries, and may mean we have to run some SQL to load a definition into the dictionary cache.

We'll ignore the work we do to parse, optimize, and execute the recursive SQL—because we're already in the middling of describing how to parse, optimize and execute SQL. Suffice to say that loading dictionary cache entries into memory may require us to free some memory from the shared pool LRU list, and attach the memory to the shared pool free lists, then find some memory on the free lists and attach it to the LRU list to hold the dictionary cache rows.

Once we have cleared the semantic checks, we can start to optimize the statement—but we need to ensure that no-one else wastes their time optimizing the same statement at the same time; so at this point we acquire some memory from the shared pool free lists (which means we may first have to release some objects from the LRU lists), and attach some chunks to the LRU to hold the *parent cursor* and the *child cursor*, and the basic information about the cursors.

■ **Note** The parent cursor holds generic information about the statement, the child cursor is appropriate to our individual working environment, such as table name translations, dependencies, optimizer environment, and ultimately the execution plan.

Having put the parent and child cursors in place we *pin* them exclusively so that (a) they don't immediately go onto the "LRU unpinned recreatable" list with the threat of being discarded and (b) so that no one else can touch them until we've finished optimizing. If any other session tries to optimize the same statement at the same time it will go into a wait state (`cursor: pin S wait on X` for the latest version of Oracle, `library cache pin` for older versions).

At this point we can do all the work of creating an execution plan—and since I've written a whole book on that topic I won't describe how this happens; suffice to say that it's basically CPU and private memory—once we've got the table, index and column information from the dictionary cache we don't have to visit shared memory again until we have a plan ready.

■ **Note** The following is a thumbnail sketch of what the optimizer has to do: work out the best join order for the tables in your query, decide the best join method between adjacent pairs of tables, and the best access method into each table. At each step of the way, the choice of the best strategy is dictated by the optimizer's estimate of the volume of data and the physical scattering of that data.

Eventually we have a plan and need to attach it to the child cursor—at which point we acquire memory from the shared pool free list (possibly freeing some objects on the LRU list) and start attaching chunks to the child cursor. Plans can be quite large so we may have to allocate several memory chunks, of which the first will appear in the *recreate* class, and the rest as *freeable*.

Finally we can unpin the parent and child cursors, pin the child in shared mode execute it, and unpin it. (Dropping from exclusive to shared means that any session waiting to optimize the same statement can now see that the plan is available and ready to use, so can acquire its own pin and execute the statement at the same time.)

You can appreciate that there's a lot of activity going on, and scope for a lot of interference in the shared pool as we search for objects, make space, and acquire space—and we can go through that cycle many times in the course of optimizing a single statement—remember, we need to check all that information from the dictionary cache before we can start creating an execution plan, then we might want to acquire a lot of space (relatively speaking) for library cache objects. Optimizing is an activity we should avoid. Just to give you an idea of the complexity of the work involved in dealing with all the memory chunks, Figure 7-5 is a *simplified* schematic of a parent cursor with two child cursors.

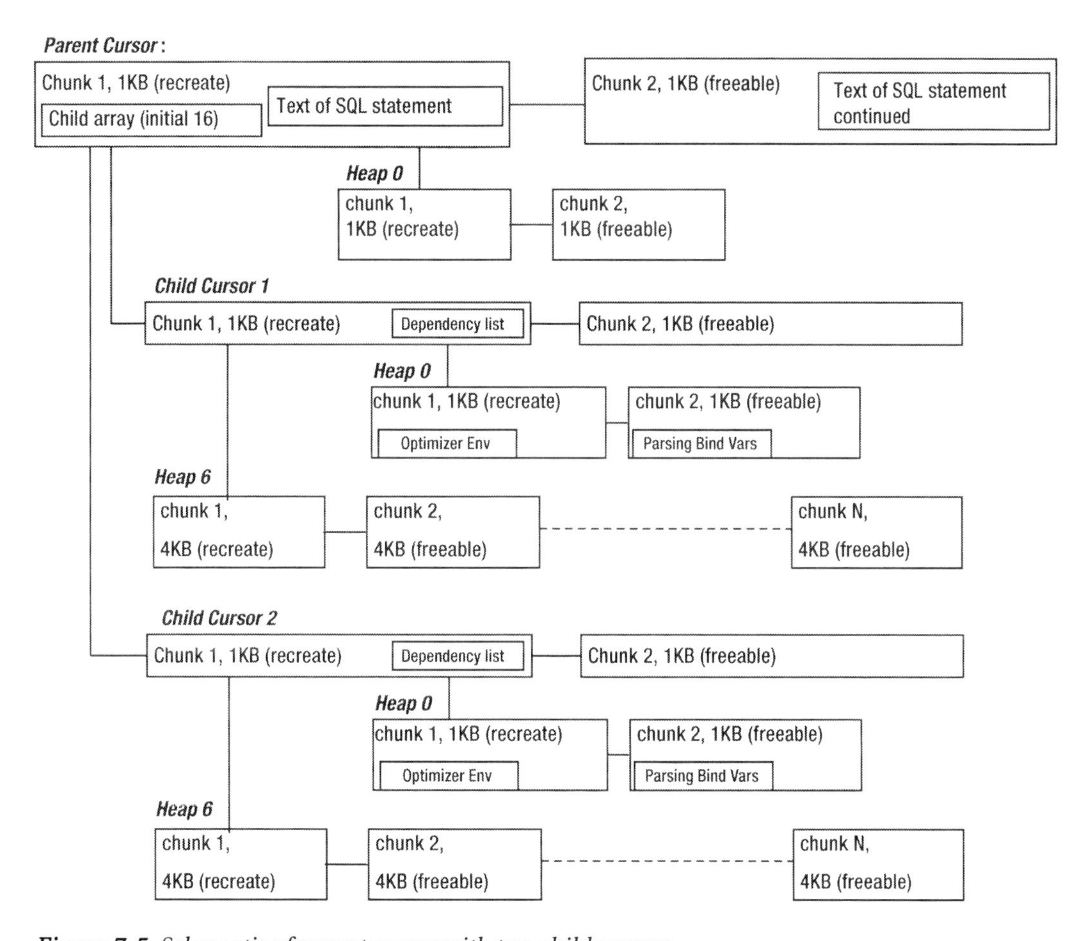

Figure 7-5. *Schematic of parent cursor with two child cursors*

The image in Figure 7-5 isn't exactly the way that Oracle allocates and links memory chunks for cursors, and the various pieces of information such as the dependency lists, optimizer environment and so on aren't really placed as tidily as I've shown them—but I've allowed myself a little poetic license in an attempt to keep the picture fairly simple.

You'll note, in particular, that I've shown two child cursors and when you look at the information they carry (parsing bind variables, optimizer environment, dependency lists, you can see why a single SQL text may need several execution plans. My initial description of optimizing didn't mention the possibility of having multiple child cursors in place already, but the first time you pass a statement to Oracle it has to check if everything about that statement matches an existing child cursor. Every child cursor for a given parent is on the same library cache latch, so Oracle has to hold that latch while checking. This, of course, is one of the threats of setting `cursor_sharing` to `similar`—you could end up with a very long list of child cursors to check.

I've mentioned pinning a couple of times in the course of describing the parsing and optimizing of a statement; pinning also occurs on execution of statements, and the mechanisms have changed in the last few releases of Oracle, so we'll finish our rummage through the library cache and shared pool with a discussion on executing, locking and pinning.

Executing, Locking, and Pinning

Assuming I want to run a query and there is a suitable child cursor in the library cache with an execution plan ready and waiting, I still have to do a little work to find it and prepare to execute it. In the worst case I will simply call Oracle passing in a piece of text and an instruction to "get the answer." To handle the text Oracle will check syntax, hash the text to a value, then search the library cache for a match; this means going to the right library cache hash bucket, searching along the chain, finding the child cursor, checking it is appropriate, and executing the plan. It's possible at this point to discover that the plan has been removed from memory, in which case we would have to re-optimize the statement—reporting a `parse count (hard)` in the session stats and incrementing `Misses in library cache during execute` if we were running a trace. You can get an idea of how often this happens by checking the statistic `v$librarycache.reloads` for the `'SQL AREA'` row.

Note `V$librarycache` will report reloads of execution plans for two reasons, either a plan has been flushed because of demand for memory, or it has been invalidated because some DDL has been run against a dependent object. As a rough guide, `reloads—invalidations` will give you an idea of how much work you are doing because of an issue relating to the availability of free memory.

At various stages in the process, though, we have to worry about concurrent activity. Historically we would get and hold the library cache hash latch while we walked along the chain searching for the correct cursor. We would create a library cache lock (KGL lock) for Heap 0 to make sure that it didn't get flushed from memory and we would create a library cache pin (KGL pin) to make sure that the plan (Heap 6 / SQL Area) didn't get flushed from memory while we were executing the query. However, you may recall all those latches relating to the library cache that appeared in 10g—like the `library cache pin allocation` latch—pins and locks are little chunks of memory that have to be allocated from, and returned to, the shared pool. So, the act of pinning a cursor meant you had to get a couple of latches, allocate some memory and so on. This is expensive stuff if your rate of execution is extremely high.

Oracle has introduced many strategies for minimizing the "infrastructure" cost of finding and executing statements. In 10.2 they introduced code to allow KGL pins to be cached by sessions (hidden parameter `_session_kept_cursor_pins`) with similar intent, though different mechanisms, to the way they allow sessions to cache buffer handles. In 11g KGL pins and locks are allocated in pages (rather than individually) that a session can acquire, reducing memory allocation requests and fragmentation. Apart from these recent changes, we can always hold cursors open—which basically means keeping the library cache lock in place all the time and this results in Heap 0 being pinned in memory (though it's not a KGL pin, in this case the "pin" is a flag set by the heap manager); this is the function of the structure **`x$kgllk`**–made officially visible through **`v$open_cursor`**. We also have the *session cursor cache*, which allows an Oracle library function to keep cursors open even when the end-user code hasn't tried to keep cursors open.

We can go one step further by keeping the pin (**`x$kglpn`**) in place on heap 6—the execution plan—by setting `cursor_space_for_time` to true (which isn't a good idea unless you have a really good application, because the side effect of pinning heap 6 whenever you have heap 0 pinned is that you limit the number of unpinned recreatable objects that can be freed when you run short of memory). However, the parameter `cursor_spare_for_time` is deprecated in 11g, possibly because Oracle now feels that the option was a solution to a problem that should no longer exist thanks to their latest strategy for pinning (started in 10g and close to completion in 11g): the introduction of mutexes.

Mutexes

Mutexes seem to have two possible functions. In the first place they behave like latches—the structure of a mutex is very small (about 24 bytes) and there is a short code path with an atomic, uninterruptible, step that changes the value of the mutex, so a mutex can be used safely to say, "The mutex is set to a blocking value—don't touch object X." But mutexes can also be used as counters, so a mutex can say, "There are currently N people reading an object—don't change the object."

Oracle has introduced mutexes to hash buckets—in particular the library cache hash buckets. Remember that we used to have just a few (between 3 and 67) latches to cover tens of thousands of library cache hash buckets. In 11.2 every single hash bucket has its own mutex; whatever else this does, it cuts down the contention on the library cache hash latches and eliminates false contention (i.e., the cases where you want bucket 1 and I want bucket 131,071 and we both go for the same latch). This is an example of the mutex as latch.

■ **Note** One of the biggest differences between mutexes and latches is that Oracle knows where *all* the latches are *all* the time—so it's possible for the internal code to accumulate and report statistics about all latch activity quite cheaply. Mutexes are dynamic—if you create a new child cursor you create new mutexes as part of that child cursor; this makes it impossible to accumulate statistics about *all* mutex activity efficiently—the cost of walking through a linked list of mutexes would be high, and if the mutexes tried to maintain a central pool of statistics this would re-introduce the contention problem that mutexes were supposed to address. So a mutex only records statistics about the problems (i.e. sleeps) that it sees—in theory there won't be many, so the contention problems of every piece of mutex code having to update a small central memory area shouldn't appear.

Back in Chapter 4 I made the point that a mutex could be held for a "long" time. This is because a mutex can take the place of a library cache pin (`x$kglpn`). Rather than attaching a structure to the child cursor to pin Heap 6 in memory, a session can simply increment (with an atomic CPU operation) a mutex that is part of the child cursor structure before executing the query, then decrement the counter afterwards. In theory it seems likely that the library cache lock (`x$kgllk`) on Heap 0 could be replaced in the same way, and there are, indeed, two mutexes built into the child cursor structure—in fact `x$kglob` (the structure under `v$sql`) reports three mutexes, but I think one of those is really just pointing to the hash bucket mutex—so perhaps this change is also on its way.

Despite the introduction of mutexes as pin mechanisms, the structure `x$kglpn` is still around (as is `x$kgllk`) in 11g; and there are still places where the mutex for pin mechanism is still not in place—for example, if you try to recompile a pl/sql procedure while it is running you will see your session waiting on a `library cache pin`. You might want to try one of the standard tests that I perform on upgrading, which is to compile and run the following stored procedure code:

```
create or replace procedure self_deadlock as
begin
        execute immediate 'alter procedure self_deadlock compile';
end;
/
```

One day you may find that library cache locks and library cache pins simply disappear—but it's not in 11.2. There have been changes, though—the bottleneck of thrashing memory and latches to create and discard locks and pins has disappeared. In 11g (and even in 10g) a session acquires a larger chunk of memory once, and then creates locks and pins from that memory, so it doesn't cause contention in the shared memory.

Summary

When you compare the buffer cache with the shared pool, you can recognize that they have to handle similar problems and have adopted similar strategies as a consequence. The function and behavior of the *cache buffers LRU chains* latch is similar to that of the *shared pool* latch; and we can also see similarities between the *cache buffers chains* latches and the *library cache* latches.

The shared pool latch controls the movement of memory from the free pool to the used pool, moving chunks on and off an LRU list; the cache buffers LRU chains latch controls the movement of buffer memory between the auxiliary (don't mind too much if we forget the block) list and the main (recently used blocks) list. The library cache latches serialize access to code and metadata objects according to hash value; the cache buffers chains latches serialize access to data blocks according to hash values.

There are interesting variations in the number and use of the latches, and different strategies involved in pinning and using items; because the buffer cache (or, at least, each working data set) works on a single unit size of memory (the relevant block size) memory management in the buffer cache is simpler than it is in the shared pool where memory allocations can, effectively, be any size. For performance reasons, this means we have multiple lists of free memory in the shared pool (compared to the one auxiliary list), and various strategies for minimizing the effects of memory fragmentation.

You should always view parsing and optimizing as two separate operations; and you should also remember the difference between a parse call and the action of parsing.

Optimizing is expensive, parsing can be expensive—on an OLTP system where most of the SQL ought to be lightweight queries for small amounts of data, you should avoid constructing SQL with embedded literal values because of the parsing and optimizing costs.

A parse call in your code may do the following:

- Vanish— particularly from pl/sql code
- Do a syntax check, library cache search, semantic analysis, and optimization
- Do a syntax check and jump to the correct cursor (from the session cursor cache)
- Do nothing but jump directly to the correct cursor (if it's in the pl/sql cache)

The steps needed to parse and optimize a new SQL statement involve Oracle visiting (and possibly loading) the dictionary cache—which requires dictionary cache latch activity and could require some activity in the shared pool to make memory available; more significantly, as the statement and it's cursor are loaded into the library cache we will see more activity in the shared pool, and may see a lot of activity as current objects are ejected and free memory is coalesced to make space for the new objects.

Although the optimizations and caching available to minimize the cost of parse calls can be very helpful, there are usually a few cases in any busy OLTP system where the reduction in contention you get from explicitly creating and holding cursors is worth a little bit of extra complexity in the code.

CHAPTER 8

RAC and Ruin

Everything's Negotiable!

Up to this point, everything I've said has been about a single instance addressing a single database; but Oracle allows multiple instances to share access to a single database, which means multiple independent data caches, multiple independent log buffers, and multiple independent SGAs—all accessing the same set of physical files, all using the same data dictionary. Without a constant stream of negotiation going on between instances, it would be impossible to ensure that the multiple instances behaved consistently, and we would see cases where data changes made by one instance were lost due to interference from another instance. This need for cross-instance traffic is the only significant new concept that we need to focus on when we think about RAC—the *Real Application Cluster.*

The ideas we need to consider are as follows: How can latch activity work if the thing you want to protect is in the memory of another instance? How can you modify your copy of a data block when another instance may have a copy that is a newer version? If you have an execution plan that includes a particular indexed access path, how do you become aware of the fact that another instance has dropped that index? If you are trying to create a read-consistent copy of a data block, how do you ensure that the SCNs of all instances that might have changed that block are kept in synch?

There are only two pieces of functionality that we need to address all these questions—global enqueues, and cache coherency—and these are the main topics we will examine in this chapter. This will give us a chance to revisit and refine our understanding of locks and latches while focusing on the critical changes that can cause problems with RAC.

Before looking at the mechanics, however, we will spend a little time looking at an overview of what RAC is, why you might want it, and the threats that the Oracle developers addressed when creating the product. We'll also take a look at the way the recovery mechanisms we've reviewed fold neatly into RAC to allow one instance to take over when another fails. Since most of the discussion relating to RAC is fairly abstract, I've also picked a commonly-used programming feature to make concrete points about creating an application that performs well on RAC.

Note I felt the need for a little alliteration in the chapter title, and it is very easy to ruin things if you don't understand a little bit about how RAC works; but RAC doesn't necessarily lead to ruin.

The Big Picture

To my mind, understanding how RAC works when it's up and running isn't the really difficult bit —it's getting it installed and running in the first place that's complicated. There are many layers that have to be configured correctly before the installation is complete. No matter what Oracle does to make things easier, there is an inherent volume of complexity involved in making sure that all the individual pieces are working correctly and cooperating; and each time you do it or, at least, each time *I* do it, there are some new bits to worry about.

Luckily, I don't feel compelled to tell you how to install RAC because there are several blog items (such as the series by Tim Hall at `www.oracle-base.com`), massive installation notes on the Oracle Technet (OTN), and entire books (such as *Pro Oracle Database 11g RAC on Linux* by Martin Bach and Steve Shaw (Apress, 2010)) written to explain it. I'm only going to give you the highlights of the run-time mechanics that show you why you need to be careful in using it.

I will, however, give you a picture of what RAC means (see Figure 8-1).

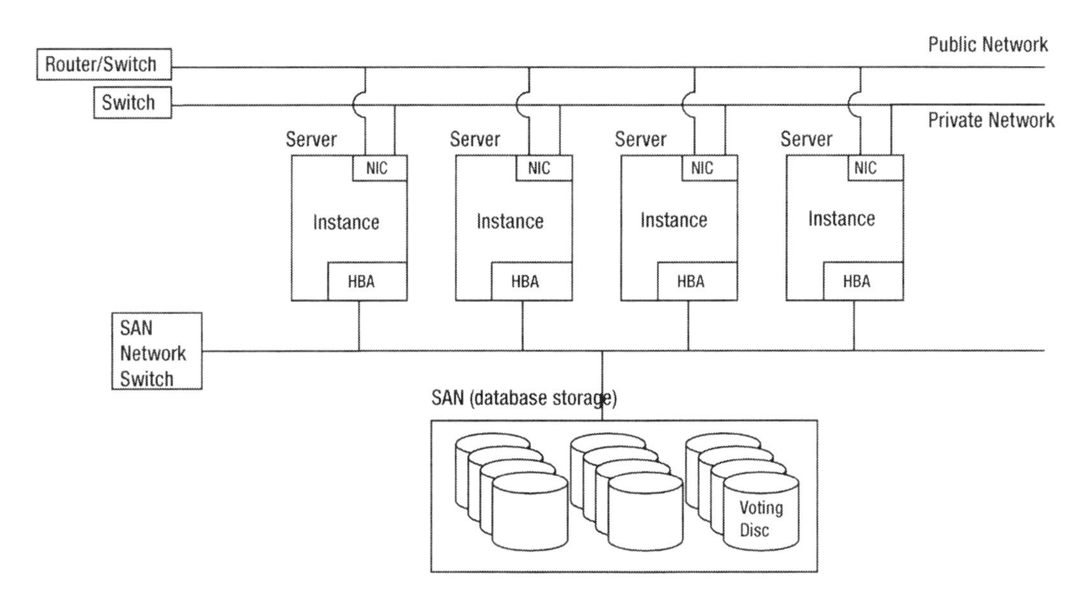

Figure 8-1. *Schematic of a RAC system*

The following are key points to pick up from this schematic:

- Each machine (generally referred to as a node) that runs an instance must be attached to two networks—one is a public network used to accept connections from end-user programs, the other is a private network used only by the instances to talk to each other and maintain a coherent picture of the combined SGAs. The private network needs to have the lowest latency that you can afford to buy.
- All instances must be able to access all the storage.

- There is a special disc that acts as a control mechanism in the event of a breakdown in communications between the machines. (If you want to get very sophisticated with RAC—especially if you decide to stretch your RAC across long distances—you will need a minimum of three such disks, ideally in three physically separate locations).

The following are things that cannot be seen in the diagram:

- There are couple of layers of software (the cluster services) running at a level between the operating system and the Oracle instance that make sure that the machines can communicate with each other.
- There is another network involved that is invisible because it's a "virtual network," driven by Oracle's cluster software, sitting on the public network. It's actually the virtual network that client programs use to communicate with the Oracle instance. This arrangement makes it possible for Oracle to inform the client code very quickly that one of the database server machines has failed, so that the client can be redirected to a surviving machine with a minimum time-lag (see sidebar).
- If you are using Oracle Corporation's preferred installation approach there will be two instances running on each machine, the standard "database" instance, identified by parameter `instance_type` as being an instance of type RDBMS, and the "storage management" instance, identified by parameter `instance_type` as being an instance of type ASM. (If you want to run instances for several different databases on the each machine you would only need one ASM instance per machine—effectively ASM is functioning rather like a logical volume manager, as a layer between the Operating System and the normal database instances.)

VIRTUAL IP ADDRESSES AND SCAN

When you configure a RAC system, one of the tasks you have to do at the operating system level is assign each machine a "virtual" IP address (VIP). Immediately after startup the cluster service software inserts this code layer above the real IP address, and the machines switch to communicating through the VIPs.

The big difference between real and virtual IP addresses is that the real IP address is logically bound to a specific piece of hardware (technically the MAC address on the network card); whereas the VIP address is controlled by software and its association with a particular piece of hardware can be changed dynamically.

If a database machine were to fail when a client program was attached to it through the real IP, the client program would wait a long time (tens to hundreds of seconds) for a response from the server before deciding that the server machine had failed. Because Oracle is using virtual IPs, when a machine fails, one of the other instances will detect the failure very rapidly and take on the virtual IP of the failed machine to handle current requests. This reconfigures the system to stop future connections going to a failed VIP (until the machine and instance are live again). This means that clients will not experience a long wait if the instance they are addressing fails.

As another aid to minimize waits caused by network problems, Oracle 11.2 has introduced the SCAN (Single Client Access Name) as part of its Grid Infrastructure. Before you can use SCAN, you have to get your system administrator to set up some new DNS (Domain Name Service) entries, or assist you in setting up a subsection of the DNS to use Oracle's GNS (Grid Naming Service). Once this has been set up, any client programs will be able to reference the system by SCAN and you won't have to reconfigure any client settings if you need to move the system to different hardware, or add or remove nodes.

Staying Alive

Looking at Figure 8-1, you might start to wonder what happens if the network fails and the different instances can't talk to each other. If the network breaks, you could end up with two sets of instances that are convinced that they have exclusive access to the database—with the result that they keep overwriting each others' changes.

There are two layers at which this threat could occur: an Oracle instance may seem to lose contact with the rest of the instances, or a machine may lose contact with the rest of the machines. We'll work from the bottom of the stack upwards and worry about the machine level first.

The Machine Defenses

The cluster services on each machine can keep in touch with each other through the network, but they also keep in touch through the voting disc shown in Figure 8-1, and this leads to several options for dealing with communication problems.

Every second, every machine writes to the "voting" disc—there is a file on the disc holding one block per machine, and each machine simply increments a counter in its block. In the simplest case, a machine may discover that it can't write to the file—in which case it takes itself out of the cluster and may reboot itself to protect the cluster. (At this point, of course, the instance will also terminate abruptly, and one of the other instances will have to go through crash recovery for it.)

As each machine writes its block, however, it also checks the blocks written by every other machine in the cluster, so it can detect any cases of a machine that hasn't updated its own block in the recent past. (It's possible that a machine in this state could have cluster software that is misbehaving but still be running, and have a live instance on it—and that poses a threat to the database.) In this case, the discovering machine is allowed to terminate the guilty machine with extreme prejudice.

It's possible that every machine can write to the file, but suffer from a network problem that stops some machines from hearing each other across the network. In this case one machine will attempt to ring-fence the voting disc and start counting how many other machines it can talk to. If it finds that it belongs to a networked group that contains more than half the machines or, if the total number of machines is even, half the machines *including* the machine with the lowest known cluster id—it will force the remaining machines out of the cluster and make them reboot. If it can't get the necessary quorum (hence the alternative name of "quorum disk" for the voting disk), it will take itself out of the cluster.

Inevitably things are more complex than the outline I've given, but you can appreciate that the cluster software has to be quite clever (and chooses to be very pessimistic) when it comes to ensuring that a machine doesn't jeopardize the health of the database by running with links to the rest of the cluster that are suspect.

The Oracle Defenses

There is a similar type of strategy at the Oracle level. As each instance starts up it broadcasts its presence to the other instances, so every instance always knows how many other instances should be alive. Similarly, when an instance shuts down (properly) it says goodbye. There is a brief period during both startup and shutdown when the latest state of the instance group is passed around and instances "rebalance" themselves to cater for the change in number. From this point onward, every instance is in constant communication over the network with every other instance (with LMON in particular acting as the network heartbeat process).

There's also a file-based heartbeat going on; as we saw in Chapter 6, the checkpoint process (CKPT) updates the control file roughly every three seconds. In RAC every instance has its own CKPT process, so the control file can act as the heartbeat file for Oracle. If you dump the control file at level 3 (see Appendix) you will see the Checkpoint Progress Records—that's the critical section of the control file that contains one record for each instance that the instance has to keep up to date.

In principle, therefore, it's possible for an instance to detect that it can no longer write to the control file, and terminate itself for the good of the system. It's also possible, in principle, for another instance to notice that an instance has hung (and, as we shall see shortly, if one instance hangs then eventually every other instance is liable to end up waiting for it to do something). We might hope, therefore, that Oracle could include code to allow one instance (if it's in the quorum, of course) to take down another instance. Unfortunately, I don't think that this can happen until 11.2, where yet another new process called *LMHB* (lock manager heart beat monitor) has been introduced to determine very rapidly that some lock processes are getting hung up waiting for lock requests to be serviced.

So we have a way of putting together several pieces of equipment to create something that behaves like a single, large system; and we have ways to protect the entire system from the problems caused by its parts. But it's complicated, and why would you want to deal with something complicated?

What's the Point?

Whenever you look at any technology, or any feature within a technology, it's worth asking why you might want to use it—what's the benefit? If you can't describe what you hope to achieve, then you can't decide how best to use the technology and how to measure your degree of success.

There are two arguments put forward for RAC—scalability and high availability, and the scalability argument comes in two flavors: throughput and response time. So, before you start chasing RAC, you need to decide which of these two arguments matters to you, and how best to implement RAC on your site to ensure that you turn the theory into reality.

High Availability

The theory of high availability says that if one of the nodes in your RAC system fails, it will only be moments before one of the other nodes recovers the redo from the failed node, the nodes rebalance, and everything then keeps on running. The failover should be virtually transparent to the front-end (although transparency isn't something that applies to transactions that are in flight unless you recode the application). There are four obvious questions to ask in response to this argument, as follows:

- How important is it to restart, say, within 10 seconds? Can we live with an alternative that might be just a little slower?

- How often does a machine fail compared to a disk or a network? (Assuming that we're not going to cover every possible single point of failure (SPOF)). How much benefit do we get from RAC?
- Do we have the human resources to deal with the added complexity of the RAC software stack and the level of skill that is still needed to handle patches and upgrades?
- How many nodes do we need to run before the workload for N nodes can run on N-1 nodes without having a performance impact that would make us uncomfortable?

Alternative technologies include things like basic cluster failover as supplied by the operating system vendor, or a simple physical standby database if we want to stick to pure Oracle technology—options where another machine can be available to take on the role of the database server. The drawbacks are that the time to failover will be longer and the other machine is an idle machine, or used for something else but with spare capacity, or it's going to give you degraded response time while it's acting as the failover machine. It's quite easy to set up the database server to fail over fairly quickly—but don't forget that every little piece of your application has to find the new machine as well.

Looking at SPOFs—how many options are you going to cover? Doubling up network cards is easy, the same goes for switches, but doubling up the storage and the actual network cabling is harder—and what's the strategy for a power outage in the data centre? You might also look at the complexity of the whole RAC stack and ask how much time you're going to lose on patching and upgrading. Oracle Corp. is constantly working towards "rolling upgrades"—but it still has a way to go.

Scalability

There are two different concepts that people tend to think of when thinking about scalability. These are as follows:

- Get the same job done more quickly—improved response time
- Get more copies of the same job done at the same time—improved throughput

It's quite helpful to think of the first option in terms of individual big jobs, and the second in terms of a large number of small jobs. If you have a batch process or report that takes 40 minutes to complete, then sharing it across two instances *may* allow it to complete in 20 minutes, sharing it across four nodes *may* allow it to complete in 10 minutes. This image probably carries faint echoes of parallel execution—and the association is quite good; if you hope to get a shorter completion time without rewriting the job you're probably going to have to take advantage of the extra nodes through *parallel execution.* If parallel execution comes to your aid, the threat is the extra cost of messaging. There are overheads in passing messages between layers of parallel execution slaves, and the overheads are even greater if the slaves are running in different instances. If you want to make big jobs faster (and can't improve the code), maybe all you need is more memory, or more CPUs or faster CPUs before you move to greater complexity.

If your aim is to allow more jobs to run in the same time—let's say you're growing a business and simply have more employees doing the same sort of thing on the system—then adding more instances allows more employees to work concurrently. If you can run 50 employees at a time on one instance, then *maybe* you can run 100 at a time on two, and 200 at a time on four. You simply add instances as you add employees.

In favor of this strategy is the fact that each instance has its own log writer (*lgwr*) and set of redo log files—and the rate at which an instance can handle redo generation is the ultimate bottleneck in an Oracle system. On the downside, if you have more processes (spread across more instances) doing the same sort of work, you are more likely to have hot spots in the data. In RAC, a hot spot means more traffic moving between instances—and that's the specific performance problem you always have to be aware of.

Again you might ask why you don't simply increase the size of a single machine as your number of users grows. In this case, there's an obvious response: it's not that easy to "grow" a machine, especially when compared to buying another "commodity" machine and hanging it off the network. Indeed, one of the marketing points for RAC was that it's easier to plan for growth—you don't have to buy a big machine on day one and have it running at very low capacity (but high cost) for a couple of years. You can start cheap and grow the cluster with the user base.

■ **Note** One of the unfortunate side effects of the "start big" strategy that I've seen a couple of times is that a big machine with a small user base can have so much spare capacity that it hides the worst performance issues for a long time—until the user base grows large enough to make fixing the performance issues an emergency.

The Grid

There is another facet to using a cluster of commodity machines rather than relying on individual large machines, and that's where the grid concept came from—and it's where some of the enhancements in Oracle 11.2 are finally taking it. If you have a large number of small machines in a cluster (not yet running any Oracle instances), you can then set up a number of different databases on your disk farm, and choose how many instances should run on each machine for each application, and redistribute the workload dynamically. Figure 8-2 shows such a configuration with two possible configurations—one for standard week day processing, where every machine runs just a single database instance (ignoring the ASM instances) during the week, but two of the GL machines start up a WEB instance at week end, when the load on the general ledger system is likely to decrease, and the load on the web application is likely to increase.

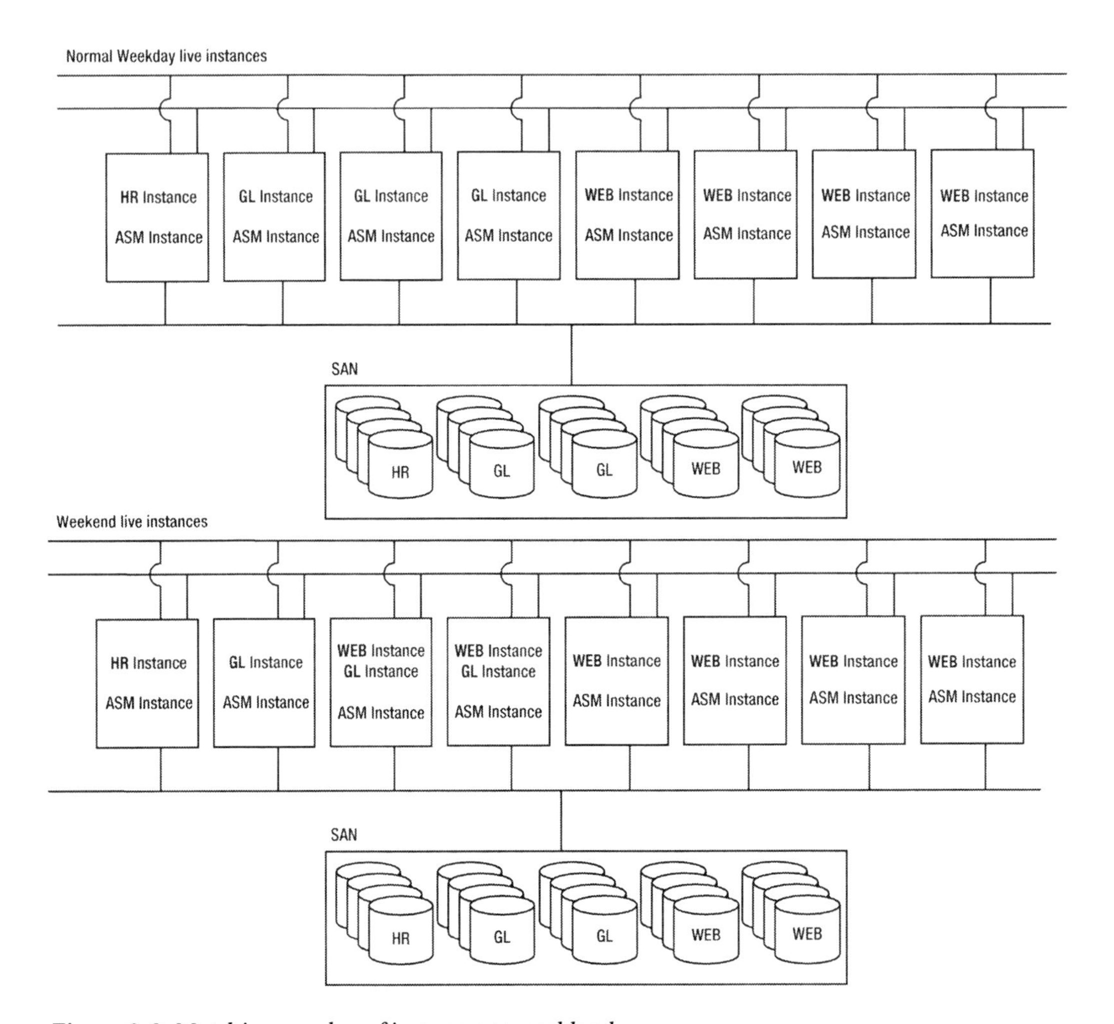

***Figure 8-2.** Matching number of instances to workload*

If you look closely at this picture you'll notice a little hint that I like to follow the "Sane SAN" strategy (proposed by James Morle) for dealing with multiple databases on a single SAN—try to break the SAN down into areas dedicated to individual databases.

In this scenario you could also imagine starting up an extra GL instance on the HR machine at the month end; and for reasons of high availability you might even have two HR instances running (with the second instance running on one of the GL machines) in Oracle's special two-instance active/passive mode (see note) in case the single HR instance failed for some reason.

■ **Note** I have mentioned the communications between instances as an important aspect of how RAC works. There is a special case implementation for two-node RAC that eliminates this cost by using one instance to do the work and the other instance to do nothing (in principle) but wait for the first instance to fail. This is the option known as the active/passive setup, and is an interesting strategy if you have a need to run two or more databases on a small cluster with rapid failover.

I have seen a couple of sites that have taken advantage of this type of multi-instance cluster, but I can't help thinking that you would be hard pushed to find many sites with a realistic requirement to move entire instances in and out of play as workload changes; however, Oracle is trying to make exactly that type of movement easier, and automatic, even in the latest releases. (I have to say that one of my client sites using this type of setup was very happy with what they had achieved, but they had a cluster of eight machines, with a standby cluster of eight machines, and it had taken a few weeks for a visiting consultant to get the whole thing working.)

How Can It Work?

When you look at a picture of a cluster of eight machines, all running an instance of Oracle against the same database, you've got to wonder how one instance can make sure that the block it wants to modify isn't being modified by the other seven instances at the same time—and won't the problem become harder as the number of instances increases. This is where the genius of the implementation comes in—*once you've got to three instances the level of overhead doesn't get any worse.* To see how this works we'll start by looking at the global resource directory or *GRD* that is a distributed mechanism for controlling access to "things," and *cache fusion* that allows the most important things (the data blocks) to move around the cluster in a timely fashion.

■ **Note** I've often pointed out to clients that if they want to investigate RAC with a view to gradual expansion to many instances then the minimum number of instances they should start with is four. For reasons we will be looking at, two instances is a very special case, and three instances is the first generic case. This makes four the minimum number for testing, because if you want to test for a generic failure you need to fail to three instances, which means starting with four.

The GRD

There are two major mechanisms that operate in RAC to handle the problems of keeping multiple instances coordinated.

- *GES*: The *global enqueue service* that handles the normal aspects of locking that we have already considered for single-instance Oracle—for example, you cannot lock a table in mode 6 (exclusive) in your instance if I am locking it in mode 3 (row-share) in my instance. There has to be a mechanism that ensures we both know about each other's lock requests. The functionality for GES is essentially handled by three background processes LCK0, LMD, and LMON—but we don't really need to know exactly what they do or how they work.
- *GCS*: The *global cache service* that handles block management (or cache coherency as it's usually called). You cannot modify your buffered copy of a block if I've modified my buffered copy because only one of those copies can end up being copied to disc, so there has to be a mechanism that ensures we both know what the other is doing and are both aware of a single current copy of the block. The functionality of GCS is essentially handled by LMSn (the n representing the fact that we can have many LMS processes for each instance—directives on the number vary, but generally focus on the number of CPUs on a machine or the number of instances in the cluster.

■ **Note** As we start to talk about things like GCS and cache fusion, it's worth mentioning that instances do not read each other's SGAs directly, they pass messages to each other, requesting information, mostly by way of LMSn and LMD.

In Chapter 4 we examined the way that Oracle creates resources to represent objects. In RAC we just need to create more resources because we have to protect many more objects—and we have to have a mechanism for locking (or queuing on) those resources, and making them highly visible across all the instances. This leads us to the two views **v$dlm_ress** (the distributed lock manager resources) and **v$ges_enqueue** (the global enqueues services enqueues—formerly **v$dlm_locks**), and the strategy of the GRD (the global resource directory).

There are two major problems that Oracle has to deal with in the GRD. First, it has to cover a very large number of objects—every item in the dictionary cache, every database block that's in memory somewhere, and so on—so the scale is much larger with a much finer granularity than the issue we tackled with locking tables, files, etc. in Chapter 4. Secondly we have multiple instances—and we might worry that we have to keep replicating the locking information to every node leading not only to a massive volume of information, but a geometrically increasing volume of lock-related traffic as the number of instances in the cluster grows. Fortunately the second problem simply doesn't exist—we don't clone the same GRD to every instance, we share one copy equally across all instances in the cluster, and the way we share it and use it is, as we shall see, very cunning.

■ **Note** Earlier versions of RAC (and OPS, its predecessor) generally used a single lock to cover either a range, or a regular “pattern” of blocks, using “fine-grained locking” as an occasional special case. In newer versions of Oracle fine-grained locking (one lock = one block) is the default approach and the option for using a single lock to cover multiple blocks is the special case. The principle exception is for read-only tablespaces, which need only one lock for each file.

Let’s start with the memory structures—we have `v$dlm_ress` that is analogous to `v$resources`—it lists the things that are lockable—and `v$ges_enqueue` that is analogous to `v$lock`—it lists the things doing the locking. Apart from the views themselves, we can see the scale of these structures in two other ways—in `v$sgastat`, and in `v$resource_limit`.

Querying these two views, we can see the memory allocated in the SGA for the global resources and locks and the number of items involved. The following (with a little editing to reduce the size of the outputs) are some key results:

```
select
        resource_name, current_utilization, max_utilization
from
        v$resource_limit
where
        resource_name like '%g_s%'
order by
        resource_name
;

RESOURCE_NAME   CURRENT_UTILIZATION MAX_UTILIZATION
--------------- ------------------- ---------------
gcs_resources                  6615            6615
gcs_shadows                    9716            9716
ges_cache_ress                 1218            1364
ges_locks                      4911            5071
ges_ress                       7772            7872

select
        *
from
        v$sgastat
where
        name like '%gcs%'
or      name like '%ges%'
order by
        name
;
```

```
POOL         NAME                            BYTES
------------ -------------------------- ----------
shared pool  gcs resources                 4927120
shared pool  gcs shadows                   3630512
shared pool  ges resource                  2602392
shared pool  ges enqueues                  5171824
```

There are many more rows in `v$sgastat` than the four I've shown, but the few results I've show here from the two views provide an important starting point to the GRD. You'll notice that `v$sgastat` shows only *GES enqueues* and `v$resource_limit` shows *GES_locks*, there are no enqueues or locks reported for *GCS*. The lock/enqueue mechanics are handled by GES whether the locks/enqueues apply to the cache resources or the more traditional resources.

Another important piece of information is visible in both views from the presence of the *GCS shadows*. Oracle separates general enqueue handling from the cache handling because the frequency of activity and the size of the packets that needs to be passed across the interconnect is so much higher for cache manipulation—so we get a separate structure for the global cache resources; but there are other reasons for creating a separate structure. When an instance crashes we don't have to worry very much about what (general) locks or dictionary cache, or library cache items it held. We do worry about which data blocks it had in its cache and the state of those blocks—so the work that GCS does to keep track of the location and state of blocks is more sophisticated and requires some extra infrastructure. So Oracle has separate structure for the global cache resources—even though some of the v$ objects then hide the separation.

But there's more than just a separate list of resources—the views are showing us *gcs RESOURCES* and *gcs SHADOWS*. And this is where we get the clue about how Oracle handles the global resource directory. Oracle shares responsibility for controlling (or *mastering*) resources equally across all instances in the cluster; but every other instance that is currently using a resource keeps a *shadow* resource that contains a critical subset of the information from the *master* resource—and in the case of cache resources we have an explicit view of the memory this takes.

Masters and Shadows

Before dealing with the subtleties of global cache management, I'll just make a few comments about how Oracle handles resource mastering. Essentially it's based on random distribution using a hashing function. If your instance wants to check up on the global state of a resource, it calculates a hash value from the resource identity, and that tells it which instance is the master instance for that resource. So, for example, if you want to attach a lock to table XYZ, your instance could do some arithmetic with the object id of the table and find out which node ought to hold the master TM resource for that table. It would then check with that node to find out whether some other instance currently had it locked in an incompatible mode.

REMASTERING

I've said that Oracle knows how to find the master resource for an object by doing arithmetic. The rules of how this works have changed over versions of Oracle and, on top of everything, there are special cases for data blocks.

If Oracle detects that a *data object* is used in one instance far more than it is in any another instance, it can bypass the normal address-based arithmetic and make the instance the resource master for all blocks from that object. (Historically, this process went through three stages (a) not working at all, (b) targeted at the file level, (c) targeted at the object (data segment) level).

Since the number of data objects in a database tends to be relatively small compared to the number of blocks in the database it is possible for each instance to keep a map of all the data objects that have a specific resource master and run a short code path to check for data object mastering before going into the generic arithmetic for deriving the master for an individual block. The main impact on the algorithm is that Oracle will dynamically remaster objects—and as it does so it has to freeze the GRD briefly (which means freezing every instance) so that existing master resources for an object can be moved to the correct instance. This can take a few seconds—and if you're unlucky you may find that the nature of your processing results in a few objects being remastered on a fairly regular basis. Recent versions of Statspack and AWR report statistics about the number of remastering events and objects remastered, which can help to alert you to a potential problem.

On my little RAC system, object_id 6334 (to pick a random example) corresponds to table WRH$_LATCH, and 6334 = 0x18be in hexadecimal, so I can get a global view of what's going on with the TM resource for that table by querying the views **gv$dlm_ress** and **gv$ges_enqueue**. Note that I'm using the gv$ global versions of the view in the following:

```
select
        *
from    gv$dlm_ress
where   resource_name like '%0x18be%TM%'
;

select
        *
from    gv$ges_enqueue
where   resource_name1 like '%0x18be%TM%'
;
```

In this case the results showed me that there was a resource (**v$dlm_ress**) with the relevant name on all three nodes; but it was only node 1 that showed the allocation of enqueues (**gv$ges_enqueue**)—in other words, node 1 is the master node, it knows everything that's going on with that TM resource, but the other two nodes have some information about the state of the resource because they are currently interested parties. The following are a few columns (rearranged vertically, through Tom Kyte's famous **print_table** routine) from the **gv$ges_enqueue** view:

```
INST_ID                     : 1
HANDLE                      : 000000008D2537C0
GRANT_LEVEL                 : KJUSERCW
REQUEST_LEVEL               : KJUSERCW
RESOURCE_NAME1              : [0x18be][0x0],[TM][ext 0x0,0x0
RESOURCE_NAME2              : 6334,0,TM
STATE                       : GRANTED
OWNER_NODE                  : 2
-----------------
```

```
INST_ID                    : 1
HANDLE                     : 000000008D256E60
GRANT_LEVEL                : KJUSERCW
REQUEST_LEVEL              : KJUSERCW
RESOURCE_NAME1             : [0x18be][0x0],[TM][ext 0x0,0x0
RESOURCE_NAME2             : 6334,0,TM
STATE                      : GRANTED
OWNER_NODE                 : 1
-----------------
```

■ **Note** The dynamic performance views in single-instance Oracle are often referred to as the v$ views since most of them have names starting with v$. These views are often defined internally as subsets of the global views, starting with gv$, and restricted to a single instance. If you are running RAC and query one of the gv$ views the node you are on will invoke a parallel query slave process on the other instances, typically with a name like PZ99 (rather than the usual Pnnn)—and even if you have attempted to disable parallel query by setting `parallel_max_servers` to zero these slaves will still be available to RAC.

The results show us that instance number 1is the one recording these enqueues—which means it's the master for the TM resource—and that there are two other instances (`owner_node`) currently maintaining an interest. It's not apparent in this output but the `inst_id` starts counting from one and the `owner_node` starts counting from zero! In this particular example the master node doesn't have an enqueue on the resource, even though (as we see from the numbers) it is the master for the resource.

You will also notice that the enqueues have a `grant_level` and `request_level`—in this case both showing `KJUSERCW` (*concurrent write*—the equivalent of the *row-exclusive* lock we normally see in `v$lock` when updating a table). Although none of the support structures are visible in the view, or even in the underlying x$, the same patterns of hash tables, pointers and linked lists support global enqueues in much the same way they support single instance enqueues.

It's possible that different resource types behave slightly differently (and the resources for a buffer cache are a very special case anyway), and it's possible that different lock levels result in different behavior but you may see shadow *resources* with enqueues attached. If you do, you will find that the enqueues attached to the shadow resources are only for the shadow's node. The following, for example is a list of the global enqueues for a particular resource (the QQ resource is one of the dictionary cache types relating to histograms):

```
select
        inst_id, owner_node, grant_level, resource_name1
from
        gv$ges_enqueue
where
        resource_name1 like '%[0xf13e8525][0xa660035f],[QQ]%'
order by
        inst_id, owner_node
;
```

```
   INST_ID OWNER_NODE GRANT_LEV RESOURCE_NAME1
---------- ---------- --------- ------------------------------
         1          0 KJUSERPR  [0xf13e8525][0xa660035f],[QQ][

         2          0 KJUSERPR  [0xf13e8525][0xa660035f],[QQ][
                    1 KJUSERPR  [0xf13e8525][0xa660035f],[QQ][
                    2 KJUSERPR  [0xf13e8525][0xa660035f],[QQ][

         3          2 KJUSERPR  [0xf13e8525][0xa660035f],[QQ][
```

Note that the grant level is KJUSERPR—protected read, equivalent to mode 4 (share) in v$lock)—this higher level may explain why the enqueues are attached to both the master and the shadow resources. Checking the value for inst_id and owner_node you can infer that inst_id 2 (node 1!) is the master for this resource, and the nodes with inst_id 1 and 3 are the shadows. Figure 8-3 is a graphic representation of this more generic case—where I've chosen to show you data about a BL (block) resource, and avoided the numeric oddities of naming by referring to the different instances as A, B, and C.

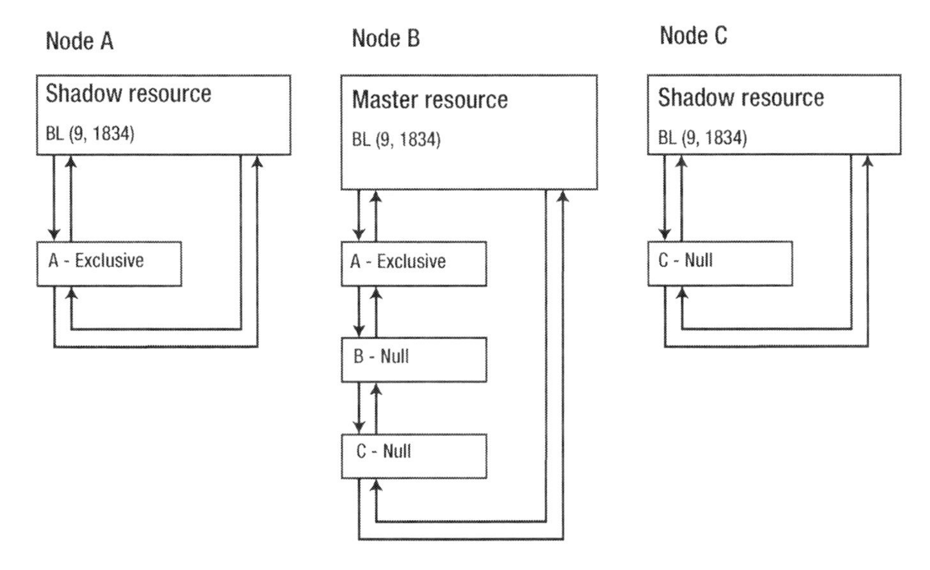

Figure 8-3. *A graphic representation of master and shadows for a three-node cluster*

As we shall see shortly the shadow resources, with their shadow enqueues, will become very important when the resource is of type BL—the buffer cache (or, more accurately, BL for block) resources.

GCS and GES

It's worth highlighting one last little point—the sheer numbers of resources Oracle has to handle. The following are a couple of queries I ran against a single node in a three-node cluster just a few minutes after starting the instances. The messy bits of instr() and substr() are there to pick up just the resource type (the two letter codes correspond to the types reported in v$locktype) and I've trimmed the output to show only the largest counts, as follows:

```
select  -- resources
        substr(resource_name, instr(resource_name,',')+2,2) , count(*)
from
        v$dlm_ress
group by
        substr(resource_name, instr(resource_name,',')+2,2)
order by
        count(*)
;

SUBSTR(R   COUNT(*)
-------- ----------
...
TM              558
QC             1061             -- dictionary cache, segments
BL             2802
QQ             3899             -- dictionary cache, histograms
QI             3959             -- dictionary cache, objects


select  -- enqueues
        substr(resource_name2,-2) , grant_level, request_level, count(*)
from
        v$ges_enqueue
group by
        substr(resource_name2,-2) , grant_level, request_level
order by
        count(*)
;

SUBSTR(R GRANT_LEV REQUEST_L   COUNT(*)
-------- --------- --------- ----------
...
QC       KJUSERPR  KJUSERPR        1060
BL       KJUSEREX  KJUSERNL        2552
BL       KJUSERPR  KJUSERNL        3891
QI       KJUSERPR  KJUSERPR        4888
QQ       KJUSERPR  KJUSERPR        6140
```

As you can see, the Qx resources—representing the dictionary cache—are fairly numerous, and the numbers can get very large when you have partitioned tables with large numbers of partitions and lots of histograms. The other resource type with a very high count is the BL type—covering blocks. In this example the number of BL resources and enqueues is significantly lower than the number of Qx resources and enqueues, but that number will increase as the database sees more use.

Essentially a BL resource is associated with a single block, although that isn't true for things like global temporary tables and read-only tablespaces. And while a given block is in a buffer cache in one of the instances, there will be a BL resource associated with it. In theory, then, the total number of master BL resources across the whole system could match the total number of buffers available to the system—

but that would require every single buffer across the entire system to hold a different block from the database.

In practice, databases tend to have popular areas, with multiple copies of each block in each instance—so the number of master BL resources is likely to be much less than the total number of buffers. On the other hand, a large fraction of the data buffers in an instance will hold blocks that need to be protected—and an instance that doesn't hold the master resource for a block will hold a shadow resource for it, so the total number of BL resources (masters plus shadows) will be in same ballpark as the total number of buffers. Fortunately, the memory allocation for a single shadow resource is significantly smaller than the memory required for a master resource.

■ **Note** When we talk about the buffer cache we try to think about blocks and buffers separately. We use buffers temporarily to hold copies (current, out of date, or constructed read consistent copies) of blocks, and the work we do tends to be about managing linked lists of *buffers*. However, when we search for data we search and locate it by *block* address—and there is no connection between the memory address of a buffer and the disc address of a block. In RAC we use the BL resource type to protect blocks—and the id1/id2 values that go with a BL resource identify the block address—we are not protecting buffers.

Even though the number of Qx resources can be very large, possibly even a significant fraction of the BL resources—there are two important differences between the two resource types. First, the dictionary cache (Qx) tends to be quite stable; a few minutes after startup the dictionary cache has probably loaded most of the information it needs and it's only likely to change slowly over time as, for example, you collect new statistics for objects. This slow rate of change means the size is not a threat to performance—although an extreme number histograms can do astonishing things to the size of the dictionary cache, and can cause problems.

On the other hand the contents of the buffer cache can change dramatically over time—blocks are read in, blocks are pushed out, and the list of resources has to keep changing to match the blocks that are cached; blocks are modified by different instances, so the lock modes have to change constantly to ensure that the only node that can change a block is the node that currently holds an exclusive lock on the resource.

And then there's the really big difference—BL resources cover objects (blocks) that actually have to move from one instance to another. Most of the resources simply act as guards, but if anyone wants a BL *lock*, they're going to want the *block* it covers immediately afterwards; this is why we have the GCS mechanism with the LMS processes—GES handles the *right* to access a block, GCS handles the actual block.

Cache Fusion

In general, most of the messaging that goes on in a RAC cluster is about blocks—we have GES dealing with the right to access blocks, and we have GCS moving copies of blocks from one instance to another. In this section we're going to look at how block movement (or *cache fusion*, as it is known) takes place, and the side effects that it causes.

Every time a RAC instance reads a block from disk into memory it will have to trigger the creation of a resource to represent the state of that block. In fact, before an instance reads a block from disc it will work out where the appropriate resource ought to be and interrogate the master instance for that resource to see if the block is already in a cache somewhere else, because if it is it can request that the current holder of the block to send it across the interconnect. There are two possible sequences of steps as far as the reader is concerned. Option one is:

1. Calculate location of master resource from block address.
2. Send message to master instance to create an enqueue on the resource.
3. If the resource does not exist, the master creates a resource, attaches an enqueue to it, and tells the reader to go ahead.
4. The reader creates a shadow resource and enqueue, and reads the block from disk into memory.

Option two (see Figure 8-4) is:

1. Calculate location of master resource from block address.
2. Send message to master instance to create an enqueue on the resource.
3. Master determines that the resource exists, and therefore is in memory somewhere in the cluster. The current enqueues attached to the resource tell it which instance is the best choice to supply the block. The master adds an enqueue to the resource, modifies the other enqueues on the resource as necessary (which may mean sending messages to some other instances), and instructs the chosen instance to forward the block to the reader.
4. When the block has arrived the reader sends a message to the master to inform it that the transfer has completed, and creates a shadow resource and enqueue.

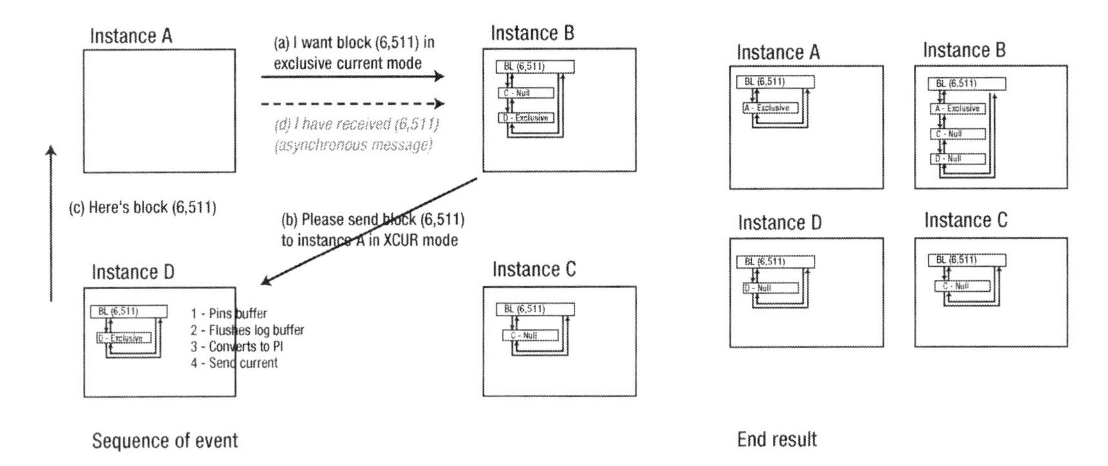

Figure 8-4. *A three-way block transfer in a four-node cluster*

If you look at Figure 8-4, with its image of a four-node RAC cluster, you can recognize an important point about the RAC implementation—it doesn't matter how many nodes there are in the cluster, the worst possible scenario is that a maximum of three nodes are involved in moving a block around the cluster:

- The node that wants the block
- The node that is the master for the corresponding resource
- The node that currently holds the "best" copy of the block

This is why you see waits for events like: `gc current block 2-way` and `gc current block 3-way` and why two-node RAC is such a special case. Two-node RAC is the only version of RAC that doesn't have to handle three-way messaging, and there are various parts of the messaging code that have been optimized to take advantage of this fact.

Despite the fact that a cache fusion operation never exceeds three steps there is still an increased performance impact as the number of nodes increases because of the increased probability that you will have to do a three-step operation.

Consider the following: in a three node RAC system, there is one chance in three that you are the master for the relevant resource—that is, one chance in three that you know that you have to read it or who to demand it from (two-way). If you aren't the master you send a message to the instance that is the master, and if the block is somewhere in memory there's a 50/50 chance that the master is also holding the block and can send it to you (two-way), rather than telling the other instance to send it to you (three-way).

Think about how the odds change if you have four nodes. There's only one chance in four that you're the master; and if you're not the master there's only one chance in three that the master is also the holder. So more nodes does mean more traffic—but after about 10 nodes the marginal difference in messaging from adding more nodes is ignorable.

It may help to look at a few real numbers (from a strictly controlled scenario) to demonstrate the point. I've set up a three-node RAC and then run one session on each node to do 100 select-and-updates each (with commits) in a fast loop on a single block. The following are the three sets of wait events (restricted to the most interesting ones) that I see:

```
Event                           Waits  Time_outs       Csec    Avg Csec    Max Csec
-----                           -----  ---------       ----    --------    --------
gc cr block 2-way                  98          0          4        .043           0
gc current block 2-way             98          0          4        .044           0

gc cr block 2-way                  49          0          2        .036           2
gc cr block 3-way                  47          0          3        .063           0
gc current block 2-way             48          0          2        .033           0
gc current block 3-way             46          0          2        .053           0

gc cr block 2-way                  50          0          2        .049           0
gc cr block 3-way                  47          0          3        .064           1
gc current block 2-way             50          0          2        .035           0
gc current block 3-way             46          0          2        .051           5
```

It's not hard to see that the results aren't symmetrical—and with a little thought you might work out that the first set of figures comes from the node that holds the master resource for the block in question. Whenever it needs to get the latest version of the block back into its cache it knows who's got that copy, so it always reports a two-way operation. (The `gc cr block 2-way` is for the select, the `gc current block 2-way` is for the update.) The other two nodes, however, have to ask the first node to work out how to get the block to them—half of the time the first node says "I've got the latest copy" and we see a two-way operation; the other half of the time the first node says "the other node has the latest copy" and we see a three-way operation.

If you extended this test to four nodes you would still see the master node doing nothing but two-way operations, but you would have three sets of results for the other nodes with roughly 33 two-way operations and 66 three-way operations of each kind. And you might note that, although the figures are not themselves conclusive, three-way operations are slower than two-way operations.

Note When you look at the messaging that goes on in RAC, particularly the way that instances pass data blocks around, there are two ways of looking at the work done. You could say that it's a positive benefit that you can get blocks across the network—it's faster than reading them from disc. You could say that it's an overhead—why not get rid of the cluster and increase your RAM? If you think the work that RAC does is an overhead, you have to ask yourself why you chose RAC at all, if your choice was made for the right reasons the cost of the traffic shouldn't be viewed as an overhead. (That doesn't mean you should ignore it, it's always nice to get rid of excess work when it's cost-effective to do so—and in RAC you do this by trying to minimize the number of blocks that every one wants to see.)

Consequences

There are all sorts of little side effects to the transfer of blocks around the cluster. In general, you may hardly notice them, but there are probably some odd boundary cases where a small side effect actually turns into a significant performance problem.

CUR or CR

When we ask another node to send a block the impact this has depends on whether we want a consistent read copy of the block, or the current block. If we want the current version of the block then the other node has to pin the relevant buffer in exclusive mode and flush the current content of the log buffer to disc before sending it—which we can see in the system statistics `gc current block pin time` and `gc current block flush time` (both reported in centiseconds). Once the other node has sent the block to us though, the copy in its buffer is no longer current— we've got the current—but it's a little better than a consistent read copy because it's a version of the block that really was current for a time, so Oracle gives it the state of PI (past image).

Past image blocks are important—and a potential nuisance. If my instance crashes after modifying the current copy that I've got, the recovery process can take advantage of past images to reduce the time to recover, and that's a potential plus.

On the other hand, if my instance writes the current block to disc what should be done with the PI in the other instance? We don't need it any more but how should we deal with it? Looking at it from the other end of the link—if the other instance wants to remove the PI from memory to use the buffer to read another block, should the instance take any special action because it's handling a PI—and does it make any difference whether the PI is clean or dirty ? You might also ask if the other node could create a local read-consistent copy by starting with a PI rather than asking another node to build a read-consistent copy from the current block.

■ **Note** There are many little details where we can ask questions, and find that no-one has documented the answer, or where the answers may have changed over time (and version). A few answers to the questions I've asked about past images. If you write a current (XCUR) block then you have to tell any instance holding a PI of that block to downgrade it to CR. If you are holding a PI copy of a block and have to flush it from memory to make a buffer free then you have to send a message to the holder of the XCUR to write the current copy to disc before you release the PI (this may only be true if the PI is currently dirty). Finally, it doesn't look as if Oracle will use a PI in the local instance to create a read-consistent copy of a block, it always seems to start with a message to the holder of the XCUR.

Things are better if your instance is only after a consistent copy of a block. The request goes to the holder of the current copy, which builds and sends the consistent read copy. Again we get two time-related statistics about CR copies: `gc cr block build time` and `gc cr block flush time`. Isn't it interesting that Oracle again flushes the log buffer before building a CR copy—I can't think of a good reason for doing so—unless it's to avoid an anomaly that could arise from the new `commit write nowait` option that we saw in Chapter 5.

Again we can ask some detailed questions about the process, and find that answers may have changed over time. Here's an interesting question—is there ever a time when the instance holding the current block refuses to build the CR copy and sends the current block instead, leaving it to the calling instance to build the copy?

I think the answer may be (or may once have been) yes. If the instance determines that it can't build the copy from blocks that it already has in memory, or finds that it's going to have to query yet another instance for undo blocks, then it won't build the CR copy—it will pass the problem to the calling instance. (Unfortunately, I have been told that it will always build the CR copy, so until I actually do a few tests myself I'm not going to make any assumptions about what really happens.)

Current Reads

It's not just requests for blocks that could cause messages about blocks to fly across the interconnect. We've already seen how the existence of past images may require some extra cross-instance chatter (and subsequent action) to take place. There are other considerations to do with the state (as in `x$bh.state`) of a block when it's read into a data buffer.

When a session reads a block from disc into memory in single-instance Oracle, it will typically arrive in the state XCUR (exclusive current) because (a) it's the current version of the block, and (b) there is only one instance and one buffer holding that version of the block so it is exclusive. In RAC it will typically arrive as SCUR (shared current) because it's perfectly reasonable for several instances to get exactly the same copy of the block into memory—and every copy is the current copy. (If it's being read for an update statement though, it will arrive in the state XCUR.)

Note If you have SYS privileges you can run the following query to see how many blocks you have in what state: `select state, count(*) from x$bh group by state;` The commonest states are: 0—free, 1—XCUR (exclusive current), 2—SCUR (shared current), 3—CR (available only for consistent read), 8—PI (past image). This isn't a nice thing to do to your buffer cache, so resist the temptation to do it on a busy production system with a large cache.

Imagine, now, that you have eight nodes in your cluster and all eight of them have a block in SCUR mode—and one of them updates the block. What happens to the other seven copies? They can't stay at SCUR any more because they're not the current copy. So the updating instance has to send a message to every other instance (by way of the resource master) to tell them to change to CR. I don't, however, know if the instance has to wait to receive any type of confirmation that the conversion has happened—possibly it's a "fire and forget" message, perhaps it only has to wait for the resource master to confirm that it has received and forwarded the message.

By now you will realize that there is a lot of unknown, or unpublished, information about the way that RAC works. But with a few ideas about how things *must* work, it's possible to devise fairly simple (though tedious) experiments that help you explain where performance anomalies come from when you see some RAC-related statistic showing a value that doesn't seem to make sense.

It's all about the fact that there can be only one current block, but the trail of past images and read-consistent copies, and the actions that cause them to appear, can be very varied and lead to unexpected levels of messaging.

Note An odd little example to highlight the strange details that appear in RAC: if you issue a call to `alter system flush buffer_cache`, this flushes the caches of *all* the instances. However, in 11.2 if no other version, PIs survive the flush and change to state CR. Don't ask why—it's probably a side effect rather than a deliberate design decision.

I don't think there's much more to say about cache coherency and the global cache services, but before I go on to a more concrete example to make use of RAC, I'd like to say a few words about instance recovery with RAC—partly to pick up on the benefits of past images.

Recovery

The first thing to do when discussing recovery and RAC is to dismiss media recovery—it's not really any different from media recovery for single-instance Oracle. You take a backup copy of the database and a list of (archived) redo log files and work through them applying the redo log entries that need to be applied; and since Oracle does a two-phase recovery (working out which blocks need recovering from which redo byte address) it doesn't really make much difference that the recovery process has to keep log files from multiple instances in synch as it reads and applies them.

There are, inevitably, a couple of interesting little details. For example, the need to (logically) merge all the log files means that when you set up a physical standby for a RAC system, only one of the standby instances can perform the actual redo read and merge. (That's not as bad as it sounds, since that one instance can hand off the redo records to the other instances in much the same way that single-instance Oracle can do parallel recovery.)

The more important aspect of recovery is instance recovery—after all, one of the arguments for RAC is high availability, and the fact that "the system" survives even if an instance (or the machine it's running on) fails. It's worth taking a look at how this works.

The different instances are constantly talking to each other—so if one instance disappears, the other instances find out about it fairly promptly. At this point they will all race to acquire the single instance recovery (IR) lock—and the instance that gets it will perform instance recovery for the failed instance.

Part of the work involves recovering the changes that had been made to blocks in the failed instance's cache and then rolling back the uncommitted changes; part of it involves reconstructing the master resources that the failed instance was holding, and cleaning out all references to the failed instance from the GRD; and part of it entails "rebalancing" the GRD because the cluster is now a different size and the hashing algorithm that allowed an instance to find a resource won't work any more.

REBALANCING

The way in which Oracle redistributes master resources keeps changing, but part of it has remained stable since 9i. Oracle keeps a very small map of "logical" and "physical" instances, and at steady state logical instance N will be physical instance N.

When an instance leaves the cluster, Oracle simply adjusts the map to assign the physical instance that has left to a different logical instance, and recreates the lost master resources on that physical instance. This avoids the need to redistribute all the resources because of one instance failure—but it does mean that the resource mastery is no longer operating a fair-share system.

It's possible that a secondary mechanism subsequently takes over and gradually migrates master resources to a fairer distribution by mapping the correct location for a master when there are N-1 nodes in play, but also keeping a note of where it might be immediately after a failure from N nodes.

It's probably appropriate to mention at this point that when it comes to BL resources, the hashing algorithm used by Oracle is based on a unit size of 256 blocks (in 11.2). Each datafile is split into chunks of 256 consecutive blocks, and the same instance will be the master for every block in a chunk. Conveniently, this means that during a tablescan, each multiblock read request is likely to cover blocks that all belong to a single instance—especially if you are using locally managed tablespaces that essentially operate on a 1 MB boundary.

It's a little difficult to work out Oracle's algorithm for redistributing BL resources when you add an instance to a cluster—particularly if you only have a small cluster to work with—but it looks as if the move from N-1 instance to N instances simply involves each instance passing mastery of every Nth chunk to the new node. This doesn't produce a regular pattern of ownership across a file, but it produces fair shares with a minimum of disruption.

There are two key points to the recovery. On the plus side, it's fully automatic (and if you're lucky and you've configured it the failed instance will be restarted automatically anyway). On the minus side, rebuilding and rebalancing the GRD freezes the instance briefly—and it's not possible to say how long that might be; ideally, it's only a handful of seconds.

Shadow resources and past images play an interesting role in what goes on during recovery. Oracle can scan all the shadow resources on the surviving nodes to reconstruct images of the master resources from the failed instance—this is probably the step that is responsible for most of the time spent in the system freeze—and as it rebuilds the master resources it can discard any master resources (from any instance) holding enqueues for only the failed instance except master resources that show exclusive locks on BL resources as these are possibly blocks that will need recovery.

When it comes to the recovery, Oracle can reduce the amount of work it has to do with the redo logs because Past Images are known to be recent copies of blocks that would have been written to disc if another instance had not called them across the network. So any time Oracle finds a redo record for a block that exists as a past image somewhere it can discard the redo if its SCN is lower than the last change SCN on the past image. This helps to reduce the recovery time, but you will still see sessions waiting for blocks that are still pinned by the recovery process.

Sequences

I'll spend the rest of this chapter on a more concrete example of the problems you can run into, and the way you have to look at RAC, by picking a single, simple piece of functionality and examining the anomalies that start to appear when RAC gets thrown into the equation. There's no specific reason why I picked *sequences* as the focus of this section—they just happen to offer an easy way of producing results that make the type of generic points I want to raise. We'll start by clearing up a couple of common misconceptions about sequences, then examine the way that the internal implementation of sequences is subject to a couple of problems in RAC, then we'll see how one of the commonest methods of using sequences needs to be reconsidered in the light of RAC.

Although Oracle sequences can be used in several different ways, the most common is as a source of unique, consecutive, whole numbers that, basically, are what you get if you use the default syntax to create a sequence, as follows:

```
create sequence test_sequence;
```

If you use the `dbms_metadata` package to read the full definition of this sequence from the data dictionary, you'll see the following important features that need some careful thought when you move to RAC:

```
select
        dbms_metadata.get_ddl('SEQUENCE','TEST_SEQUENCE',user) defn
from dual;

DEFN
-----------------------------------------------------
CREATE SEQUENCE  "TEST_USER"."TEST_SEQUENCE"
MINVALUE 1 MAXVALUE 999999999999999999999999999
INCREMENT BY 1 START WITH 1 CACHE 20 NOORDER
NOCYCLE
```

The two points I want to pick up on are the `CACHE 20` clause (where the 20 could be replaced with any positive whole number or the entire clause could be replaced with `NOCACHE`) and the `NOORDER` clause.

The cache size can make a big difference to single-instance and to RAC, and if you switch from NOORDER to ORDER it can make a catastrophic difference to RAC.

Caching Sequences

There are two misconceptions about sequences and their caches that need to be corrected. The "cache" isn't, as many people think, quite like a traditional cache—it's just a target; if you set a cache of 100 for a sequence Oracle doesn't have to create 100 numbers and store them somewhere in anticipation of them being used—which means it doesn't cost you anything to have a very large cache value.

The second erroneous belief is about where sequences are cached—and they're cached in the SGA. Some people think that sequences are cached by sessions, which would mean that if two sessions were using a sequence with a cache of 1,000 then one session would (for example) be generating number between 1 and 1,000 and the other session would be generating numbers from 1,001 to 2,000. It's possible that this belief came into existence because you can request the currval (current value) as well as the nextval (next value) from a sequence—and this does carry a faint implication that the sequence may be cached locally to the sessions, but really it's just the session remembering currval as the result from the last time it called nextval, it's only one number, not "the whole cache size."

Sequence Internals

Oracle sequences really don't do anything particularly clever, and it's very easy to find out almost everything about how they work by simply tracing a couple of sessions and examining the resulting trace files. Essentially they work as follows:

- A sequence is defined internally as a single row in a table called seq$.
- When you first use the sequence, the starting value of the sequence is incremented by the cache size and written to the row.
- Oracle then tracks two things in memory—the current value (starting from the original value on the row) and the target value.
- Every time anyone calls for nextval, Oracle increments the current value and checks it against the target value before supplying it.
- If the current value and the target value match, Oracle updates the row in the table by adding the cache size to the value that was the target value, producing a new in-memory target.

It's easy to demonstrate the principle. The following example is coded for 11g, where the syntax to assign a sequence value to a variable becomes legal in PL/SQL (even though the internal implementation still runs a select {sequence}.nextval from dual):

```
create sequence test_sequence;

declare
        m_n     number;
begin
        for i in 1..1000 loop
                m_n := test_sequence.nextval;
        end loop;
```

```
end;
/
```

If you run this code with `sql_trace` enabled, and then process the trace file through `tkprof`, you will find the following results (and some other bits that I've deleted):

```
insert into seq$(obj#,increment$,minvalue,maxvalue,cycle#,order$,cache,
  highwater,audit$,flags)
values (:1,:2,:3,:4,:5,:6,:7,:8,:9,:10)

call     count       cpu    elapsed       disk      query    current        rows
------- ------  -------- ---------- ---------- ---------- ----------  ----------
Parse        1      0.00       0.00          0          0          0           0
Execute      1      0.00       0.00          0          1          4           1
Fetch        0      0.00       0.00          0          0          0           0
------- ------  -------- ---------- ---------- ---------- ----------  ----------
total        2      0.00       0.00          0          1          4           1

update seq$ set increment$=:2,minvalue=:3,maxvalue=:4,cycle#=:5,order$=:6,
  cache=:7,highwater=:8,audit$=:9,flags=:10
where obj#=:1

call     count       cpu    elapsed       disk      query    current        rows
------- ------  -------- ---------- ---------- ---------- ----------  ----------
Parse       50      0.00       0.00          0          0          0           0
Execute     50      0.00       0.00          1         50        102          50
Fetch        0      0.00       0.00          0          0          0           0
------- ------  -------- ---------- ---------- ---------- ----------  ----------
total      100      0.00       0.00          1         50        102          50
```

The first statement is Oracle creating our sequence by inserting a row into the `seq$` table with a `highwater` of 1 and a `cache` of 20. The first time we select `nextval` (which is 1) this row is updated to get a `highwater` of 21, and on every twentieth call thereafter it gets updated again—which is why we can see the update taking place 50 (= 1000/20) times. There are two important consequences to this mechanism.

- If you make a lot of calls to `nextval` and don't change the default cache size, you will be generating a lot of updates and redo. That's bad for your session and database anyway—whether RAC or single instance. You may also see waits for the `SQ` lock, which is the lock a session takes while it updates the highwater mark, and on the latch covering the dictionary cache line for `dc_sequences`.
- In a RAC system, things are worse because the block from `seq$` holding the row that you're updating could be constantly traveling round the cluster as different instances make use of the same sequence and have to update the same row in the table. You also have the problem that a single instance may need to read the row back from the table before updating it—because other instances have been updating it more or less concurrently.

In fact, things can be much worse in RAC because the `seq$` table can hold 80 or 90 rows per block—so if you've got a few popular sequences you could have a huge amount of cross-instance traffic and extra reads on the table even when users on different instances are using *different* sequences. Even in single-instance Oracle this can lead to `buffer busy waits`, in RAC it leads to `gc buffer busy` waits.

(Many years ago Oracle even had a note on Metalink about recreating the data dictionary table `seq$` with a very large `pctfree` to limit the damage this behavior could cause in what was then OPS.)

■ **Note** In the tkprof output we saw 50 updates to the `seq$` table when we called for `nextval` 1,000 times from a sequence with a cache size of 20. The number 50 would be repeated in `v$enqueue_stat` with 50 gets for enqueues of type TX (transaction), TM (table), and SQ (sequence). Moreover, we would also see 50 gets, modifications and flushes on the `dc_sequences` parameter in `v$rowcache`—every time we update the table we first update the row cache entry, then copy it to the database.

Ordered Sequences

I've already pointed out that the sequence is cached at the instance level, but there are multiple instances in RAC that lead to another interesting issue: by default each instance will generate its own set of values. If you have four nodes and a cache size of 20, then you will see things like one instance using values 101 to 120, the next using 121 to 140, and so on. This means that the order in which the values are generated and used is unlikely to be purely sequential, and this can make people unhappy. This arrangement also means that if you shut the system down, you will lose some sequence numbers. The instance aiming for the current highwater value on the table can update the `seq$` table to say it stopped prematurely, but there's no way for the other instances to record the numbers they will lose on shutdown.

SEQUENCES, ORDER, AND AUDIT

Occasionally people use sequences with the `nocache` option because they want to guarantee that there are no gaps in the data they produce. Sometimes this is for business applications such as generating purchase order numbers; sometimes it's for a more abstract audit-like purpose. It's important to realize that you can't use Oracle sequences for this type of functionality.

Sequences are non-transactional and Oracle makes no guarantee that you will not lose some values. If, for example, you select `nextval` and then your code does a rollback for some reason, you will have lost a value. Not only can you fail to meet the requirements if you think that setting `nocache` (combined, perhaps with the `order` option) will make it possible to use Oracle sequences, you will also have produced an inherently non-scalable application.

If you need to guarantee no loss and ordering, you will have to employ a mechanism that populates a pool of numbers, and an algorithm that guarantees that you either use a number or retain a physical record of any number that was "allocated but not used." (I described a possible mechanism for this in Practical Oracle 8i a few years ago.)

A common response to the problem of "losing" values is either to set the cache size to zero (nocache)—which causes a dramatic volume of cache transfers as the seq$ block moves from instance to instance in a RAC system—or to leave the sequence with a non-zero (preferably large) cache but apply the order clause—which is nearly as bad for traffic though less nasty in terms of generating *undo* and *redo*.

The order option is specifically aimed at RAC. Instead of allowing each instance to have its own cache for the sequence there is just one highwater value, and one memory location with the current value; however, that memory location is controlled by a special global lock (an SV lock) and the current value of the sequence is passed around in the negotiations for the lock. So the values are generated in order because there is only one live value at any one moment, and only one instance can increment it—which means you've serialized the sequence generation across your instances (but you still haven't got a guarantee that a session or instance crash, or rollback, will stop you from losing the occasional value).

The SV lock is a little strange, and highlights another of the oddities that appear when you start looking closely at implementation details in RAC. If you look in v$lock_type you will find that there is an SV lock type with the description: *Lock to ensure ordered sequence allocation in RAC mode*, and its first parameter (the id1 of view v$lock—although you won't see it appearing there) is the object id of the sequence. However, when a process tries to acquire the SV lock you don't see any sign of it in v$lock, and you won't see a wait for an enqueue as you would, for example in a trace file or in v$session_wait. Instead you'll see a wait for DFS lock handle (which is one of the many waits that is subsequently summarized in v$session_event to the blanket events in waitclass Other) and it's only by decoding the value of the first parameter that you'll discover that it's an SV lock.

There are still more surprises to come though. You might expect the SV lock to be held in mode 6 (exclusive) when one instance wants to acquire it to generate the next sequence value—but decoding the first parameter value of the DFS lock handle wait event you'll find that the lock mode is 5. Believe it or not this is an exclusive lock in RAC! Don't ask why but instead of the six lock modes we saw for non-RAC resources in Chapter 4, RAC uses fives values, which I've listed in Table 8-1.

■ **Note** You will find various documents telling you how to decode the parameters that go with wait events; in many cases you need only query v$event_name to get meaningful descriptions. For example, many of the enqueues waits have the text name|mode for the description of their first parameter. The pipeline symbol ("|") is a clue to convert the value to hexadecimal for ease of translation. In my case I got a value of 1398145029 for my DFS lock handle, which converts to 0x53560005. The 5 on the end is the lock mode, and if you know your ASCII you'll recognize 0x53 as 'S' and 0x56 as 'V'.

Table 8-1. RAC Lock Modes

Mode	Name	Description	V$lock equivalent
0	KJUSERNL	No permission	0 (Null)
1	KJUSERCR	Concurrent read	2 (Row-share)
2	KJUSERCW	Concurrent write	3 (Row-exclusive)
3	KJUSERPR	Protected read	4 (Share)
4	KJUSERPW	Protected Write	5 (Share Row Exclusive)
5	KJUSEREX	Exclusive access	6 (Exclusive)

The other events you're likely to see appearing if you use the order option for a popular sequence are the `latch: ges resource hash list` and the `row cache lock` wait. The former is just telling us that RAC-related resources use the same hash table and linked list strategies that we've seen so many times before. The latter is reminding us that sequences are closely linked to their entries in **`v$rowcache`** and the work (and time) needed to modify and flush an entry in the row cache is higher in RAC than it is in single-instance Oracle.

Sequences and Indexes

There's still more that we can learn about RAC by looking closely at sequences. The next problem comes with the commonest use of sequences—the "meaningless primary key." If you are using sequence to generate consecutive numbers and then using those numbers as a primary or unique key you will have an index on the column holding those numbers—and everyone, from every instance, who inserts a row into the table will want to insert the latest high value into that index. In other words, you've created a cross-instance hot spot—guaranteed to lead to `gc buffer busy` waits. This problem isn't restricted to sequences, of course, all it requires is that the values inserted are always increasing—an index on a simple "current timestamp" column would have the same problem.

INDEX ITL ISSUES

There is a long-standing defect (or bug, perhaps) in Oracle's implementation of B-tree indexes. When a leaf block split takes place and several processes are trying to insert index entries into the splitting block at the same time there is a strange race condition that results in far too many ITL entries being created in the two leaf blocks produced. Since the ITL list in a new index leaf block is always at least as large as it was before the split, the excess ITL entries never disappear—and it is possible to get to a point where every index leaf block loses half its space to the ITL entries as the block is created..

Any index based on a sequence (or real-time timestamp) is a prime candidate for running into this problem, and any index that is regularly subject to even fairly low rates of concurrent insert on hot spots (and that can be as low as one session per CPU) can easily end up running with 50 percent wasted space. In earlier versions of Oracle the workaround was simple: define a suitable value for `maxtrans` on the index. Unfortunately, from 10g onwards, Oracle ignores `maxtrans`.

I have written several articles on this topic on my blog under the category of "index explosion." A bug fix has been released for Oracle 12.1 and there are already a few backports to versions in the 10.2 timeline.

Prior to the introduction of ASSM (automatic segment space management) it was possible to define multiple *free lists* and (sometimes more importantly) multiple *free list groups* to reduce the problem of concurrent inserts on *tables*. ASSM, which allows different RAC instances to claim different bitmap blocks from a segment thereby isolating inserts from each other, made it virtually unnecessary for DBAs to think about the problem of buffer busy waits on tables. But you can't do anything to spread *index* hot spots; an index entry can't be randomly placed, it has to go in the right location.

There have been several suggestions about how to deal with this hot-spot problem. One of them is to reconstruct the index as a *reverse-key* index

---

■ **Note** In a reverse-key index the bytes of each individual column (except the rowid, in the case of a non-unique index with its embedded rowid) are reversed before the entry is stored in the index. This has the effect of making values that initially look similar end up looking very different from each other. For example comparing 329,002 and 329,003 before and after reversal we would see: (c3, 21, 5b, 3) and (c3, 21, 5b, 4) turning into: (3, 5b, 21, c3) and (4, 5b, 21, c3).

At first sight this looks like a good idea—but there is a side effect. If most of your queries are about "recent" data, you may need to cache only a tiny percentage of the total index to keep the relevant part of a "hot" primary key in memory; but if you reverse it the *intent* is to spread the hot spot across a larger area of the index, and the effect is often that you have to cache most (or even all) of the index to get the same caching benefit. Figure 8-5 is a graphic demonstration of the point

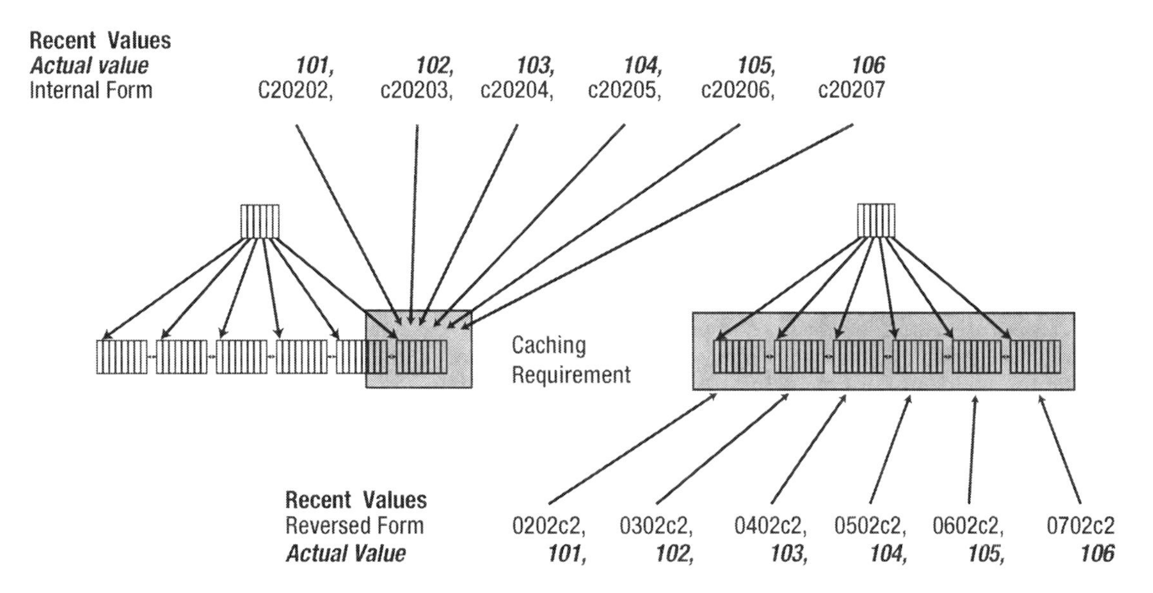

Figure 8-5. *The caching impact of reverse key indexes*

There are two alternative strategies. The simplest one is to ensure that the sequence you use has a very large cache size—5,000 to 50,000 would not be unreasonable (remember, we are talking about high rates of insert so we expect to get through a cache of that size fairly quickly. If you do this, each instance will be inserting rows that have values that differ by thousands so each instance will spend most of its time inserting into its own isolated area in the index. The drawback to this plan is that most of the time leaf block splits will be 50/50 leaf block splits (except for the instance currently inserting the highest values)—in fact, given the concurrency problem mentioned in the side bar, you could see space usage running as low as 25 percent. As a variant on the idea of introducing a large difference between the values used by different nodes, Oracle has, in the past, suggested adding 10^N times the instance id as you use a sequence value, where N is sufficiently large that the sequence won't get near 10^N for a few years.

The other strategy—if you've paid for the partitioning option—is to hash partition the index. Split the index into (say) 16 different pieces by hashing on the sequence number and you've turned the one high-value hot spot into 16 (the number of hash partitions should always be a power of two for best effect) warm spots. You will still get contention on the highest block on each partition, but the reduction in contention may be enough that you can live with the result.

Whatever strategy you choose to address this problem, remember to keep the scale of the problem in perspective. Buffer busy waits are not good—but unless they really waste a lot of critical processing time it's possible to live with them. Be careful that your solution to buffer busy waits doesn't introduce a worse problem. Tragically, I have known sites that introduced RAC because they thought it would get them out of trouble—and then found that it made their troubles worse because the nature of their problems (such buffer busy waits) is exaggerated by the way that RAC works.

Summary

There are two main reasons for looking at RAC—high availability and scalability. As far as high availability is concerned, setting up RAC is not a trivial operation and you should think carefully about your minimum acceptable down time before introducing such a complex stack into your business. As far as scalability is concerned, you need to be aware that badly designed applications may get worse in a RAC environment because of the traffic between instances; on the other hand, a well-designed application may allow you to match your user base with the number of commodity machines you group into a cluster in a nearly linear fashion.

A core feature of the implementation of RAC is that instances need to inform each other of the objects they are using, and the need to protect them properly. Oracle handles this in a distributed Global Resource Directory (GRD). Every object—down to the granularity of the block for data segments—has a master resource that lists the interest that every instance has in the resource. In general, the location of the master resource can be derived by simple arithmetic. Each instance that has attached an enqueue to the master resource will also keep a local "shadow" resource—as far as the data buffer is concerned this allows Oracle to ensure that only one instance can update a block at a time, and that the instance that is holding the master resource for a block coordinates its movement across the network when the block is needed by another instance. The implementation that Oracle uses for the GRD ensures that, no matter how many instances there are in the cluster, the largest number of steps required for an instance to acquire a block is three—this is how Oracle offers the potential for near perfect scalability as you add nodes. However, the probability of a three-way negotiation taking place increases as the number of instances increases, and three-way transfers are slower than two-way transfers.

When an instance crashes, one of the other instances will detect the crash very rapidly—and take control of recovery on behalf of that instance; this involves two steps. First it reverse engineers the master resources held by the crashed instance, which it can do by interrogating the other instances for the relevant shadow resources; then it simply reads the redo log files of the crashed instance in a way that virtually mirrors an absolutely standard recovery—pinning the blocks that need recovery in its buffer cache until the recovery is complete. It will also freeze the GRD temporarily while adjusting the algorithm that the cluster needs to follow to calculate where each master resource should now be located.

There are many small details to consider when converting from single instance to RAC, and lots of little ways you can engineer your design for optimum performance. In this chapter I have selected *sequences* as a showcase to highlight the patterns of thought that you need to follow to avoid the traps that RAC can lead you into. Sequences in RAC are a threat—you need to think carefully about what costs you are prepared to suffer if you really want to use them. At a minimum you should set the cache size for popular sequences to something much larger than the Oracle default. Don't use `nocache`, and don't use `order` unless the sequence sees very little activity.

Since sequences are often used to generate artificial keys, they also introduce hot spots at the "high-value" end of indexes; be cautious about using reverse key indexes to combat this problem as the strategy can lead to increased levels of disk activity—hash partitioned indexes may be a good idea, if you've already paid for the partitioning license.

APPENDIX

Dumping and Debugging

A Summary of This Book's Hackery

Over the past eight chapters, I've been casually mentioning symbolic dumps, peeking at memory, internal structures, and setting events. This appendix is a summary of the methods I've used in the book to investigate or demonstrate some of the things that Oracle does.

oradebug

There are various ways in which one session can affect how another session behaves. One of the oldest and easiest is the `oradebug` utility, which you can take advantage of if your account has sysdba privileges. Many of the things you can do with oradebug you can also do by setting events, so some of the tricks listed in this section will reappear in different guises later on.

Suspending Processes

Some of the things I did to get a better understanding of dbwr and lgwr required those processes to stop. Oradebug allows you *suspend* and *resume* a process. The first thing to do is to attach to an Oracle process, which I tend to do by using the `pid` from `v$process`. There are many simple queries you can write to find the process id for a background process, and the following is an example that probably works across many versions of Oracle (though there are simpler options from 10*g* and later):

```
select
        prc.pid
from
        v$bgprocess     bgp,
        v$process       prc
where
        bgp.name = 'LGWR'
and     prc.addr = bgp.paddr
;
```

On the system I'm looking at right now this query returns the value 6, which I use as follows (warning: do not do this on a system that anyone else is using—you may find that the instance crashes, or that the process can't be made to resume):

```
SQL> oradebug setorapid 6
Windows thread id: 1052, image: ORACLE.EXE (LGWR)
SQL> oradebug suspend
Statement processed.
SQL> -- get some other session to do a little work and commit
SQL> -- it will hang on the commit, waiting on log file sync.
SQL> oradebug resume
Statement processed.
SQL>
```

Suspending lgwr is particularly risky. Don't forget that there may be some recursive SQL going on that will make sessions hang; for example, if you have database auditing enabled with `audit connect`, any ordinary end-user sessions trying to connect or disconnect will hang because their connection will try to commit after inserting or updating a row in `sys.aud$`.

One particular use I made of the suspend mechanism was to demonstrate that one of my long-held assumptions (that pmon detected local instance deadlocks) was wrong. I had actually made this observation in the original manuscript, and one of my reviewers pointed out that I was wrong—so I suspended pmon, set up a deadlock situation, and waited for the ORA-00060 "Deadlock detected" error; sure enough, even with pmon suspended, the deadlock was still trapped and reported within the (fairly standard) 3 seconds.

Dumps

You can use oradebug to dump memory structures to trace files. When I do this I usually connect as sys and then attach oradebug to my own process to generate the dumps. Once you're in oradebug, there is a command to show the trace file name, but it seems to work only after the first use of the trace file; however, you can modify the trace file name by setting the `tracefile_identifier`, and this counts as a first use:

```
SQL> oradebug setmypid
Statement processed.
SQL> oradebug tracefile_name
Statement processed.
SQL> alter session set tracefile_identifier = xxx;

Session altered.

SQL> oradebug tracefile_name
c:\oracle\admin\d10g\udump\d10g_ora_2256_xxx.trc
SQL>
```

If you want to see a list of all the available dumps, the command is `oradebug dumplist`. Many `dump` commands take two parameters—the name of the dump and the level at which to dump. The dump level then tends to follow two patterns: one is simply the higher the level the more that gets dumped; the other is a bitmap approach, where different powers of 2 result in different dumps. Table A-1 lists the `dump` commands I used in the course of writing this book. The effects are not consistent across versions; this table covers 10g+.

Table A-1. A Selection of the **oradebug** *dump Commands*

Option	Result
buffers *N*	Dumps information about buffers, buffer headers, and the various linked lists. Any dump above level 1 is likely to be large even if you start with a buffer cache that is small; with an 8MB cache I got a 28MB dump at level 2 and 49MB at level 3. Unfortunately, it's only level 4 that gives you all the linked list information from the working data sets. 1 = buffer headers only 2 = 1 + raw dumps of blocks + transaction headers 3 = 2 + complete symbolic dump of blocks 4 = working data sets, and buffers headers and raw blocks in hash chain order
enqueues *N*	Dumps information about the resources and enqueues. Level 3 is the most useful (though a little messy until you add a few blank lines), and is the one I used in Chapter 4 on locks. The size of the output is fairly closely dictated by the current number of rows visible in **v$lock**. It's likely to be much less than 1MB. 1 = enqueue resource hash table 2 = 1 + list of currently used resources 3 = 2 + active enqueues on each resource
file_hdrs *N*	Dumps the data file headers. There isn't much to look at, but if you want to check the effect of checkpointing, you need file header dumps to see the checkpoint SCN. A few kilobytes per data file. 1 = standard 2 = adds a little about v10-style header 3 = adds tablespace information, and extended file information. At this level you can also find the **root dba:** entry in file 0 which gives the location of the bootstrap table sys.bootstrap$.
redohdr *N*	Dumps the headers of the online redo log files. Levels 1–3 show increasing (small) amounts of information. Level 1 is sufficient to get the first and next SCN. 1 = standard 2 = adds a little about file header compatibility 3 = adds a little extra detail

Continued

Option	Result
`controlf` *N*	Dumps the contents of the control file. Level 10 is a raw dump, while levels 1 to 9 and 11 dump larger and larger selections of the different control file record types. Level 2 gives a few critical SCNs and RBAs (redo block addresses),
`library_cache` *N*	Dumps library cache information. This dump uses a bitmap strategy. Contents are combined by adding the dump values. Strangely, some of the 11*g* dumps contain less information than the 10*g* equivalents. `1` = `v$librarycache` (approximately) and (for 10*g*) summaries of permanent space allocated for key structures `2` = hash chain summary and (for 10*g*) permanent allocation summaries `4` = list of buckets with header structures for objects, and linked lists on hash chains (sufficient to see details of the lock/pin/mutex information for an object) `8` = 4 + dependencies, "data" blocks, accesses, translations, etc. `16` = 8 + heap dumps of each object's "data" blocks; file will be very big `32` = 16 + complete raw dump of all chunks in the heaps; file will be huge {`x$kglob.kglhdadr`} (e.g., `v$sql.child_address`). For versions prior to 11g, if you convert an object (child) address to decimal, you can dump the summary information for the object. If you want to use the address in the hexadecimal form you get from the x$ or v$ structures, it has to start with "0x". {`x$kglob.kglhdpar`} (e.g., `v$sql.address`). For versions prior to 11g, if you convert an object (parent) address to decimal, you can dump the summary information for the object with a short list of the handles of its children. Again, you can prepend hexadecimal versions of the addresses with 0x.
`library_cache_object {level} {address}`	For 11.2 only (it is recognized in 11.1, but always seems to fail with an "in-flux" error. This is the 11g replacement for the object-level dump in 10g. Dumps details of a single library cache object. The address should be the {`x$kglob.kglhdadr`} (e.g. `v$sql.child_address`), or {`x$kglob.kglhdpar`} (e.g. `v$sql.address`). Hexadecimal addresses should have "0x" prepended, or you can convert to decimal. The levels use the bitmap method; levels I have found useful are: 0 – simple, short, dump 16 – detailed dump 48 – highly detailed dump, including child details if you supply a parent address

Option	Result
heapdump *N*	Dumps the contents of a top-level heap. Again, the dump uses a bitmap strategy; in this case each bit represents a different heap. The main use I've made of this is to dump the SGA heap to show the free memory hash chains and LRU list(s) for used memory. Be very cautious about using this command on the SGA – it can hang your system or, at best, cause a massive latch contention problem for a few minutes. 1 = dump the PGA heap 1025 (0x401) = PGA heap with raw dump of memory chunks 2 = dump the SGA heap 2050 (0x802) = SGA heap with raw dump of memory chunks 4 = dump the session (UGA) heap 4100 (0x1004) = session heap with raw dump of memory chunks 8 (8200/0x2008) = current call heap (with raw dump of memory chunks) 16 (16400/0x4010) = user call heap (with raw dump of memory chunks) 32 (32800/0x8020) = large pool heap (with raw dump of memory chunks) 64 (65600/0x10040) = streams pool heap (with raw dump of memory chunks) 128 (131200/0x20080) = java pool heap (with raw dump of memory chunks) It is also possible to add power(2,29) = 0x2000,0000 = 536,870,912 to the base heap number to get the top five subheaps dumped in detail, and power(2,30) = 0x4000,0000 = 1,073,741,824 to get a recursive dump of the top 5 sub-heaps of each dumped sub-heap

Peeking at Memory

There are two main strategies I use to examine the contents of particular memory locations: knowing the names and peeking at memory. If you know the name of an Oracle variable, you can use the `dumpvar` command to see its value. For example, I happen to know that there is a variable called `kcbnhb` (*kcb* is about the buffer cache, *nhb* is the number of hash buckets) in the SGA, so I can use oradebug as follows:

```
SQL> oradebug setmypid
Statement processed.
SQL> oradebug dumpvar sga kcbnhb
uword kcbnhb_ [3D387B4, 3D387B8) = 00008000
SQL>
```

Generically, that's `dumpvar {area} {variable}`. So, for example, since I know that the current *session* value for `use_stored_outlines` is in a variable called `ugauso_p`, I can do the following:

```
SQL> alter session set use_stored_outlines = rule_based;

Session altered.

SQL> oradebug setmypid
Statement processed.
SQL> oradebug dumpvar uga ugauso_p
qolprm ugauso_p [7867A44, 7867A68) = 00000001 5552000A 425F454C 44455341
SQL>
```

If you know your hex and ASCII you will be able to see the text “RULE_BASED” in the last 12 bytes of the dump, starting with the length of 10 (0x000A).

If you need to find out the names of the variables in the SGA, you can query the structure x$ksmfsv (in this example I’ve picked a subset, but there are several thousand to choose from) and start making guesses about what the names and types mean:

```
select
        *
from    x$ksmfsv
where   ksmfsnam like 'kcbn%'
;

ADDR      INDX INST_ID KSMFSNAM     KSMFSTYP KSMFSADR KSMFSSIZ
-------- ----- ------- ------------ -------- -------- --------
034F9E50  2285       1 kcbnbh_      word     03D37B28        4
034F9E60  2286       1 kcbnbha_     word *   03D37B2C        4
034F9E80  2288       1 kcbnwp_      word     03D37B34        4
034FAF00  2552       1 kcbnbf_      word     03D387B0        4
034FAF10  2553       1 kcbnhb_      uword    03D387B4        4
034FAF20  2554       1 kcbnhbsft_   uword    03D387B8        4
034FB090  2577       1 kcbnpg_      ub4      03D38814        4
034FB160  2590       1 kcbnchkl_    ub1      03D38868        1
034FB170  2591       1 kcbnchk_     int      03D3886C        4
034FBA40  2732       1 kcbnf01_     uword    03D38CE0        4
034FBA50  2733       1 kcbnf02_     uword    03D38CE4        4
```

Each row in x$ksmfsv holds the starting address of a variable (you will notice that the names—ksmfsnam—in this view have an underscore at the end, which you have to remove when you use them with the dumpvar option).

■ **Note** If you don’t want to query x$ksmfsv (that’s kernel services – memory – fixed SGA variables, by the way), there is a special dump command for it, and for the equivalent structure in your PGA and UGA: oradebug dump global_area *N*, where—like the heapdump references in Table A-1, but with a short list of legal values—*N* is 1 for the PGA, 2 for the SGA, and 4 for the UGA. (You can also multiply each by 1025 to see a raw dump of the large structures referenced by the various pointers.)

We could access the variables by name using dumpvar, but most of these variable are simple numbers (although one is a pointer to a number) so we have two other strategies to access them very easily. First, we can peek at the address—remembering to show that it is a hex value. For example, here's another way to check the number of hash buckets is

```
SQL> oradebug setmypid
Statement processed.
SQL> oradebug peek 0x03D387B4 4
[3D387B4, 3D387B4) = 00008000
```

The peek command takes two mandatory parameters and one optional one. The first two are the address and length, the last is a flag to tell Oracle to dump the result to your trace file. In this example I've told Oracle to display 4 bytes (which is the minimum on this platform anyway) but not send the result to the trace file.

But if you've got the address, you can query memory directly. The structure x$ksmmem is indirectly a memory map of the SGA, so we can query the contents of memory 4 bytes at a time. Here's another check on the number of hash buckets:

```
SQL> select * from x$ksmmem where addr = hextoraw('3D387B4');

ADDR       INDX INST_ID KSMMMVAL
-------- ------ ------- --------
03D387B4  12069       1 00008000

1 row selected.
```

You have to be very careful in the way you use x$ksmmem. If you use an address that isn't currently mapped, your session will crash with Oracle error ORA-03113, "end-of-file on communication channel," and the same will happen if your SQL manages to produce an execution path with any predicate that Oracle can't turn into addr = raw_value.

The option to query memory directly may seem fairly limited, but there aren't any good methods to query memory from, which is why some companies (and adventurous individuals) have written low-level programs that attach directly to Oracle's memory to read it. However, I did feel the need to check the content of the log buffer from time to time while writing this book, so when I wanted to look at it, peeking was a good enough start.

Here's a little SQL that will extract a few details about the public redo threads:

```
select
        first_buf_kcrfa,
        last_buf_kcrfa,
        pnext_buf_kcrfa_cln,
        next_buf_num_kcrfa_cln
from
        x$kcrfstrand
where
        last_buf_written_kcrfa != '00'
order by
        indx
;
```

```
FIRST_BU LAST_BUF PNEXT_BU NEXT_BUF_NUM_KCRFA_CLN
-------- -------- -------- ----------------------
05450000 057A4800 05552E00                   2070
057A4A00 05AF9200 05AF9400                   6820

2 rows selected.
```

The `first_buf_kcrfa` and `last_buf_kcrfa` are the addresses of the first and last buffers (i.e., pages matching the log file block size) of the two public log buffers in my system. The `pnext_buf_kcrfa` is the address of the next buffer that will be used and then written to disk. With this information I could, with a little effort, and after getting some easily identifiable data into the log buffer, use oradebug to peek at the contents of the log buffer. Since each page in the log buffer is 512 bytes (which is more than Oracle will display onscreen) I would normally use `oradebug peek {address} 512 1` to dump the data to the trace file one page at a time; but for the purposes of the book, here's a dump of the next few buffer pages, showing only the first 16 bytes of each page—which happen to be the header bytes for the page:

```
SQL> oradebug peek 0x05552e00 16
[5552E00, 5552E10) = 00002201 000022BE 000002E9 D67F80A8
SQL> oradebug peek 0x05553000 16
[5553000, 5553010) = 00002201 000022BF 000002E9 9B6B8010
SQL> oradebug peek 0x05553200 16
[5553200, 5553210) = 00002201 000022C0 000002E9 509980D0
SQL>
```

You will notice that the third word in each page (`000002e9`) evaluates to 745, which is the `sequence#` of my current redo log. The second word is the block id within the log file that this page of memory will be written to. (Unfortunately, I have no idea what the leading 00002201 represents.) I was more interested in checking the data, and cross-checking the raw dump of memory with the symbolic dump from the file—which we will be coming to shortly.

Dumps from SQL

Many of the oradebug commands to dump structures are also available from SQL*Plus, sometimes with options to refine or restrict the content of the dump. Many of the dumps shown in the previous section can be done with a call to `alter session`, or to the package `dbms_system`. Then there are further dumps that you can get through `alter system` calls.

oradebug Alternatives

If you don't want to use oradebug, the following, as a representative sample, is how you can dump the buffer cache from an ordinary SQL*Plus session:

```
alter session set tracefile_identifier = 'alter_session';
execute dbms_system.ksdwrt(1,'Example using alter session')
alter session set events 'immediate trace name buffers level 1';
```

I usually try to dump some text comments whenever I want to dump data through a looping program, which is where `dbms_system.ksdwrt` is useful. It takes two parameters: the second is a piece of text, while the first tells Oracle where to write the text. The options are `1` for the trace file, `2` for the alert log, and `3` to write to both.

The typical oradebug dump turns into an `immediate` event, with the word `level` appearing between the dump name and the level at which to dump.

■ **Note** Although many oradebug dump commands have an SQL equivalent, there will be some translations that don't work. An example is `oradebug dump library_cache {address}` to dump an individual library cache object. You will probably get a trace file containing nothing but the comment "In-flux value for handle."

You may already be familiar with `dbms_system.set_ev()` as one of the many methods for enabling `sql_trace` (or event 10046 as it is often known). However, there is a dummy event number (65,535) that can be used to make the call perform the named dumps:

```
alter session set tracefile_identifier = 'dbms_system';
execute dbms_system.ksdwrt(1,'Example using dbms_system')

declare
        m_serial        number(15,0);
begin
        select  serial#
        into    m_serial
        from    v$session
        where   sid = dbms_support.mysid
        ;

        dbms_system.set_ev(
                si => dbms_support.mysid,
                se => m_serial,
                ev => 65535,
                le => 1,
                nm => 'buffers'
        );
end;
/
```

To give them their full names, the five parameters for `dbms_system.set_ev` are `sid`, `serial#`, `event`, `level`, and `name`. If you set the event to 65535, then the `name` and `level` parameters can take on the names and levels used in the oradebug command.

Data File Blocks

The first of the `alter system` commands that I use regularly (often wrapped in a little PL/SQL procedure to identify index root blocks, or segment header blocks) is the call to dump a block or group of blocks. The syntax is

```
alter system dump datafile {File no} block {Block no};
alter system dump datafile 4 block 129;
alter system dump datafile {File no} block min {Block min} block max {Block max};
alter system dump datafile 4 block min 129 block max 133;
```

In recent versions of Oracle this version of the call will dump the on-disk copy and all the copies of the selected blocks from memory and, thanks to the complexity of the private redo mechanism, may report one of the memory copies as being corrupted. There is a variation on this command that uses the data file name rather than a file number:

```
alter system dump datafile '{name}' block {Block no};
alter system dump datafile '{name}' block min {Block min} block max {Block max};
```

If you use this version of the call, the blocks obviously have to be read from disk (which means you have to issue a checkpoint to make sure that you're looking at the latest version, of course).

Although you can dump virtually any data file block with the previous calls (file headers are the one exception I know of, but there may be others), there is a special case that I use occasionally for undo segment headers, which dumps the block by segment name:

```
alter system dump undo header '{segment name}';
alter system dump undo header ' _SYSSMU3$';
```

Log Files

The other thing that I dump fairly regularly is the log file. The basic syntax for this is very simple:

```
alter system dump logfile '{filename}';
alter system dump logfile 'C:\ORACLE\ORADATA\D10G\REDO01.LOG'
```

In most cases I tend to issue `alter system switch logfile;` before doing a little bit of work and then dumping the whole file, but there are many options for being selective about which bits of the file you want to dump. My Oracle Support (the application formerly known as MetaLink) has a note (ID 1031381.6) giving you some of the possible options. The document is not quite complete, however. As far as I know the full syntax is

```
alter system dump logfile '{filename}'
        scn min {first SCN to dump}
        scn max {last SCN to dump}
        time min {seconds since an oddly arbitrary point in time}
        time max {ditto}
        layer {integer}
        opcode {integer}
        xid {usn} {slot} {sequence}          -- 10g and later but breaks on IMU redo
        Objno {object id}                    -- 10g and later but breaks on IMU redo
        dba min {datafile no} . {blockno}    -- remove the dot for 10g and later
        dba max {datafile no} . {blockno}    -- remove the dot for 10g and later
        rba min {log file seq#} . {blockno}  -- remove the dot for 10g and later
        rba max {log file seq#} . {blockno}  -- remove the dot for 10g and later
```

As you can see, there are options to be selective. The ones that I find more useful are the ones that specify a database block, the object id, and the transaction id. I have, on occasion, used all the other options on production systems apart from the redo block address. The option I've used most commonly is to dump all the redo related to a given database block—and this has usually been to find when, or how, the block was corrupted.

For example, for 9*i* and 10*g* respectively:

```
alter system
        dump logfile 'C:\ORACLE\ORADATA\D920\REDO02.LOG'
        dba min 11 . 10  dba max 11 . 10
;

alter system
        dump logfile 'C:\ORACLE\ORADATA\D10G\REDO02.LOG'
        dba min 5 10 dba max 5 10
;
```

Note that the spaces either side of the dot are needed for 9*i* and earlier, but the dot is not needed from 10*g* and later (the same is true for the `rba min` and `rba max` options). Remember, also, that the file number is the *absolute* file number, not the *relative* file number. Since the absolute and relative files numbers are usually equal in small databases (up to 1023 files) you may want to set event 10120 before creating a couple of files as this will allow you to create files where the absolute and relative files numbers don't match.

If you want to scan all the redo generated for a time period, you first have to do a little experimentation (probably). You can specify a time, but it's expressed as the number of seconds since an internally selected starting point—except that there is an error in the code converting seconds to dates: it thinks there are 31 days in *every* month of the year.

I have a simple script that I use (modifying it as necessary) to dump a small time range in the recent past—the following code, followed by the first few lines of the dump, was for a 5-minute range starting 10 minutes ago on the date that I wrote this appendix:

```
select
        (
                (sysdate - 10/(24*60)) -
                to_date('25/7/1987 00:00:00','dd/mm/yyyy hh24:mi:ss')
        ) * 86400       start_time,
        (
                (sysdate -  5/(24*60)) -
                to_date('25/7/1987 00:00:00','dd/mm/yyyy hh24:mi:ss')
        ) * 86400       end_time
from
        dual
;

alter system
dump logfile 'C:\ORACLE\ORADATA\D10G\REDO02.LOG'
        time min 760100786
        time max 760101086

DUMP OF REDO FROM FILE 'C:\ORACLE\ORADATA\D10G\REDO02.LOG'
 Opcodes *.*
 RBAs: 0x000000.00000000.0000 thru 0xffffffff.ffffffff.ffff
 SCNs: scn: 0x0000.00000000 thru scn: 0xffff.ffffffff
 Times: 08/25/2011 11:06:26 thru 08/25/2011 11:11:26
```

The last thing that's worth a mention is the layer/opcode pair. I've mentioned OP codes in the context of redo records in a couple of chapters, and pointed out, for example, that OP code 5.4 is a commit record. The code actually breaks down into two parts, the layer and the opcode within the layer (in this context the word "layer" carries no implication of there being a hierarchy, by the way). Layer 5 is the transaction management layer, layer 10 is the index layer, layer 11 is the table layer, and so on.

■ **Note** If you want to know more about the possible layers and OP codes, one of the more comprehensive lists of OP codes can be found on Julian Dyke's website at `www.juliandyke.com/Internals/Redo/Redo.html`.

It can be useful, occasionally, to analyze what sort of activity had been going on for a period when you think the redo generation has been extreme. I do know of people that have written C programs to read the raw redo log and analyze the appearance of the redo opcodes—and I have to admit that there was one occasion when I could have used such a program—but if you need to do something of this sort, you can always dump the redo for a specified time period and then use something like `grep` to pick out the OP codes or, as I have done occasionally, read the file into an external table and analyze it with SQL or PL/SQL. The problem with this approach, of course, is that the trace file is likely to be *enormous*.

The following, for example, is the call to dump the redo only for records that include opcode 10.11 (set pointer to previous leaf block)—one of the actions that occurs when you split an index leaf block and have to set up the links that logically put the new block in the right place. This is followed by the first few lines of output from running the Windows `find` command against the trace file, looking for the text `OP:10.11`:

```
alter system dump logfile 'C:\ORACLE\ORADATA\D10G\REDO01.LOG'
layer 10 opcode 11 ;

---------- C:\ORACLE\ADMIN\D10G\UDUMP\D10G_ORA_3028.TRC
CHG #2 TYP:0 CLS: 1 AFN:5 DBA:0x01800c1b OBJ:88098 SCN:0x0.04a9ab0a SEQ: 1 OP:10.11
CHG #2 TYP:0 CLS: 1 AFN:5 DBA:0x01800c1c OBJ:88098 SCN:0x0.04a9ab13 SEQ: 1 OP:10.11
CHG #2 TYP:0 CLS: 1 AFN:5 DBA:0x01800c1d OBJ:88098 SCN:0x0.04a9ab19 SEQ: 1 OP:10.11
CHG #2 TYP:0 CLS: 1 AFN:5 DBA:0x01800c1e OBJ:88098 SCN:0x0.04a9ab20 SEQ: 1 OP:10.11
CHG #2 TYP:0 CLS: 1 AFN:5 DBA:0x01800c1f OBJ:88098 SCN:0x0.04a9ab26 SEQ: 1 OP:10.11
CHG #2 TYP:0 CLS: 1 AFN:5 DBA:0x01800c20 OBJ:88098 SCN:0x0.04a9ab2d SEQ: 1 OP:10.11
```

I've had to do a little cosmetic edit on the trace file lines to fit the page, but I haven't lost any information by doing so. There are two things you might see as suspicious if this were from a production system. The first is that the OBJ is always the same—we have one index only, which is growing. The second is that the DBA is increasing by one block at a time—every time we add a block to this index, the next block we add is a new block that we add "to the left" of the previous block, meaning we have an index that is accepting lots of data one (or a few) row at a time in descending order.

I've mentioned this example only as an indication of how you may spot a pattern of activity if you can extract a subset of the redo records easily. In this case, from a 5-minute window on the log file, the full trace file was about 38MB—for this particular opcode the trace file was only 160KB, making the option for detailed investigation viable.

One last thought: if you try to dump `layer 9999 opcode 9999`, Oracle will scan the entire redo log file for an opcode that doesn't exist, so this is a way of validating the integrity of a log file.

■ **Note** The instance that you use to dump a file, whether it's a redo log file or a data file, doesn't have to be the instance that created the file. It doesn't even have to be the same version of Oracle, although you usually run into problems if you try to use an older version of Oracle to dump a newer file.

Guesswork

It's worth closing with a few comments on how you can unravel the mysteries of Oracle—especially when you're wading through trace files and X$ structures and wondering what the strange names mean. A good starting point is to look at the My Oracle Support (MOS) document *175982.1 ORA-600 Lookup Error Categories*, which includes a large table of mnemonics that are often used as the first three or four letters of the weird and wonderful names that you're likely to find.

With a couple of clues in hand, it's surprising how much more you can find on MOS—usually by searching the bug database, where temporary workarounds to bugs often reveal little snippets of information about how things work, or which parameters are significant in which areas of code.

Finally, you can always search the Internet. There are a few sources of trustworthy information. But remember, a lot of the material on the Internet (and quite a lot that's on MOS) is just gossip and speculation that's been handed down over the years. Good information ought to include a date, an Oracle version, and some supporting evidence: base your level of belief on what these three things (or absence thereof) tell you.

Glossary

"When I use a word, it means just what I choose it to mean."

—Humpty Dumpty

2PC: (*See* two-phase commit)

ACID: The properties of a reliable transactional system: Atomic, Consistent, Isolated and Durable.

archived redo logfile: (*See* log file(archived))

array: A list of related items of uniform size. If you know the size of an item, you can calculate the location of the nth item in the list.

AMM (automatic memory management): Introduced in 11g, this allows you to tell the instance how much memory it is allowed to acquire, but lets the instance decide dynamically how to share the memory between the server processes and the SGA.

ASM (automatic storage management): Introduced in 10g, this is the feature that uses a special version of an Oracle instance to act like a logical volume manager, mapping the connection between database files and disk devices.

ASMM (automatic shared memory management): Introduced in 10g, this allows you to tell the instance how much memory to allocate for the SGA as a whole, allowing the instance to decide dynamically how much should be allocated to each large-scale structure within the SGA.

ASSM (automatic segment space management): The default space management mechanism for tablespaces, originally introduced in 9i to relieve the DBA of a need to worry about setting the number of freelists or freelist groups for a data object.

AUM (automatic undo management): Introduced in 9i as a mechanism to relieve the DBA of a need to specify the number and size of undo (rollback) segments.

block: The smallest unit of file handling in an Oracle database. It generally refers to the data block.

block address: The absolute address of a block in a database. For datafiles it is made up of the absolute file number and the block number within file.

block header: An area at the start of each block holding various pieces of information about the contents of the block.

buffer: (a) Memory used as a high-speed storage layer between the user and the discs. (b) The memory used to hold copies of recently accessed data blocks (typical Oracle usage). (c) A unit of memory sized to hold exactly one data block (alternate Oracle usage). (d) A copy of the latest section of the redo log file currently being written to (*log buffer*).

buffer handle: (*See* buffer pin)

buffer header: A chunk of memory describing the content of a single data buffer and holding various pointers and flags describing the state of the buffer. Buffer headers are stored in an array in the same memory granule as the buffers they describe.

buffer pin (also buffer handle): A small chunk of memory from the shared pool that connects a user to a data buffer. It is associated with the buffer through one of two linked lists attached to the buffer header.

change vector: (*See* redo change)

checkpoint: (a) As a noun, the moment Oracle starts copying the content of current blocks from buffers to disc in order to bring (some part of) the datafiles up-to-date with respect to the redo log files. (b) As a verb, the action of copying buffers to disc. Checkpoints may be full (e.g., at database shutdown) or partial (e.g., at tablespace read only calls).

checkpoint (incremental): A checkpoint that is invoked every three seconds to copy data blocks with the oldest recorded changes from the data buffer to disc (rather than copying datablocks of a specific part of the database, such as a table or tablespace). The database control file is updated with a timestamp (in the form of an SCN and Redo Byte Address) of the oldest change to a data block that has not yet been protected by this copy. There will be occasions when there are no blocks in the data buffer that need copying.

child cursor: A collection of objects in the library cache that define the execution plan, dependencies, and environment that allow a session to execute an SQL statement. A single statement may end up generating multiple child cursors.

circular reference: (*See* reference, circular)

cluster (1): A data structure available to Oracle that allows rows with related values to be stored in the same data blocks. There are two options, hash clusters and index clusters. A cluster may hold multiple tables.

cluster (2): A network of closely coupled computers engineered to behave as a single unit through the constant exchange of messages.

commit: Instruction to Oracle to allow the changes made by a transaction to become visible to other users of the database, and ensure that the changes are made durable by writing the relevant part of the log buffer to disc.

commit cleanout: The action of revisiting blocks to update a transaction's ITL entry in each block with the commit SCN at the moment the transaction commits (Oracle-specific).

commit SCN: The SCN generated at the moment a transaction commits.

consistent get: The act of visiting a buffer that contains a copy of a block processed to show only those changes committed at a required target SCN. Getting to this state sometimes needs no work done.

current get: The act of visiting a buffer that is known to contain the most up-to-date version of a block.

database: The physical storage component of an Oracle system, comprised at a minimum of datafiles, tempfiles, online redo log files, control files, and parameter files.

database writer (dbwr): The process (dbw*N*, if there are multiple processes) responsible for copying the current version of blocks from the buffer to disc.

datafile: A file holding persistent data, which may be end-user data, Oracle's data and metadata, or the recent history (in the undo records) of data generated by Oracle.

dbwr (also dbwN): (*See* database writer)

delayed block cleanout: If a block has not been updated with a commit SCN by a committing transaction, the next session to read the block will be required to update the relevant ITL entry with a suitable commit SCN, and clear out any locking information that the transaction left behind.

delayed logging block cleanout: When a commit cleanout occurs, the session does not log the change made to the ITL. Instead, the next session to modify the block finishes the cleanout and writes the complete log of all the changes that the committing session should have made – hence the logging for the committing session has been delayed.

dynamic performance views: Generic name for the x$ memory structures and (more commonly) v$ and gv$ views that allow the SYS account to see some of the internal structures used by the Oracle program as it runs.

enqueue: Used to serialize access to objects. The code path for enqueues is longer that the code path for latches and mutexes, but enqueues allow for a greater variation in the options for how restrictive the serialization can be. Enqueues tend to be used to protect "real" physical parts of the database.

enqueue resource: A chunk of memory labeled to represent an object in the database. RAC has two layers of resources—the local ones that we see in single instance Oracle, and a much greater volume of global ones that are used to coordinate multiple SGAs.

fast commit: The term used to describe Oracle's mechanism for doing the smallest amount of work possible when a transaction commits.

free space credit: Part of an ITL entry that reports the number of bytes of space in a block that would become free if the transaction owning the ITL entry commits. (Note: This is never set to a value less than zero.)

GCS (global cache services): In RAC, the mechanism that deals with keeping the data caches of all the SGAs coherent.

GES (global enqueues services): In RAC, the mechanism that coordinates locking activity (other than simple row-locking) across all instances.

granule (also memory granule): The large-scale unit of memory that Oracle uses to organize the SGA and allow memory to be transferred between the different functions of the SGA. Possible granule sizes are 4 MB, 8 MB, 16 MB and 64MB , dependent on version and SGA size.

GRD (global resource directory): In RAC, the set of distributed resources used to coordinate the activity of the multiple SGAs. The GRD is shared across all instances, and Oracle has an algorithm for calculating where to find a particular master resource.

group commit: When the log writer (lgwr) is posted to write, it will write the contents of the log buffer up to the highest used point. This means that any transactions that happen to have their commit record in the log buffer between the start and end of the write are all made durable at the same time. On completing the write, lgwr will post all sessions that are waiting for a block to be written if that has a lower address than the last block written.

hash bucket: A single location in a hash table used as the starting point of a linked list of items that produce a matching value when a particular arithmetic function is applied to a key attribute of the item. (Sometimes used synonymously with *hash chain.*)

hash chain: A linked list of items in a single hash bucket.

Hash Function: A mathematical algorithm that will always give the same output value for a given input value and will attempt to distribute all allowable input values evenly across the allowed output values.

hash table: An array of hash buckets used as the basis of an access method, allowing rapid location of a data item through a key value.

in-memory undo: Along with private redo, Oracle 10g introduced "private undo." This is memory in the SGA that acts as a set of miniature log buffers that may be allocated to individual sessions for the duration of a transaction; however, these buffers will only hold redo relating to the changes a transaction should make to undo blocks. When a transaction commits, the in-memory undo will be copied into the public logbuffer immediately after the private redo. There are various reasons why this copy may happen prematurely.

incremental checkpoint: (*See* checkpoint, incremental)

initrans: A parameter in an object (table, index, or cluster) definition specifying, and reserving space for, the minimum number of concurrent transactions that will be allowed to modify any given block in the object. (*See also* maxtrans)

instance: The collective name for the shared memory segment and the Oracle processes that access it. Many instances can have concurrent access to a single database.

Interested Transaction List: (*See* ITL)

ITL (interested transaction list): An area in each block of a data object (table, index, cluster) holding information about transactions that recently modified that block.

Java pool: One of the subheaps of the SGA. It is reserved for use by the Java Virtual Machine.

KGL lock: A small chunk of memory that can be attached, through a linked list, to an item in the library cache to associate it with a session that has been using it. KGL locks are exposed through the *dynamic performance view* `v$open_cursor`.

KGL pin: A small chunk of memory that can be attached, through a linked list, to an item in the library cache to associate it with a session that is currently using it. KGL pins have largely been replaced in 11.2 by *mutexes*.

large pool: One of the subheaps of the SGA. It is reserved for allocations of large chunks of memory of a fairly uniform size. Created as a way to reduce fragmentation of the shared pool, the large pool tends to hold memory chunks allocated by RMAN, parallel execution slaves and, for systems using shared_server technology, session heaps.

last change SCN: An SCN value recorded on each data block that, in combination with a single byte counter, records the SCN at the moment the block was last modified. The counter is restarted at one when a change is made at a new SCN, and the SCN is incremented after the counter reaches 254.

latch: A small chunk of memory, combined with an atomic CPU operation, which can be used to act as a serialization mechanism. The structure is larger and the code path is longer than it is for a *mutex* because the latch allows more space and code for instrumentation. Latches tend to be used to protect objects that are fixed, in-memory structures.

lgwr (log writer): The background process responsible for copying the log buffer to disc. The log writer is scheduled to run on a very regular basis to ensure that the log buffer stays nearly empty at all times.

library cache: The collection of items in the shared pool relating to SQL and PL/SQL statements, including object dependencies, privileges, and execution plans for statements.

linked list: A collection of related data items that are connected only by a series of pointers. Each item in the list points to the next one, and the only way to find a specific item is to follow pointers along the list until you get to the item you want. Oracle makes frequent use of linked lists (and especially doubly-linked lists, where each item points forward to the next item and backwards to the previous item).

lock: (*See* enqueues and KGL lock)

lock byte: An attribute of a row (or index entry). When any rows in a block have been modified by a given transaction, there will be an ITL entry in that block identifying the transaction. The index of the ITL entry used by that transaction will be written into a single-byte location at the start of the row. This allows other processes to see that the row has been locked, and which transaction locked it.

lock mode: Although locks (enqueues) act to serialize access to objects, there are ways in which sessions may share, or partially share, objects. Oracle allows for six different levels (i.e., modes) of locking, and a complex arrangement of lock compatibility.

log buffer: Sometimes called the public log buffer or public redo thread, this is a relatively small chunk of memory in the SGA used as a window into the current redo log file. Most Oracle processes may copy change records into the log buffer, but only the log writer can transfer the contents of the buffer to disc. Since 9i it has been possible to have multiple log buffers, and this happens automatically in 10g. (10g also introduced "private" log buffers.)

log buffer, private: (*See* private redo thread)

log file (redo log file): A file holding the stream of change records produced by sessions as they modify data blocks. Each instance in RAC will have its own set of log files. An instance usually has a small number of "online" redo log files that are constantly reused.

log file (archived): If a database is running in archivelog mode, then each online redo log file has to be copied to an alternative location before it can be reused. These copies are referred to as archived redo log files.

log writer: (*See* lgwr)

logical standby: A copy of a live database opened in a special mode that allows the redo information from the live database to be translated into SQL statements, which can be run against the standby. The standby will be open in read/write mode and can be used for other work. The redo selected can be a subset of the full redo.

LRU (least recently used): An algorithm for optimizing the effectiveness of a buffer by arranging the contents in a list and promoting popular (recently used) items to the top of the list while allowing unpopular items to drift to the end of the list and fall off.

master resource: In RAC, the global resource directory (GRD) holds a list of resources representing individual items (blocks, sequences, transactions) at a fine level of granularity. One instance will hold a complete record for an item listing all the interested instances—this complete record is the master resource.

maxtrans: A parameter in an object (table, index or cluster) definition that limits the number of concurrent transactions that can modify any given block in the object. (*See also* initrans)

memory granule: (*See* granule)

multi-threaded server: (*See* shared server)

mutex: A small chunk of memory combined with an atomic CPU operation, which can be used to act as either a serialization mechanism or (with a longer hold time) a pinning mechanism. The structure is significantly smaller and the code path is much shorter than it is for a *latch* because a mutex has very little instrumentation. Mutexes are generally embedded in objects, so can be created dynamically, making them more numerous (offering reduced contention), but harder to track. Mutexes tend to be used to protect objects that are fairly transient, in-memory structures.

online redo log: (*See* log file)

oradebug: A debugging utility supplied by Oracle, which can be run by a suitably privileged user connected to an instance through SQL*Plus. Oradebug allows you to examine structures (physical database and in-memory instance) and manipulate the code path and memory content of a running instance.

physical standby: A copy of the live database started in recovery mode so that the raw information from the redo log of the live database can be applied to it to keep it in synch (with a small delay) with the live database. 11g introduced a (licensed) option to open a physical standby for reporting while the redo is still being applied.

piggyback commit: (*See* group commit)

pmon (process monitor): One of the basic background processes in an Oracle instance that deals with cleaning up any memory structures that have been left by a failed session (or end-user process).

pointer: A memory location holding the address of another memory location.

private redo thread: Since 10g, Oracle has allocated chunks of memory in the SGA to act as mini log buffers that may be allocated to individual sessions for the duration of a transaction. When a session commits it will copy the content of its private log buffer into the public log buffer. (There are various reasons why this copy can take place prematurely).

RAC (real application cluster): A version of the Oracle code that allows multiple instances to share the same set of database files, which, if implemented correctly, can offer benefits of scalability and availability.

read consistent: As in “a read consistent copy of block X.” A way of describing a copy of a block that shows only the transactions committed as at a specific SCN. (*See* consistent get)

real application cluster: (*See* RAC)

recovery: The process of taking an old copy of a database and bringing the copy up-to-date by applying the redo that has been generated since the copy was made—and rolling back any uncommitted transactions that are still visible in the database once all the relevant redo has been applied.

redo change: The description of the effects of a single atomic change to a datafile block.

redo record: A group of redo change vectors which constitutes a single contiguous item to copy into the log buffer (and on to the log file).

redo strand, private: (*See* private redo thread)

reference, circular: (*See* circular reference)

rocket science: A generic term suggesting that a topic is technically too complex for an ordinary individual to understand; for example, "Oracle is complicated, but it's not rocket science."

rollback: A command to apply the undo records generated by a transaction so that the changes made by that transaction are effectively removed from the database; also the action of applying undo records.

rollback segments: A common term used to describe undo segments before automatic undo management was introduced in 9i.

row directory: A section of an index or table block that contains a list of offsets (pointers) to the starting position of rows (index entries) in the block.

savepoint: It is possible to create named savepoints part way through a transaction so that, prior to commit, the transaction can be partially undone by a call to roll back to a specific savepoint.

science: A mechanism for establishing the degree to which an abstract model of the real world matches the real world.

SCN (system change/commit number): A counter stored in the SGA of an instance that acts as a clocking mechanism. Each time a session commits a transaction (and on a few other occasions) the SCN is incremented. In a RAC environment, the different instances are constantly re-synchronizing their SCNs.

SCN, commit: (*See* commit SCN)

SCN, last change: (*See* last change SCN)

segment header: A special block (once guaranteed to be the first block in a segment) holding metadata about the segment. In an ASSM tablespace there will be a few segment space management blocks before the segment header block.

segmented array: An array that is broken into a number of chunks. This allows the array to grow as needed without having to pre-allocate a large amount of memory. Oracle makes frequent use of segmented arrays to build simple lists.

SGA (also known as system global area and shared global area): The memory that is made publicly available (i.e., shared memory) to all processes accessing the database. The combination of the memory and processes is known collectively as the *instance*.

SGA heap: In computing terms, the shared pool is structured as a "heap," and a heapdump at level 2 will dump the shared pool—labeling it as the SGA heap.

shadow resource: In RAC, the global resource directory (GRD) holds a list of resources representing individual items (blocks, sequences, transactions) at a fine level of granularity. One instance will hold a complete record for an item, listing all the interested instances. Every other instance that has an interest in that item will hold a smaller record holding information only about that instance's interest. These smaller records are the shadow resources.

Shared Global Area: (*See* SGA)

shared pool: Apart from the data cache, the largest allocation of memory in the SGA. It holds information about SQL and PL/SQL statements, object definitions, dependencies and privileges, and a few other structures.

single point of failure: (*See* SPOF)

smon (system monitor): A background process that wakes up every five minutes to check the state of health of the instance and do various housekeeping tasks, such as dropping undo segments and deleting temporary segments from failed index builds.

SPOF (single point of failure): Is there one piece of equipment in your system that you could destroy to make your system unusable? If there is, you are looking at a single point of failure.

state object (SO): A chunk of memory in a session's heap that, typically, keeps track of an object in the SGA; for example if a session has a transaction active, the session memory will hold a 'transaction state object' corresponding to the row it is using in `x$ktcxb`.

standby database: A generic label for a copy of a production database that uses the content of the live redo log files to keep itself automatically up-to-date in near real time. (*See also* logical standby and physical standby.)

streams pool: One of the subheaps of the SGA. It is reserved for use by Oracle's Streams technology to avoid excess disk I/O when forwarding data to other databases.

System Change Number: (*See* SCN)

System Commit Number: (*See* SCN)

sysaux tablespace: (*See* tablespace (sysaux))

System Global Area: (*See* SGA)

system tablespace: (*See* tablespace (system))

table directory: A section of a table block that identifies the starting point in the row directory for each of the tables stored in the block. It is only relevant to blocks belonging to clusters (1).

tablespace: The "large scale" unit of storage in Oracle. A tablespace may be made up of many files that can be recovered individually, but logically it is better to think of the tablespace as the unit of recovery. In 10g Oracle introduced the "bigfile" tablespace which is limited to a single file.

tablespace (sysaux): A tablespace introduced in 10g to hold the high-volume, non-critical information associated with various Oracle tools and features. Although there is no special internal handling for the sysaux tablespace, user data should not be stored in the sysaux tablespace.

tablespace (system): The primary tablespace in the database that holds the data dictionary and a few other system related objects. There are a few special mechanisms involved in the way Oracle handles the system tablespace and user data should not be stored in the system tablespace.

tablespace (temporary): A special type of tablespace used by Oracle to hold transient data and the intermediate results of in-memory operations that are large enough to require "virtual" memory. Temporary tablespaces are subject to some very special internal handling. Although transient user data in the form of instantiated global temporary tables may be stored in the temporary tablespaces, user objects cannot be defined to use temporary tablespaces.

tablespace (undo): A special tablespace (or set of tablespaces), one active per instance, used to store undo information. The undo tablespace is subject to some very special internal handling, and user objects cannot be stored in the undo tablespaces.

temporary tablespace: (*See* tablespace (temporary))

trace file: A text file dumped in response to an error raised by Oracle or due to an event set by the user. The default location of trace files varies with version of Oracle and according to parameters that may be set by the DBA.

transaction: A set of changes that takes the database from one consistent state to another consistent state. The set of changes becomes publicly visible only when the session making the changes issues a commit. No other session is allowed to see any of the changes until it is allowed to see all of the changes.

transaction table: A short list in each undo segment header block that holds reference details for recent transactions.

transaction control: A section in each undo segment header block that holds summary information about the state of the segment's transaction table.

two-phase commit (2PC): A protocol used in distributed transactions to ensure that all the components of the transactions end up in the same state, that is, all committed or all rolled back.

undo record: The unit of information stored in an undo tablespace describing how to reverse out a single change to a data block.

undo segment: Segment created in the undo tablespace for storing undo information.

undo segment header: The first block of an undo segment holding, in particular, the transaction table and transaction control for the segment.

undo tablespace: (*See* tablespace (undo))

upper bound commit: The SCN written to an ITL during delayed block cleanout. The transaction may have committed before this SCN, but the process doing the cleanout doesn't need to know exactly when the commit took place.

Index

D

J

K

L

M

N

O

P

S

U

V

W, X, Y, Z

CPSIA information can be obtained at www.ICGtesting.com
Printed in the USA
LVOW110351141211

259329LV00004B/4/P

9 781430 239543